Complete Arabic

Jack Smart and Frances Altorfer

Revised by
Frances Amrani

First published in Great Britain in 2001 as Teach Yourself Arabic by Hodder Education. An Hachette UK company.

First published in US in 2001 by The McGraw-Hill Companies, Inc.

This edition published in 2017 by John Murray Learning

British Library Cataloguing in Publication Data: a catalogue record for this title is available from the British Library.

Library of Congress Catalog Card Number: on file.

ISBN: 978 1 444 19516 3

4

Cover image © Shutterstock.com

Typeset by Datapage India (Pvt.) Ltd.

Printed and bound by CPI Group (UK) Ltd, Croydon, CR0 4YY

John Murray Learning policy is to use papers that are natural, renewable and recyclable products and made from wood grown in sustainable forests. The logging and manufacturing processes are expected to conform to the environmental regulations of the country of origin.

Carmelite House

50 Victoria Embankment

London EC4Y 0DZ

www.hodder.co.uk

Contents

Acknowledgements

We would like to thank Brian Pridham, Mike Pinder, Sharjah Television, Bob Coles and Ruth Butler at the Institute for Arab and Islamic Studies at Exeter University, and Frances Taylor, for helping us with realia and materials.

We are most grateful to Western Union for permission to use material.

Thanks also to Lynne and Brent Noble, Denise Mountford and Kirsty Christer, Amira Nowaira, and to Mairi Smart and Ahmed Chbib for their generous help with this edition.

We are particularly grateful to our editors at Hodder & Stoughton, Sarah Bauer, Victoria Roddam, Cecilia Bembibre, Robert Williams and Cheryl Hutty, for their patience and encouragement during the preparation of this new edition.

We would also like to thank Mr Jim Doran and H. Russell for their helpful comments on earlier editions.

Meet the authors

The authors are linguists with much experience, and are familiar with the Arab countries, their society, religion and culture.

Jack Smart taught Arabic at university level for over 30 years, specializing in the learning of the language, his students ranging from beginners to candidates for a doctoral degree. He was familiar with the written language from its earliest pre-Islamic period to the present day, and researched widely into spoken Arabic dialects, in several of which he was fluent. He lived and worked in Egypt, Sudan and the Gulf countries, and made short or extended visits and study trips to virtually all of the other Arab states.

Frances Altorfer has also lived in the Middle East. She knows several European languages as well as Swahili and Arabic, and has many years of experience of teaching languages, using the most up-to-date learning methods.

Working in partnership, Jack provided the linguistic material, and Frances the teaching expertise. The result is, we are sure, a balanced self-teaching book with a broad scope, mainly linguistic, but also with useful sections on the Arabic and Islamic culture, in a clear and easily digestible format.

The current edition has been updated with the assistance of Frances Amrani.

Frances Amrani studied Arabic at the University of Manchester and has over 25 years' experience as a language teacher and teacher trainer. She specializes in materials design, methodology and publishing for language teaching. Frances has lived and worked in Jordan, Algeria, Morocco and the Gulf and is a regular visitor to the MENA region.

Introduction

Welcome to *Complete Arabic!*

The aims of the course

If you are an adult learner with no previous knowledge of Arabic and studying on your own, then this is the course for you. Perhaps you are taking up Arabic again after a break or perhaps you are intending to learn with the support of a class. Again, you will find this course very well suited to your purposes.

The language you will learn is based on the kind of material seen in international Arabic newspapers, magazines and websites or heard on radio and television news broadcasts. The main emphasis is on understanding Arabic, but we also aim to give you an idea of how the language works, so that you can create sentences of your own.

If you are working on your own, the audio recordings will be all the more important, as they will provide you with the essential opportunity to listen to Arabic and to speak it within a controlled framework.

How to use this course

All the important information that you need for the basic structures of Arabic is given in Units 1–10. Units 11–16 introduce more advanced but essential structures, through texts and conversations. Make sure you have mastered the principles given in Units 1–10 before moving on. Throughout the units you will find 'Discovery' questions to get you thinking about the way Arabic works, as well as short الآن دورك **al-'aan dawrak** '*Your turn*' exercises to immediately have a go at new concepts.

Statement of aims

At the beginning of each unit is a summary of what you can expect to learn by the end of that unit. There is also an overview of how the unit relates to the Common European Framework of Reference for languages (CEFR).

Cultural background

These highlight some of the social and cultural aspects of life in the Arab world and introduce an element of the topic covered in each unit.

Presentation of new language

This is in the form of Vocabulary builders and the conversations or texts introducing the new language, which are also recorded. These are followed by questions and phrase-matching exercises to help you check your comprehension. The answers to these and a translation of the texts are at the end of the book. The language is presented in manageable chunks, building carefully on what you have learned. At the beginning of the course the texts and vocabulary are given both in Arabic script and in transliteration, that is, in English letters. As the course progresses the transliteration is dropped to encourage you to rely less on the transliteration as you work through the units.

Language discovery

In this section the forms of the language are explained and illustrated. Main grammatical concepts have often been grouped together for ease of reference and they gradually build up to provide you with all the structures you need to read and write Arabic.

Word discovery

This section will help you familiarize yourself with the way in which Arabic words are formed.

Practice

The practice sections provide a variety of activities so that you can start using the new words and structures. Practice is graded so that activities which require mainly recognition come first. As you grow in confidence in manipulating language forms, you will be encouraged to write and speak the language yourself. The answers can be found at the end of the course, in the Answer key. Transcripts of listening comprehension exercises follow the Answer key.

Reference

The reference section contains a Grammar summary of the main structures of the Arabic language and a set of Verb tables, so that every verb you come across in the book can be matched in the tables to a verb which works in the same way.

Selected Arabic–English and English–Arabic vocabularies are provided so that you can look up words alphabetically.

STUDY TIPS

Remember that the first step in learning a language is listening and understanding. Concentrate initially on that and then work on your writing skills, using the information in the units and, if possible, by listening to native speakers.

In using a course such as this, it is important to pace yourself, with a view to consolidating what you have learned before moving on. Due to the nature of the language, the units are of varying length and complexity. There is no need to attempt to absorb a whole unit in one sitting.

Our suggestion is that you concentrate on the texts first, with reference to the transcripts and the audio if you have it. This includes mastering the vocabulary as far as possible. The translations are there to help you if you get stuck. You should then look at the Language discovery section and make sure you understand how the language is working. Finally, work through the exercises and Test Yourself sections. These are based on the constructions explained in the unit and will help you consolidate what you have learned. Try to do each exercise before checking your work in the Answer key.

HINTS FOR FURTHER STUDY

This course covers all the main structures of Arabic and a reasonable amount of vocabulary. If you want to dig deeper, you will first need one or two of these dictionaries.

▶ Arabic–English: Hans Wehr *A Dictionary of Modern Written Arabic* (edited by J. Milton Cowan) is an essential tool.

▶ English–Arabic: the best available is Munir Ba'albaki Al-Mawrid, *A Modern English–Arabic Dictionary*. This very comprehensive work was designed for use by native Arabic speakers and so, to select the correct word for a given context, some cross-referencing with Wehr may be necessary.

▶ Arabic–English and English–Arabic: *Oxford Arabic Dictionary*. This dictionary is also available online and is corpus-based. The online version is updated regularly.

These three dictionaries are the best for the serious student, but there are others available.

There is a multitude of Arabic grammars on the market, of widely differing merits. David Cowan, *Modern Literary Arabic* provides a concise look at the structures of written Arabic at a slightly deeper level than this book.

There are two additional reference books which will help you with vocabulary and script, *Essential Arabic Vocabulary: A Handbook of Core Terms* and *Read and Write Arabic Script* both written by Mourad Diouri.

Spoken Arabic varies widely from country to country, and you should choose from the wide selection of material available according to which country you intend to visit. Very roughly the Arabic dialects divide into the following groups: North Africa from Morocco to Libya; Egypt and the Sudan; the Lebanon, Jordan and Syria; Iraq and the Arabian Peninsula.

The Arabic of the last of these is covered by the present writers' *Complete Gulf Arabic* in the same series.

You can read and hear Arabic on the BBC Arabic, CNN and Al-Jazeera websites, although you should not expect to understand everything straight away. These websites give news items in small chunks, which are ideal pieces of 'real' Arabic.

Good luck! We hope you will enjoy learning Arabic!

Learn to learn

THE DISCOVERY METHOD

There are lots of approaches to language learning, some practical and some quite unconventional. Perhaps you know of a few, or even have some techniques of your own. In this book we have incorporated the Discovery method of learning, a sort of DIY approach to language learning. What this means is that you will be encouraged throughout the course to engage your mind and figure out the language for yourself, through identifying patterns, understanding grammar concepts, noticing words that are similar to English, and more. This method promotes language awareness, a critical skill in acquiring a new language. As a result of your own efforts, you will be able to better retain what you have learned, use it with confidence, and, even better, apply those same skills to continuing to learn the language (or, indeed, another one) on your own after you've finished this book.

Everyone can succeed in learning a language – the key is to know how to learn it. Learning is more than just reading or memorizing grammar and vocabulary. It's about being an active learner, learning in real contexts, and, most importantly, using what you've learned in different situations. Simply put, if you figure something out for yourself, you're more likely to understand it. And when you use what you've learned, you're more likely to remember it.

And because many of the essential but (let's admit it!) dull details, such as grammar rules, are taught through the Discovery Method, you'll have more fun while learning. Soon, the language will start to make sense and you'll be relying on your own intuition to construct original sentences independently, not just listening and repeating.

Enjoy yourself!

BECOME A SUCCESSFUL LANGUAGE LEARNER

1 Make a habit out of learning

Study a little every day, between 20 and 30 minutes if possible, rather than two to three hours in one session. Give yourself short-term goals, e.g. work out how long you'll spend on a particular unit and work within the time limit. This will help you to create a study habit, much in the same way you would a sport or music. You will need to concentrate, so try to create an environment conducive to learning which is calm and quiet and free from distractions. As you study, do not worry about your mistakes or the things you can't remember or understand. Languages settle differently in our brains, but gradually the language will become clearer as your brain starts to make new connections. Just give yourself enough time and you will succeed.

2 Expand your language contact

As part of your study habit try to take other opportunities to expose yourself to the language. As well as using this course, you could try listening to radio and television or reading articles and blogs. Remember that as well as listening to online radio live you can use catch-up services to listen more than once. Perhaps you could find information in Arabic about a personal passion or hobby or even a news story that interests you. Subtitles are often available with television and films both in Arabic on English films and English on Arabic films. These can often provide an additional support while listening. In time you'll find that your vocabulary and language recognition deepen and you'll become used to a range of writing and speaking styles.

3 Vocabulary

To organize your study of vocabulary, group new words under:

   a generic categories, e.g. food, furniture.

   b situations in which they occur, e.g. under restaurant you can write *waiter, table, menu.*

c functions, e.g. greetings, parting, thanks, apologizing.

d words that come from the same root system.

▶ Say the words out loud as you read them.

▶ Write the words over and over again. Remember that if you want to keep lists on your smartphone or tablet you can usually switch the keyboard language to make sure you are able to include all accents and special characters.

▶ Listen to the audio several times.

▶ Cover up the English side of the vocabulary list and see if you remember the meaning of the word.

▶ Associate the words with similar sounding words in English, e.g. The word *forbidden* in Arabic sounds a bit like 'Mum + no(r)' **mamnuu:** ممنوع. If you imagine your mum telling you that you can't do something, it will help you remember the word for *forbidden*.

Smoking is forbidden ➜ **mamnuu: at-tadkhiin** ممنوع التدخين

Photography is forbidden ➜ **mamnuu: at-tasuwiir** ممنوع التصوير

▶ Create flash cards, drawings and mind maps.

▶ Write words for objects around your house and stick them to objects.

▶ Pay attention to patterns in words, particularly how they relate to the root system e.g. The root **K-T-B** ك – ت – ب *to write* is linked to **KiTāB** كتَاب *book*, **KuTuB** كُتُب *books*, **KāTiB** كاتِب *writer*, **KuTTāB** كُتَّاب *writers*, **maKTūB** مَكْتُوْب *letter*, **maKāTīB** مَكَاتِيْب *letters*, **maKTaB** مَكْتَب *desk, office*, **maKāTiB** مَكَاتِب *offices*.

▶ Experiment with words. Use the words that you learn in new contexts and find out if they are correct. For example, you learn in Unit 6 that one of the meanings of **márkaz** مركز means *centre* in the context of a centre for something, e.g. **márkaz ash-shurTah** مركز الشرطة *police station*. Experiment with and look out for examples of **márkaz** مركز in new contexts, e.g. **márkaz tasawwuq** مركز تسوق *shopping centre*. Check the new phrases in this book, in a dictionary or with Arabic speakers.

▶ Make the best of words you already know. When you start thinking about it you will realize that there are quite a few Arabic words and expressions which are commonly used in English: e.g. *Inshallah, caravan, mufti, bint, mullah, alcohol, fatwa, shariah, jihad, alchemy, algebra*.

4 Grammar

▶ To organize the study of grammar, write your own grammar glossary and add new information and examples as you go along.

▶ Experiment with grammar rules. Sit back and reflect on the rules you learn. See how they compare with your own language or other languages you may already speak. Try to find out some rules on your own and be ready to spot the exceptions. By doing this you'll remember the rules better and get a feel for the language.

▶ Try to find examples of grammar in conversations or other articles.

▶ Keep a 'pattern bank' that organizes examples that can be listed under the structures you've learned.

▶ Use old vocabulary to practise new grammar structures.

▶ When you learn a new verb form, write the conjugation of several different verbs you know that follow the same form.

5 PRONUNCIATION

▶ When organizing the study of pronunciation keep a section of your notebook for pronunciation rules and practise those that trouble you.

▶ Repeat all of the conversations, line by line. Listen to yourself and try to mimic what you hear.

▶ Record yourself and compare yourself to a native speaker.

▶ Make a list of words that give you trouble and practise them.

▶ Study individual sounds, then full words.

▶ Don't forget, it's not just about pronouncing letters and words correctly, but using the right intonation. So, when practising words and sentences, mimic the rising and falling intonation of native speakers.

6 Listening and reading

The conversations in this book include questions to help guide you in your understanding. But you can go further by following some of these tips.

▶ Imagine the situation. When listening to or reading the conversations, try to imagine where the scene is taking place and who the main characters are. Let your experience of the world help you guess the meaning of the conversation, e.g. if a conversation takes place in a snack bar you can predict the kind of vocabulary that is being used.

- Concentrate on the main part. When watching a foreign film you usually get the meaning of the whole story from a few individual shots. Understanding a foreign conversation or article is similar. Concentrate on the main parts to get the message and don't worry about individual words.

- Guess the key words; if you cannot, ask or look them up. When there are key words you don't understand, try to guess what they mean from the context. If you're listening to an Arabic speaker and cannot get the gist of a whole passage because of one word or phrase, try to repeat that word with a questioning tone; the speaker will probably paraphrase it, giving you the chance to understand it.

7 Speaking

Rehearse in the foreign language. As all language teachers will assure you, the successful learners are those students who overcome their inhibitions and get into situations where they must speak, write and listen to the foreign language. Here are some useful tips to help you practise speaking Arabic:

- Hold a conversation with yourself, using the conversations of the units as models and the structures you have learned previously.

- After you have conducted a transaction with a salesperson, clerk or waiter in your own language, pretend that you have to do it in Arabic, e.g. buying groceries, ordering food, drinks and so on.

- Look at objects around you and try to name them in Arabic.

- Look at people around you and try to describe them in detail.

- Try to answer all of the questions in the book out loud.

- Say the conversations out loud then try to replace sentences with ones that are true for you.

- Try to role-play different situations in the book.

8 Learn from your errors

- Don't let errors interfere with getting your message across. Making errors is part of any normal learning process, but some people get so worried that they won't say anything unless they are sure it is correct. This leads to a vicious circle as the less they say, the less practice they get and the more mistakes they make.

- Note the seriousness of errors. Many errors are not serious, as they do not effect the meaning; for example, if you use the wrong gender (**húwa** هو *he* for **híya** هي *she, it*), or the wrong adjective form (**al-'azraq** الأزرق for **al-zarqaa'** الزرقاء *blue*). So, concentrate on getting your message across and learn from your mistakes.

9 Learn to cope with uncertainty

- Don't over-use your dictionary. When reading a text in Arabic, don't be tempted to look up every word you don't know. Underline the words you do not understand and read the passage several times, concentrating on trying to get the gist of the passage. If after the third time there are still words which prevent you from getting the general meaning of the passage, look them up in the dictionary.

- Don't panic if you don't understand. If at some point you feel you don't understand what you are told, don't panic or give up listening. Either try and guess what is being said and keep following the conversation or, if you cannot, isolate the expression or words you haven't understood and have them explained to you. The speaker might paraphrase them and the conversation will carry on.

- Keep talking. The best way to improve your fluency in the foreign language is to talk every time you have the opportunity to do so: keep the conversations flowing and don't worry about the mistakes. If you get stuck for a particular word, don't let the conversation stop; paraphrase or replace the unknown word with one you do know, even if you have to simplify what you want to say. As a last resort use the word from your own language and pronounce it in the foreign accent.

- Remember most Arabs will actually use a dialect at home, so sometimes you might actually be using the correct Arabic word, but it isn't the one they expect or the one which would be their first choice in a speaking situation.

Arabic script and pronunciation guide

1 Basic characteristics

The Arabic script looks difficult because it is so different from what we are used to. In fact, it is easy to master and, with one or two easily definable exceptions, all sounds are written as they are pronounced. There are no combinations of vowels (diphthongs) which result in a totally different sound, such as, e.g. the English words *plough, dough, through, enough*.

Some important facts about the Arabic script:

▶ Arabic is written from right to left. As a result of this, what we would regard as the back cover of a book, magazine or newspaper is, in fact, the front cover of an Arabic publication.

▶ Arabic script is always joined, or cursive, like traditional English handwriting. There is no equivalent of the English text you are now reading, where all the letters have separate forms with spaces between them.

▶ There are no capital letters.

▶ The joining strokes between letters, called ligatures, have the effect of slightly altering the shape of the letters on either side. As a result, Arabic letters have varying forms, depending on whether they come at the beginning, in the middle or at the end of a word.

▶ A few letters do not join to the following letter.

▶ The three short vowels, **a**, **i** or **u**, as opposed to the long vowels **aa**, **uu** and **ii**, are not shown in the script. For example, the word **bank** (borrowed from English) is written **b-n-k**. This is not so much of a problem as you might think, since the number of shapes or forms which Arabic words take is limited. There is a system (not normally used in Modern Arabic) to show the short vowels, which is explained below. As almost all Modern Arabic is written without the short vowels, we have generally not included them in the Arabic script in this course, although the transliteration (pronunciation guide) given for all the Arabic vocabulary and structures will show you what they are. However, we have included the short vowels in the Arabic script in some places where it is especially helpful.

2 The alphabet

Because Arabic is a cursive script, we have given the initial, medial and final forms of each letter, used depending on where they occur in the word. A separate form has also been included, since some letters do not join to the one after them. If you look at the letters carefully you will see that there are really only two shapes, although four forms of the non-joining letters have been given.

The Arabic alphabet is given in its traditional order.

 00.01

ص ش س ز ر ذ د خ ح ج ث ت ب ا

ي و ه ن م ل ك ق ف غ ع ظ ط ض

In most cases, the initial form of the letter can be regarded as the basic or nucleus form. For example, if you look at **baa'** (the second letter in the following list of Arabic Letters), you will see that its basic (initial) form is a small left-facing hook with a single dot below it. The medial form is more or less the same, with a ligature coming in from the right (remember Arabic reads from right to left). The final form is the same as the medial, with a little flourish to the left, at the end of the word, and the separate form is the same as the initial, but again with the flourish to the left. Study the letters bearing these features in mind, as many of them follow the same principle.

The term 'final' in the table should be interpreted as meaning 'final after a joining letter'. If the preceding letter is a non-joiner, the separate form will be used. If you look closely, you can see that final and separate letters are usually elongated in form or have a 'flourish' after them.

Fuller descriptions and other hints on deciphering will be given in the units.

Here are the four shapes of **baa'** in enlarged type:

بـ   ـبـ   ـب   ب

initial   medial   final   separate

You will see that the nucleus is the hook with a dot under it (the initial form). The medial shape has joining strokes before and after the letter, and the final form has an elongation or flourish. Letters which do not join to the following one are marked with an asterisk (*).

THE ARABIC LETTERS

 00.02

Name	Initial	Medial	Final	Separate	Pronunciation
alif*	ا	ـا	ـا	ا	see below
baa'	بـ	ـبـ	ـب	ب	b
taa'	تـ	ـتـ	ـت	ت	t
thaa'	ثـ	ـثـ	ـث	ث	th
jiim	جـ	ـجـ	ـج	ج	j
Haa'	حـ	ـحـ	ـح	ح	H
khaa'	خـ	ـخـ	ـخ	خ	kh
daal*	د	ـد	ـد	د	d
dhaal*	ذ	ـذ	ـذ	ذ	dh
raa'*	ر	ـر	ـر	ر	r
zaay*	ز	ـز	ـز	ز	z
siin	سـ	ـسـ	ـس	س	s
shiin	شـ	ـشـ	ـش	ش	sh
Saad	صـ	ـصـ	ـص	ص	S
Daad	ضـ	ـضـ	ـض	ض	D
Taa'	طـ	ـطـ	ـط	ط	T
DHaa'	ظـ	ـظـ	ـظ	ظ	DH
:ain	عـ	ـعـ	ـع	ع	:
ghain	غـ	ـغـ	ـغ	غ	gh
faa'	فـ	ـفـ	ـف	ف	f
qaaf	قـ	ـقـ	ـق	ق	q
kaaf	كـ	ـكـ	ـك	ك	k
laam	لـ	ـلـ	ـل	ل	l
miim	مـ	ـمـ	ـم	م	m
nuun	نـ	ـنـ	ـن	ن	n

haa'	ـهـ	ـه	ـ	ه	h
waaw*	و	ـو	ـو	و	w
yaa'	ـيـ	ـيـ	ـي	ي	y

There is one combination consonant, **laam-alif**. This must be used when this series of letters occurs and it is a non-joiner:

Name	Initial	Medial/Final	Separate	Pronunciation
laam-alif	لا	لا	لا	laa

The **taa' marbuuTah**, referred to in this book as the 'hidden **-t**', is the Arabic feminine ending. As it only occurs at the end of words, it has only two forms: final (after joiners) and separate (after non-joiners). It is always preceded by a short vowel:

Final	Separate
ـة	ة

If you look carefully at this letter, you will see that it is a **haa'** with the two dots above of the **taa'** added. It is normally ignored in speech, or rendered as a very weak **h**, but in certain combinations of words, it is pronounced as **t**. It has therefore been transcribed as **h** or **t** accordingly.

The **hamzah** is regarded by the Arabs as a supplementary sign, not as a letter of the alphabet. Its official pronunciation is a 'glottal stop' (as the *ts* in the Cockney pronunciation of *bottle*), and it has been transliterated by means of an apostrophe ('). It is sometimes omitted in speech, but should be shown in written Arabic, where it occurs either on its own, or written over an **alif**, **waaw** or **yaa'**. In the last case, the two dots under the **yaa'** are omitted. It can also occur written below an **alif**, but this is less common. The actual **hamzah** never joins to anything, but its 'supporting' letters take the form required by their position in the word:

	Initial	Medial	Final	Separate
independent		ء in all cases		
over **alif**	أ	ـأ	ـأ	أ
under **alif**	إ	does not occur		إ
over **waaw**	—	ـؤ	ـؤ	ؤ
over **yaa'**	—	ـئـ	ـئ	ئ

Note that, at the beginning of a word, **hamzah** is always written above or below **alif**.

The writing of the **hamzah** is a frequent source of spelling errors among native speakers and it is often omitted in print and writing.

In foreign loanwords the letter *p* is usually written as a **baa'** and the letter *v* is written either as **faa'** or with the Persian letter ڤ – a **faa'** with three dots above it instead of one.

الآن دورك al-'aan dawrak

1 **In the photograph, which well-known international companies are sponsors of this racecourse?**

3 Vowels

The letters of the Arabic alphabet are all regarded as consonants.

In Arabic writing, the short vowels are not usually marked except in children's school textbooks, the Holy Qur'an and ancient classical poetry. They appear in Qur'an so there is no confusion about the meaning. Otherwise they do not appear in most modern written Arabic, but an educated reader will know where they are. In some ways it is similar to knowing spelling conventions in English e.g. where most educated speakers know which letters are silent.

The long vowels are expressed by the three letters **alif**, **waaw** and **yaa'**. **Alif** almost always expresses the vowel **aa**, but **waaw** and **yaa'** can also be the consonant *w* or *y* (as in English *wish* and *yes*).

الآن دورك al-'aan dawrak

2 What does the writing on the side of the bus say?

The most important factors to consider in Arabic words are, first, the consonants and, second, the long vowels. It will not make much difference in most cases whether you pronounce a word with **a**, **u** or **i** (short vowels), but it is important to get the long vowels right. (See Sections 7 and 8 for more details on vowels.)

4 Variations in handwriting

Think of the Arabic script as essentially handwriting (since it is always cursive, no matter how it is produced – by hand or on a computer). Since calligraphy is a highly developed art in the Arab world, there are more variations in the form of the letters than is the case in English.

The most common of these is that two dots above or below a letter are frequently combined into one dash, and three dots (which only occur above) into an inverted 'v' like the French circumflex (ˆ). Here is an example showing **taa'** and **thaa'**:

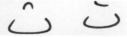

Another common variation is the writing of **siin** (**s**) and **shiin** (**sh**) simply as long lines, ironing out their 'spikes', and often with a small hook below at the beginning:

This occurs frequently in handwriting, signwriting and newspaper and advert headings – in fact, everywhere where the original copy has been prepared by a calligrapher rather than typeset.

Above all, Arabic writing is fun. Look at it as an art form!

5 Transliteration

Transliteration means expressing a language that uses a different writing system (like Arabic) in letters and symbols based on the Roman alphabet, usually for teaching purposes. There is no standard way of doing this and we have tried to keep the system used in *Complete Arabic* as simple as possible.

The essential feature of a transliteration system is that it has to have a precise equivalent for every sound used in the target language. This differs from conventional spelling, e.g. in English the letter *s* has totally different sounds in the two words *loafs* and *loaves*. Consider also that the same sound in the former can be spelled *ce*, e.g. *mince*. Transliteration systems have to iron out such discrepancies.

We have adapted the English alphabet, using capital letters to distinguish between Arabic sounds that seem related to speakers of English. For instance, Arabic has two sorts of 't', which we have distinguished in this way: **rattab** means *arranged*, whereas **raTTab** means *moistened*. Consequently, you will not find capital letters used as they are conventionally, e.g. in personal and place names. (An exception has, however, been made in the case of **Al-laah** *God, Allah*.)

6 The Arabic sounds

We have divided the pronunciation guide into three groups:

Group 1: Sounds that are more or less as in English.

Group 2: Sounds that do not occur in English, but are found in other European languages.

Group 3: Sounds that are specific to Arabic.

Note: The letter **alif** has no sound of its own and is used only to express the long vowel **aa** and as a support for the **hamzah** (see the relevant sections).

GROUP 1

00.03

b	baa'	as in باب **baab** *door*
d	daal	as in درس **dars** *lesson*
dh	dhal	as in ذلك **dháalik** *that*

Do not confuse this with the sound **th** (see below), as they convey entirely different meanings in Arabic (**dhawb** *melting*, **thawb** *a garment*).

f	faa'	as in فلفل **fílfil** *pepper*
h	haa'	as in هو **húwwa** *he*, but never omitted in speech as it very often is in English (e.g. *vehement*). An exception is the common feminine ending **-ah**, see Section 2 above.
j	jiim	as in جديد **jadíid** *new*
k	kaaf	as in كبير **kabíir** *big*
l	laam	mostly as in لا **laa** *not*, but sometimes has a duller sound, roughly as in English *alter*.
m	miim	as in ممكن **múmkin** *possible*
n	nun	as in نور **nuur** *light*
s	siin	as in سمسم **símsim** *sesame* (it is never pronounced *z* as in *things*: see **z** below)
sh	shin	as in شريعة **sharíi:ah** *sharia (Islamic law)*
t	taa'	as in تاجر **táajir** *merchant*
th	thaa'	as in ثلاثة **thaláthah** *three*
w	waaw	as in واحد **wáaHid** *one*
y	yaa'	as in يوم **yawm** *day*
z	zaay	as in زوج **zawj** *husband*

الآن دورك al-'aan dawrak

3 Practise saying these words:

درجة *degree* or *step*   بستان *orchard*   فهد *leopard*   وزارة *ministry*

GROUP 2

 00.04

r	raa'	as in رجل **rájul** *man*. This is the trilled *r* of Scottish *very* ('verry'), and common in Italian and Spanish (*Parma, Barcelona*).
gh	ghain	as in غرب **gharb** *west*. Similar to the *r* of Parisian French.
kh	khaa'	as in خارج **kháarij** *outside*. Like the sound of *ch* in Scottish *loch* and *och aye*.

الآن دورك al-'aan dawrak

4 Practise saying these words:

الرياض *Riyadh*   المغرب *Morocco*   الخليج *The Gulf*

GROUP 3

 00.05 These sounds are particular to Arabic. To pronounce them requires practice and it is best to listen to native speakers if you can.

S, T,		With the exception of **H** (see below), the capitalized consonants are
D, DH		pronounced in a way similar to their small letter versions **s**, **t**, **d** and **dh**, except that the tongue is pressed into a spoon shape and the sound is more forceful. These sounds have an effect on any surrounding vowels, which makes them sound more hollow. A rough (British) English equivalent is the difference in the *a* as in *Sam* and in *psalm*.

S   Saad   as in صغير **Saghíir** *small*

T   Taa'   as in طالب **Táalib** *student*

D   Daad   as in ضيف **Dayf** *guest*

DH   DHaa'   as in ظهر **DHuhr** *noon*

:   :ain   as in عمل **:ámal** *work*. You will find that what is normally called gagging in English is actually a restriction in the deep part of the throat. If you begin to gag and then immediately relax the muscles in order to release the airstream from the lungs, you will have produced a perfect **:ain**.

H   Haa'   as in حج **Hajj** *pilgrimage*. Pronounced in exactly the same way as **:ain**, except that, instead of completely closing the muscles referred to above, they are just constricted and the air allowed to escape. The only time English speakers come near to a (weakish) **H** is when they breathe on their glasses before cleaning them. Both **:ain** and **Haa'** should always be pronounced with the mouth fairly wide open (say 'ah').

'   hamza   as in أمل **'ámal** *hope*. The **hamzah** or glottal stop occurs in English between words pronounced deliberately and emphatically (e.g. 'She (pause) is (pause) awful.'), but is probably more familiar as the Cockney or Glaswegian pronunciation of *t* or *tt* as in *bottle*.

q   qaaf   as in قريب **qaríib** *near*. Officially pronounced as a 'back of the throat' English *c* or *k* and not related to *qu* in English. A rough equivalent is the pronunciation of the letter *c* in (British) English *calm*.

LOCAL VARIATIONS

As with any language spoken over such a wide area, regional pronunciations occur. The versions of pronunciation in Group 3 above are the officially correct ones, always used in reciting the Holy Qur'an, but local variants often slip into the pronunciation of politicians, radio and TV announcers etc. The most important of these affect the following letters:

th   Many speakers in the north and west of the Arab world find this sound difficult to pronounce and render it as either *t* or *s*.

j   In Egypt and a few other areas, this is rendered *g* as in *gold*. In the Lebanon, parts of Syria and Jordan, it sounds like the *j* of French *Jacques* (which is the same as the *s* in English *pleasure*).

dh   Sometimes becomes *d* or *z*.

D   Pronounced identically to **DH** in most of the eastern Arab world (Iraq, the Gulf and Saudi Arabia).

DH   See **D** above. Additionally, in many urban parts of Egypt, the Lebanon, Syria and Jordan it often becomes a sort of emphatic *z*-sound.

q   In informal speech, this is often pronounced as *g* in many parts of the Arab world. In the spoken Arabic of urban areas of Egypt, the Lebanon and Syria it is pronounced as a glottal stop (**hamzah**).

> **LANGUAGE TIP**
>
> The variants are given to help you avoid confusion when listening to 'live' Arabic in various parts of the Arab world. It is probably better to stick to the more formal values until your ear becomes attuned but if – as we highly recommend – you enlist the help of a native speaker, imitate his or her pronunciation.

7 Vowels

 00.06 There are only five common vowels, three of which occur both long and short. These have been transcribed as follows:

aa   as in ثالث **tháalith** *third*, a long emphatic a as in the word and in: 'Did he really eat a whole chicken? Yes he did and he ate steak as well.'

a   as in أبدا **ábadan** *never*

ii   as in كبير **kabíir** *big*

i   as in جبن **jíbin** *cheese*

uu   as in فلوس **filúus** *money*

u   as in بلدان **buldáan** *countries*

oo   as in تلفون **tilifóon** *telephone*, like *rose* as pronounced in Scotland

ai   as in بيت **bait** *house*

ay   as in دبي **dubáy** *Dubai*, like *aye*

8 Writing vowels and other signs

As short vowels are not normally written in Modern Arabic, it is better to become used to recognizing Arabic words without them. However, the transliterated Arabic throughout this course will show you which short vowel should be pronounced and the short vowels are also sometimes included on the Arabic script where helpful to understanding the patterns of words. Short vowels are normally only written in religious texts such as Qur'an (or in primary school educational texts teaching the alphabet and some dictionaries). They appear in Qur'an so there is no confusion about the meaning. Otherwise they do not appear in most modern written Arabic, but an educated reader will know where they are. In some ways it is similar to spelling conventions in English e.g. where most educated speakers know which letters are silent.

All these signs are written above or below (as indicated) the consonant they follow. For instance, to express the word **kutiba**, you write the (Arabic) consonant **k** + the vowel sign for **u**, consonant **t** + the sign for **i**, **b** + the sign for **a**, like this:

$$كُتِبَ$$

As all three letters are joining letters, the **k** has the initial form, the **t** the medial form and the **b** the final form.

The long vowels are the same signs, but followed by **alif** for **aa**, **waaw** for **uu** and **yaa'** for **ii**. For example, if the above word had all three vowels long (**kuutiibaa** – an imaginary word, for purposes of illustration only), it would be written like this:

$$كُوتِيبَا$$

A similar means is used to express the diphthong vowels **aw** and **ay**, except that, as you would expect, the vowel sign preceding the و or ي is always **a**, for example:

تَي   كَو

tay   **kaw**

ZERO VOWEL SIGN

When a consonant has no vowel after it, this is marked by writing a miniature circle (like a zero) above it; here above the **k**:

maktab

This sign is omitted at the end of words, in this case the **b**. It is often referred to as *sukun*.

DOUBLED CONSONANTS

 00.07

Doubled consonants (written in the transliteration as **bb**, **nn**, **ss**, etc.) are very important in Arabic, as they can change the meanings of words radically. They are only pronounced in English when they span two words, e.g. 'But Tim, my young friend…'. In Arabic, however, they must always be pronounced carefully, wherever they occur, with a slight hesitation between them. For example, **mathal** means *a proverb*, **maththal** means *he acted, represented*.

In Arabic, the consonant is written once only, with the following sign (a little Arabic **s** س) without the tail) above it, for example:

maththal

The sign for the vowel following the doubled letter – here an **a** – is written above the doubling sign. It is often referred to as *shada*. As you have already learned, an **i** vowel is expressed by writing a short oblique stroke under the letter. However, by convention, when a letter already has the doubling sign, the stroke is put under the sign but actually above the letter.

maththil

These double consonants must be clearly pronounced twice in Arabic. Imagine a sort of hyphen between them. Another example should make this clear:

Hamaam حمام   *pigeons*

Hammaam حمام   *bathroom*

OTHER SIGNS

The letter **alif** occasionally appears with a longer, curved stroke above it (similar to a stretched out Spanish tilde as in *cañon*). It is then pronounced as a **hamzah** (glottal stop) followed by a long **aa** vowel. An important word which you will meet often and should take pains to learn to write and pronounce correctly is the Arabic word for the Qur'an:

اَلْقُرْآن

al-qur'aan

Finally, a sign used on only a very few (but common) words is a vertical stroke above the preceding letter, often called the 'dagger **alif**'. This is simply a shorthand way of writing the long **aa** vowel. Another very important word in Arab culture is *God*, or *Allah*:

Al-laah

Here the vertical stroke is written over the doubling sign. Pronounce this **alláah** with the stress on the second syllable. (It is usually uttered with the 'dark' **l**, i.e. an **l** pronounced with the tongue hollowed at the back of the upper teeth. This gives the **aa** a 'hollow' sound.)

9 Irregular spellings

The letter **yaa'** occurs frequently at the end of words in Arabic. It is usually pronounced **-ii**, but also sometimes **-aa**. In the former case, it is usually written with two dots under it (ي) and in the latter, without them (ى), but this rule is not, unfortunately, always adhered to.

banaa

Note that in this case, the vowel preceding the **yaa'** is **a**. Words showing this characteristic will be explained as they occur.

The hybrid letter ة, the 'hidden **-t**', is always preceded by a (ـَة) (see Section 2).

Note: Both of these spellings can only occur at the end of a word. If any suffix is added to the word, they become ا and ت respectively. (This will be explained fully later in the book.)

10 One-letter words

By convention, Arabic words consisting only of one consonantal letter (and usually a short vowel) are joined to the following word. Thus **wa** *and* + **anta** *you* is written:

وَأَنْتَ

To make things clearer in transliteration, such words are separated by a hyphen: **wa-anta** in this book.

11 Stress

00.08 The best way to learn where the stress in each new word falls is to listen to the audio as often as you can, and practise saying the words and phrases out loud. Listening to native Arabic speakers and Arab TV and radio as much as possible will also help you 'get your ear in'.

One simple general rule, however, is that if a word contains a long vowel (**aa**, **uu**, etc.) the stress falls on this; and if there is more than one (long vowel), the stress falls on the one nearest the end of the word:

مَكَاتِب **makáatib** but مَكَاتِيب **makaatíib**

The stress will be on the last long syllable before a vowel ending.

To help you get used to where the stress falls, the stressed syllables of words have been marked with an acute accent: **á**, **áa**, etc. in the first few units.

12 Case endings

Classical Arabic had a set of three grammatical case endings for nouns and adjectives, but these are nowadays largely ignored in all but very formal speech such as Qur'anic recitation and ancient poetry.

The only one of these that concerns us is the so-called 'indefinite accusative', because this shows in the script. This is known as the accusative marker.

Its form is an **alif** attached to the end of the noun or adjective, technically with two slashes above the preceding consonant: ـًا It is pronounced **-an**, e.g. كتاب **kitáab**, but with accusative marker كتابًا **kitáaban**. In practice, the two slashes before the **alif** are usually omitted: كتابا.

Practice

Try writing the following words in Arabic script (without vowel signs).

a	*prince*	amíir	_____
b	*tree*	shájarah	_____
c	*doctor*	Tabíib	_____
d	*cinema*	síinima	_____
e	*film*	fíilm	_____

ﻓﻠﻨﺒﺪأ
fal-nábda'

Let's get started!

In this unit you will learn how to:
▸ *greet people*
▸ *say some essential survival words and phrases*
▸ *form short descriptive phrases*
▸ *use definites and indefinites (e.g. the articles the and a/an).*

CEFR: (A1) *Can use basic greetings and leave-taking expressions; can ask how people are.*

 ## Greetings

When spending time in Arab countries, there are some common phrases you can use as greetings. For example, the universal greeting السلام عليكم **as-salaamu :alaykum!** *peace be upon you* has a standard reply: وعليكم السلام **wa-:alaykum as-salaam** *and peace upon you*. In the same way, the reply to صباح الخير **SabáaH al-kháyr** *good morning* is صباح النور **SabáaH an-núur**, or to مساء الخير **masáa' al-kháyr** *good afternoon* or *good evening* it's مساء النور **masáa' an-núur**, and after كيف حالك؟ **káyfa Háal-ak?** *How are you?* you'd say الحمد لله **al-Hámdu lil-láah** *fine*, (lit. *'praise be to God'*). Arabs often use one greeting after another when they meet. This is done in a very ritualistic way and is considered to be good manners.

Arabs are traditionally polite people and, no matter how busy they are, they regard the use of these greetings as essential, to be said before any business is done, so keep practising the greetings until you feel confident that you can understand them and use them without difficulty.

People don't usually use terms like *Mr* and *Mrs*. In Egypt and some other northern Arab countries, people say سيدي **síidi** where we might say *Sir*, but in other countries this term is reserved for certain classes of nobility. Its correct formal pronunciation is **sáyyidi**, but this does not show in the Arabic script.

What do you think the Arabic word for *morning* is?

a صباح **SabáaH**
b الخير **al-kháyr**
c النور **an-núur**

Vocabulary builder

01.01 Listen to the new expressions and repeat them until you can say them with confidence. Listen again and complete the gaps.

GREETINGS

صباح الخير	SabáaH al-kháyr	*Good morning (lit. 'morning (of) the goodness')*
صباح النور	SabáaH an-núur	*Good morning (reply) (lit. 'morning (of) the light')*
مساء الخير	masáa' al-kháyr	*Good afternoon/good evening (lit. 'evening (of) the goodness')*
مساء النور	masáa' an-núur	*Good afternoon/good evening (reply) (lit. 'evening (of) the light')*
كيف حالك؟	kayfa Háal-ak?	*How are you? (to a man) (lit. 'How (is) condition-your?')*
كيف حالك؟	kayfa Háal-ik?	*How are you? (to a _____)*
الحمد لله	al-Hámdu lil-láah	*Fine (reply) (lit. 'praise be to God')*
أهلا وسهلا	áhlan wa-sáhlan	*Hello/welcome*
أهلا بك	áhlan bi-k	*(reply to a man)*
أهلا بك	áhlan bi-ki	*(reply to a _____)*
وأنت؟	wa-ánta/ánti	*And you? (sing. m./f.)*
بخير	bi-khayr	*Well (lit. 'in well-being')*

> **LANGUAGE TIP**
>
> In Arabic you must distinguish between a man and a woman when you are speaking to people. To say *you* to a man you say **ánta**, and to a woman you say **ánti**.

ESSENTIALS

يا	yaa	*(obligatory before anyone's name or title when addressing them)*
من فضلك	min fáDl-ak	*please (to a _____)*
من فضلك	min fáDl-ik	*please (to a woman)*
شكرا	shúkran	*thank you*
نعم	ná:am	*yes*
لا	laa	*no*
تفضل	tafáDDal	*Here you are, welcome (to a man)*
تفضلي	tafáDDali	*Here you are, welcome (to a _____)*
و	wa-	*and*
بـ	bi-	*with*
بدون	bi-dúun	*without*

Conversation 1

 السلام عليكم as-saláamu :aláy-kum *HELLO*

01.02 Let's listen to two people greeting each other.

| السلام عليكم | as-saláamu :aláy-kum | *Hello* |
| وعليكم السلام | wa- :aláy-kum as-saláam | *Hello (reply)* |

 01.03 Now listen and repeat the conversation.

| Kamáal | السلام عليكم يا جون! | as-saláamu : aláy-kum yaa John! |
| John | وعليكم السلام يا كمال! | wa :aláy-kum as-saláam, yaa Kamáal! |

 Cover up each part and say it yourself several times until you feel confident.

> **LANGUAGE TIP**
>
> Remember to pronounce the stress on every word where it is shown.

You go to visit your Arabic-speaking friend Nadia. She welcomes you into her house. What do you say to her?

Conversation 2

تحيات taHiyyaat *GREETINGS*

01.04 Suad is about to begin teaching an Arabic class at the university in Cairo. Before she starts she greets a new student.

| Suad (سعاد) | صباح الخير | SabáaH al-kháyr |
| Student (طالبة) | صباح النور | SabáaH an-núur |

1 What time of day is it?

2 Complete the greetings with the words from the box.

صباح النور مساء الخير

_____ a

_____ b

_____ c

_____ d

3 Give the appropriate greeting for these scenarios.

   a It is 11 a.m. and you go to the bank. Greet the bank clerk.

   b You are in a restaurant one evening and an acquaintance comes up and greets you. What would you say?

   c Your partner comes home from work at 7 p.m. What does he/she say to you?

   d You go into a shop. Say hello to the shopkeeper.

   e You see your neighbour in the street and she says hello to you. How would you reply?

4 Can you pick out the letters Suad says which mean _the_ in Arabic?

Conversation 3

كيف حالك؟ kayfa Háal-ak? _HOW ARE YOU?_

01.05 _Suad has a short conversation with one of the students._

1 How is the student today?

Suad (سعاد)	كيف حالك؟	káyfa Háal-ak?
Student (طالب)	الحمد لله.	al-Hámdu lil-láah
Suad (سعاد)	أهلا وسهلا.	áhlan wa-sáhlan
Student (طالب)	أهلا بك وأنت كيف حالك؟	áhlan bi-ki. wa ánti, káyfa Háal-ik?
Suad (سعاد)	الحمد لله، بخير.	al-Hámdu lil-láah, bi-kháyr

> **LANGUAGE TIP**
>
> Note the spelling of **ahlan** and **sahlan** with a final **alif**.

2 What does the student ask Suad?

> **LANGUAGE TIP**
>
> If you are speaking to a woman, you must say **káyfa Háal-ik** instead of **káyfa Háal-ak**, although there is no difference in most written Arabic. If you are talking a group of people, you must say كيف حالكم؟ **káyfa Háal-kum**. Similarly, you must say **áhlan bi-ki** to a woman (same spelling), rather than **áhlan bi-k**, or أهلا بكم **áhlan bi-kum** to a group of people.

> **LANGUAGE TIP**
>
> الحمد لله **al-Hámdu lil-láah** _Thanks be to God_ never changes and is used in many situations. Even if something unfortunate or unpleasant has happened, the devout Muslim must submit to the will of Allah and praise Him for what He has decreed. إن شاء الله **Inshá Al-láah** _If God wills_ is also used in a similar way and is often used to say no or refuse an invitation indirectly.

4

Language discovery

بيت، بيوت	**bayt, buyúut**	*house*
صغير	**Saghíir**	*young (person), small (thing)*
ولد، أولاد	**wálad, awláad**	*boy (pl. also children)*
طويل	**Tawíil**	*tall (person), long (thing)*
كتاب، كتب	**kitáab, kútub**	*book*
كبير	**kabíir**	*big*
جميل جميلة	**jamíil/jamíilah**	*beautiful, handsome*

> **LANGUAGE TIP**
>
> The feminine of most nouns and adjectives is formed by adding ة pronounced as a weak -h sound.
> This is preceded by an **a-** vowel which is not written, but it is transcribed as **-ah** in this book, e.g. **jamíil**
> (f. **jamíilah**). The feminine will not be given in this book, unless it is an exception to this simple rule.

> **LANGUAGE TIP**
>
> The plurals of nouns and adjectives in Arabic do not follow a logical system, so it is better to learn them
> along with the singular from the beginning. They are given after the singular noun in the vocabulary,
> separated by a comma.

1 DEFINITE OR INDEFINITE?

It is important in Arabic to be able to distinguish between **definite** words and phrases
and **indefinites**.

Indefinite words have *a* or *an* before them in English. There is no indefinite article or word
for *a* or *an* in Arabic.

بيت	**bayt**	*(a) house*
سندويتش	**sandawíitsh**	*(a) sandwich*

There are three types of **definite** word in English:

▶ words that have the definite article *the* – *the house*

▶ proper nouns – *Mohammed, Cairo, Egypt*

▶ pronouns such as *he, I, you,* etc.

In Arabic the definite article *the* never varies in writing, and is always ‎ال‎ **al-**. The hyphen shows that, in the Arabic script, **al-** is always attached to the word that follows it.

البيت	**al-bayt**	*the house*
الاهرام	**al-ahráam**	*the pyramids*

 ## 2 IMPORTANT PRONUNCIATION

We're going to look at two important points of Arabic pronunciation.

 01.06 For the first, listen to the example and repeat what you hear.

Note the difference between what's spoken and what's written.

Written	Pronounced
after a preceding consonant	after a preceding vowel
باب البيت **baab al-bayt** *the door of the house*	في البيت **fi l-bayt** *in the house*

> If the preceding word ends in a vowel or **-ah**, the a of **al-** in the word that follows is omitted when you speak but is still used when writing.

 01.07 Now for the second point. Listen to the example and repeat what you hear.

Note the difference between what's written and what's said.

Written	Pronounced	
	after a consonant	after a vowel
الشمس	**ash-shams** *the sun*	**sh-shams**
النور	**an-nuur** *the light*	**n-nuur**
السندويتش	**as-sandawíitsh** *the sandwich*	**s-sandawíitsh**

> If the word to which **al-** is attached begins with one of the following consonants, the l of the **al-** isn't pronounced and the following letter is doubled.

t	th	d	dh	r	z	s	sh	S	D	T	DH	l	n
ت	ث	د	ذ	ر	ز	س	ش	ص	ض	ط	ظ	ل	ن

You are pronouncing the word properly if you make a small hesitation on the doubled letters.

An easy way to remember these letters is to pronounce them all out loud. With the slight exception of **sh**, you will notice that the tip of your tongue is contacting somewhere in the region of your front teeth or the gum above them – where the letter **l** is pronounced, which is why the assimilation occurs. No other Arabic consonants are pronounced in this area.

Arabs call these the 'sun letters', simply because the word شمس **shams** *sun* begins with one of them. The remaining letters are called the 'moon letters', because قمر **qamar** *moon* does not begin with an assimilated letter.

Remember: the written form remains the same; it is only the pronunciation that varies. However, to help you, the assimilations have been represented in the transliteration. This pronunciation is not optional. If you don't follow these two aspects of pronunciation your pronunciation when speaking will be incorrect.

الآن دورك al-'aan dawrak

1 01.08 **Listen to the following words. Which begin with sun letters and which begin with moon letters?**

a	الشاي
b	الاهرام
c	السلام
d	سندويتش
e	النور
f	الكبير
g	الصغير

3 NOUNS AND ADJECTIVES

Arabic adjectives (e.g. *big, beautiful, blue*) behave like nouns but:

▶ they always follow the noun

▶ they must agree with the noun in definiteness and in gender

▶ additional adjectives are simply added after the first one with no punctuation or joining word.

If the noun is definite, the adjectives must all be definite and have the definite article.

It will be a great help when you are learning Arabic if you can come to look on nouns and adjectives as being virtually the same thing. This only happens in slightly archaic English in phrases such as 'the great and the good', 'the meek shall inherit the earth'. More commonly we use the helping word *one*: 'Which dress do you prefer?', 'The blue one'.

Arabic grammar will become easier if you mentally add the word *one* to Arabic adjectives, so that you are effectively equating them with nouns. In Arabic, the reply to the question above would have been simply, 'The blue'.

 01.09 Listen and repeat.

بيت صغير	**bayt Saghíir**	*a small house = (a) house (a) small(-one)*
الولد الطويل	**al-wálad aT-Tawiil**	*the tall boy = the-boy the-tall(-one)*
بريطانيا العظمى	**briiTáanyaa l-:úDHma**	*Great Britain = Britain the-great(-one)*
كتاب كبير جديد	**kitáab kabíir jadíid**	*a big new book = (a) book (a) big(-one) (a) new(-one)*
البنت الجميلة الصغيرة	**al-bint al-jamíilah aS-Saghíirah**	*the beautiful young girl = the-girl the-beautiful(-one) the-young(-one)*

الآن دورك **al-'aan dawrak**

2 Now match the following.

a the new house

b the small boy

c a beautiful book

d a tall girl

١ الولد الصغير

٢ كتاب جميل

٣ البيت الجديد

٤ بنت طويلة

هرم كبير
háram kabíir
a big pyramid
(a) pyramid (a) big(-one)

هرم صغير
háram Saghíir
a small pyramid
(a) pyramid (a) small(-one)

الآن دورك al-'aan dawrak

3 How do you say *the big pyramid*?

> **LANGUAGE TIP**
>
> إلى المركز التجاري
> **TO THE COMMERCIAL CENTRE**
> ←
>
> Some words end with a final ى (written without the two dots), which is pronounced **-a** (strictly **-aa**, but often shortened). إلى **ila(a)** *to/towards* is an example of this.

Word discovery

 1 Which of these words is the odd one out and why?

| سندويتش sandawíitsh | كتاب kitáab | بيت bayt | قمر qamar |

The majority of Arabic words are built around a three-consonant root. If you come across words that don't follow the three-consonant root pattern, this is likely to be because they are loan words.

When learning Arabic we usually call the first consonant of the root C^1 – i.e. first consonant – and later consonants C^2 and C^3. The vowels between are usually stated as they are (**a, i, u, aa, uu, ii** and so on) or, where they are variable, simply by v, meaning vowel.

The word pattern for this unit is $C^1aC^2iiC^3$, for example كبير **kabíir**.

The word كبير **kabíir** means *big* (or *old* when applied to people).

2 Look at the list and match the Arabic with the English.

a	البيت الكبير	**1**	a big sandwich
b	الكتاب الكبير	**2**	the big book
c	القمر الكبير	**3**	the big house
d	سندويتش كبير	**4**	the big moon

In Arabic, anything to do with the root **k-b-r** will have something to do with bigness, large size and so on. This is a very useful concept, noticed long ago by Arab philologists. Most dictionaries are still arranged according to these three-letter roots.

Here we have the three consonants **k-b-r**. In Arabic, they are fleshed out with long and short vowels. You can see that in the word كبير **kabíir** *big*, the first consonant of the root (**k**) has

fal-nábda' Let's get started! فلنبدأ 1   **9**

a vowel after it and the second consonant (**b**) has a long **ii** after it. This is a very common pattern for adjectives in Arabic.

 01.10 To help you feel the cadences (modulated sounds) of the Arabic sounds, you'll hear an English equivalent (or one as near as possible). Such words which are familiar to you will also help with the Arabic stress patterns.

Pattern	Arabic example	English sound-alike vowels
C^{1}aC^{2}iiC^3	كبير **kabíir** *big*	*marine*

It will help you greatly in learning Arabic if you learn and listen for these patterns.

Here are some more words to show the pattern:

a	صغير	**Saghíir**	*young (person), small (thing)*
b	طويل	**Tawíil**	*tall (person), long (thing)*
c	بعيد	**ba:íid**	*far, distant*
d	قريب	**qaríib**	*near*
e	جديد	**jadíid**	*new*
f	قديم	**qadíim**	*old (things)*
g	جميل	**jamíil**	*beautiful, handsome*
h	لطيف	**laTíif**	*pleasant, nice*
i	كريم	**karíim**	*noble, generous*
j	صحيح	**SaHíiH**	*correct, right*

الآن دورك **al-'aan dawrak**

3 Write down the roots for the ten words above (in Arabic or transliteration with hyphens between the letters).

Note: For this type of exercise, use the independent forms of the letters in the Arabic script.

Listen and understand
WHAT DO THEY WANT?

تاكسي	**táaksii**	*taxi*
مصباح	**miSbáaH**	*lamp*
شاي	**shaay**	*tea*
سكر	**súkkar**	*sugar*
بكم هذا؟	**bi-kam háadha?**	*how much is this?*
ثلاثة جنيهات	**thaláathah junayháat**	*three pounds*

01.11 *Some tourists are spending the day in Cairo.*

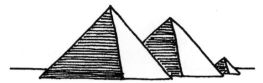

1 Listen to the conversations. Which picture belongs with each conversation?

a    b   c

_____   _____   _____

Conversation one

táaksi! al-ahráam, min faDl-ak!   تاكسي! الأهرام من فضلك.

ná:am, ya sáyyid-i!   نعم، يا سيدي!

Conversation two

al-miSbáaH min fáDl-ak   المصباح من فضلك.

tafáDDal   تفضل

shúkran   شكرا

Conversation three

shaay wa-sandawíitsh minfáDl-ak   شاي و سندويتش من فضلك.

shaay bi-súkkar?   شاي بسكر؟

laa shúkran, bidúun súkkar. bi-kam háadhaa?   لا شكرا، بدون سكر. بكم هذا؟

thaláathah junayháat   ثلاثة جنيهات

2 Which conversation takes place:
   a in a café beside the Nile? _____
   b in Khan al-Khalili market? _____
   c in Tahrir Square, in the centre of Cairo? _____

3 Find the Arabic words for the following items:
   a tea with sugar _____
   b the lamp _____
   c the pyramids _____
   d a sandwich _____

Practice

1 Match the following greetings with the appropriate reply.

a	شكرا.	١	السلام عليكم.
b	مساء النور.	٢	مساء الخير.
c	ثلاثة جنيهات.	٣	كيف حالك؟
d	وعليكم السلام.	٤	بكم هذا؟
e	الحمد لله.	٥	تفضل!

 2 01.12 Listen to some conversations in a café. What is being ordered?

a   قهو ة من فضلك.   qáhwah min fáDl-ak

b   ليمون من فضلك.   laymóon min fáDl-ak

c   كوكا كولا صغيرة من فضلك.   kookakóola Saghíirah min fáDl-ak

d   أيس كريم بشوكولاتة من فضلك.   ays kriim bi-shokoláatah min fáDl-ak

3 What does من فضلك min fáDl-ak mean?

 4 01.13 Now listen to some people talking about going places. Where do they want to be taken?

a   السينما من فضلك.   as-síinimaa min fáDl-ak

b   البنك من فضلك.   al-bank min fáDl-ak

5 See if you can match the words with the pictures.

سندويتش sandawiitsh a   تلفون tilifúun b   بيت bayt c

طماطم TamáaTim d   سينما síinima e   بيرة صغيرة biirah Saghíirah f

راديو جديد ráadyo jadíid h   برجر كبير bárgar kabíir g

1
_____

2
_____

3
_____

4
_____

5
_____

6
_____

7
_____

8
_____

6 Choose the correct word to complete the phrases.

a the new cinema   السينما الجديدة/جديدة

b a small girl   بنت الصغيرة/صغيرة

c a beautiful book   كتاب الجميل/جميل

d a long film   فيلم الطويل/طويل

e the big roomy house   البيت الكبير واسع/الواسع

> **LANGUAGE TIP**
>
> واسع **wáasi:** means *roomy, spacious*

7 Mohammed is having a party and his British friend, John, arrives. Complete the gaps.

Mohammed	كيف ـــــــــــــ ؟	káyfa ـــــــــ ?
John	ــــــــــــــــــ	
Mohammed	ــــــــــــ وسهلا.	ـــــــــ wa sáhlan
John	أهلا ـــــــــــ	áhlan ـــــــــ

8 You meet some friends. How do you ask them how they are? _____

9 A colleague comes into your office and you greet him. What do you say? _____

? Test yourself

1 How would you say these greetings in Arabic?

a Good morning. _____

b I'm fine. _____

c How are you? (to a man) _____

d Hello. _____

e Good evening. _____

2 In transliteration, change these words and phrases from indefinite to definite. (Remember to check whether they begin with sun or moon letters.)

a   سندويتش   **sandawíitsh**   _____

b   تلفون   **tilifúun**   _____

c   بيت   **bayt**   _____

d   طماطم   **TamáaTim**   _____

e   سينما   **síinima**   _____

f   بيرة صغيرة   **bíirah Saghíirah**   _____

g   برجر كبير   **bárgar kabíir**   _____

h   راديو جديد   **ráadyo jadíid**   _____

SELF CHECK	
I CAN. . .	
⬤	. . .greet people.
⬤	. . .say some essential survival words and phrases.
⬤	. . .form short descriptive phrases.
⬤	. . .use definites and indefinites.

2 التفاصيل الشخصية

at-tafaaSiil ash-shakhSíyyah

Personal details

In this unit you will learn how to:

▶ *ask someone's name and give your own name.*
▶ *say where you are from.*
▶ *form simple sentences with* **is/are.**
▶ *say* **there is/there are.**
▶ *use the numbers 1–10.*

CEFR: (A1) *Can introduce himself/herself and others, and can ask and answer questions about personal details such as where he lives; can handle numbers.*

 ## Arabic names

In most of the Middle East, people's legal names include their father and paternal grandfather's first name followed by the family or tribe name, e.g. مصطفى يوسف محمد حسن **Mustapha Yousef** (father) **Mohammed** (grandfather) **Hassan.** Mustapha's father's full name would be يوسف محمد صالح حسن **Yousef Mohammed Saleh Hassan.** If Mustapha had a sister, her name would follow the same paternal pattern, e.g. **Safia Yousef Mohammed Hassan.** Historically the names would be connected with the words ابن **ibn (bin)** *son* or بنت **bint** *daughter* to indicate the relationships, but this is increasingly rare except in the Gulf. Once people have children, they are traditionally referred to as أبو **Abu** *Father* or أم **Umm** *Mother* of (eldest (male) child's name). So, for example, Yousef would be **Abu Mustapha** أبو مصطفى.

 What do you think Yousef's wife would be known as?

Vocabulary builder

 02.01 Listen to the new expressions and repeat them until you can say them with confidence. Listen again and complete the gaps with the places from the box.

PLACES

Dubai	Egypt	Alexandria	Cairo
Sudan	France	London	Manchester

مصر	miSr	_____
الإسكندرية	al-iskandaríyyah	_____
القاهرة	al-qáahirah	_____
دبي	dubáy	_____
لندن	lándan	_____
مانشستر	mánshestar	_____
السودان	as-suudáan	_____
فرنسا	faránsa	_____

> **LANGUAGE TIP**
>
> Most, although not all, place names are regarded as feminine.

NUMBERS

واحد	wáaHid	one	سبعة	sáb:ah	seven
اثنين	ithnáyn	two	ثمانية	thamáanyah	eight
ثلاثة	thaláathah	three	تسعة	tís:ah	nine
أربعة	árba:ah	four	عشرة	:áshrah	ten
خمسة	khámsah	five	صفر	Sifr	zero
ستة	síttah	six			

KEY PHRASES

ما اسمك؟	maa ísm-ak/ísm-ik (m./f.)?	What is your name?
اسمي...	ísm-i...	My name is…
من أين أنت؟	min áyna ánta/ánti (m./f.)?	Where are you from?
أنا من...	ána min...	I am from…
أنا من الخرطوم.	ána min al-kharTúum	I am from Khartoum.
كم رقم تلفونك؟	kam raqm tilifóon-ak?/-ik?(m./f.)	What's your telephone number?

> **LANGUAGE TIP**
>
> In Arabic, some possessive pronouns, e.g. *your*, vary according to whether you are speaking to a man, a woman or several people.

Conversation 1

 من أين أنت؟ min áyna ánta? *Where are you from?*

حسنا	**Hásanan** (note spelling)	*well, right, OK*
من	**min**	*from*
في	**fii**	*in*

02.02 *Suad introduces herself to her students and asks one of them some questions.*

1 What is the student's name?

Suad	حسنا. أنا اسمي سعاد. ما اسمك؟
Student	أنا اسمي مايكل.
Suad	أهلا وسهلا يا مايكل. من أين أنت؟
Student	أنا من مانشستر في إنجلترا. وأنت؟
Suad	أنا من الإسكندرية في مصر.

2 Answer the questions.
   a Where does the student come from? _____
   b Where does Suad come from? _____

Now read the conversation.

3 Find the Arabic for:
   a I'm from Manchester. _____
   b I'm from Alexandria. _____

 4 Can you see an Arabic word meaning *to be*?

 Now cover up each part and say it yourself several times until you feel confident.

Conversation 2

مصر جميلة miSr jamíilah Egypt is beautiful

جدا	**jíddan** (note spelling)	*very*
مدينة، مدن	**madíinah**	*city*
هي	**híya**	*she, it (f.)*
قديم / قديمة	**qadíimah/qadíim**	*old (of things only)*
المتحف المصري	**al-mátHaf al-míSri**	*The Egyptian Museum*
ميدان التحرير	**maydáan at-taHríir**	*Tahrir Square*
قريب من	**qaríib min**	*near to (lit. 'from')*
فندق النيل	**fúnduq an-níil**	*Nile Hotel*
هناك	**hunáaka**	*there is/are*
مطعم، مطاعم	**máT:am**	*restaurant*
ممتاز	**mumtáaz**	*excellent*
طبعا	**Táb:an** (note spelling)	*naturally, of course*
الجيزة	**al-jíizah/geezah**	*Giza, a district of Cairo (in Egypt the letter ج is pronounced like g in garden)*

 02.03 *Suad tells her students a little about Egypt.*

1 What does she say about Cairo?

> مصر جميلة جدا. القاهرة مدينة كبيرة، وهي قديمة جدا.
> المتحف المصري في ميدان التحرير قريب من فندق النيل.
> هناك مطعم ممتاز في فندق النيل في ميدان التحرير. وطبعا هناك الأهرام في الجيزة.

2 Answer the questions.
   a Where is the Egyptian Museum? _____
   b What does Suad recommend in the hotel? _____

3 How would you say *There is an excellent hotel in the city* in Arabic?

Conversation 3

رقم تلفونك كم؟ raqm tilifóon-ak kam? *What's your telephone number?*

0	1	2	3	4	5	6	7	8	9	10
.	١	٢	٣	٤	٥	٦	٧	٨	٩	١٠

 02.04 After the class, some of the students want to arrange to meet up. They exchange telephone numbers.

1 Listen to the audio while looking at the conversation. Do you notice anything unexpected about the way the numbers are written?

> زكي   رقم تلفونك كم يا حامد؟
>
> حامد   رقم تلفوني ٦٣٤٧٢١١. ورقم تلفونك أنت؟
>
> زكي   رقم تلفوني ٦٢١٥٥٠٠. يا ماري، رقم تلفونك كم؟
>
> ماري   رقم تلفوني ٦٢٠٧٥٨٩

2 What is Zaki's telephone number? And what is Marie's? _____

3 Find the Arabic for *telephone number*. _____

4 How would you say *My telephone number is 33075*? _____

 5 Which question would you use when asking *What's his number*?

a رقم تلفونك كم؟

b رقم تلفونه كم؟

 # Language discovery

1 HOW TO SAY *IS* AND *ARE* IN ARABIC

There is no equivalent of the verb *to be* in the present tense in Arabic. Sentences which contain the words *is* or *are* in English are constructed in Arabic by putting together the following:

▶ any definite noun with an indefinite noun or adjective:

البيت كبير	**al-bayt kabíir**	*the house (is a) big(-one) = The house is big*
محمد مشغول	**muHámmad mashghúul**	*Mohammed (is a) busy(-person) = Mohammed is busy*
هو مدير	**húwa mudíir**	*He (is a) director = He is a director*

▶ a definite noun or a pronoun with a phrase beginning with a preposition:

| أنا من الإسكندرية. | **ána min al-iskandaríyyah** | I (am) from Alexandria = I am from Alexandria |
| بيروت في لبنان. | **bayrúut fii lubnáan** | Beirut (is) in the Lebanon = Beirut is in the Lebanon |

If a definite noun is put with a definite noun or adjective, a separating pronoun must be inserted, to make the meaning clear:

| محمد هو المدير | **muHámmad <u>húwa</u> al-mudíir** | Mohammed he (is) the director = Mohammed is the director |

Here is a summary of how to make definite and indefinite phrases and sentences in Arabic:

بيت كبير	**bayt kabíir**	a big house (lit. '(a) house (a) big(-one)')
البيت الكبير	**al-bayt al-kabíir**	the big house (lit. 'the-house the-big(-one)')
البيت كبير	**al-bayt kabíir**	the house is big (lit. 'the-house (is a) big(-one)')
ناصر هو الرئيس	**náaSir húwa r-ra'íis**	Nasser is the boss (lit. 'Nasser he the-boss')

2 HOW TO SAY *THERE IS, THERE ARE*

This is expressed in modern Arabic by starting the sentence with هناك **hunáaka** *there*:

| هناك مطعم في الميدان | **hunáaka máT:am fi l-maydáan** | There is a restaurant in the square |
| هناك غرف واسعة في الفندق | **hunáaka ghúraf wáasi:ah fi l-fúnduq** | There are spacious rooms in the hotel |

3 THE ARABIC NUMBERS 1–10

We have given the numbers in their spoken or colloquial forms. In strictly grammatical Arabic, the use of the numbers is complicated and so these forms are the ones nearly always used.

There are two main points to remember when writing Arabic numbers:

▶ The numerals are written from left to right (the opposite direction of the script), for example:

| ٦٢ | ٧٣١ | ٨٥٤ | ٧٥٩١ | ٤٠٠٢ |
| 62 | 731 | 854 | 7591 | 4002 |

▶ The written forms given are the standard ones used in most of the Arab world, but some countries (mainly in North Africa) use the same forms as in English (1, 2, 3, 4, etc.), and this tendency seems to be spreading even in the Middle East.

We call our numerical system 'Arabic' to distinguish it from Roman, but the forms of the numbers have changed slightly over time. Still, if you use a little imagination – and turn some of them through 90˚ – you should spot the similarities.

0	1	2	3	4	5	6	7	8	9	10
.	١	٢	٣	٤	٥	٦	٧	٨	٩	١.

4 PERSONAL PRONOUNS

Personal pronouns are always definite, i.e. if you say *he*, you are talking about one particular person.

These are the personal pronouns:

أنا	**ána**	*I*		نحن	**náHnu**	*we*
أنت	**ánta**	*you (m.)*		أنتم	**ántum**	*you (m. pl.)*
أنت	**ánti**	*you (f.)*		أنتن	**antúnna**	*you (f. pl.)*
هو	**húwa**	*he*		هم	**hum**	*they (m. pl. or a mixed group)*
هي	**híya**	*she*		هن	**húnna**	*they (f. pl.)*

> **LANGUAGE TIP**
>
> The final **alif** of أنا **ana** is there to distinguish it from other similarly spelled words. Pronounce it short, and accent the first syllable. (In fact most final **-aa** sounds in informal modern Arabic tend to be pronounced short.)

The male and female forms of *you* (singular) are identical in unvowelled writing. The context usually makes it clear which is intended.

Since all Arabic words are either masculine or feminine, in English it must be translated as *he* or *she*, depending on the gender of the word:

الميدان كبير	**al-maydáan kabíir**	*the square (m.) is big*
هو كبير	**húwa kabíir**	*it is big*
السيارة صغيرة	**as-sayyáarah Saghíirah**	*the car (f.) is small*
هي صغيرة	**híya Saghíirah**	*it is small*

5 ASKING QUESTIONS IN ARABIC

There are several ways to ask questions in Arabic:

▶ by using a question word such as *which?*, *what?* or *where?*:

 1 Look back and find any question words you can in the conversations and in Unit 1.

ما اسمك؟	**maa ísm-ak?**	*What is your name?*
من أين أنت؟	**min áyna ánta?**	*Where are you from? (lit. 'from where you?')*

▶ by placing هل **hal** or أ **'a** at the beginning of the sentence, acting as a verbal question mark if no question word is present:

هل محمد مشغول؟	**hal muHámmad mashghúul**	*Is Mohammed busy? (lit. '(?) Mohammed (is a) busy (-person)')*
أهو مشغول؟	**'a-húwa mashghúul**	*Is he busy? (lit. '(?) He (is a) busy (-person)')*

There is no precise rule about which to use, except that أ **a** is usually used with personal pronouns. Written question marks are also used in modern Arabic, in addition to these question words.

Arabic words which consist of only one letter plus a short vowel, such as أ **a** or و **wa**, must not be written alone but are attached to the following word.

 ## 6 PRONUNCIATION OF AL- AFTER LONG VOWELS

When Arabic prepositions ending with a long vowel, such as **fii** *in* are placed before a word beginning with **al-** *the*, the **a** of **al-** disappears and the vowel of the preposition is pronounced short:

في المدينة	**fii al-madíinah → fi l-madíinah**	*in the city*

If the word begins with one of the 'sun letters', the doubling of the initial consonant still applies.

في السعودية	**fi s-sa:uudíyyah**	*in Saudi (Arabia)*

IRREGULAR SPELLINGS

Some of the most common prepositions (e.g. على **:álaa** *on*, إلى **ílaa** *to/towards*) have an irregular spelling of the final **aa** vowel which is written as a **yaa'** without the dots. This is also shortened before **al-**.

Word discovery

The root of a word gives an idea of its meaning. For example, the root ب-ر-د **b-r-d** means the word has something to do with *cold*:

بارد   <u>**báarid**</u>   *cold* (adjective: not used for people)

 1 Given the above example, how do you think you can make adjectives out of some roots?

 02.05 The word pattern for this unit is: C¹aaC²iC³; the example بارد **báarid** sounds like the English *calmish*.

Listen to the following examples.

a	عادل	:áadil	*just, upright*
b	لازم	láazim	*necessary*
c	ناشف	náashif	*dry*
d	كامل	káamil	*complete, perfect*
e	نافع	náafi:	*useful*
f	صالح	SáaliH	*doing right, upright, honest*
g	سالم	sáalim	*safe, sound*

الآن دورك **al-'aan dawrak**

2 Extract the roots from the seven words above, using Arabic script.

Practice

1 Look at pictures a–f. Using the phrase أنا من...، complete what each person would say.

a _____   b _____   c _____

d _____   e _____   f _____

2 Change the indefinite following noun/adjective phrases into definite phrases.

e.g.   كتاب كبير ← الكتاب الكبير

kitaab kabiir   ➔   al-kitaab al-kabiir

a بيت صغير	d سكرتير جديد
b سيارة جميلة	e مدير مشغول
c ولد طويل	

3 Change the phrases in the previous exercise into *is/are* sentences.

e.g.   الكتاب كبير ← الكتاب الكبير

al-kitaab al-kabiir   ➔   al-kitaab kabiir

4 Now substitute a pronoun for the noun in the sentences in the previous exercise.

e.g.   هو كبير ← الكتاب كبير

al-kitaab kabiir   ➔   huwa kabiir

5 Change the following statements into questions.

d الكتاب جديد	a أنت من مصر
e يتكلم عربي	b محمد في دبي
	c هي أمريكية

> **LANGUAGE TIP**
>
> يتكلم yatakállam mean *he speaks*; and عربي: árabi means *Arab, Arabic* and is more informal than the standard عربية which can also be used for the language.

6 Change the following questions into statements.

a هل السيارة جديدة؟   d هل محمد هنا؟

b أهي مشغولة؟   e أهو مشغول؟

c هل الفندق قريب من الأهرام؟

 7 02.06 Where do you think the following people are from? Listen and repeat what they are saying.

a أنا من تونس.   d أنا من اسكتلاندا.

b أنا من لبنان.   e أنا من أبو ظبي.

c أنا من باريس.   f أنا من إيطاليا.

8 In the telephone directory, all the UAE airports are listed together. Which of the six airports would you get if you dialled:

a 245555?   **1** Abu Dhabi

b 448111?   **2** Dubai

c 757611?   **3** Sharjah

4 Ras al Khaimah

5 Fujairah

6 Al Ain

مطارات الإمارات
• مطار أبو ظبي الدولي ٧٥٧٦١١
• مطار دبي الدولي ٢٤٥٥٥٥
• مطار الشارقة الدولي ٥٨١٠٠٠
• مطار رأس الخيمة الدولي ٤٤٨١١١
• مطار الفجيرة الدولي ٢٧٦٢٢٢
• مطار العين الدولي ٨٥٥٥٥٥

LANGUAGE TIP

مطار، ات maTáar, -áat means *airport*

---

9 Here is a list of international dialling codes from a Jordanian telephone directory.

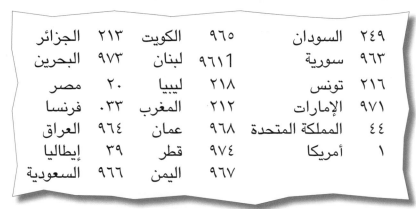

الجزائر ٢١٣	الكويت ٩٦٥	السودان ٢٤٩
البحرين ٩٧٣	لبنان ٩٦١١	سورية ٩٦٣
مصر ٢٠	ليبيا ٢١٨	تونس ٢١٦
فرنسا ٠٣٣	المغرب ٢١٢	الإمارات ٩٧١
العراق ٩٦٤	عمان ٩٦٨	المملكة المتحدة ٤٤
إيطاليا ٣٩	قطر ٩٧٤	أمريكا ١
السعودية ٩٦٦	اليمن ٩٦٧	

What is the code for:

a Bahrain? _____   **d** Qatar? _____

b Egypt? _____   **e** Saudi Arabia? _____

c America? _____   **f** Italy? _____

Test yourself

1 How would you say these questions and phrases in Arabic?

  a What is your name? _____

  b Where are you from? _____

  c What's your telephone number? _____

  d My name is… _____

  e I am from London. _____

  f Is the car small? _____

2 Complete the number table.

اثنين	ithnáyn	_____ **a**	2
_____ **b**	wáaHid	_____ **c**	_____ **d**
_____ **e**	_____ **f**	_____ **g**	5
اثنين صفر أربعة خمسة ستة	ithnáyn Sifr árba:ah khámsah síttah	٢٠٤٥٦	_____ **h**
تسعة ثلاثة ثمانية سبعة	tís:ah thaláathah tamáanyah sáb:ah	_____ **i**	9387

SELF CHECK

	I CAN...
○	. . . ask someone's name and give my own name.
○	. . . say where I am from.
○	. . . construct simple sentences with *is/are*.
○	. . . say *there is/there are*.
○	. . . use the numbers 1–10.

كيف تصف نفسك
kayfa taSif nafs-ak

How you describe yourself

In this unit you will learn how to:
▶ *say your nationality*
▶ *say which languages you speak*
▶ *talk about more than one object*
▶ *say the names of some places around town*
▶ *talk about professions.*

CEFR: (A1) *Can use a series of phrases and sentences to describe educational background and present or most recent job; can understand sentences and frequently used expressions related to areas of most immediate relevance (basic personal or family info, employment).*

📷 Arabic professions

While there are lots of words for different professions in Arabic, there are two words which cover many different jobs and are therefore used a great deal: مدير **mudíir** *manager* and مهندس **muhándis** *engineer*.

مدير can be used for most jobs which have an administrative element, so any type of manager or director.

مهندس can be used for most jobs which have a technical element, e.g. civil engineer, architect, electrical engineer, mechanical engineer, etc. It is linked to the word for geometry الهندسة **al-handasah**. Sometimes, particularly in Egyptian Arabic, you will hear the term باش مهندس **baash muhandis**, which means *chief engineer*. This is an honorary title which is commonly used in spoken language. The word باش comes from Ottoman Turkish and means *head*.

What do you think مدير الفندق means?

Vocabulary builder

03.01 Listen to the new expressions and repeat them until you can say them with confidence. Listen again and complete the gaps.

PEOPLE, PLACES AND LANGUAGES

عمان	:ammáan	*Amman*
إنجلترا	ingiltárra (with g as in garden)	_____
العربية	al-:arabíyyah	*Arabic, the Arabic language (more formal than :árabi)*
أردني	úrdunii	*Jordanian*

COMMON PHRASES

مرحباً	márHaban	*Welcome, hello*
عن إذنك	:an ídhn-ak/:an ídhn-ik	*excuse me, by your leave (to a man/woman)*
مع الأسف	má:a l-ásaf	*I'm sorry./Unfortunately* (It is used when an English speaker would use 'Sorry' as a rhetorical device rather than a genuine apology.)
لا	laa	*no, not*
فقط	fáqaT	*only*
_____ / كثيرة	kathíirah/kathíir	*much, many*

USEFUL PHRASES

أتكلم الإنجليزية	atakállam al ingliiziah	*I speak _____*
لا أتكلم العربية	laa atakállam al:árabiah	*I don't speak Arabic*
بطلاقة	bi-Taláaqah	*fluently*
_____ / قليل	qalíilah/qalíil	*a little, few*
يتكلم فرنساوي	yatakállam faransáawi	*he speaks French*
تتكلم _____	tatakállam al:árabiah	*she speaks _____*
ما عملك؟	maa :ámal-ak/:ámal-ik?	*What is your occupation? (to a man/woman)*

28

Conversation 1

 أأنت سوداني؟ 'a-ánta suudáani? *ARE YOU SUDANESE?*

طنطا   **TánTaa**   *Tanta (a town in Egypt)*

 03.02 *Two of the students in Suad's class are asking each other where they come from.*

Listen to the first part of this conversation.

1 How does Zaki ask 'Where is Tanta?'

حسام	مرحبا . أأنت مصري؟
زكي	لا، أنا سوداني من الخرطوم. وأنت؟
حسام	أنا مصري من طنطا .
زكي	أين طنطا؟
حسام	طنطا قريبة من القاهرة.

2 Answer the questions.
   a What nationality is Zaki? _____
   b What town does he come from? _____

03.03 *The students in Suad's class all begin to talk about their nationalities.*

Now listen to the rest of this conversation.

3 What is the Arabic word for *I*?

سعاد	أنا مصرية، وأنت يا مايك؟
مايك	أنا إنجليزي.
كايلي	أنا أسترالية.
يونس	أنا لبناني. أنا من بيروت.
ماري	أنا فرنسية.

4 Where does everyone come from?
   a Suad _____   **d** Younis _____
   b Mike _____   **e** Marie _____
   c Kylie _____

Conversation 2

 هل تتكلم إنجليزي؟ hal tatakállam inglíizii? *DO YOU SPEAK ENGLISH?*

راكب   **ráakib**   *passenger*

 03.04 On a flight to Jordan, Julie, an English girl, gets talking to one of the other passengers.

Listen to the conversation several times.

1 Which language(s) does the passenger speak/not speak?

عن إذنك. من أين أنت؟	راكب
أنا من إنجلترا. وأنت؟	جولي
أنا من عمان. أنا أردني.	راكب
هل تتكلم إنجليزي؟	جولي
لا، مع الأسف، لا أتكلم إنجليزي. أتكلم عربي فقط.	راكب
تتكلمين العربية بطلاقة!	
لا، قليلة فقط.	جولي

2 Listen again and find the Arabic for the following:
   a Do you speak English?   **b** A little.

3 The passenger thinks Julie speaks good Arabic. True or false?

Conversation 3

 ما عملك؟ maa :ámal-ak? *WHAT'S YOUR OCCUPATION?*

جامعة لندن   **jáami:at lándan**   *University (of) London*

طبيب، أطباء   **Tabíib, (pl.) aTibbaa'***   *doctor*

 03.05 During the flight the passenger asks Julie what she does.

1 What is Julie's occupation at the moment?

ما عملك؟	راكب
أنا طالبة في جامعة لندن. وأنت؟	جولي
أنا طبيب في عمان.	راكب

2 Where does the passenger work?

3 Find the Arabic equivalent for:

a What's your occupation? _____

b I am a doctor. _____

LANGUAGE TIP

When you refer to a woman's profession in Arabic, add **-ah (ة)** to the masculine.

Masculine		Feminine		
طبيب	**Tabíib**	طبيبة		doctor
طالب	**Táalib**	طالبة		student
مدرس	**mudárris**	مدرسة		teacher
مهندس	**muhándis**	مهندسة		engineer
مدير	**mudíir**	مديرة		manager
رئيس	**ra'íis**	رئيسة		boss
محمد مدير		**muHámmad mudíir**		Mohammed is a manager
ليلى مدرسة		**láylaa mudárrisah**		Leila is a teacher

Conversation 4

 هل لندن مدينة كبيرة؟ **hal lándan madíinah kabíirah? *IS LONDON A BIG CITY?***

جسر، جسور	**jisr, (pl.) jusúur**	bridge
محل، محلات	**maHáll, (pl.) maHalláat**	shop, store
جامعة	**jáami:ah**	university
وسط	**wasT** or **wasaT**	middle

 03.06 The passenger asks Julie about London.

1 Name one of the places Julie mentions in London.

هل لندن مدينة كبيرة؟	راكب
نعم، هي مدينة كبيرة جدا. هناك متاحف كبيرة كثيرة وجسور ومحلات.	جولي
أين الجامعة؟	راكب
هي في وسط المدينة، قريبة من المتحف البريطاني.	جولي

2 Which institution does the passenger ask her about?

Language discovery

حقيبة	Haqíibah	bag
بعيد / بعيدة	ba:íid/ba:íidah	far/far away
نظيف/ نظيفة	naDHíif/naDHíifah	clean
وسخ / وسخة	wásikh/wásikhah	dirty

1 MASCULINE AND FEMININE: REMINDER

All words in Arabic are either masculine or feminine in gender. Where we use the word *it* in English for objects, Arabic uses *he* or *she* depending on the gender of the object:

المكتب نظيف	al-máktab naDHíif	the office is clean
هو نظيف	húwa naDHíif	it is clean
الجامعة بعيدة	al-jáami:ah ba:íidah	the university is far (away)
هي بعيدة	híya ba:íidah	it is far (away)

2 FEMININE ENDINGS

There is no marker for masculine words, but most feminine words are marked by the ending ة.

This is pronounced as a weak *h* sound and is always preceded by an **a-** vowel, which is not written. The ending has been transcribed as **-ah** in this book.

A few Arabic words for female family members, for example أم **umm** *mother*, have no feminine gender marker, but are naturally dealt with as feminine.

3 AGREEMENT

Adjectives agree in gender, number and definiteness with the noun they are describing. This applies to the three types of construction you already know: indefinite phrases, definite phrases and *is/are* sentences:

حقيبة ثقيلة	Haqíibah thaqíilah	a heavy bag
الميدان الكبير	al-maydáan al-kabíir	the big square
الغرفة وسخة	al-ghúrfah wásikhah	The room is dirty.

Unless otherwise stated, you can assume that the feminine of any word is formed by adding
ـة as shown.

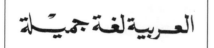 **al-:arabíyyah lúghah jamíilah**
Arabic is a beautiful language.

4 NATIONALITY ADJECTIVES

1 Look at the countries and then look at the nationality adjectives. How do you change a country name into a masculine adjective? How do you change a country name into a feminine adjective?

| مصر | **miSr** | *Egypt* | مصري/مصرية | **míSrii/miSríyyah** | *Egyptian* |
| لبنان | **lubnáan** | *Lebanon* | لبناني/لبنانية | **lubnáanii/lubnaaníyyah** | *Lebanese* |

> **LANGUAGE TIP**
>
> The final **-ii** of the masculine is technically **-iyy**, but this is not normally reflected in the pronunciation.
>
> أنا سوداني/أنا سودانية   **suudaaníyyah/ána suudáanii**   *I am Sudanese*

Where the name of a country ends in **-aa** or **-ah**, this is omitted:

بريطانيا	**briiTáanya**	*Britain*	بريطاني/بريطانية	**briiTáanii/briiTaaníyyah**	*British*
أمريكا	**amríikaa**	*America*	أمريكي/أمريكية	**amríikii/amriikíyyah**	*American*
مكة	**mákkah**	*Mecca*	مكي/مكية	**mákkii/makkíyyah**	*Meccan*

Many Arabic place names have the word *the* (**al-**) in front of them, as in English *Canada*, but *the United States*. When this occurs, the Arabic **al-** is omitted from the nationality adjective:

| المغرب | **al-mághrib** | *Morocco* | مغربي/مغربية | **mághribii/maghribíyyah** | *Moroccan* |
| الكويت | **al-kuwáyt** | *Kuwait* | كويتي/كويتية | **kuwáytii/kuwaytíyyah** | *Kuwaiti* |

5 MORE THAN ONE

There are no particular rules for forming Arabic plurals and they should be learned along with the singular, as they are given in the vocabulary. The word **al-** *the* does not change in the plural:

| الغرفة | **al-ghúrfah** | *the room* |
| الغرف | **al-ghúraf** | *the rooms* |

6 PLURALS OF PEOPLE AND OBJECTS

Plurals of objects and abstracts are regarded in Arabic as feminine singular. So all adjectives agree by using their feminine singular, and the pronoun **híya** *she* is used to refer to *them*:

كتب طويلة	**kútub Tawíilah**	*long books*
الكتب الطويلة	**al-kútub aT-Tawíilah**	*the long books*
الكتب طويلة.	**al-kútub Tawíilah**	*The books are long.*
هي طويلة.	**híya Tawíilah**	*They are long.*

7 TALKING ABOUT ONE OF SOMETHING

The word for *one* is an adjective and therefore comes after its noun and agrees with it like any other adjective:

| فندق واحد | **fúnduq wáaHid** | *one hotel* |
| غرفة واحدة | **ghúrfah wáHidah** | *one room* |

8 THE VERB TO SPEAK

Here are the singular present tense forms of the verb تكلم **takállam** *to speak*.

2 Complete the gaps with the correct English pronoun, e.g. *he, she, you.*

أتكلم	**atakállam**	_____ *speak*
تتكلم	**tatakállam**	_____ *speak (m.)*
تتكلمين	**tatakallamíin**	_____ *speak (f.)*
يتكلم	**yatakállam**	_____ *speaks*
تتكلم	**tatakállam**	_____ *speaks*

> **LANGUAGE TIP**
>
> The same set of prefixes is used for the present tense of all Arabic verbs, so you must learn these thoroughly. Note that the *you* (m.) and *she* forms are identical.

| هل يتكلم جون عربي؟ | **hal yatakállam juun :árabi?** | *Does John speak Arabic?* |
| يتكلم عربي بطلاقة. | **yatakállam :árabi bi-Taláaqah** | *He speaks Arabic fluently.* |

Word discovery

 03.07 The word pattern for this unit is maC¹C²uuC³, for example, **mashghúul** مشغول, which sounds like the English *Mam(e)luke.*

This word pattern expresses something or someone to which an action has been done, called a <u>passive participle</u> in English.

Mashghúul, comes from the root **sh-gh-l**, *work*; so **mashghúul** means *made to work*, i.e. *busy*.

Mamlúuk is an Arabic word meaning *owned*, as the Mam(e)luke rulers in Egypt originally were, having been brought in as soldier slaves.

The **ma-** never changes. It is a prefix and can be applied to any root, but is not part of it.

Here are some more examples.

a	مكتوم	maktúum	*concealed*
b	مكتوب	maktúub	*written*
c	مسموح	masmúuH	*permitted*
d	ممنوع	mamnúu:	*forbidden*
e	مبسوط	mabsúuT	*contented, happy*
f	مفروض	mafrúuD	*necessary, obligatory*

الآن دورك al-'aan dawrak
Extract the roots from the six words above.

_____

_____

_____

_____

_____

 Practice

 1 03.08 **Listen to the audio and work out which country in the box these people say they come from.**

| 1 عمان   2 الأردن   3 الكويت   4 المغرب   5 البحرين |

a	مرحبا، أنا مغربية	márHaban, ánaa maghribíyyah
b	صباح الخير، أنا أردني	SabáaH al-khayr, ána úrdunii
c	أهلا، أنا عماني	áhlan, ánaa :umáanii
d	مرحبا، أنا بحرينية	márHaban, ánaa baHrayníyyah
e	وأنا كويتي	wa-ánaa kuwáytii

كيف تصف نفسك 3 *kayfa taSif nafs-ak How you describe yourself*   **35**

2 How many of these countries do you recognize? Match them with their corresponding nationality and language.

Country	Nationality	Language
a إيطاليا	1 تونسي	A الإسبانية
b هولندا	2 أسترالي	B العربية
c إسبانيا	3 ألماني	C الهولندية
d أستراليا	4 إيطالي	D الألمانية
e تونس	5 فرنسي	E الإيطالية
f ألمانيا	6 إسباني	F الفرنسية
g فرنسا	7 هولندي	G الإنجليزية

3 Michael is writing to an Arabic-speaking friend about someone he has met. Read this part of his letter and answer the questions.

> اسمها سلمى وهي سورية من دمشق. تتكلم اللغة العربية والانجليزية والفرنسية. هي مدرسة.

a What is her name? _____

b Where does she come from? _____

Now find the Arabic for the following expressions:

c She is a teacher. _____

d She speaks Arabic. _____

جنسية	**jinsíyyah**	*nationality*
أية	**áyyah**	*any*
غيرِ	**ghayr**	*other than*
قليلاً	**qalíilan**	*slightly, a bit*

4 Read the information about Martin Romano.

مارتن رومانو من أمريكا. هو طالب. يتكلم انجليزي و إيطالي بطلاقة وعربي قليلا.

03.09 Martin is registering with a college in Cairo for an evening class. The secretary asks him some questions about himself. Imagine that you are Martin. How would you answer the following questions?

السكرتيرة ما اسمك؟	
مارتن	a _____
السكرتيرة ما جنسيتك؟	

	مارتن	b ——————
	السكرتيرة	ما عملك؟
	مارتن	c ——————
	السكرتيرة	هل تتكلم عربي؟
	مارتن	d ——————
	السكرتيرة	تتكلم إنجليزي بطلاقة طبعا؟
	مارتن	e ——————
	السكرتيرة	وأية لغة غير الإنجليزية؟
	مارتن	f ——————

مشهور	**mashhúur**	*famous*
سعيد	**sa:íid**	*happy, joyful*
صيدلية، ـات	**Saydalíyyah, -aat**	*pharmacy*

5 Give the correct adjectives from the masculine words in brackets.

١ السكرتيرة (مشغول)

٢ الأهرام (المصري) (مشهور)

٣ الفيلم (جديد)

٤ السيارة (الكبير) (أمريكي)

٥ سميرة طالبة (جديد)

٦ هل اللغة (الانجليزي) (نافع)؟

٧ هناك في دبي فنادق (جديد) (كثير)

٨ هناك في الميدان صيدلية (واحد)

٩ فاطمة بنت (سعيد)

6 What are the professions of these people? Write a sentence using a personal pronoun, as in the example.

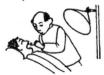

هو طبيب اسنان *húwa Tabíib asnáan He is a dentist.*

طبيب أسنان **Tabíib asnáan** *dentist*

Test yourself

1 How would you say these questions and phrases in Arabic?

a Are you Sudanese? _____

b Do you speak Arabic? _____

c Is Mecca a big city? _____

d What's your occupation? _____

e Where's the museum? _____

f He is a doctor. _____

2 03.06 Complete the gaps from Conversation 4 without looking back. Then listen to the audio to check.

راكب   هل لندن a _____ كبيرة؟

جولي   نعم، هي مدينة b _____ جدا. هناك متاحف كبيرة كثيرة وجسور ومحلات.

راكب   c _____ الجامعة؟

جولي   هي في d _____ المدينة، قريبة من المتحف البريطاني.

SELF CHECK

	I CAN. . .
○	. . . say my nationality.
○	. . . say which languages I speak.
○	. . . talk about more than one object.
○	. . . say the names of some places around town.
○	. . . talk about professions.

هذا وذلك
háadhaa wa-dháalik
This and that

In this unit you will learn how to:
▶ *tell the time*
▶ *ask about opening times*
▶ *say the days of the week*
▶ *say the numbers 11–20*
▶ *form phrases and sentences with* this, that, those, *etc.*

CEFR: (A1/A2) *Can indicate time by such phrases as next week, last Friday, in November, 3:00; can handle numbers, quantities, cost and time.*

Telling the time

In Arab countries, particularly in the Muslim communities, it is still very common to time things according to prayer times. This is fairly easy, as the call to prayer can be heard everywhere and provides a rhythm to the day. There are five main prayer times in Islam: **Fajr**, **Dhur**, **Asr**, **Maghrib** and **Isha**, which relate to the position of the sun. Often a coffee or lunch invitation might be for بعد الظهر **ba:d aDH-DHúhr** (this is also the normal word for *afternoon*) or an evening dinner invitation will be indicated as بعد المغرب **ba:d al-maghrib** *after Maghrib/sunset*.

If it is not clear from the context whether a time referred to is a.m. or p.m., these additional words may be placed after the time: الصبح **aS-SúbH** *morning, forenoon,* الظهر **aDH-DHúhr** *(around) noon,* بعد الظهر **ba:d aDH-DHúhr** *afternoon,* العصر **al-:áSr** *late afternoon* (about 4 p.m.), and المساء **al-masáa'** *evening,* الليل **al-layl** *night.*

If someone invited you to their house at الساعة تسعة الصبح **as-sáa:ah tís:ah aS-SubH**, what time would they be expecting you? And at الساعة سبعة المساء **as-sáa:ah sáb:ah al-masáa'**?

Vocabulary builder

04.01 Listen to the new expressions and repeat them until you can say them with confidence. Listen again and complete the gaps.

TALKING ABOUT TIME

الساعة كم؟	as-sáa:ah kam?	*What time is it?*
الساعة واحدة	as-sáa:ah wáaHidah	*it's one o'clock*
الساعة اثنين وربع/إلا ربع	as-sáa:ah ithnáyn wa-rub:/íllaa rub:	*it's quarter past/to two*
الساعة ثلاثة و/إلا ثلث	as-sáa:ah thaláathah wa/íllaa thulth	*it's twenty past/to three*
الساعة عشرة ونصف	as-sáa:ah :áshrah wa-níSf	*it's half past ten*
يفتح/يقفل الساعة كم؟	yáftaH/yáqfil as-sáa:ah kam?	*What time does it _____ ?*
يفتح/يقفل الساعة سبعة.	yáftaH/yáqfil as-sáa:ah sáb:ah	*It opens/closes at _____ o'clock.*

MORE TIME-RELATED WORDS

اليوم	al-yawm	*today*
الغد	al-ghad	*tomorrow*
أمس	ams	*yesterday*
بعد الغد	ba:d al-ghad	*the day after _____*
أمس الأول	ams al-áwwal	*the day before yesterday*
قبل ثلاثة أيام	qabl thaláathat ayyáam	*three days ago*
بعد أربعة _____	ba:d arba:at ayyáam	*in four days*

THE DAYS OF THE WEEK

يوم الأحد	yawm al-áHad	*Sunday*
يوم الاثنين	yawm al-ithnayn	*_____*
يوم الثلاثاء	yawm ath-thalaatháa'	*Tuesday*
يوم الأربعاء	yawm al-arbi:áa'	*Wednesday*
يوم الخميس	yawm al-khamíis	*_____*
يوم الجمعة	yawm al-júm:ah	*Friday*
يوم السبت	yawm as-sabt	*Saturday*

> **LANGUAGE TIP**
>
> Sometimes the word **yawm** is omitted: الغد الأحد **al-ghad al-áHad** *tomorrow is Sunday.*

ASKING THE PRICE OF SOMETHING

	bi-kám	how much (lit. 'for how much')
التذكرة بكم؟	at-tádhkirah bi-kám?	How much is a ticket?
هذا بكم؟	háadhaa bi-kám?	This is how much?
هذا بخمسة دراهم.	háadha bi-khámsah daráahim	This is _____ dirhams.
بكم تلك المجلة؟	bi-kám tílka l-majállah?	How much is that magazine?
هي بدينار واحد.	híya bi-diináar wáaHid	It is one dinar.

> **LANGUAGE TIP**
>
> In English we say *How much is this?*, but the same question in Arabic can be بكم هذا؟ **bi-kám háadhaa?** or هذا بكم؟ **háadhaa bi-kám?**

Conversation 1

أين المتاحف؟ **áyna l-matáaHif?** *WHERE ARE THE MUSEUMS?*

هذا/هذه	**háadha/háadhih(i)**	this (m./f.)
خريطة، خرائط	**kharíiTah, kharáa'iT**	map
الشارقة	**ash-sháariqah**	Sharjah
سوق، أسواق	**suuq, aswáaq**	market
سمك	**sámak**	fish (collective)
تاريخ	**taaríikh**	history
طبيعي	**Tabíi:ii**	natural
فن، فنون	**fann, funúun**	art
شارع، شوارع	**sháari:, shawáari:**	street, road
ذلك/ تلك	**dháalik(a)/tílka**	that (m./f.)
صحيح	**SaHíiH**	true
انظري	**únDHuri**	look! (to a woman)
حصن، حصون	**HiSn, HuSúun**	fort, fortress
برج، أبراج	**burj, abráaj**	tower
من الممكن أن	**min al-múmkin an**	maybe (before a verb)
نذهب	**nádhhab**	we go

> **LANGUAGE TIP**
>
> The word **suuq** *market* is usually regarded as feminine.

04.02 *Bridget and Jim Hayes are visiting Sharjah and an Arabic-speaking friend, Hassan, is showing them around. Today they plan to visit some of the new museums in the city.*

1 What does Hassan point out on the map first?

حسن   هذه خريطة الشارقة. هذه هي المدينة القديمة، وهذا سوق السمك.

جيم   أين المتاحف؟

حسن   هذه هي المتاحف، هنا وهنا. هذا هو متحف الفنون، وهذا هو متحف التاريخ الطبيعي في شارع المطار.

بريجت   ذلك المتحف بعيد.

جيم   نعم، هذا صحيح. انظري، متحف الحصن هنا في شارع البرج. هو متحف ممتاز، ومن الممكن أن نذهب إلى المدينة القديمة بعد ذلك.

بريجت   حسنا. نذهب إلى متحف الحصن.

2 Answer the questions.

   a Why don't they want to go to the Natural History Museum? _____

   b Which museum do they decide to visit eventually? _____

3 Link the English phrases to their Arabic equivalents.

   a This is the Old Town/City.   ١ من الممكن أن نذهب إلى المدينة القديمة.

   b That museum is far away.   ٢ ذلك المتحف بعيد.

   c That's true.   ٣ هذا صحيح.

   d Maybe we can go to the Old Town/City.   ٤ هذه هي المدينة القديمة.

Conversation 2

يقفل الساعة كم؟ **yáqfil as-sáa:ah kam?** *WHAT TIME DOES IT CLOSE?*

يقفل	yáqfil	he/it closes, shuts
مسؤول، ـون	mas'úul, -uun	official
مسؤول المتحف/ مسؤولة المتحف	mas'úul al-mátHaf / mas'úulat al-mátHaf	Museum attendant (m./f.)
ساعة، ـات	sáa:ah, -aat	hour, time, watch, clock
دقيقة، دقائق	daqiiqah, daqaa'iq	minute
يفتح	yáftaH	he/it opens

عندنا	:índanaa	we have
وقت، أوقات	waqt, awqáat	time
تفضلوا	tafáDDaluu	come in, here you are (pl.)
كتيّب	kutáyyib	booklet, brochure
عن	:an	about, concerning
الآن	al-'aan	now

> **LANGUAGE TIP**
>
> تفضلوا **tafáDDaluu** is used when inviting someone to come in, sit down, or when giving them something. The final **alif** is not pronounced.

 04.03 *Hassan, Jim and Bridget arrive at the museum. They ask the attendants about opening hours.*

1 What is the time now?

حسن	صباح الخير. المتحف يقفل الساعة كم؟
مسؤول المتحف	صباح النور. يقفل الساعة واحدة ويفتح الساعة أربعة بعد الظهر.
بريجت	كم الساعة الآن؟
حسن	الساعة عشرة وربع.
بريجت	حسنا، عندنا وقت كثير.
مسؤولة المتحف	مرحبا، تفضلوا. هذا هو كتيّب عن المتحف.
حسن	شكرا.

2 Answer the questions.

   a What time does the museum close for lunch? _____

   b When does the museum open again after lunch? _____

   c What does the attendant give them? _____

3 Link the English phrases to the appropriate Arabic.

a	It closes.	١	يفتح.
b	It opens.	٢	الساعة عشرة وربع.
c	What's the time?	٣	هذا هو كتيّب عن المتحف.
d	It's a quarter past ten.	٤	يقفل.
e	Welcome, come in.	٥	مرحبا، تفضلوا.
f	This is a brochure of the museum.	٦	الساعة كم؟

Conversation 3

بكم...؟ bi-kam...? *HOW MUCH (DOES IT COST)?*

تذكرة، تذاكر	**tádhkirah, tadháakir**	ticket
بالغ/ بالغون	**baaligh/baalighúun**	adults
درهم، دراهم	**dírham, daráahim**	dirham (unit of currency, Dhs.)
طفل، أطفال	**Tifl, aTfáal**	child

04.04 *They go to the admission desk to buy tickets.*

1 How much does a child's ticket cost?

السلام عليكم.	حسن
وعليكم السلام.	مسؤولة المتحف
التذكرة بكم من فضلك؟	حسن
البالغون بستة دراهم، والأطفال بثلاثة دراهم.	مسؤولة المتحف
ثلاث تذاكر بستة دراهم من فضلك.	حسن
ثمانية عشر درهما من فضلك. شكرا. تفضلوا التذاكر.	مسؤولة المتحف
شكرا.	حسن

2 Now answer these questions.

a How much does an adult ticket cost? _____

b How much does Hassan have to pay? _____

3 Link the English to the appropriate Arabic expressions.

a How much is a ticket, please?

b Adults are six dirhams.

c Three six-dirham tickets, please.

d Here are the tickets.

١ البالغون بستة دراهم.

٢ ثلاث تذاكر بستة دراهم، من فضلك.

٣ تفضلوا التذاكر.

٤ التذكرة بكم، من فضلك؟

Language discovery

1 DEMONSTRATIVES – *THIS* AND *THAT*

The words *this, that*, etc. are called <u>demonstratives</u>. In English, they behave in two ways:

▶ as an adjective: *this book is expensive*. The word *this* describes which book we mean.

▶ as a pronoun: *that was an excellent film*. Here the word *that* represents a noun (the film).

> **LANGUAGE TIP**
>
> It will help you in the use of the Arabic demonstratives if you bear in mind that, in Arabic, they are <u>always</u> pronouns and <u>never</u> adjectives. Arabic really says *this* (object, person) *the-big* (thing, one).

 1 Looking back at the conversations, what do you notice about the plural forms of Arabic demonstratives (i.e. *these* and *those*)?

Singular

m.	هذا المتحف	**háadhaa l-mátHaf**	*this museum*
f.	هذه الخريطة	**háadhihi l-kharíiTah**	*this map*
m.	ذلك الشارع	**dháalika sh-sháari:**	*that street*
f.	تلك المدينة	**tílka l-madíinah**	*that town*

Plural

هؤلاء الأولاد/البنات	**haa'uláa'i l-awláad/l-banáat**	*these boys/girls*
أولئك البنات/أولئك الأولاد	**uuláa'ika l-banáat/ l-awláad**	*those girls/boys*

Agreement

Demonstratives agree with the noun in gender:

háadhaa l-mátHaf   هذا المتحف

this(thing) the-museum   *this museum (m.)*

háadhihi l-madíinah   هذه المدينة

this(thing) the-town   *this town (f.)*

Adjectives

Adjectives come after nouns in the usual way:

háadha l-maktab al-jadíid   هذا المكتب الجديد

this(thing) the-office the-new(one)   *this new office*

háadhihi l-jaríidah t-tuunisíyyah   هذه الجريدة التونسية

this(thing) the-newspaper the-Tunisian(one)   *this Tunisian newspaper*

Demonstrative sentences with indefinites

háadhaa kitáab

this(thing) (is) book

هذا كتاب

this is a book

háadhihi sayyáarah

this (thing) (is) car

هذه سيارة

this is a car

dháalika qálam jadíid

that(thing) (is) pen new(one)

ذلك قلم جديد

that is a new pen

tílka jaríidah yawmíyyah

that (thing) (is) newspaper daily(one)

تلك جريدة يومية

that is a daily newspaper

Demonstrative sentences with definites

The pronoun agreeing with the subject noun is always put between the demonstrative and the rest of the sentence. This is necessary as otherwise we would get a definite phrase (see Unit 1):

háadhaa sh-sháari:

this the-street

هذا الشارع

this street

háadhaa húwa sh-sháari:

this(thing) he (is) the-street

هذا هو
الشارع

this is the street

tílka híya l-bint

that(person) she (is) the-girl

تلك هي البنت

that's the girl

The same procedure is often followed with names of people or places:

háadhaa húwa muHámmad

this (person) he Mohammed

هذا هو محمد

this is Mohammed

Remember that since plurals of inanimate objects are regarded in Arabic as being feminine singular, the demonstrative used is feminine singular and the pronoun used for *they* is actually *she*:

tílka híya l-kútub al-:arabíyyah

those (things) they (are) the-books the-Arabic

تلك هي الكتب العربية

those are the Arabic books

Spelling and pronunciation

▶ Note that **háadhaa**, **haadhíhi** and **dháalika** are nominally spelled with the dagger **alif** for the first long **a**. This is usually omitted in print, but a normal **alif** cannot be used.

▶ Although spelled long, the final vowel of **háadhaa** is usually pronounced short.

▶ When these words – or any word ending in a vowel – come before **al-** *the*, the **a** of the latter is omitted:

هذا المتحف	**háadhaa l-matHaf**
تلك المدرسة الكبيرة	**tilka l-mádrasah l-kabíirah**

▶ When **dháalika** comes at the end of a sentence, its final **a** is usually omitted.

2 TELLING THE TIME

The way of telling the time in Standard Arabic is complicated and used only in the most formal situations. For this reason, the following section is given in the more common colloquial (transliterated) form, without Arabic script, except for the main terms.

as-sáa:ah wáaHidah
it's one o'clock

as-sáa:ah ithnáyn wa-rúb:
the hour is two and a quarter

as-sáa:ah thaláathah ílla thulth
the hour is three less a third (of an hour), 20 minutes

as-sáa:ah iHdá:shar waa-niSf
the hour is eleven and a half

Note that:

▶ *one o'clock*, and in some dialects *two o'clock*, use the feminine form of the numeral (**wáaHidah**, **ithnáyn/thintáyn**)

▶ *three o'clock* to *ten o'clock* inclusive use the independent form ending in **-ah**

- for *eleven* and *twelve o'clock* there is only one possible form

- **niSf**, *half*, is often pronounced **nuSS**

- for the English *past*, Arabic uses و **wa**- *and*:

  as-sáa:ah iHdá:shar wa-rúb: *quarter past eleven*

- for the English *to*, Arabic uses إلا **ílla** *except for, less*:

  as-sáa:ah thaláathah ílla rúb: *quarter to three*

> **LANGUAGE TIP**
>
> To say *at* a particular time Arabic requires no additional word, so **as-saa:ah khamsah** can mean *(it is)* *five o'clock* or *at five o'clock*.

| **as-saa:ah sittah wa khamsah** | **as-saa:ah waaHidah wa nuSS** | **as-saa:ah arba:ah illa thulth** |

Twenty-five past and *twenty-five to* the hour are expressed in Arabic as 'the hour and a half less five' and 'the hour and a half and five' respectively:

as-sáa:ah khámsah wa-niSf ílla khámsah   *twenty-five past five*

as-sáa:ah khámsah wa-niSf wa-khámsah   *twenty-five to six*

More formally (and less commonly) all times can be stated using the preceding hour plus the number of minutes:

as-sáa:ah :ásharah wa khámsah wa-arba:íin daqíiqah   *10:45*

This is the method used by speaking clocks, etc., and also sometimes on official radio and television announcements. These, however, use the literary Arabic forms of the numbers, which differ significantly.

3 NUMBERS 11–20

 04.05 The numbers are given here in the colloquial form, as they were in Unit 2.

١١	iHdá:shar	11	١٦	sittá:shar	16
١٢	ithná:shar	12	١٧	sab:atá:shar	17
١٣	thalaathtá:shar	13	١٨	thamantá:shar	18
١٤	arba:atá:shar	14	١٩	tis:atá:shar	19
١٥	khamsatá:shar	15	٢٠	:ishríin	20

 Did you notice the common element á:shar (equivalent to English -teen)? This is a slightly altered form of the written :áshar.

Agreement with nouns

▶ In written Arabic, the numbers must agree with their nouns in gender.

▶ With the numbers 11–99 inclusive, the noun is in the accusative singular. This is shown on most nouns without an **-ah** ending by the **alif** accusative marker and pronounced **-an** in formal speech.

أربعة عشر كتابا   **arba:atá:shar kitáaban**   *14 books*

but

خمسة عشر تذكرة   **khamstá:shar tádhkirah**   *15 tickets*

▶ In Arabic, the noun is plural only after the numerals 3–10 inclusive. Talking about two of anything requires a special ending known as the dual. This is dealt with in Unit 13.

خمسة بيوت   **khámsat buyúut**   *five houses*

4 ASKING THE PRICE OF SOMETHING

Here Arabic uses the preposition **bi-**:

بكم تلك المجلة؟   **bi-kám tílka l-majállah?**   *How much is that magazine?*
هي بدينار واحد.   **híya bi-diináar wáaHid**   *It is one dinar.*

Word discovery

The word pattern for this unit is maC^{1}C^{2}aC^3, for example, **máktab** مكتب *office, desk*, which sounds like the English *madman*.

The root **k-t-b** refers to *writing*, and **máktab** literally means *a place where you write*.

1 Given the above example, what meaning do you think this word pattern usually represents?

 04.06 Sometimes this pattern adds a feminine ending **-ah**. Thus, from the root **d-r-s** to do with studying, we have **mádrasah** مدرسة, meaning *a place of study*, i.e. *school*. Occasionally, the two forms exist side by side:

مكتب	**máktab**	*office*
مكتبة	**máktabah**	*library, bookshop*

الآن دورك al-'aan dawrak

2 Here are some more examples. Complete the English, using the roots to help you.

مدخل	**mádkhal**	_____
مخرج	**mákhraj**	_____
متحف	**mátHaf**	*museum*
ملعب	**mál:ab**	_____
مسرح	**másraH**	*theatre*
مسبح	**másbaH**	_____
مقبرة	**máqbarah**	*cemetery*

LANGUAGE TIP

دخل	*enter*	لعب	*play*	سبح	*swim*

Practice

 1 04.07 **Listen to the times of day while looking at the times. Decide in each case what the correct time is.**

a as-sáa:ah wáaHidah wa-niSf   1:15, 1:20 or 1:30?

b as-sáa:ah sáb:ah ílla khámsah   6:25, 6:35 or 6:55?

c	as-sáa:ah :ásharah wa-rub:	10:15, 10:30 or 10:45?
d	as-sáa:ah khámsah	4:55, 5:00 or 5:05?
e	as-sáa:ah tís:ah aS-SubH	9 a.m. or 9 p.m.?

 2 04.08 **Ask what time it is and say the time shown on the clock. Listen to the audio to see if you are right.**

Example:

| as-sáa:ah kam? | *What time is it?* |
| as-sáa:ah thamáanyah | *It is eight o' clock.* |

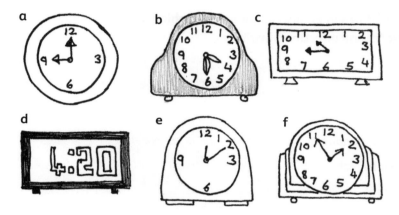

3 **Do you remember the days of the week? See if you can complete these sentences in Arabic.**

١ اليوم _____ الثلاثاء.

٢ الغد _____

٣ كان _____ يوم الاثنين.

٤ كان أمس الأول _____.

٥ _____ يوم الخميس

٦ _____ بعد ثلاثة أيام

LANGUAGE TIP

كان   **kaan(a)**   *was* (see Unit 8)

شـجـرة، أشـجـار	**shájarah, ashjáar**	*tree*
حديقة، حدائق	**Hadíiqah, Hadáa'iq**	*garden, park*
جار، جيران	**jaar, jiiráan**	*neighbour*
قارب، قوارب	**qáarib, qawáarib**	*(small) boat*
بحر، بحار	**baHr, biHáar**	*sea, large river*

4 Your Arabic-speaking friend is showing you some photographs of his home and family. Choose the correct demonstrative:

١ هذا\هذه هو البيت الجديد.

٢ هذا\هذه هي الأشجار في الحديقة.

٣ أولئك\ذلك هم الأولاد.

٤ هذا\هذه هي فاطمة.

٥ أولئك\تلك هم الجيران.

٦ ذلك\تلك هي القوارب في البحر.

5 Write out the following dates in English in numerical fashion, e.g. 10/6/1989 (day/month/year). Watch the direction of writing!

d ١٩٩٠-٢-٢٨   a ١٩٥٢-١٢-٣

e ١٨٣٦-٤-١٧   b ١٩٦٧-١١-١٩

c ٢٠٠٠-١-١

دينار دنانير	diináar, danaaníir	dinar (unit of currency)
مسرحية، ـات	masraHíyyah, -aat	play (theatrical)
تبتدئ	tabtádi'	she/it begins

6 Write out the following times in Arabic words and practise saying them out loud.

f ٥:٣٠   a ٢:٣٥

g ١:١٥   b ٨:١٠

h ١٢:٠٠   c ٩:٢٥

i ٣:٢٠   d ٧:٠٠

j ١٠:٠٥   e ٣:٤٥

 # Reading

 مواقيت المتحف mawaaqíit al-mátHaf *MUSEUM OPENING TIMES*

مواقيت	mawaaqíit	appointments, times (of opening, etc.)
إجازة	ijáazah	holiday, vacation, closing day
زيارة ـات	ziyáarah, -aat	visit
لـ	li-	to, for
امرأة	imráah	woman
نساء	nisáa'	women (This is an irregular plural.)
للنساء	li-n-nisáa'	(lit. 'for the women' (by convention, the **alif** of **al** is omitted after **li-**))

Read the notice for the museum opening times, then answer
the questions.

مواقيت المتحف		
يوم السبت	١٣:٠٠-٩:٠٠	١٧:٠٠- ٢٠:٠٠
يوم الأحد	١٢:٠٠-٩:٠٠	١٧:٠٠- ٢٠:٠٠
يوم الاثنين	إجازة	
يوم الثلاثاء	١٣:٠٠-٩:٠٠	١٧:٠٠- ٢٠:٠٠
	(الزيارة للنساء فقط)	
يوم الأربعاء	١٣:٠٠-٩:٠٠	١٧:٠٠- ٢٠:٠٠
يوم الخميس	١٣:٠٠-٩:٠٠	١٧:٠٠- ٢٠:٠٠
يوم الجمعة	١٦:٣٠- ٢٠:٣٠	

a When are women particularly welcome? _____

b Which day is the museum closed? _____

c When does the museum close on Friday evening? _____

d When does the museum usually open in the morning? _____

e On which day does the museum not open in the morning? _____

f How many days have the same opening times? _____

 Speaking

1 04.09 **You want to buy tickets for a performance at the National Theatre in
Kuwait. Complete your part in the conversation, using the prompts given.**

a أنت Say 'good evening'.

كاتب مساء النور.

b أنت Ask how much a ticket costs.

كاتب التذكرة بأربعة دنانير

c أنت Ask for four tickets.

كاتب ١٦ دينارا من فضلك

d أنت Offer the ticket clerk your money.

كاتب شكرا.

e   أنت   Ask the ticket clerk when the theatre opens.

كاتب   يفتح الساعة سبعة، والمسرحية تبتدئ الساعة سبعة ونصف.

f   أنت   Say 'thank you'.

2 Now answer the following questions.

a How much does a ticket cost? _____

b When does the theatre open? _____

c When does the play begin? _____

Test yourself

1 How would you say these questions and phrases in Arabic?

a What time is it? _____

b What time does it open? _____

c It opens at half past ten. _____

d How much is a ticket, please? _____

e This is Mohammed. _____

2 Complete the days of the week.

_____a	yawm al-áHad	*Sunday*
يوم الاثنين	yawm al-ithnayn	*Monday*
_____b	yawm ath-thalaatháa'	*Tuesday*
يوم الأربعاء	yawm al-arbi:áa'	_____c
يوم الخميس	yawm al-khamíis	*Thursday*
_____d	yawm al-júm:ah	*Friday*
يوم السبت	yawm as-sabt	_____e

SELF CHECK

I CAN...	
○	...tell the time.
○	...ask about opening times.
○	...say the days of the week.
○	...say the numbers 11–20.
○	...form phrases and sentences with *this, that, those*, etc.

5 بيتنا بيتكم

báyt-naa báyt-kum

Our house is your house

In this unit you will learn how to:
▶ *talk about your family*
▶ *say who things belong to*
▶ *describe possessions*
▶ *use the numbers 21–100.*

CEFR: (A1/A2) *Can handle numbers, quantities, cost and time; can understand sentences and frequently used expressions related to areas of most immediate relevance (basic personal or family info).*

 ## Segregated social events

Within the framework of the Islamic way of life, customs vary widely in the Arab world. For example, in more conservative areas, a man visiting a family will never see any of the women and should not even ask about them except in a very general way, e.g. ؟كيف العائلة **kayf al-:aa'ilah** *How's the family?* However, in more liberal countries, he can behave much as he would in a European country. It is best to err on the safe side until you are sure of your ground, taking your cue from your hosts.

In very traditional areas, if a man is invited with his wife, she may be taken to the women's quarters on arrival and be entertained and fed with the women, while her husband stays with the men. She will be reunited with her husband when they leave.

What should you not ask your host if you don't know him very well?

Vocabulary builder

05.01 **Listen to the new expressions and repeat them until you can say them with confidence. Listen again and complete the gaps.**

INTRODUCING PEOPLE

هذا توم	háadha Tom	*This is Tom. (for a man)*
هذه هي زوجتي، سلمى	háadhihi híya záwjat-ii, sálma	*This is my wife, Salma. (for a woman)*

ASKING AND SAYING HOW OLD SOMEONE IS

كم عمره؟	kam :úmr-uh	*How old is he?*
تميم كم عمره؟	tamíim kam :umr-uh	*How old is Tameem? (lit. 'how much his-life')*
عمره ٨ سنوات	:umr-uh thamáany sanawáat	*He is _____ years old.*

MEMBERS OF THE FAMILY

والد	wáalid	*father (lit. 'male parent', formal)*
والدة	wáalidah	*mother (lit. 'female parent', formal)*
والد	ab	*father (this is the most commonly used word)*
والدة	umm	*mother (this is the most commonly used word)*
ابن، أبناء	ibn, abnáa'	*son*
بنت، بنات	bint, banáat	*daughter, girl*
أولاد	awláad	*boys, children*
أخ، إخوان/إخوة	akh, ikhwáan/íkhwah	*brother*
أخت، أخوات	ukht, akhawáat	*sister*
زوج	zawj	*husband*
زوجة	záwjah	_____
عم/خال	:ámm/kháal	*uncle (father's/mother's side)*
عمة/خالة	:ámmah/kháalah	_____
جد	jadd	_____
جدة	jáddah	*grandmother*
ابن عم/خال	ibn :amm/khaal	*(male) cousin (father's/mother's side)*
بنت عم/خال	_____/_____	*(female) cousin (father's/mother's side)*

Conversation

 هذه هي زوجتي **háadhihi híya záwjat-ii** *THIS IS MY WIFE*

لك	**lá-ki**	*for you (to a woman)*
هدية، هدايا	**hadíyyah, hadáayaa**	*present, gift*
اجلس، اجلسي	**íjlis, íjlisii**	*sit down! (to a man/woman)*
سنة، سنوات	**sánah, sanawáat**	*year*

 05.02 *Hamed has invited his English friend, Tom, to his flat in Cairo for dinner. The whole family is there, so Tom has the chance to meet them all.*

1 Can you spot a quick way to tell if Tom's children are older or younger than Hamed's?

حامد	تفضل يا توم!
توم	شكرا يا حامد.
حامد	هذه هي زوجتي سلمى. سلمى، هذا توم، من المكتب.
توم	مساء الخير يا سلمى، كيف حالك؟
سلمى	بخير الحمد لله. أهلا وسهلا. و كيف حالك أنت؟
توم	الحمد لله. هذه هدية لك!
سلمى	شكرا يا توم. هذا والدي، وهذه والدتي... وهذا ابننا تميم. تفضل، اجلس.
توم	تميم كم عمره؟
سلمى	عمره ١٥ سنة، وبنتنا فريدة عمرها ١٢ سنة.
حامد	أولادك أنت، كم عمرهم، يا توم؟
توم	أولادنا صغار - ابننا عمره ٥ سنوات، وبنتنا عمرها ٣ سنوات.

2 Listen to the conversation again and answer the questions.

a Who does Hamed introduce to Tom first? _____

b How old is Tameem? _____

c How old is their daughter? _____

3 Find the Arabic for:

a This is my father. _____

b Please sit down. _____

c This is our son. _____

d How old are your children? _____

e Our daughter is three years old. _____

Language discovery

1 NUMBERS 21–100

05.03 **Listen to the audio and repeat each number as you hear it.**

1 Complete the missing numbers.

٢٠	20	_____		٤٤	_____	44
٢١	21	wáaHid wa-:ishríin		٥٠	khamsíin	50
٢٢	22	ithnáyn wa-:ishríin		٥١	wáaHid wa-khamsíin	51
٢٣	23	thaláathah wa-:ishríin		٥٧	_____	57
٢٤	24	árba:ah wa-:ishríin		٦٠	sittíin	60
٢٥	25	khámsah wa-:ishríin		٦٣	thaláathah wa-sittíin	63
٢٦	26	síttah wa-:ishríin		٦٨	_____	68
٢٧	27	sab:ah wa-:ishríin		٧٠	sab:íin	70
٢٨	28	thamáaniyah wa-:ishríin		٧٦	_____	76
٢٩	29	tís:ah wa-:ishríin		٨٠	thamaaníin	80
٣٠	30	thalaathíin		٨٥	_____	85
٣١	31	wáaHid wa-thalaathíin		٩٠	tis:íin	90
٣٣	33	_____		٩٩	_____	99
___	40	arba:íin		١٠٠	míiyah	100
٤٢	42	ithnáyn wa-arba:íin				

In Arabic, units are placed before the tens, as in *five-and-twenty*, like the blackbirds in the pie of the nursery rhyme:

| ٢٣/23 | **thaláathah wa-:ishríin** | *three and twenty* |
| ٦٥/65 | **khámsah wa-sittíin** | *five and sixty* |

Pronunciation

The tens have a slightly different written form ending in ون **-uun** in some contexts, but they are universally pronounced with the **-iin** ending in everyday speech. They are easy to remember, as, with the exception of *twenty*, they closely resemble the equivalent unit numbers, with the addition of **-iin**.

2 POSSESSIVE PRONOUNS

Possessives describe who or what something belongs to. English expresses this in several ways:
This is my shirt.   *This shirt is mine.*   *This shirt belongs to me.*

There are several points to note in Arabic:

▶ Written Arabic has only one way to express the possessive, using the equivalents of English *my, your, his,* etc. We call these words <u>possessive pronouns</u>. There is no equivalent in Arabic of the English *mine, yours,* etc. In Arabic, these pronouns are suffixes, which are joined on to the object that is possessed:

their house becomes in Arabic   بيتهم **báyt-hum** *house-their*

this is my car becomes   هذه سيارتي **háadhihi sayyáarat-i** *this(-one) (is) car-my*

الآن دورك al-'aan dawrak

2 What does سيارتها mean?

▶ Arabic distinguishes, in the case of *his* and *her, your* and *their* (but not *my* or *our*), whether the owner of the thing is a man or a woman. In the following list (and throughout this book), some of these possessive pronouns are given in a slightly simplified form, much as they are used in spoken Arabic.

▶ Since they are suffixes, the Arabic script versions of these pronouns have been given here as if they were joined to a word ending in a joining letter.

Singular		Plural	
ـي -ii	*my*	ـنا -na(a)	*our*
ـك -ak	*your (m.)*	ـكم -kum	*your (m.)*
ـك -ik	*your (f.)*	ـكن kúnna	*your (f.)*
ـه -uh	*his*	ـهم -hum	*their (m.)*
ـها -ha(a)	*her*	ـهن -húnna	*their (f.)*

Pronunciation

▶ **-haa** and **-naa** are generally pronounced short, although written with long vowels.

▶ The following changes in pronunciation are not reflected in the Arabic script:

▷ After words ending in long vowels or **-ay**:

-ii, *my*, becomes **-ya**.

يداي   **yadáa-ya**   *my hands* (**yadaa** *hands*)

-ak and **-uh** lose their vowels:

يداك، يداه   **yadáa-k, yadáa-h**

-ik becomes **-ki**:

يداك   **yadáa-ki**

▷ When preceded by **i**, **ii** or **ay**:

-hum and **-hunna** change to **-him** and **-hinna**:

مبانيهم   **mabaaníi-him**   *their buildings*

The hidden t

You will remember that ـة is the most common feminine ending in Arabic and is written with a hybrid letter, a cross between **h** and **t**. If a possessive pronoun suffix is added to a feminine word, the ـة **h** changes into an ordinary ـت **t**:

السيارة الجديدة   *the-car the new-one*
as-sayyáarah l-jadíidah   *the new car*

سيارته الجديدة   *car-his the new-one*
sayyáarat-uh al-jadíidah   *his new car*

Definites

All Arabic possessives are regarded as definite and follow the agreement rules for definites.
This is because if you say *my book*, you are referring to one specific book (see Unit 3)

a-háadha báyt-ak?   أهذا بيتك؟

This (thing) house-your?   *Is this your house?*

ná:am, háadha báyt-ii   نعم، هذا بيتي

Yes, this (thing) house-my. *Yes, this is my house.*

a-haadhíhi sayyaarát-haa?   أهذه سيارتها؟

This (thing) car-her?   *Is this her car?*

laa, láysat haadhíhi sayyaarát-haa   لا، ليست هذه سيارتها

No, is-not this (thing) car-her.   *No, this is not her car.*

> **LANGUAGE TIP**
>
> ليست **láysat** means *is not* (f.)

Word discovery

05.04 The pattern for this unit is C¹uC²úuC³, for example, **buyúut** بيوت *houses*, which sounds like the English *to lose*.

This shape usually represents one of two things:

▶ the plural of simple nouns whose singular shape is C¹vC²C³; for example:

    b-y-t singular **bayt** *house* → plural **buyúut** *houses*

    فلس/فلوس **fils/fulúus** *piastre, small unit of currency*

    شعب/شعوب **sha:b/shu:úub** *people, folk*

▶ nouns expressing the action of a verb – usually formed in English by adding the ending -ing (e.g. do ➜ doing, think ➜ thinking). In English we call this a <u>verbal noun</u>:

| دخول | dukhúul | from **d-kh-l** enter, meaning entering, entrance |
| خروج | khurúuj | from **kh-r-j** exiting, leaving; the act of going out |

Note that, as is the case with many shapes, $C^1uC^2úuC^3$ cannot be formed from every noun or verb root. The benefit of learning the shapes is in recognition, not formation. However, any noun which you come across in this form will be either a plural or a verbal noun.

الآن دورك al-ʾaan dawrak

Based on this pattern, turn the following words into plurals or verbal nouns.

a جيب _____ pocket/pockets

b صحن _____ dish/dishes

c جسر _____ bridge/bridges

d عبر _____ to cross/crossing

e جلس _____ to sit/seating

Practice

1 Put the following numbers into numerical order:

١٤   ٢٨   ٥٣   ٤٢   ٨٨   ٢٤   ٩٦   ٥٨   ٣١   ٦٧

____ ____ ____ ____ ____ ____ ____ ____ ____ ____

2 05.05 You are planning a camping trip with some Arab friends and see the following advertisement in an Arabic paper. You want to tell your friends about it. Read aloud the prices of the following items several times. Then listen to the audio to check that you were correct, and write the prices in English.

3 You have invited an Arab friend and her husband for dinner. Match the English phrases with the appropriate Arabic ones:

a Please come in.

b This is my husband.

c How are you?

d This is a present for you.

e Sit down

f Welcome

١ هذا هو زوجي.

٢ أهلا وسهلا.

٣ كيف حالك؟

٤ تفضل.

٥ اجلس.

٦ هذه هدية لك.

قميص، قمصان	qamíiS, qumSáan	shirt
وسخ	wásikh	dirty
حقيبة، حقائب	Haqíibah, Haqáa'ib	bag, suitcase

4 Complete the sentences with a possessive, using the correct suffix endings. The first one has been done for you.

١ قميص ــــــــ وسخ. (قميصك وسخ.)

٢ والدة ــــــــ إيطالية.

٣ هرم ــــــــ هو الكبير.

٤ هذه أخت ــــــــ مريم.

٥ ليست هذه السيارة سيارة ــــــــ

٦ أهذا مكتب ــــــــ الجديد؟

٧ جد ــــــــ من تونس.

٨ أين حقائب ــــــــ؟

5 Now match the English sentences with the Arabic ones in exercise 4.

a My pyramid is the big one. _____

b My mother is Italian. _____

c Your shirt is dirty! _____

d Where are our suitcases? _____

e Is this his new office? _____

f Their grandfather is from Tunis. _____

g This car is not mine. _____

h This is my sister, Miriam. _____

6 Study the family tree, then answer the questions in Arabic, using the examples as a guide:

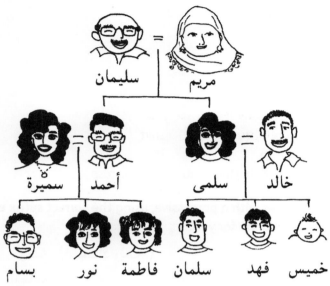

a Imagine that you are Salma:

Example: من أخوك **man akhúu-ki** *Who is your brother?*

Answer: أخي أحمد **ákh-ii áHmad** *My brother is Ahmed.*

1 Who is your husband? _____
2 Who is your mother? _____
3 Who are your children? _____

b What relation are the following people to Ahmed?

Example: سميرة **Samíirah**

Answer: هي زوجته **híya záwjat-uh** *She is his wife.*

1 Bassam _____
2 Fatima _____
3 Suleiman _____
4 Salma _____

c Answer the following questions in Arabic.

1 What relation is Fatimah to Fahad? _____
2 What relation is Khalid to Bassam? _____
3 What relation is Suleiman to Bassam, Noor and Fatima? _____

1 **How would you say these questions and phrases in Arabic?**
   a Is this your house? _____
   b How old are your children? _____
   c I'm well, praise be to God. _____
   d No, this is not her car. _____
   e This is a present for you. _____

2 **Complete the number table.**

_____**a**	wáaHid wa-:ishríin	واحد وعشرون
٥١	wáaHid wa-khamsíin	_____**b**
٢٣	thaláathah wa-:ishríin	_____**c**
_____**d**	árba:ah wa thamaaníin	أربعة وثمانون
٦٣	thaláathah wa-sittíin	_____**e**
_____**f**	síttah wa- sab:íin	ستة وسبعون
_____**g**	míiyah	مائة

SELF CHECK

	I CAN. . .
○	. . . talk about my family.
○	. . . say who things belong to.
○	. . . describe possessions.
○	. . . use the numbers 21–100.

6 أين وسط المدينة؟
áyna wásT al-madíinah?
Where is the town centre?

In this unit you will learn how to:
▶ *give simple directions*
▶ *talk about more places in town and their location*
▶ *say what belongs to whom*
▶ *express nationalities.*

CEFR: (A2) *Can understand everyday signs and notices; can make arrangements to meet, decide where to go and what to do; can write about everyday aspects of his environment.*

Arabic place names and compass points

There are many Arabic words which are familiar to English speakers even if only as place names, for example the Maghreb المغرب (lit. 'the west', from the root غرب meaning *disappearing*, as in the sun setting) and the Mashreq المشرق (lit. 'the east', from the root شرق meaning *sunrise*), souk سوق (*market*) and medina مدينة (*city/town*).

The points of the compass are:

ash-shamáal الشمال

al-gharb الغرب — الشرق ash-sharq

al-janúub الجنوب

Some world areas derived from the points of the compass are الغرب **al-gharb** *the West*, الشرق الأوسط **ash-sharq al-awsaT** *the Middle East*, الشرق الأقصى **ash-sharq al-aqSaa** *the Far East*, and جنوب أفريقيا **jinub afriikiiya** *South Africa*.

___

What is the Arabic word for *middle* or *centre*?

a شرق   b وسط   c أقصى

Vocabulary builder

06.01 Listen to the new expressions and repeat them until you can say them with confidence. Listen again and complete the gaps.

PREPOSITIONS

يمين	yamíin	*right (side)*
شمال	shimáal	*left (side) (similar to* north, *but notice different vowels)*
يسار	yasaar	*left (side)*
عند	:ind	*at*
بجانب	bi-jáanib	*next to, beside*
أمام	amáam	*in front of*
على طول	:ála Tuul	*straight ahead*
وراء	waráa'	*behind*

USEFUL PHRASES

عن إذنك	:an ídhn-ak	*excuse me (lit. 'by your leave')*
خلني أفكر	khallí-nii ufákkir	*let me think*
لف	liff	*turn! (to a man)*
اذهب	ídh-hab	*go! (to a man)*
حوالي	Hawáalii	*approximately, about*
متر، أمتار	mitr, amtáar	_____
أشكرك	ashkúr-ak	*thank you (lit. 'I thank you', to a man)*
شكرا جزيلا	shúkran jazíilan	*thank you very much; many thanks*
عفوا	:áfwan	*you're welcome*

ASKING AND GIVING SIMPLE DIRECTIONS

أين الفندق؟	áyna l-fúnduq	*Where is the hotel?*
لف يمين	liff yamíin	*turn* _____
اذهب على طول	ídh-hab :ála Tuul	_____
على اليمين	:ála l-yamíin	*on the right*
بجانب مكتب البريد	bi-jáanib máktab al-baríid	*beside/next to the post office*
أمام محطة الباص	amáama maHáTTat al-baaS	*opposite/in front of the bus station*
وراء البنك	waráa' al-bank	_____ *the bank*
بين الصيدلية ومحطة البنزين	báyna aS-Saydalíyyah wa-maHáTTat al-banzíin	*between the pharmacy and the petrol station*
بعد الجسر	ba:d al-jisr	_____ *the bridge*

Conversation

أين وسط المدينة من فضلك؟ áyna wásT al-madíinah, min fáDl-ak?
WHERE IS THE TOWN CENTRE, PLEASE?

وسط	**wásT**	*centre (of town, etc.)*
رجل، رجال	**rájul, rijáal**	*man*
ذهب	**dh-hab**	*to go*
مكتب، مكاتب	**máktab, makáatib**	*office*
عرف	**:árafa**	*to know*
جامع، جوامع	**jáami:, jawáami:**	*main mosque*
إشارة، ــات	**isháarah, -aat**	*(traffic) signal*
ملك، ملوك	**málik, mulúuk**	*king*
فاهم	**fáahim**	*understanding*
محطة، ــات	**maHáTTah, -aat**	*station*
بنزين	**banzíin**	*petrol*
موقف، مواقف	**máwqif, mawáaqif**	*stopping, parking place*

06.02 *Andy Fraser, a Scot working in Jordan, has to go to a small town near Amman to visit a client. He stops a passer-by to ask directions.*

1 What does Andy say to get the man's attention?

أندي عن إذنك! أين وسط المدينة؟

الرجل على طول. إلى أين تذهب؟

أندي أذهب إلى مكتب علي المبروك. هل تعرفه؟ هذه هي خريطة المدينة.

الرجل نعم، أعرفه. خلني أفكر. نعم هو هنا. بعد الجامع الكبير لف شمال عند الإشارة. هذا شارع الملك حسين. اذهب على طول حوالي ١٠٠ متر.

أندي نعم، أنا فاهم.

الرجل مكتب علي المبروك على اليمين، بجانب محطة البنزين، أمام سينما البلازا

أندي نعم، أشكرك. هل هناك موقف للسيارات؟

الرجل نعم، هناك موقف كبير للسيارات وراء مكتب علي المبروك.

أندي شكرا جزيلا!

الرجل عفوا!

2 Answer the questions.

a What is the first thing Andy has to look out for:

  1 a mosque?   **2** traffic lights?   **3** King Hussein Street?

b In which direction should he turn at the traffic lights? _____

c How far should he go along the street? _____

d What is the office next to? _____

e Is the car park:

  1 on the left?   **2** on the right?   **3** behind the office?

3 Link the English phrases with the equivalent Arabic expressions:

a excuse me   ١ أنا فاهم

b straight ahead   ٢ على طول

c let me think   ٣ لف شمال

d turn left   ٤ هل هناك موقف للسيارات؟

e on the right   ٥ خلني أفكر

f I understand   ٦ على اليمين

g Is there a car park there?   ٧ عن إذنك

Language discovery
1 FORMING ADJECTIVES FROM NOUNS

To describe persons or things associated with the noun, English uses a variety of suffixes:

history → *historic*   *man* → *manly*   *America* → *American*   *Japan* → *Japanese*

Arabic adds the following endings to the noun:

Gender	Transliteration	Arabic
m. sing.	-ii	ـِي
f. sing.	-iyyah	ـِية
m. plural	-iyyuun/-iyyiin	ـِيون / ـِين
f. plural	-iyyaat	ـِيات

They should all have the doubling sign over the ي, but this is almost always omitted.

الآن دورك al-'aan dawrak

Turn these words into adjectives by adding the correct endings.

a مصر (m. sing.)   **c** تاريخ (f. plural)

b يابان (f. sing.)   **d** رجل (m. sing.)

> **LANGUAGE TIP**
>
> The ending ـِيون changes to ـِين when affected by the possessive or the requirement for an
> accusative marker (see Unit 12).

There are irregular plurals (masculine only) which will be given with the singulars where required.

The noun sometimes has to be altered slightly:

▶ If it has **al-** in front – as in some countries and places – this is dropped:

مغربي – المغرب   *Morocco* → *Moroccan*

▶ The feminine ending ة and certain other endings are dropped:

صناعي – صناعة   *industry* → *industrial*
أمريكي – أمريكا   *America* → *American*

▶ Some words change their internal vowelling before the ending:

مدني – مدينة   **madiinah → madanii**   *city* → *urban, civilian*

2 POSSESSIVES WITH TWO NOUNS

Possessive constructions have two elements: the possessor, or owner, and the thing possessed, or property. In *the doctor's car, the doctor* is the 'owner' and *the car* is the 'property'.

Owner (of)	Property
the doctor's	*car*

The most usual way to say this in English is by the use of an apostrophe *s*: *'s*, in which case the order is 'owner' before 'property'. However, sometimes we use the word *of* and reverse the order:

Property	(of)	Owner
the title	*of*	*the book*
The Dogs	*of*	*War*

Arabic is similar to the above, except that:

▶ no word for *of* is used

▶ the first possessed noun (*title, Dogs*) never has the definite article **al-**. So the normal form in Arabic looks like this:

noun without al- máktab	followed by	noun with al- al-mudíir
office		*(of) the manager*
(the possessed object/property)		(the owner/possessor)

> **LANGUAGE TIP**
>
> The phrase **al-maktab al-mudíir** does not make sense to an Arab.
>
> ▶ If the first (possessed) noun has the feminine ending ة this is pronounced **-t** but – unlike with the possessive pronouns in Unit 5 – does not change its form when written. This is because it is still at the end of a word.
>
> | سيارة محمد | **sayyáarat muHámmad** | *Mohammed's car* |
> |---|---|---|

> **LANGUAGE TIP**
>
>
>
> The second element of a possessive may also be a proper name.
>
> | **Saydalíyyat sáarah** | *Sarah's pharmacy* |
> |---|---|

▶ With the exception of the demonstratives *this*, *that*, etc., no word may be inserted between the two nouns, so any additional words such as adjectives have to come at the end.

Note that possessives are frequently used in Arabic to associate two concepts that English would express in another way.

márkaz ash-shúrTah   مركز الشرطة

station (lit. 'centre') (of) the-police   *the police station*

maHáTTat al-baaS   محطة الباص

station (of) the-bus   *the bus station*

3 PROPER NAMES

You will remember that all proper names are regarded as definite, whether or not they begin with the definite article **al-**, *the*, such as القاهرة **al-qáahirah** *Cairo*. In either case they refer to a specific person or place.

بيت أحمد   **bayt áHmad**   *Ahmed's house*

جامعة القاهرة   **jáami:at al-qáahirah**   *University of Cairo, Cairo University*

4 SIMPLE SENTENCES WITH POSSESSIVE CONSTRUCTIONS

The formula <u>definite + indefinite</u> gives a simple sentence in Arabic (see Unit 2) implying the word *is/are* in English. Since nearly all possessive constructions are by nature definite, you can use them in the same way. The last part of the sentence can be a simple adjective (e.g. *Mohammed's house is <u>big</u>*), but can also be a phrase with a preposition (using words such as *in*, *under*, *on*, etc.), telling you where something is located. The possessive construction must not be split up:

jáami:at al-qáahirah kabíirah   جامعة القاهرة كبيرة

university (of)(the) Cairo (is) big   *Cairo University is big*

bayt muHámmad fii wásT al-madíinah   بيت محمد في وسط المدينة

house (of) Mohammed (is) in (the) centre (of)   *Mohammed's house is in the centre of*

   the-town   *town*

If both possessive terms are of the same gender, it will strike you that these adjectives placed at the end of the phrase might describe either of the possessive terms. However, the context usually makes everything clear:

waziir ad-daakhilíyyah al-jadíid

minister (of) the-interior the-new

وزير الداخلية الجديد

the new minister of the interior

kútub al-ustáadh al-jadíidah

books (of) the-professor the-new

كتب الأستاذ الجديدة

the professor's new books

> **LANGUAGE TIP**
>
> Ministries, embassies and government departments usually have the possessive construction:
>
> | | | |
> |---|---|---|
> | وزارة السياحة | **wizáarat as-siyáaHah** | *the ministry of tourism* |
> | وزارة التعليم قريبة من الميدان. | **wizáarat at-ta:líim qaríibah min al-maydáan** | *the ministry of education is near the square.* |
> | دائرة المرور | **dáa'irat al-murúur** | *the traffic department* |
>
> If the name of a country is mentioned, place the nationality adjective after the noun, in which case there is no hidden **-t**.
>
> | | | |
> |---|---|---|
> | السفارة البريطانية | **as-sifáarah al-briiTaaníyyah** | *the British embassy* |

5 DEMONSTRATIVES WITH POSSESSIVES

Demonstratives (*this, that, those,* etc.) are the only words that can go between the two terms of a possessive:

▶ If the demonstrative applies to the second (possessor) word, it goes between, usually taking the form: noun without **al-** + demonstrative + noun with **al-**:

qálam háadhaa t-tilmíidh

pen (of) this(person) the-pupil

قلم هذا التلميذ

this pupil's pen

▶ If the demonstrative applies to the first (possessed) word, it comes at the end: noun without **al-** + noun with **al-** + demonstrative:

sayyáarat al-mudíir haadhíhi

car (of) the-manager this (one)

سيارة المدير هذه

this car of the manager's

In both cases, the demonstrative must agree in gender with the word to which it applies.

Word discovery

 06.03 The word pattern for this unit is C¹iC²aaC³ah, for example, **wizáarah** وزارة *ministry*, which sounds like the English *banana*.

This type of noun is usually derived from a word of the CaCíiC shape (see Unit 1), which refers to a man:

| وزير | **wazíir** | *minister* | → | وزارة | **wizáarah** | *ministry* |
| سفير | **safíir** | *ambassador* | → | سفارة | **sifáarah** | *embassy* |

 الآن دورك **al-'aan dawrak**

1 **Given these examples, what do you think the meaning of this word pattern is?**

2 **Based on these patterns, complete the sentence by using the correct word (in English and Arabic).**

In the Gulf, *the Emirates* (إمارات **imaaráat**, plural of إمارة **imáarah**) are so named because they were each originally ruled by an _____.

Listen and understand

في المدينة **fi l-madíinah** *IN THE TOWN*

 1 06.04 **Look at the town map and read through the names of all the places. Then listen to the audio to hear how they are pronounced.**

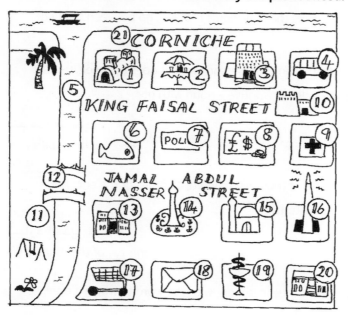

1	سوق الذهب	suuq adh-dháhab	gold market
2	مطعم	máT:am	restaurant
3	فندق	fúnduq	hotel
4	محطة الباص	maHáTTat al-báaS	bus station
5	الخور	al-khawr	the creek
6	سوق السمك	suuq as-sámak	fish market
7	مركز الشرطة	márkaz ash-shúrTah	police station
8	بنك الشارقة	bank ash-sháariqah	Bank of Sharjah
9	مستشفى	mustáshfaa	hospital
10	الحصن القديم	al-HiSn al-qadíim	the old fort
11	حديقة	Hadíiqah	park, garden
12	جسر	jisr	bridge
13	البلدية	al-baladíyyah	town hall
14	ميدان	maydáan	square
15	جامع	jáami:	mosque
16	برج الاتصالات	burj al-ittiSáalaat	telecommunications tower
17	سوبرماركت	suubarmáarkit	supermarket
18	مكتب البريد	máktab al-baríid	post office
19	صيدلية	Saydalíyyah	pharmacy
20	مركز التسوق	márkaz at-tasáwwuq	shopping centre
21	الكورنيش	al-koorníish	the Corniche

 2 06.05 **Now listen to the audio while you read the text and decide which places are being asked for.**

a على الكورنيش، بين مطعم شهرزاد ومحطة الباص.

b على اليمين في الميدان، بجانب برج الاتصالات.

c قريب من الخور، بين الجسر وسوق الذهب.

d بين السوبرماركت وصيدلية ابن سينا.

e اذهب على طول في شارع جمال عبد الناصر وهو على الشمال بعد الجسر.

f في شارع الملك فيصل، وراء المستشفى.

Practice

1 Here are some common word combinations, many of which you will see on road signs, in shops, etc. Look at the two nouns and put them together, making the second noun into an adjective. Some are given in the definite form.

Example: مركز **markaz** *centre* – تجارة **tijaarah** *commerce*
→ مركز تجاري *markaz tijaarii commercial (shopping) centre*

a منطقة **minTaqah** *area, zone* – زراعة **ziraa:ah** *agriculture*

b قمر **qamar** *moon* – صناعة **Sinaa:ah** *manufacturing*

c البنك **al-bank** *the bank* – الوطن **al-waTan** *the nation*

d الشؤون **ash-shu'uun** *the affairs* – الخارج **al-khaarij** *the exterior*

e منطقة **minTaqah** *area, zone* – عسكر **:askar** *army, troops*

f الآثار **al-aathaar** *the remains* – التاريخ **at-taariikh** *the history*

g الدراسات **ad-diraasaat** *the studies* – الأدب **al-adab** *the literature*

h العلوم **al-:uluum** *the sciences* – الطبيعة **aT-Tabii:ah** *the nature*

i القصر **al-qaSr** *the palace* – الملك **al-malik** *the king*

j المستشفى **al-mustashfaa** *the hospital* – المركز **al-markaz** *the centre*

k بريد **bariid** *post* – داخل **daakhil** *interior*

l الأجهزة **al-ajhizah** *equipment (pl.)* – الكهرباء **al-kahrabaa'** *the electricity*

> **LANGUAGE TIP**
>
> Here, صناعة **Sinaa:ah** means *artificial*: 'artificial moon', i.e. *satellite*.

2 Fit two words together to make places found around an Arab city.

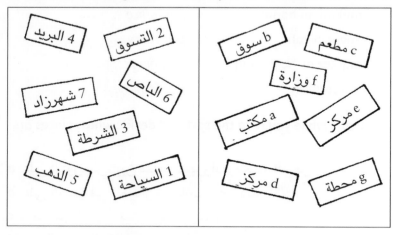

3 06.06 Ask where the following places are. Check your answers with the audio.

a the town hall

b the police station

c al-Bustan shopping centre

d King Faisal Street

e Sheherazade restaurant

4 06.07 Look at the town map in the Listen and understand section and imagine that you are standing on the bridge when someone asks you the way. Give the locations of the places in the last exercise. Possible answers are given on the audio.

عجلة، ــات	ájalah, -aat:	bicycle
عاصمة، عواصم	áaSimah, :awáaSim:	capital (political)
شركة، ــات	shárikah, -aat	company (commercial)
بلد، بلاد/ بلدان	balad, biláad/buldáan	country, nation

5 Combine the two nouns to form a possessive construction.

Example: boy – bicycle

→ عجلة الولد: ajalat al-walad the boy's bicycle

a bank – manager _____

b town – centre _____

c country – capital _____

d company – office _____

e Rashid – sister _____

عريض	aríiD:	wide
قصر، قصور	qaSr, quSúur	palace/castle
غرفة، غرف	ghúrfah, ghúraf	room
شقة، شقق	sháqqah, shíqaq	flat, apartment
طبيخ	Tabíikh	cooking, cuisine
لذيذ	ladhíidh	delicious, tasty
دكان، دكاكين	dukkáan, dakaakíin	small shop, stall

6 Make *is/are* sentences from these words, making sure that the adjectives agree.

Example: watch – Faisal – new

→ ساعة فيصل جديدة *Faisal's watch is new*

a streets – Abu Dhabi – wide _____

b gardens – palace – beautiful _____

c rooms – apartment – spacious _____

d cuisine – Morocco – delicious _____

e shops – market – small _____

? Test yourself

1 How would you say these sentences and phrases in Arabic?

   a The University of Cairo is big. _____

   b the country's capital _____

   c The Ministry of Justice is near the square. _____

   d Where is the Moroccan embassy? _____

   e Is there a police station there? _____

2 Combine the two nouns into a compound noun in Arabic.

   a منطقة **minTaqah** *zone* – صناعة **Sinaa:ah** *industry* ➔ _____ industrial zone

   b طبيخ **Tabiikh** *cuisine* – عرب: **arab** *Arabs* ➔ _____ Arab cuisine

   c المتحف **al-matHaf** *the museum* – الشعب **ash-sha:b** *the people, folk* ➔ _____ the folk museum

   d القنصلية **al-qunSuliyyah** *the consulate* – أمريكا **amriikaa** *America* ➔ _____ the American consulate

   e الإدارة **al-idaarah** *the administration* – البلد **al-balad** *the town, municipality* ➔ _____ the town council/administration

SELF CHECK

I CAN...
○ ... give simple directions.
○ ... talk about more places in town and their location.
○ ... say what belongs to whom.
○ ... express nationalities.

ماذا فعلت؟

máadhaa fa:ált?

What did you do?

In this unit you will learn how to:
▶ *talk about things that happened in the past*
▶ *describe means of transport*
▶ *use Arabic verbs*
▶ *say me, him, them, etc.*

CEFR: (A2) *Can get simple information about travel, use of public transport and buy tickets; can describe plans, arrangements, habits and routines, past activities and personal experiences.*

Arab travellers and their influence

The Arab people have always been great travellers. Perhaps the most famous traveller in the Arab world was Ibn Battuta, who was born in Tangier, Morocco, in 1304. He set off on hajj الحج (*religious pilgrimage to Mecca* مكّة) in his early twenties, but carried on travelling and only returned home nearly 30 years later having covered over 73,000 miles.

We often think about journeys Arabs have made across the desert, but they have also been associated with major sea routes, and their influence stretches around the globe. Even places in Mexico such as Guadalajara وادي الحجارة **Wādī al-Ḥejārah** ('river bed of stones') have names of Arabic origin.

Several common English words linked to travel are Arabic in origin. Match the words with their original Arabic word and meaning:

a	safari	**1**	السفاري	**A**	desert
b	caravan	**2**	أمير البحر	**B**	fee associated with international trade
c	tariff	**3**	صحارى	**C**	journey
d	sahara	**4**	كاروان	**D**	prince of the sea
e	admiral	**5**	تعاريف	**E**	company of travellers

Vocabulary builder

 07.01 Listen to the new expressions and repeat them until you can say them with confidence. Listen again and complete the gaps.

TALKING ABOUT HOW YOU TRAVELLED

سافر	**sáafara**	to travel

HE TRAVELLED TO JEDDAH … … سافر إلى جدة

بالسيارة	by car
بالطائرة	by plane
بالباص	by _____ /coach
بالقطار	by train
بالتاكسي	by_____
بالسفينة	by ship

FURTHER EXPRESSIONS OF TIME

I met him…	قابلته …
last night	أمس بالليل
last week/month	الأسبوع/الشهر الماضي
last year	السنة الماضية
three years ago	قبل ثلاث سنوات
in 1995	في سنة ١٩٩٥
a week/month ago	قبل أسبوع/شهر
a year ago	قبل سنة

Reading

أَخي فهد *ákhii fahd* **MY BROTHER, FAHD**

شهر، شهور/أشهر	shahr, shuhúur/ásh-hur	month
مارس	maars	March
عمل	:ámila	to work, do
سكن	sákana	to reside, live, stay
رسالة، رسائل	risáalah, rasáa'il	letter, message
كل	kull	every, each
أسبوع، أسابيع	usbúu: asaabíi:	week
رجع	rája:a	to return, come/go back
سبتمبر	sabtámbar	September

07.02 *Samira, a Kuwaiti girl, writes to a friend about her brother who was working abroad.*

1 When did Samira's brother return to Kuwait?

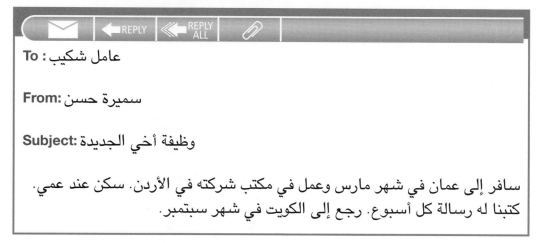

To : عامل شكيب

From: سميرة حسن

Subject: وظيفة أخي الجديدة

سافر إلى عمان في شهر مارس وعمل في مكتب شركته في الأردن. سكن عند عمي.
كتبنا له رسالة كل أسبوع. رجع إلى الكويت في شهر سبتمبر.

2 Listen to the audio again and say whether the following are true or false:

a Samira's brother went to Amman in March.

b He wrote to Samira every week.

3 Link the English phrases with the equivalent Arabic:

a He worked in the office.

b He stayed with my uncle.

c We wrote him a letter every week.

١ سكن عند عمي.

٢ كتبنا له رسالة كل أسبوع.

٣ عمل في المكتب.

Conversation

ماذا فعلت أمس؟ máadhaa fa:ált ams? *WHAT DID YOU DO YESTERDAY?*

فعل	**fá:ala**	*to do*
عائلة، ـات	**:áa'ilah, -aat**	*family*
يسكنون	**yaskunúun**	*they live, reside, stay*
قابل	**qáabala**	*to meet, encounter*
طبخ	**Tábakha**	*to cook*
غداء	**ghadáa'**	*lunch*
شرب	**sháriba**	*to drink*
قهوة	**qáhwah**	*coffee*
هل أعجبتك؟	**hal a:jábat-ik**	*did you (f.) like it (f.)?*
ما	**maa**	*not*
وصل	**wáSSala**	*to transport, take, give a lift*

07.03 *Zaki, a student at the college in Cairo, asks Sonya, an English friend, what she did the day before.*

1 What did Sonya do yesterday?

زكي	ماذا فعلت أمس؟
سونية	أمس ذهبت إلى بيت أحمد.
زكي	كيف ذهبت إلى هناك؟
سونية	ذهبت بالتاكسي. هو وعائلته يسكنون في الزمالك.
زكي	ماذا فعلتم؟
سونية	قابلت والده ووالدته وأخواته. طبخت والدته الغداء. بعد الغداء شربنا قهوة عربية.
زكي	وهل أعجبتك؟
سونية	نعم، هي لذيذة.
زكي	هل رجعت بالتاكسي؟
سونية	لا، ما رجعت بالتاكسي. أحمد وصلني إلى البيت في سيارته.

2 Listen to the conversation again, then answer the questions.

    a How did Sonya go to Ahmed's house?

        1 by train   **2** by taxi   **3** by bike

    b Where do Ahmed and his family live?

        1 Zamalek   **2** Helwan   **3** Maadi

    c What meal did they eat together?

        1 breakfast   **2** lunch   **3** dinner

    d Who cooked the meal?

        1 Ahmed   **2** Ahmed's father **3** Ahmed's mother

    e What did they have after lunch?

        1 Arabic coffee   **2** Turkish coffee   **3** American coffee

    f How did Sonya get home?

        1 by taxi   **2** by bus   **3** by car

3 Match the English with the Arabic.

    a yesterday   ١ كيف ذهبت إلى هناك؟

    b How did you go there?   ٢ هل أعجبتك؟

    c I went by taxi.   ٣ وصلني إلى البيت.

    d Did you like it?   ٤ أمس

    e He gave me a lift home.   ٥ ذهبت بالتاكسي.

Language discovery

1 THE ARABIC VERB: GENERAL

The Arabic verb differs from the English verb in two ways:

    a It has only two full tenses (i.e. ways to express when an action took place):

▶ the past tense is used for all completed actions

▶ the present tense is used for all actions not yet complete

▶ the future tense is just the present tense with the prefix - سـ **sa-**.

    b Most verbs can be reduced to a past stem and a present stem, and a standard set of prefixes and suffixes can be added to these stems to form meaningful words.

Arabic verbs fit into a limited number of categories, but there are virtually no truly irregular verbs in Arabic – apparent irregularities can usually be explained by the occurrence of the weak letters و **waaw** and ي **yaa'** as one of the letters in the stem. (For further details, see Verb tables.)

2 PAST TENSE

The verb **kátaba** belongs to Type S-I in the Verb tables. The root **k-t-b** indicates *writing*.

Note: study the following in conjunction with the S section of the Verb tables, which contains further information.

Singular			Plural		
كتب	**kátab(a)**	*he wrote*	كتبوا	**kátab-uu**	*they (m.) wrote*
كتبت	**kátab-at**	*she wrote*	كتبن	**katáb-na**	*they (f.) wrote*
كتبت	**katáb-t(a)**	*you (m.) wrote*	كتبتم	**katáb-tum**	*you (m.) wrote*
كتبت	**katáb-ti**	*you (f.) wrote*	كتبتن	**katab-túnna**	*you (f.) wrote*
كتبت	**katáb-t(u)**	*I wrote*	كتبنا	**katáb-na(a)**	*we wrote*

Here is a list of some commonly used verbs. Remember that these are all in the *he* form of the past tense and, in the past tense, they can all be formed in the same way as **kátaba**.

ذهب	**dháhaba**	*go*
سافر	**sáafara**	*travel*
وصل	**wáSala**	*arrive*
رجع	**rája:a**	*return, go back*
عمل	**:ámila**	*do, work*
تفرج على	**tafárraja :álaa**	*watch, spectate*
خبر	**khábbara**	*tell, inform*
قابل	**qáabala**	*meet*
غسل	**ghásala**	*wash*
غادر	**gháadara**	*leave, depart*

كلم	**kállama**	speak to
وجد	**wájada**	find
قرأ	**qára'a**	read
فعل	**fá:ala**	do, act
ركب	**rákiba**	ride
سكن	**sákana**	live, reside
أكل	**'ákala**	eat
شرب	**sháriba**	drink
لعب	**lá:iba**	play
طبخ	**Tábakha**	cook
شاهد	**sháahada**	see, look at
وضع	**wáDa:a**	put, place
رقص	**ráqaSa**	dance
دخل	**dákhala**	enter
خرج	**kháraja**	go out (of)
كسر	**kásara**	break
تأخر	**ta'ákhkhara**	be late
فتح	**fátaHa**	open
قفل	**qáfala**	close

3 NOUN AND PRONOUN SUBJECTS

The subject of a verb is the person or thing doing the action. It is important in Arabic to distinguish between noun and pronoun subjects.

Verbs with pronoun subjects

When you say *they arrived, he said, it opened*, you are using a pronoun subject and the suffix ending of the verb indicates who or what the subject is. The separate pronouns, which you learned in Unit 2, are not normally used with verbs, except for emphasis:

وصلت من المغرب أمس	**waSalat min al-maghrib ams**	*She arrived from Morocco yesterday.*
سافر إلى الرباط الأسبوع الماضي	**saafara ila r-ribaaT al-usbuu: al-maaDii**	*He travelled to Rabat last week.*

الآن دورك al-'aan dawrak

1 How would you say *They (m.) arrived from Rabat last week*?

Verbs with noun subjects

When the subject of a sentence is a noun (*the workmen arrived, Ahmed said*):

▶ the verb usually comes first, followed by the subject

▶ the verb is always in the *he* or *she* form, no matter what the subject.

In English, we usually say who or what we are talking about (the subject), then go on to say what the subject did (the verb). This is followed with any other information such as who or what he did it to, where and when he did it (the object or predicate), so that the word order is usually: subject–verb–the rest:

Subject	Verb	Object/predicate
The man	*wrote*	*the letter.*

The normal word order in Arabic, however, is: verb–subject–the rest.

Note that, because Arabic is written right to left, these appear in the opposite order in the examples.

Verb	Subject	Object/predicate
كتب الرجل الرسالة **kataba** *wrote(-he)*	**r-rajul** *the man*	**ar-risaalah** *the letter*
سافرت المدرسة مع تلامذتها **saafarat** *travelled(-she)*	**al-mudarrisah** *the teacher*	**ma:a talaamidhat-haa** *with her students*
وصلت الطائرة الصبح **waSalat** *arrived(-she)*	**aT-Taa'irah** *the plane*	**S-SubH** *in the morning*
دخل الوزراء القصر **dakhala** *entered(-he)*	**l-wuzaraa'** *the ministers*	**al-qaSr** *the palace*

The fact that the verb in these cases is either in the *he* or *she* form, i.e. always singular, never plural, should be noted carefully. Remember that the plural of things (inanimate objects or abstracts) is regarded as feminine singular, so that the rule for verbs which precede their subjects looks like this:

Subject	Example	Verb
one or more male human beings; singular inanimate noun of m. gender	*man, boys, book*	*he* form
one or more female human beings; singular inanimate noun of f. gender; plural of inanimate noun of either gender	*woman, girls, car, books, cars*	*she* form

4 SAYING *NOT* IN THE PAST TENSE

To negate something that happened in the past, the word ما **maa** *not* can be placed before the verb:

maa sharibt al-qahwah   ما شربت القهوة

Not I-drank the-coffee   *I didn't drink the coffee.*

[V]

عامل، عمال	**:áamil, :ummáal**	*workman*
رئيس، رؤساء	**ra'íis, ru'asáa'**	*boss, chief*
خبز	**khubz**	*bread*

الآن دورك al-'aan dawrak

2 Turn the following sentences into negatives, then translate them.

a تأخرت الطائرة _____

b كلم العمال الرئيس _____

c أكلت الخبز _____

_____

_____

_____

5 SENTENCES IN WHICH THE VERB COMES AFTER THE SUBJECT

The verb–subject–object/predicate word order is the most common in Arabic, but it is possible to have verbs that come after their subjects. This occurs most frequently in sentences with more than one verb, e.g. *The workmen arrived on the site and started to dig the foundations.*

wáSala l-:ummaal wa-badat fii hafir asasat   وصل العمال وبدأت في حفر أساسات

If a sentence starting with a noun subject has more than one verb, the first one comes before the noun subject and obeys the *he/she* form agreement rule, and any subsequent verb comes after the subject and must agree with it completely, in number (singular or plural) and gender (male or female).

So if the subject refers to men, the second and any subsequent verbs must end in **-uu** (masculine plural). If it refers to women, it must end in **-na** (feminine plural). The plural of things, regarded as feminine singular, will have the ending **-at** on both verbs:

وصل العمال وصلحوا الباب	**wáSala l-:ummaal wa-SallaHuu l-baab**	*The workmen arrived and mended the door.*
دخلت البنات الغرفة وشربن القهوة	**dakhalat al-banaat al-ghurfah wa-sharibna l-qahwah**	*The girls entered the room and drank the coffee.*
وقعت الكتب من الرف وأصابت المدرس	**waqa:at al-kutub min ar-raff wa-aSaabat al-mudarris**	*The books fell from the shelf and struck the teacher.*

> **VOCABULARY**
>
> وقع **wáqa:a** means *to fall*; رف، رفوف **raff, rufúuf** *shelf*; أصاب **aSáaba** *to hit, strike*

5 *ME, IT, THEM* – OBJECT PRONOUNS

To say *me, it, them* Arabic uses – with one exception – the same pronoun suffixes as the possessive pronoun suffixes that mean *my, its, their* (see Unit 5).

They are added to the verb to express the object of the sentence, to which the action of the verb is applied:

Singular

ني	**-nii**	*me*
ـك	**-ak**	*you (to a man)*
ـك	**-ik**	*your (to a woman)*
ـه	**-uh**	*him*
ـها	**-haa**	*her*

Plural

ـنا	**-naa**	*us*
ـكم	**-kum**	*you (to men)*
ـكن	**-kúnna**	*you (to women)*
ـهم	**-hum**	*them (men)*
ـهن	**-húnna**	*them (women)*

> **LANGUAGE TIP**
>
> As the table shows, the only one that differs is the suffix for *me*, which is ـني **-nii** after verbs (as opposed to ـي **-ii** after other types of word).
>
> | | | |
> |---|---|---|
> | خبرني ناصر | **khabbara-nii naaSir** | *Nasser told me.* |
> | كلمته أمس | **kallamt-uh ams** | *I spoke to him yesterday.* |
> | قابلناهم في السوق | **qaabalnaa-hum fi s-suuq** | *We met them in the market.* |

When **-ak** and **-uh** come after a vowel, they are reduced to **-k** and **-h** respectively and **-ik** becomes **-ki**. This is another example of elision (when words blend together):

شاهدناك	**shaahadnáa-k/ki**	*We saw you (m./f.).*
شربوه	**sharibúu-h**	*They (m.) drank it.*

> **LANGUAGE TIP**
>
> The masculine plural ending **-uu** is written with a 'silent' **alif** at the end (ـوا – see Verb tables). This is omitted when any suffix is joined onto the verb.

Pronunciation
ELISION

Here are some conventions of Arabic pronunciation. They will help to improve your Arabic.

1 Definition of elision

Elision in Arabic usually means that a preceding vowel swallows up a following one.

al- *the* becomes **l-** after vowels:

صلحوا الباب	**SállaHuu l-baab**	*They repaired the gate.*

Elision also occurs with the sun letters (see Unit 1):

صلحوا السيارة	**SállaHuu s-sayyáarah**	*They repaired the car.*

2 Elision of fii

When the word **fii** *in* precedes **al-** *the*, the **a** of **al-** is omitted and the vowel of **fii** is shortened to make **fi**. Technically, this applies to all words ending in long vowels, but it is most noticeable with **fii**:

في البيت   **fi l-bayt**   *in the house*

3 Initial i

Standard Arabic does not allow words to begin with two consonants like English does (e.g. *trip, blank*). Instead it adds an **i-** vowel prefix (in Arabic, expressed by an **alif** with an **i** vowel below it). In practice, however, this vowel sign is rarely written:

اِجتماع   **ijtimáa:**   *meeting*

When this vowel is preceded by a word ending in a vowel, the **i** vowel is elided: واجتماع **wa-ijtimáa:** *and (a) meeting* is pronounced **wa-jtimaa:**. This is a refinement in pronunciation and it will do no harm if you fail to observe it meticulously.

> **LANGUAGE TIP**
>
> Some words beginning with **alif** use this to carry a radical **hamzah** (i.e. one which is part of the root) and this should not be elided. This kind of **hamzah** is quite often – but not always – marked in print, and we have tried to follow the Arab convention:
>
> أكل   **ákala**   *he ate*
>
> أمير   **amíir**   *prince, Emir*
>
> أخذ   **ákhadha**   *he took*

Word discovery

 07.04 The word pattern for this unit is taC¹áaC²uC³, for example, **ta:áawun** تعاون *co-operation*, which sounds like the English *to our one*.

Some more examples are:

تكاتب   **takáatub**   *correspondence, writing to each other*
تفاهم   **tafáahum**   *mutual understanding*
تضامن   **taDáamun**   *solidarity*
تبادل   **tabáadul**   *exchange, exchanging*

Looking at the nouns above, decide whether they mean:

    a doing something with someone else

or

    b doing something alone

Practice

1 How did Mohammed travel to Cairo? Match the pictures with the Arabic phrases.

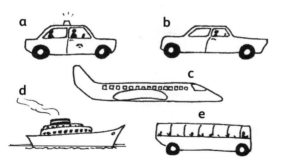

سافر محمد إلى القاهرة...

١ بالسيارة

٢ بالطائرة

٣ بالسفينة

٤ بالباص

٥ بالتاكسي

مفتاح، مفاتيح	**miftáaH, mafaatíiH**	*key*
جيب، جيوب	**jayb, juyúub**	*pocket*
مائدة، موائد	**máa'ida, mawáa'id**	*table*
جريدة، جرائد	**jaríidah, jaráa'id**	*newspaper*

2 Who did what? Match the English with the Arabic sentences.

a We read the newspapers.

b She put her bag on the table.

c We entered the room.

d You (m. sing.) wrote a letter.

e He lived in London.

f You (f. pl.) came out of the hotel.

g I found the keys in my pocket.

h They (m.) arrived at Bahrain Airport.

١ دخلنا الغرفة.

٢ وجدت المفاتيح في جيبي.

٣ وضعت حقيبتها على المائدة.

٤ وصلوا إلى مطار البحرين.

٥ خرجتن من الفندق.

٦ كتبت رسالة.

٧ سكن في لندن.

٨ قرأنا الجرائد.

3 Put the correct suffix endings on the verbs in brackets.

a They (m.) travelled to Kuwait.

b She opened the door.

c Did you (m. sing.) watch the television?

d I arrived yesterday.

e She cooked and we ate the food.

(سافر) إلى الكويت.

(فتح) الباب.

هل (تفرج) على التلفزيون؟

(وصل) أمس.

(طبخ) و(أكل) الطعام.

شاطئ	sháaTi'	shore, beach
جمل، جمال	jámal, jimáal	camel
شاب، شباب	shaabb, shabáab	youth/young person
كافيتريا	kaafitírya	cafeteria/café
عصير	:aSíir	juice

4 Jamal went on holiday to Egypt. Match the pictures with the sentences.

a

b

c

d

e

f

١ (لعب) على الشاطئ.

٢ (قابل) شبابا مصريين.

٣ (جلس) في الكافيتريا.

٤ (ركب) جملا.

٥ (شرب) عصيرا.

٦ (ذهب) إلى السوق.

5 Now write Jamal's postcard home, putting the verbs in brackets in the I-form.

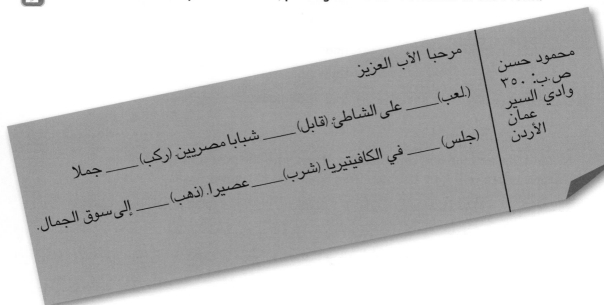

محمود حسن
ص.ب: ٣٥٠
وادي السير
عمان
الأردن

مرحبا الأب العزيز

_____ (لعب) على الشاطئ ـــــ (قابل) شبابا مصريين ـــــ (جلس)

في الكافيتيريا. (ركب) ـــــ جملا ـــــ (شرب) عصيرا. (ذهب) ـــــ إلى سوق الجمال.

تفاحة، تفاح	**tuffáaHah, tuffáaH**	*apple*
سأل	**sá'ala**	*to ask*
سؤال، أسئلة	**su'áal, ás'ilah**	*question*

6 Change the highlighted nouns to object pronouns.

Example: *I met the manager* ➔ *I met him*

قابلته. ➔ قابلت المدير.

١ كتبت <u>الرسالة</u>   ٤ سألت <u>السؤال</u>

٢ أكلت <u>التفاحة</u>   ٥ غسلن <u>القمصان</u>

٣ كلم <u>الرجال</u>   ٦ قابل <u>فاطمة</u> في عمان

سائق، ـون/ ساقة	**sáa'iq, -úun/sáaqah**	*driver*

7 Match the Arabic with the English sentences:

a My wife cooked the food.

١ قرأ الطلاب الكتب في مكتبة الجامعة.

b The driver took his boss to the airport.

٢ شربت السكرتيرات قهوة كل يوم.

c The students read the books in the
   university library.

٣ طبخت زوجتي الطعام.

d The aeroplane arrived in Beirut.

٤ وصل السائق رئيسه إلى المطار.

e The secretaries drank coffee every day.

٥ وصلت الطائرة إلى بيروت.

قعد	qá:ada	to stay, remain, sit
لمدة...	li-múddat...	for the period of...
ناس	naas	people
تنس	tánis	tennis
صديق، أصدقاء	Sadíiq, aSdiqáa'	friend
لهم	lá-hum	for them

8 Read the passage and complete the Arabic with the past tense form of an appropriate verb from the box. Then have a go at translating it.

بيل وميري والأولاد من لندن ــــــ إلى دبي في شهر مارس سنة ٢٠١٠ ــــــ. هناك ــــــ لمدة أسبوع. ــــــ في شقة كبيرة قريبة من البحر، و ــــــ ناسا كثيرين من الإمارات. يوم الاثنين ــــــ بيل تنس، و ــــــ ميري إلى الشاطئ. يوم الثلاثاء ــــــ إلى بيت صديقهم منصور، و ــــــ لهم زوجته طعاما عربيا.

قعدوا   سكنوا   لعب   سافر   ذهبوا

قابلوا   ذهبت   طبخت   ووصلوا

حضر	HáDara	to attend, be present
مؤتمر، ـات	mu'támar, -áat	conference
صحن، صحون	SaHn, SuHúun	dish

9 The following sentences all have the verb (highlighted) before the subject. Rewrite them with the verb after the subject, paying attention to the correct agreement.

Example:

المدراء رجعوا من الاجتماع.   ←   رجع المدراء من الاجتماع.

١ سافر محمد إلى القاهرة.

٢ رجع الأولاد من المدرسة.

٣ حضر المهندسون المؤتمر.

٤ طبخت البنات طعاما عربيا.

٥ وقعت الصحون من المائدة.

Test yourself

1 How would you say these questions and phrases in English?

١ كيف ذهبت إلى هناك؟ ـــــــــــــــــ

٢ ذهبت بالتاكسي. ـــــــــــــــــ

٣ قرأ الطلاب الكتب في مكتبة الجامعة. ـــــــــــــــــ

٤ سكن عند عمي. ـــــــــــــــــ

٥ شربت السكرتيرات قهوة كل يوم. ـــــــــــــــــ

٦ وجدت الرسالة في جيبي. ـــــــــــــــــ

٧ سكن في البحرين. ـــــــــــــــــ

٨ خرجتم من الغرفة. ـــــــــــــــــ

SELF CHECK	
I CAN. . .	
○	. . . talk about things that happened in the past.
○	. . . describe means of transport.
○	. . . use Arabic verbs.
○	. . . say *me, him, them,* etc.

8 كان يا ما كان
kaan yaa maa kaan

Once upon a time

In this unit you will learn how to:
▶ *say* was/were
▶ *say* is/are not
▶ *describe what something was like*
▶ *say* became
▶ *use a new type of* is/are *sentence*
▶ *say you had done something.*

CEFR: (A2) *Can tell a story or describe something in a simple list of points; can write a description of an event real or imaginary; can narrate a story.*

Storytelling

Arab culture has a long history of traditional oral storytelling. Perhaps the most famous is that of *The Arabian Nights/A Thousand and One Nights*, or ألف ليلة وليلة **alf laylah wa-laylah** (lit. 'a thousand nights and a night'). Princess Sheherazade kept her husband, the Sultan, from executing her when, for 1001 nights, she told him one tale after another, always ending at an exciting point of the story, so that he had to let her live to tell the rest of the tale the next night. These stories are very familiar and the European editions include Aladdin, Sindbad and Ali Baba. There is some debate about which stories were in the original collection and the authenticity of the different versions in print. This is largely due to the fact that the stories originate from an oral tradition of storytelling where each teller adds to and edits a story each time they tell it.

 What is the Arabic word for *night*?

Vocabulary builder

08.01 **Listen to the new expressions and repeat them until you can say them with confidence. Listen again and complete the gaps.**

DESCRIBING SOMEONE OR SOMETHING

كان ممثلا مشهورا	kaana mumaththilan mash-huuran	He was a famous actor.
كانت تعبانة جدا بعد الرحلة	kaanat ta:baanah jiddan ba:d ar-riHlah	She was very tired after the journey.
_____ شعرها أسود	kaana sha:r-haa aswad	Her hair was black.

> **LANGUAGE TIP**
>
> **aswad** *black* does not take the accusative marker. See below and Unit 15.

TALKING ABOUT WHERE SOMETHING WAS

كان المفتاح في _____	kaana l-miftaaH fii jayb-uh	The key was in his pocket.
كانت الجرائد على المائدة.	kaanat al-jaraa'id :ala -l-maa'ida	The papers were on the table.

TALKING ABOUT WHAT SOMEONE OR SOMETHING IS NOT

ليس _____ كبيرا.	laysa al-funduq kabiiran	The hotel is not large.
لست مريضا.	lastu mariiDan	I am not ill.

TALKING ABOUT WHAT YOU HAD DONE IN THE PAST

هل كنت قد شاهدت الفيلم _____ ؟	hal kunta qad shaahadta l-fiilm min qabl?	Had you seen the film before?
كنا قد وقفنا وجلسنا.	kunna qad waqafnaa wa-jalasnaa	We had stopped and sat down.

Reading 1

كان يا ما كان kaan yaa maa kaan *ONCE UPON A TIME*

خليفة، خلفاء	khaliifah, khulafáa'	caliph, head of the Islamic state (m., despite its ending)
حمال، ـون	Hammáal, -uun	porter
فقير، فقراء	faqiir, fuqaráa'	poor; poor person
في يوم من الأيام	fii yawm min al-ayyáam	one day (lit. 'in a day of the days')
كان ... يحمل	káana ... yáHmil	he was carrying
حمل، أحمال	Himl, aHmáal	load, burden
ثقيل	thaqíil	heavy
تاجر، تجار	táajir, tujjáar	merchant
صيف	Sayf	summer
حرارة	Haráarah	heat
شديد	shadíid	strong, mighty
أصبح	áSbaHa	become
تعبان	ta:báan	tired
عطشان	:aTsháan	thirsty
وقف	wáqafa	stop, stand
طريق، طرق	Taríiq, Túruq	road, way
باب، أبواب	baab, abwáab	gate, door
فخم	fakhm	magnificent
للاستراحة	li-l-istiráaHah	in order to rest (lit. 'for the resting')
عمل، أعمال	:ámal, a:máal	work, job, business
الأرض	al-árD	the ground, the earth (f.)
جلس	jálasa	sit, sit down
بينما	báynamaa	while
جالس	jáalis	sitting, seated
كـ	ka-	like (joined to following word)
سمع	sámi:a	hear, listen

98

موسيقى	**muusíiqaa**	*music (f.)*
منبعث	**munbá:ith**	*emanating*
داخل	**dáakhil**	*inside, the inside of something*
خادم، خدام، خادمة، ـات	**kháadimah, -aat kháadim, khuddáam**	*servant*
واقف	**wáaqif**	*standing, stationary*
صاحب، أصحاب	**SáaHib, aS-Háab**	*owner, master; also sometimes friend*

 08.02 *This is how Princess Sheherazade introduced the stories of Sindbad the Sailor.*

1 What was the porter (حمال) called?

   a Harun al-Rashid   **b** al-Hindbad   **c** Sindbad

في أيام الخليفة هارون الرشيد كان في بغداد حمال فقير اسمه الهندباد. وفي يوم من الأيام كان الهندباد هذا يحمل حملا ثقيلا إلى بيت تاجر في السوق. وكان ذلك في الصيف وكانت حرارة الشمس شديدة جدا. وأصبح الهندباد تعبانا وعطشانا. فوقف في الطريق عند باب قصر فخم للاستراحة من عمله. ووضع حمله على الأرض وجلس. وبينما هو جالس هكذا سمع موسيقى جميلة منبعثة من داخل القصر. وكان هناك خادم واقف أمام باب القصر، فسأله الهندباد: من صاحب هذا القصر الفخم؟

2 Answer the questions.

   a Where was the porter going? _____

   b Why did he stop? _____

   c What did he stop beside?

     1 a house   **2** a door   **3** a market

   d What did he ask the servant? _____

3 Match the English phrases with the appropriate Arabic expressions:

a beautiful music	١	كان ذلك في الصيف
b the heat of the sun was very strong	٢	أمام باب القصر
c that was in the summer	٣	في أيام الخليفة هارون الرشيد
d in the days of the Caliph Harun al-Rashid	٤	أصبح الهندباد تعبانا
e in front of the gate of the palace	٥	موسيقى جميلة
f al-Hindbad became tired	٦	كانت حرارة الشمس شديدة جدا

Reading 2

السندباد البحري as-sindibaad al-baHrii *SINDBAD THE SAILOR*

قال(له)	qáala (lá-hu)	he said (to him)
إنه	ínn-uh	it is…
من؟	man	who?
دهش	dáhisha	be surprised, astonished
ساكن	sáakin	living, residing
الذي	alládhii	who, the one who
البحار السبعة	al-biHáar as-sáb:ah	the seven seas
عجيبة،عجائب	:ajíibah, :ajáa'ib	(object of) wonder
الدنيا	ad-dúnya(a)	the world (f.)
كلها	kúll-haa	all of them
حزين	Hazíin	sad
نفسه	náfs-uh	himself
لماذا؟	li-máadha(a)	why?
غني، أغنياء	ghánii, aghniyáa'	rich, rich person
لست	lástu	I am not (see Language discovery)
كلام	kaláam	speech
أرسل	ársala	send
آخر	áakhar	other
تعال	ta:áala	come!
مع	má:a	(along) with
تبع	tábi:a	follow
جماعة، ـات	jamáa:ah, -aat	group, gathering
انسان، ناس	insáan, naas	human being; pl. = people
أجلس	ájlasa	seat, cause to sit down
قدم	qáddama	offer, present with
نوع، أنواع	naw:, anwáa:	kind, sort, type
أكل	akl	things to eat, food

رحلة، ـات	ríHlah, -aat	journey, voyage
عجيب	:ajíib	wonderful
أمر	ámara	order, command
		(بـ bi- something)
كان قد أمر	káana qad ámara	he had ordered
نقل	naql	transport, transportation

 08.03 *Who could own this magnificent palace? Listen to the rest of the story…*

1 The sailor had travelled:

a for seven years   **b** the seven seas   **c** to seven countries

وقال له الخادم: إنه قصر السندباد البحري. قال الحمال: ومن هو؟ فدهش الخادم وقال: أنت ساكن في بغداد وما سمعت عن السندباد البحري؟ قال الهندباد: لا. قال الخادم: هو الذي سافر في البحار السبعة وشاهد عجائب الدنيا كلها. فعند ذلك أصبح الحمال حزينا وسأل نفسه قال: لماذا السندباد هذا غني، وأنا لست غنيا؟ وسمع السندباد هذا الكلام من داخل القصر وأرسل خادما آخر إلى الباب. وخرج هذا الخادم من باب القصر وكلم الهندباد وقال: تعال معي. فتبعه الحمال إلى داخل القصر وشاهد هناك رجلا طويلا جالسا في وسط جماعة من الناس، وكان هذا الرجل السندباد. وقال البحري للحمال: مرحبا، أهلا وسهلا. وأجلسه بجانبه وقدم له أنواعا كثيرة من الأكل اللذيذ. وبعد ذلك خبره عن رحلاته العجيبة، وكان السندباد قد أمر خدامه بنقل حمل الهندباد إلى بيت التاجر.

2 Answer the questions.

a Why was the servant astonished? _____

b The porter become sad because:

    1 Sindbad was rich and he was poor

    2 the servant told him to leave

    3 he was hungry

c Who was with Sindbad?

    1 a group of servants   **2** his wife   **3** a group of people

d Sindbad gave him:

    1 gold   **2** food   **3** drink

e What had he ordered his servants to do? _____

3 Match the English phrases with the appropriate Arabic expressions:

a he said.

b (Indeed) it is the palace of Sindbad the Sailor.

c He has travelled the seven seas.

d I am not rich.

e Come with me.

f Greetings and welcome!

g He told him about his amazing voyages.

h He had ordered his servants.

١ تعال معي.

٢ سافر في البحار السبعة.

٣ خبره عن رحلاته العجيبة.

٤ إنه قصر السندباد البحري.

٥ كان قد أمر خدامه.

٦ قال

٧ مرحبا، أهلا وسهلا.

٨ أنا لست غنيا.

Language discovery

1 SAYING *WAS* AND *WERE*

Arabic does not use a verb for *is/are*, but when you talk about the past, the verb **kaana** for *was/were* is necessary.

This verb differs slightly from the past tense verbs that you have met in that it has two stems (**kaan-** and **kun-**). The endings are the standard past tense suffixes used on all Arabic verbs (see the Verb tables).

Singular			Plural		
he was	كان	kaana	they (m.) were	كانوا	kaan-uu
she was	كانت	kaan-at	they (f.) were	كن	kun-na
you (m.) were	كنت	kun-t(a)	you (m.) were	كنتم	kun-tum
you (f.) were	كنت	kun-ti	you (f.) were	كنتن	kun-tunna
I was	كنت	kun-t(u)	we were	كنا	kun-naa

▶ The final vowels in brackets can be omitted in informal speech.

▶ The stem **kaan-** is used in the *he*, *she* and *they* (m.) forms, and the stem **kun-** for the rest. It may help you to remember them if you notice that the shortened **kun-** stem is used before suffixes which begin with a consonant. **kaana** is a type Mw-I verb: see Verb tables.

> **LANGUAGE TIP**
>
> Since the last letter of the root of this verb is **n**, the usual shorthand spellings with the doubling sign is used when the suffix also begins with an **n** (كنّ **kunna** they (f.) were, and كنّا **kunnaa** we were).
>
> كنا في تونس في الصيف   **kunnaa fii tuunis fi S-Sayf**   *We were in Tunisia in the summer.*

Word order

The verb **kaana** usually comes first in the sentence, and the normal rules of agreement given in the previous unit apply:

كان جمال عبد الناصر قائدا عظيما.	**kaana jamaal :abd an-naaSir qaa'idan :aDHiiman**	*Jamaal Abd al-Nasir was a great leader.*
كان المدير مشغولا.	**kaana l-mudiir mashghuulan**	*The manager was busy.*
كنت مريضا.	**kunt(u) mariiDan**	*I was ill.*

الآن دورك **al-'aan dawrak**

1 Based on the patterns given, reorder the following words to make sentences in Arabic, and then give the English translation.

مشهورة الممثلة كانت   —————————————————

كانت البيوت قديمة   —————————————————

2 THE ACCUSATIVE MARKER

Formal Arabic (usually) has a set of three varying noun endings, which show the part played by a word in a sentence, similar to case endings in Latin or German. The words *he, him* and *his* show these cases in English:

Nominative	Accusative	Genitive
he	*him*	*his*

Most of these endings are only short vowel marks, which are omitted in modern written Arabic, and for the sake of simplification we have not included them in this book.

The only case ending appearing in print in contemporary written Arabic – except for a few special types of noun – is the accusative case.

How to form the accusative

This ending only affects the spelling of indefinite unsuffixed nouns or adjectives. The full form is actually ﺍً (pronounced **-an**), but only the **alif** is usually written after the noun/adjective.

'Unsuffixed' in this context normally means that the noun or adjective does not have the feminine ending ﺔ **-ah**. Nouns and adjectives that have this ending never add the **alif**.

> **LANGUAGE TIP**
>
> You may think that we could have said simply masculine nouns take the extra **alif**, but there are feminine nouns that do not have the ﺔ **-ah** ending and these have to obey the **alif** law.
>
> For example, أم **umm** *mother* is clearly feminine but has no ﺔ **-ah** ending. Its accusative indefinite is therefore أمًا **umman**. There is also a handful of nouns signifying men that have the feminine ending, such as خليفة **khaliifa** *caliph* in Reading 1. These are obviously regarded as masculine, and do not take the **alif** because of the presence of the ﺔ **-ah** ending.

> **LANGUAGE TIP**
>
> A minority of Arabic unsuffixed nouns and adjectives do not add the alif. The most common of these are the main colours, as well as some forms of the internal plural and many proper nouns. From this unit on, these are marked in the vocabulary sections with an asterisk (*) and also appear like this in the glossaries at the end of the book:
>
> | | | |
> |---|---|---|
> | كان الكلب أبيض | **kaana l-kalb abyaD** | *The dog was white.* |
> | قرأنا جرائد كثيرة أمس | **qara'naa jaraa'id kathiirah ams** | *We read many newspapers yesterday.* |
> | قابلنا أحمد في السوق | **qaabalnaa aHmad fi s-suuq** | *We met Ahmed in the market.* |

When to use the accusative

In Arabic, the accusative is used in four instances:

1 When the second noun is the object of the sentence, i.e. the thing or person the verb applies to:

شاهدوا قصرا فخما	**shaahaduu qaSran fakhman**	*They saw a magnificent castle.*

2 After the verbs كان **kaana** *was, were,* ليس **laysa** *is not, are not,* أصبح **aSbaHa** *to become,* and a few other similar verbs.

Note: ليس **laysa** alone can also take an alternative construction using the preposition **bi-** which does not take the accusative:

لست غنيا/لست بغني   **lastu ghaniyyan/lastu bi-ghanii**   *I am not rich.*

3 In some common expressions and adverbs, when the ending is most commonly heard in spoken Arabic:

أهلا وسهلا	**ahlan wa sahlan**	*hello, greetings*
مرحبا	**marHaban**	*welcome*
شكرا	**shukran**	*thanks*
جدا	**jiddan**	*very*
أبدا	**abadan**	*never*
طبعا	**Tab:an**	*naturally*

4 After certain short words, known as <u>particles</u>, such as **inna** and **anna** (see Language discovery section 6).

> **LANGUAGE TIP**
>
> The Arabs refer to these words as '**kaana** and her sisters' and '**inna** and her sisters'.

3 SAYING WHERE SOMETHING WAS

kaana can be used before prepositions (words that tell you where something is) and such sentences are the same as those verbless sentences in the present, except that **kaana** is put at the beginning (and obeys the agreement rules given in Unit 7).

كان قلمي في جيبي   **kaana qalam-ii fii jayb-ii**   *My pen was in my pocket.*

4 HOW TO SAY *IS/ARE NOT*

The word **maa** *not* is used before normal verbs (see Units 7 and 10) and can also be used before **kaana** in a past tense sentence.

To negate *is/are* sentences, however, the verb ليس **laysa** is used. This verb is unique in Arabic, as it is only used in what looks like the past tense, with past tense suffixes, but the meaning is actually present.

Like **kaana** it has two stems (**lays-** and **las-**). As with **kaan-/kun-** you will see that in both verbs the first stem is used for the *he, she* and *they* (m.) parts, and the second stem with the rest. Remember that, although it looks like a past tense, it means *isn't/aren't*.

Singular			Plural		
he isn't	ليس	lays-a	they (m.) aren't	ليسوا	lays-uu
she isn't	ليست	lays-at	they (f.) aren't	لسن	las-na
you (m.) aren't	لست	las-t(a)	you (m.) aren't	لستم	las-tum
you (f.) aren't	لست	las-ti	you (f.) aren't	لستن	las-tunna
I am not	لست	las-t(u)	we aren't	لسنا	las-naa

ليس الولد مجتهدا   **laysa l-walad mujtahidan**   *The boy is not hard working.*

> **LANGUAGE TIP**
>
> **laysa** requires the accusative marker in the same way as **kaana**. (But see also alternative construction
>
> with **bi-** described earlier.)

5 HOW TO SAY *TO BECOME*

There are several verbs in Arabic meaning *to become*, but أصبح **aSbaHa** is by far the most
common. Like **kaana** and **laysa**, it requires the accusative marker on unsuffixed indefinites,
but it has only one stem, **aSbaH-**.

> **LANGUAGE TIP**
>
> The initial **hamzah** of **aSbaH** is never elided, so if you say *and he became* it is
>
> **wa-aSbaHa**, not **wa-SbaH**.

أصبح الولد مريضا   **aSbaHa l-walad mariiDan**   *The boy became ill.*

أصبحت البنت مريضة   **aSbaHat al-bint mariiDah**   *The girl became ill.*

بنت **bint** is an example of a feminine noun without the suffix ـة. However, the adjective
mariiDah still has to have the suffix, as it refers to a female.

The verbs أصبح **aSbaHa** كان **kaana** and ليس **laysa**, have all been dealt with together
here as they share the common feature of using the accusative marker on what is not a
direct object.

6 SENTENCES WITH إن INNA AND أن ANNA

The particle **inna**, though frequently used, is virtually meaningless. However, it is translated
in this book where necessary as *indeed*, just to show it is there (older Arabic-teaching
manuals use the biblical *verily*).

إن **inna** is usually used with *is/are* sentences which require no verb in Arabic. When they are followed by an indefinite unsuffixed noun – usually the name of a person or place – this noun takes the accusative marker **-an** and this time it is the first noun in the sentence which has the accusative marker (unlike **kaana**, **laysa** and **aSbaHa** sentences where it is attached to the second noun):

| إن محمدا عامل مجتهد | **inna Mohammedan :aamil mujtahid** | *(Indeed) Mohammed is a hard worker.* |

أن **anna** is the conjunction *that* and follows the same rules as **inna**.

The Muslim Confession of Faith, as heard from the minarets every prayer time, is a good example of the use of **anna**:

| أشهد ألا إله إلا الله وأن محمدا رسول الله | **ash-hadu allaa ilaaha illa l-laah wa-anna Mohammedan rasuulu l-laah** |

> **LANGUAGE TIP**
>
> The transliteration here reflects the Classical Arabic pronunciation. **allaa** is a contraction of **an-laa** *that not, no.*
>
> It is usually translated as:
>
> *I witness that there is no god but Allah, and that Mohammed is His messenger.*

inna and anna with pronouns

Since **inna** requires an accusative after *it*, it has to use the suffixed pronouns (given in Unit 7):

| إنه خبر جيد | **inna-h khabar jayyid** | *(Indeed) it is good news.* |
| إنها بنت لطيفة | **inna-haa bint laTiifah** | *(Indeed) she is a pleasant girl.* |

7 HOW TO SAY *HAD DONE SOMETHING*

Although there are only two tenses in Arabic, past and present, the verb كان **kaana** can be used to express the meaning of *had done something*, called the <u>pluperfect</u> tense in English.

The little word قد **qad** is commonly introduced between the subject and the main verb. It emphasizes that the action has been well and truly completed, that it is over and done with.

The word order is as follows:

1 The *he* or *she* form of **kaana** (because it always precedes its noun – see Unit 7).
2 The subject of the sentence (i.e. who is doing the action) if this is stated. If it is a pronoun (*he*, *we*, etc.) it will be implicit in the verb (see Unit 7).

3 The word **qad** (optional in colloquial or informal Arabic).

4 The fully agreeing part of the main verb (i.e. the action that had been carried out). It is fully agreeing because it comes after its subject (see Unit 7).

5 Any other information (when, where it happened, etc.)

كان المدير قد وصل يوم السبت.	**kaana l-mudiir qad waSal yawm as-sabt**	The *manager had arrived* on Saturday.
كانوا قد سافروا إلى الهند من قبل.	**kaanuu qad saafaruu ila l-hind min qabl**	*They had travelled to India* before.

● SUMMARY OF THE ARABIC SENTENCE

These are the four types of Arabic sentence:

1 *Is/are sentences with no verb: (the) X (is/are) Y*

السندباد رجل غني.	**as-sindibaad rajul ghanii**	*Sindbad is a rich man.*

2 Sentences with a verb (other than the **kaana** group): *verb X Y*

شرب محمد الشاي.	**shariba Mohammed ash-shaay**	*Mohammed drank the tea.*

3 Sentences with **kaana**, **aSbaHa** and **laysa**

The second term of the sentence is accusative, marked with an **alif** when required: **kaana/aSbaHa/laysa** (the) X Y *accusative*

كان الهندباد فقيرا.	**kaana l-hindibaad faqiiran**	*Hindbad was poor.*

4 Sentences introduced by **inna** and its associates.

The first term of the sentence is accusative, marked as appropriate: **inna** (the) X *accusative* (is/are) Y

إن حسنا تلميذ مجتهد.	**inna Hasanan tilmiidh mujtahid**	*(Indeed) Hassan is a hard-working pupil.*

Remember:

▶ The accusative marker is only written after words which do not have **al-** the in front of them. It is not used after words with a suffix such as the feminine ending **-ah** or words that are one of the minority of such words which never take the accusative marker (noted with an asterisk as they occur).

▶ The negative verb ليس **laysa** *is/are* not is past in form but present in meaning.

Word discovery

 08.04 The word pattern for this unit is C¹aC²C²aaC³, for example, **Haddáad** حداد

blacksmith, which sounds like the English *had Dad* (as in *had Dad known…*).

Haddaad comes from حديد **Hadiid** *iron*. This is a formation often used for trades.

In the Sindbad story we have حمال **Hammaal** *porter*, from the root **H-m-l** *carrying*. Other

examples are:

نجار	**najjaar**	*carpenter*
خباز	**khabbaaz**	*baker*
بناء	**bannaa'**	*builder*
خياط	**khayyaaT**	*tailor*

This type of word takes the ـون **-uun** plural.

It is really an intensive form of CaaCiC (see Unit 2), in that it expresses the idea that

somebody is always, habitually or professionally performing the action of the root.

The feminine ending ة **-ah** is often added to this word shape to indicate a female member

of the trade or profession, or a machine.

دبابة	**dabbaabah**	*(military) tank* (lit. 'crawling machine',
		from the root **d-b-b** *crawling*)
غسالة	**ghassaalah**	*washing machine* (from the root **gh-s-l** *washing*)
سيارة	**sayyaarah**	*car* (lit. 'going-machine')
عصارة	**:aSSáarah**	*juicer*
دباسة	**dabbáasah**	*stapler*

These take the plural ـات **-aat**. Remember to remove the letter ة before adding the plural ending.

 What do you think the word for a female tailor or seamstress is?

 # Practice

الآن	**al-áan**	*now*
درجة، ـات	**dárajah, -aat**	*step, degree*
درجة الحرارة	**dárajat al-Haráarah**	*temperature* (lit. 'degree of heat')
صف، صفوف	**Saff, Sufúuf**	*class (in school)*
سادس	**sáadis**	*sixth*

خامس	kháamis	fifth
طويل، طوال	Tawíil, Tiwáal	long, tall
قصير، قصار	qaSíir, qiSáar	short
سعيد، سعداء	sa:íid, su:adáa'*	happy, joyful

1 Complete the following sentences with the appropriate form of كان kaana. Don't forget to add the accusative marker where necessary.

١ الآن درجة الحرارة ٣٥. الصبح ـــــــــــ ١٨.

٢ هذه السنة سميرة في الصف السادس. السنة الماضية ـــــــــــ في الصف الخامس.

 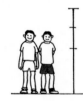

٣ الآن الأولاد طوال، في سنة ١٩٩٠ ـــــــــــ قصارا.

٤ اليوم حامد سعيد، أمس ـــــــــــ ـــــــــــ حزينا.

أمس   اليوم

2 Write these sentences in the past tense, remembering to put the accusative marker where necessary.

Example: *Mahmoud is unhappy* ➔ *Mahmoud was unhappy*

محمود حزين ➔ كان محمود حزينا

> ممثل، ـون **mumáththil, -uun** means actor, representative

١ ذلك الطعام لذيذ.

٢ حدائق الفندق واسعة.

٣ شركتنا مشهورة في الخليج.

٤ عمر الشريف ممثل مصري.

٥ الأولاد سعداء.

بهو	bahw	(hotel) lobby
بستان	bustáan	orchard
مسبح، مسابح*	másbaH, masáabiH*	swimming pool
أعمال	a:máal	(pl.) business, affairs, works
ملعب، ملاعب*	mál:ab, maláa:ib*	pitch, court, course

3 Where are they? Mahmoud and his wife Salma and their son Hamad and daughters Faridah and Sarah are staying at a hotel in Abu Dhabi. They have left a note at the desk to say where they can be found if friends or colleagues want to contact them. Answer the questions in Arabic, using ليس laysa and the accusative marker where necessary.

Example: *Is Salma in the Palm Court café?* هل سلمى في مقهى النخيل؟

No, she is not at the Palm Court café. لا، ليست في مقهى النخيل

٥ هل محمود في مركز الأعمال؟   ١ هل الساعة ١٠:٣٠ الصبح؟

٦ هل سلمى في ملعب الجولف؟   ٢ هل محمود في البهو؟

٧ هل أرقام الغرف ٥١١ و٥١٢ و٥١٣؟   ٣ هل سلمى في مطعم البستان؟

٨ هل الأولاد في ملعب التنس؟   ٤ هل سلمى وفريدة وسارة في المسبح؟

فهد، فهود	**fahd, fuhúud**	*leopard*
نمر، نمور	**námir, numúur**	*tiger*
منقط	**munáqqaT**	*spotted*
مخطط	**mukháTTaT**	*striped*

4 An Arabic proverb says:

الفهد منقط والنمر مخطط

A leopard can't change his spots.

(lit. 'the leopard is spotted and the tiger is striped')

What is wrong with this picture? Change the caption into the negative to make sense.

الفهد مخطط والنمر منقط _____

كسلان	**kasláan**	*lazy*
مستشفى، مستشفيات	**mustáshfaa, mustashfayáat**	*hospital*
قصة، قصص	**qíSSah, qíSaS**	*story, tale*

5 Change the sentences into the negative, using the verb laysa.

١ علي طالب كسلان. _____

٢ أنا تعبان بعد رحلتي. _____

٣ الفنادق الكبيرة في وسط المدينة. _____

٤ هي مشهورة جدا. _____

٥ الطبيب مشغول في المستشفى. _____

٦ هذه القصة من ألف ليلة وليلة طويلة جدا. _____

6 Change the sentences into the pluperfect tense.

Example: كان الهنداباد (قد) وجد قصر السندباد → وجد الهنداباد قصر السندباد

١ روت شهرزاد قصة جديدة كل ليلة. _____

٢ خبر البحري الحمال عن رحلاته العجيبة. _____

٣ وصل الضيف في الفنادق الكبيرة في وسط المدينة. _____

LANGUAGE TIP

روت **ráwat** means *she told*

٤ تبعته الخادمات الى داخل القصر. _____

٥ أكل الناس الأكل اللذيذ. _____

LANGUAGE TIP

The use of **qad** is optional. Watch out for the agreement of the main verb which comes after its subject in the pluperfect.

Test yourself

1 Put the sentences in the correct order and give the English translation.

a كنا في بيروت في الصيف ــــــــــــــــــــــــــــــــــ

b الحمال كان مشغولا ــــــــــــــــــــــــــــــــــ

2 Match the four types of Arabic sentences with the examples ١-٤

  a *Is/are sentences with no verb: (the) X (is/are) Y*

  b Sentences with a verb (other than the **kaana** group): *verb X Y*

  c **kaana/aSbaHa/laysa:** *(the) X Y accusative*

  d **inna:** *(the) X accusative (is/are) Y*

  Kenza drank the tea.

  The boy was thirsty.

  The manager is a busy man.

  Indeed Rashid is a hard-working baker.

١ شربت كنزة الشاي

٢ كان الولد عطشانا

٣ المدير رجل مشغول

٤ إن رشيدا خباز مجتهد

SELF CHECK

I CAN...
... say *was/were*.
... say *is/are not*.
... describe what something was like.
... say *became*.
... use a new type of *is/are* sentence.
... say *I had done something*.

٩ أكثر من واحد
akthar min waaHid
More than one

In this unit you will learn how to:
▶ *look for a job in the paper or on a website*
▶ *look for a flat or a house*
▶ *talk about more than one person or thing*
▶ *say these/those*
▶ *talk about two people or things.*

CEFR: (A2/B1) *Can understand texts that consist mainly of high frequency everyday or job-related language; can scan longer text in order to locate desired information in everyday material.*

Classified ads

For many years Arabic newspapers have carried classified advertisements with all the usual sections: وظائف شاغرة *Situations vacant,* للبيع *For sale,* مطلوب *Wanted,* للايجار *For rent* and so on. Recently these have declined in popularity and there is now a huge growth in online classified websites and social media pages which include these categories. The Arabic sites often have a search button labelled بحث to help you look for what you need.

Not all Arab countries have traditional estate agents, although you will find them in cities, particularly in the Gulf where there is a large expat population. Traditionally you hear about a housing opportunity by word of mouth or government schemes. Also until recently property has rarely been sold; it generally gets passed on to other family members.

Which verb means *to sell?*	بحث إيجار بيع طلب

Vocabulary builder

09.01 Listen to the new expressions and repeat them until you can say them with confidence. Listen again and complete the gaps.

LOOKING FOR A JOB

طلب	Tálaba	seek, want
_____	maTlúub	wanted, required
وظيفة، وظائف	waDHíifah, waDHáa'if*	job, situation
موظف، ــون موظفة، ــات	muwáDHDHaf, -úun muwáDHDHafah, -áat	employee, official
كوافيرة، ــات	kwaafíirah, -áat	hairdresser (f.), coiffeuse
فني، ــون	fánnii, -úun	technician
كهربائي	kahrabáa'ii, -úun	electrician
مدربة، ــات	mudárribah, -áat	trainer (f.)
صيدلانية، ــات	Saydalaaníyyah, -áat	pharmacist (f.)
مندوب مبيعات، مندوبو مبيعات	mandúub mabii:áat, manduubúu mabii:áat	sales representative (**mumáththil** is also used instead of **mandúub**)
بائع،، ــون بائعة، ــات	báa'i:, -úun báa'i:ah, -áat	sales assistant
مبيع، ــات	mabíi:, -áat	selling, sales
خبرة	khíbrah	experience
رخصة قيادة/سياقة	rúkhSat sáaqah	driving licence
إقامة	iqáamah	residence; residence permit
صالح	SáaliH	valid; (of people) upright
معرفة	má:rifah	knowledge
راتب	ráatib	salary
سيرة ذاتية	síirah dhaatíyyah	CV; résumé

LOOKING FOR ACCOMMODATION

_____	li-l-iijáar	for rent
الخلو مباشرة	al-khalw mubáasharat	for immediate occupation
فيلا، فيلل	fíilla, fílial	_____
صالة	Sáalah	sitting room, lounge
حمام، ــات	Hammáam, -aat	_____

دش	dushsh	_____
مطبخ	máTbakh	kitchen
سعر، أسعار	si:r, as:áar	price
مفروش	mafrúush	furnished
مركزي	márkazii	central
متجاور	mutajáawir	adjacent, neighbouring, next to each other
كامل	káamil	complete, whole
جنسية، ــات	jinsíyyah, -aat	nationality
أعزب	á:zab*	bachelor, single
متزوج	mutazáwwaj	married
عنوان، عناوين	:unwáan, :anaawíin*	address
لديك	ladáy-k	you have (lit. 'with you')

Conversation 1

وظائف شاغرة waDHáa'if sháaghirah SITUATIONS VACANT

 09.02 *John Parker is looking for a job as a salesperson in Abu Dhabi and has registered at an employment agency. Two colleagues at the agency are discussing his file.*

1 What languages does John speak? Listen and check.

حيدر	من هو جون باركر؟
عماد	جون باركر انجليزي. عمره ٣٢ سنة. هو متزوج. يتكلم عربي.
حيدر	ما له خبرة؟
عماد	له خبرة ٥ سنوات في المبيعات في الإمارات. لديه رخصة قيادة وإقامة في الإمارات.

2 John needs to fill in an application form. Imagine that you are him, and complete the form.

١ الاسم الكامل ....

٢ العمر ....

٣ الجنسية ....

٤ أعزب/متزوج ....

٥ العنوان ....

٦ رقم التلفون ....

٧ اللغات ....

٨ هل لديك رخصة قيادة صالحة؟ ....

٩ هل لديك رخصة إقامة صالحة في الإمارات؟ ....

١٠ الخبرة ....

Conversation 2

للإيجار li-l-iijáar *FOR RENT*

 09.03 *Halim, Farah, Saliha and Majid are describing where they live to Hamid.*

1 How many of them have more than one bathroom?

حميد	مرحبا حليم، كيف منزلك؟
حليم	أسكن في شقة صغيرة قريبة من وسط المدينة، فيها غرفة واحدة وصالة وحمام ومطبخ.
حميد	مرحبا فرح، كيف منزلك؟
فرح	نسكن في شقة جديدة. فيها غرفتان، واحدة لي أنا وزوجي وواحدة للأولاد، وصالة.
حميد	مرحبا صليحة، كيف منزلك؟
صالحة	نسكن في فيلا قريبة من البحر. هي جميلة جدا. عندنا أربع غرف وحمامان وصالتان وهناك مطبخ طبعا.
حميد	مرحبا مجيد، كيف منزلك؟
مجيد	نسكن في فيلا، فيلا صغيرة. هناك ثلاث غرف وصالة وحمام ومطبخ.

2 Now try to identify who lives in which of the flats or houses described:

   a A villa with four bedrooms and two bathrooms, two living rooms and a kitchen.

   b A small villa with three bedrooms, living room, bathroom and kitchen.

   c A flat with one room and living room.

   d A two-bedroomed apartment with living room.

Language discovery

1 TALKING ABOUT MORE THAN ONE OF ANYTHING

▶ Arabic plural formations are not often predictable, so they must be learned along with their singulars.

▶ In Arabic, the plural of inanimate objects or abstracts is treated in all respects as a feminine singular, so verbs and adjectives must be in the feminine singular form.

▶ In English, the word 'plural' refers to more than one (i.e. 1+). However, Arabic has a special form for two of anything, called the 'dual', so the plural in Arabic refers to more than two (2+).

Plurals of nouns

There are three ways to form the plural in Arabic:

1 The external or suffix masculine plural.

2 The external feminine/neuter plural.

3 The internal plural.

THE EXTERNAL OR SUFFIX MASCULINE PLURAL

Add the suffix ـون **-uun** to the singular noun.

For the accusative form add ـين **-iin** to the singular.

This kind of plural can only be used on words which indicate male human beings, as opposed to females and things/abstracts. The common exception to this is سنة pl. سنون (**sanah, sinuun**) *year*, and even this word has an alternative plural (سنوات **sanawáat**):

حضر المدرسون المؤتمر	HaDar al-mudarrisuun al-mu'tamar	The teachers attended the conference.
هم مقاولون	hum muqaawiluun	They are contractors.
كان المهندسون مصريين	kaana l-muhandisuun miSriyyiin	The engineers were Egyptian.
أصبحوا محاسبين	aSbaHuu muHaasibíin	They became accountants.

THE EXTERNAL FEMININE/NEUTER PLURAL

Drop the ـة (if there is one) and add ـات **-aat** to the singular word. This can be applied to words indicating females or things/abstracts and there is no special accusative form:

وصلت الطالبات يوم الجمعة	waSalat aT-Taalibaat yawm al-jum:ah	The (female) students arrived on Friday.
أصبحن مدرسات	aSbaHna mudarrisaat	They became teachers.
أأنتن ممرضات؟	a-antunna mumarriDaat?	Are you nurses?
تعلمنا كل الكلمات	ta:allam-naa kull al-kalimaat	We learned all the words.

THE INTERNAL PLURAL

This is formed by altering the internal vowelling of the word (like English *foot* ➜ *feet*). Some words also add prefixes and/or suffixes.

The internal plural is used mainly for males and things/abstracts, rarely for females. There is no general relationship between the singular word shape and the plural word shape.

Some words indicating males form a plural with the feminine ending, e.g. طالب، طلبة **Táalib, Tálabah**, *male student*. (This word also illustrates the fact that some words have alternative plurals, in this case طلاب **Tulláab**.) Such plurals are still regarded as masculine.

LANGUAGE TIP

The Arabic internal plural system cannot generally handle words consisting of more than four consonants, excluding suffixes such as ة- **-ah**, but counting doubled consonants as two. It is therefore likely that 'short' words will take an internal plural, but this is not a rule:

دخل الرجال الغرفة	dakhala r-rijaal al-ghurfah	The men entered the room.
نحن عمال في شركة السيارت	naHnu :ummaal fii sharikat as-sayyaaraat	We are workers in the car company.
الكتب على المائدة	al-kutub :alaa l-maa'ida	The books are on the table.

Plurals of adjectives

It is a good idea to think of adjectives in Arabic as another class of noun. They have the same choice as nouns in forming their plurals:

▶ **-uun** or **-aat** ending

▶ internal plurals, which must be learned with their singulars.

If no adjective plural is given in the vocabulary, use the suffixed plurals according to the following rules. Internal plurals are given for those adjectives that have them.

Noun	Adjective plural form
male human beings	internal plural if it has one, otherwise + **-uun**
female human beings	+ **-aat**
things/abstracts	+ **-ah** (f. singular)

These rules hold for nearly all adjectives with a few common exceptions, mainly relating to the primary colours (see Unit 15).

Common adjectives with internal plural forms

Adjective	Meaning	Male plural form
كسلان kasláan	lazy	كسالى kasáalaa
نشيط nashíiT	active	نشاط nisháaT
كبير kabíir	big	كبار kibáar
صغير Saghíir	small	صغار Sigháar
نحيف naHíif	thin	نحاف niHáaf
سمين samíin	fat	سمان simáan
طويل Tawíil	tall	طوال Tiwáal
قصير qaSíir	short	قصار qiSáar
ذكي dhákii	clever	أذكياء adhkiyáa'*
غبي ghábii	stupid	أغبياء aghbiyáa'*
سعيد sa:íid	happy	سعداء su:adáa'*
حزين Hazíin	sad	حزناء Huzanáa'*
غريب gharíib	strange	غرباء ghurabáa'*
أجنبي ájnabii	foreign	أجانب ajáanib*
عظيم :aDHíim	great, mighty	عظماء :uDHamáa'*
جديد jadíid	new	جدد júdud

> **LANGUAGE TIP**
>
> Many of these plurals – marked with * – do not take the accusative marker. This applies to the plural only, not the singular as well.

The plural of things in Arabic is regarded in all respects as feminine singular for the sake of grammatical agreement. Here are a few more mixed examples:

الأولاد طوال	**al-awlaad Tiwaal**	The boys are tall.
الطلبة مجتهدون	**aT-Talabah mujtahiduun**	The students are hard working.
الممثلات الجديدات	**al-mumaththilaat al-jadiidaat**	the new actresses
البيوت القديمة	**al-buyuut al-qadiimah**	the old houses

2 هؤلاء haa'uláa'(i)..., أولئك uuláa'ik(a)... (THESE..., THOSE...)

You have already learned the demonstrative pronouns هذا/هذه this and ذلك/تلك that (see Unit 4) to describe singular words which are either masculine or feminine in gender.

> **LANGUAGE TIP**
>
> Because plurals of things/abstracts in Arabic are regarded as feminine singular, all verbs, adjectives and pronouns relating to them must be feminine singular.

When speaking of plural male/female human beings, use the forms هؤلاء haa'ulaa'(i) these and أولئك uulaa'ik(a) those, respectively. The final vowels are often missed out in informal situations.

With these plural forms, there is no distinction for gender, so both of them can apply to either males or females:

هؤلاء الطلبة حاضرون	haa'ulaa'i T-Talabah HaaDiruun	These students are present.
أولئك البنات جميلات	uulaa'ika l-banaat jamiilaat	Those girls are beautiful.
تلك البيوت كبيرة	tilka l-buyuut kabiirah	Those houses are big.

3 TALKING ABOUT TWO PEOPLE OR THINGS

Arabic has a special way of talking about two of anything, called the <u>dual</u>. This is obligatory in use for both people and things (i.e. you cannot use the plural), although increasingly in some colloquial forms of Arabic it is becoming slightly archaic or considered very formal.

Formation of the dual

▶ If the noun does not have the feminine ending **-ah**, add the suffix **-aan** to the singular. This changes to **-ayn** when an accusative marker is required:

الولدان طويلان	al-waladaan Tawiilaan	The two boys are tall.
كان الولدان طويلين	kaana l-waladaan Tawiilayn	The two boys were tall.

This applies to the vast majority of nouns and adjectives.

▶ If the noun has the **-ah** ending of the feminine singular, this changes to **-at** (spelled with an ordinary ت) and the suffix **-aan/-ayn** is added to it:

السيارتان كبيرتان	as-sayyaarataan kabiirataan	The two cars are big.
كانت السيارتان كبيرتين	kaanat as-sayyaarataan kabiiratayn	The two cars were big.

Since Arabic has this dual form for *two*, it is not usually necessary to insert the numeral word. (As with the masculine plural ending ـون/ـين **-uun/-iin** the final ن of the dual is omitted if the word constitutes the first term of a possessive construction. See Unit 13.)

Dual pronouns

Arabic does not need to distinguish between one and two for the person who is speaking, so where English says *we two*, Arabic says simply *we*, but *you two*, أنتما **antumaa** (both m. and f.):

أنتما تعبانان   **antumaa ta:baanaan**   *You two are tired.*

and *they two* هما **humaa** (both m. and f.):

هما مشهوران   **humaa mashhuuraan**   *They two are famous.*

In practice, the dual is not common, except when speaking about things that always come in pairs like hands, legs, etc.

يدان	**yadáan**	*(two) hands*
رجلان	**rijláan**	*(two) legs*
أذنان	**udhnáan**	*(two) ears*
عينان	**:aynáan**	*(two) eyes*

> **LANGUAGE TIP**
>
> These words – and indeed all parts of the body that occur in pairs – are feminine.
>
> There are also special dual markers for the verb. These are given in the Verb tables, but they occur so rarely that they need only to be noted at this stage.

Word discovery

 09.04 The word pattern for this unit is muC¹aC²C²iC³, for example, **mudárris** مُدَرِّس *teacher*, which sounds like the English *molasses*.

This shape indicates the person or thing carrying out the action of Verb form II (see Table S-II), grammatically known as the active participle. It is often used to indicate trades or professions.

 1 Complete this example:

The verb دَرَّس **dárrasa** means *to teach*, so مُدَرِّس is a *teaching person*, i.e._____ .

Here are some more examples:

مدرب	**mudárrib**	_trainer_
محرر	**muHárrir**	_editor_
مفتش	**mufáttish**	_inspector_
ممرض	**mumárriD**	_(male) nurse_
مؤذن	**mu'ádhdhin**	_muezzin_

A similar shape with an **a**-vowel instead of an **i**-vowel after the middle radical is also common. This is the <u>passive participle</u>, i.e. the person or thing to which the action of the verb has been applied. An example of this is مُوَظَّف **muwáDHDHaf** _official, employee_. This comes from the verb وَظَّف **waDHDHafa** _to appoint to an official position, employ_.

All these words can be made feminine by the addition of the ending ة **-ah**. The male versions take the plural suffix ـون, and the female ـات.

> **LANGUAGE TIP**
>
> Remember that the point of learning word shapes is to be able to read and know something about Arabic words. It is not always possible to get an exact English sound-alike, but the pattern is usually easy to imitate. Say them out loud one after another until they become familiar.

الآن دورك al-'aan dawrak

2 Based on this pattern, complete the following.

_____ _____ _female teacher_

منجم **munájjim** _____ (hint: نجم means _star_)

Reading

Look at the job advertisements and answer the questions. You do not need to understand every word.

1 You are an experienced hairdresser looking for a job in Dubai. Which of these three jobs would suit you best?

a

كـوافيرة درجـة اولى بـراتب مـغر لصــالــون كــبير في الشــارقــة

b
مطلوب كوافيرة ذات خبرة لتسريح الشعر والمنكير والبـاديكر بالعين

c
مـطـلــوب كــوافيرة درجـة اولى لصــالــون راق بــدبـــي

2 Which picture is most appropriate for each of these job advertisements?

1   2   3

_____   _____   _____

a
مدربة للرشاقة والايروبيك لمركز
ريـاضـي ت:٦٥١٣٩

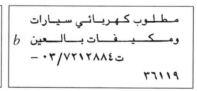

b
مـطـلــوب كهربـائـي سـيارات
ومـكـيـفـات بــالــعين
ت:٧٢١٢٨٨٤/٠٣ –
٣٦١١٩

c
مطلوب فنـي أجهـزة الكترونية
لتصليح هواتف متحركة فاكس
٧٤٧٥١

3 What people are wanted for the jobs advertised? Match the people to the jobs.

a labourers and builders

b French teacher

c manager for a ladies' fashion shop

d pharmacist

e secretary (male or female)

f employees for a restaurant

g salesmen and saleswomen

h saleswoman for a shoe shop

1

مطلوب صيدلانية للعمل في صيدلية بعجمان مرخصة من وزارة الصـــــحـــــة ت:١٨٢٦٠

2

مطلوب بائعة لمحل احذية نسائي بدبي لديها خبرة ٣ سنوات ت:٧٧١٧٣

3

مدرس لغة فرنسية مؤهل لمدرسة هـــنــديـــة ت٢٧٦٠٠ ف٢٧٦٠٦

5

مطلوب موظفات لمطعم بالعين ت٤٦٣٢٤

6

مندوبات مبيعات ذوات خبرة مع رخصة قيادة راتب ٥٠٠٠ ـ ٦٠٠٠ الرجاء ارسال السيرة الـذاتـيـة عـلـى فـاكـس ٩١٨٥٥ لعناية المهندس حسـام

7

مطلوب

مديرة

لمحل أزياء نسائي بدبي خبرة وإجادة اللغة الإنجليزية

نقال: ٤٤٠٥٩
فاكس: ٣١٩٣

8

عمـــال + بـنـائـيـين الاتصـال ٩١٥٥١

9

مندوب مبيعات خبرة في اجهزة التبريد والتكييف لاتقل عن خمس سـنـوات في الامـارات مـع لـغـة انجليزية وعربية ارسال السيرة الـذاتـيـة عـلـى الـفـاكـس ٣٩٩٢١

10

مطلوب

سكرتير
أو سكرتيرة عربية

يجيد الطباعة عربي ـ انجليزي ولديه معرفة في أمـور الهجرة والعمل

الاتصال ٣١٨٥٥
فاكس ٣٥٦١٣
الشارقة

4

شركة كبرى

تطلب :

بائعـين وبائعـات

لمحلاتها في دبي وأبوظبي

الشروط المطلوبة :

● خبرة في المبيعات
● إجادة اللغة الانجليزية محادثة وكتابة
● حسـن المظهر

يرجى ارسال السيرة الذاتية على فاكس رقم ٢٩٥٤٦

4 Which of the advertisements in the last exercise require:

    a some previous experience? _____

    b a driving licence? _____

    c a knowledge of English? _____

5 Name any three requirements applicants need for this position as a sales representative.

 Practice

1 Write the correct form of plural for the adjectives in brackets.

٤ قرأنا الجرائد (الإنجليزي)	١ بناتك (جميل)
٥ البنوك (مقفول) بعد الظهر	٢ هؤلاء الأولاد (ذكي)
٦ الرجال (المصري) (نشيط)	٣ القمصان (مخطط)

اشتريت	**ishtaráyt**	*I bought*
قميص، قمصان	**qamíiS, qumSáan**	*shirt*
جيد	**jáyyid**	*of good quality*
جوعان، جوعى	**jaw:áan*, jáw:aa***	*hungry*

2 Change the highlighted nouns, adjectives or pronouns in the following sentences into the correct plural form.

Example:

I bought a shirt last week.	اشتريت قميصا الأسبوع الماضي.
I bought three shirts last week.	اشتريت ثلاثة قمصان الأسبوع الماضي.

١ وجدنا **مطعما جيدا** في القاهرة.

٢ حضر **المدير** الاجتماع.

٣ هل أنت **جوعان**؟

٤ **السكرتيرة مشغولة**.

٥ بنتها **طالبة** في الجامعة.

٦ **هو ممثل كويتي**.

٧ كان **الفيلم طويل**.

3 Now change these whole sentences into the plural. Remember that verbs preceding their nouns remain singular, and that the -uun/-iin plural ending must show the correct case.

١ وصل العامل الجديد

٢ أين الكتاب الفرنسي؟

٣ وجدته المدرسة على الرف

٤ أصبح الولد سمينا

٥ خرج الضيف من الفندق

> **LANGUAGE TIP**
>
> سمين، سمان **samíin, simáan** means *fat*, and ضيف، ضيوف **Dayf, Duyúuf** is *guest*.

ولكن   **waláakin, walaakínna**   *but* (the latter behaves like إن **inna**)

نساء   **nisáa'***   *women (pl.)*

4 Choose the correct ending for each of these sentences.

a هذه الشقق قريبة ...

١ ولكن أولئك الطلبة المصريين قليلون.

b هؤلاء نساء نحيفات ...

٢ ولكن أولئك نساء سمينات.

c هذه الجرائد يومية ...

٣ ولكن هذه الشقق بعيدة.

d هؤلاء الطلبة اللبنانيون كثيرون ...

٤ ولكن هذه الجرائد أسبوعية.

5 Put the following sentences into the dual. (You can leave the verbs in the singular as they come before the noun.)

١ (The office is closed.) المكتب مقفول.

٢ (The technician is not present.) ليس الفني حاضرا.

٣ (The bathroom is spacious.) الحمام واسع.

٤ (The employee worked in the ministry.) عمل الموظف في الوزارة.

٥ (The manageress spoke to the workman.) كلمت المديرة العامل.

6 Match the Arabic abbreviations with the English words:

a	room, bedroom	ت	١
b	bathroom	ش	٢
c	telephone	غ	٣
d	Post Office (PO) Box No.	ح	٤
e	street	ص ب	٥

 7 You are looking for accommodation. Read the advertisements and answer the questions.

للايجار

1
فيلا ٤ غرف وحمام ومطبخ في حي الخليل ت ٣٢٩٨٤ أوقات العمل

5
فيلتان متجاورتان تكييف مركزي دبي ت ٤٠٢٦٢

2
شقق فندقية مفروشة يوميا وأسبوعيا وشهريا الشارقة ت ١٨٢٢٢

6
فرصة ٤ غرف + ٢ ح + ١ مطبخ ١٣٠٠٠ سنوي على البحر مباشرة الخلو ٥٠٠٠ ألف عجمان ٥٤٥١٤

3
فيلا للايجار جديدة تكييف مركزي بسعر مغر جداً ٦٥٠٠٠ درهم

7
شقق للايجار غرفتان + صالة + حمامان مقابل جريدة الخليج ت ٩١١٨٨

4
شقة ثلاث غرف وصالة قريبة من حديقة ت ٦٩٤٣٠٩٩

a You want to rent somewhere for your large family. Which place has the most bedrooms and bathrooms?

b You are looking for two villas close to each other for your firm. Are there any which would be suitable?

c You want to rent a villa for just a few weeks. Is there anything available?

d You have found a villa that you like, but can only call the owner during office hours. Which one is it?

e You would like to rent a villa near a park. Which one could you choose?

f You work for the *al-Khaleej* newspaper. Which flat would be most convenient for you?

g Where could you find a villa to rent, which is not too expensive, with air conditioning if possible?

Test yourself

1 How would you say these sentences and phrases in English?

١ أصبحن طالبات _____

٢ حضر المهندسون المؤتمر _____

٣ الكتب على الرف _____

٤ الأولاد نشاط _____

٥ أولئك البنات جديدات _____

2 Make these into dual sentences by changing the adjective in brackets. Then translate into English.

١ أنتما (ذكي) _____

٢ أنتما (غريب) _____

٣ القدمان (صغير) _____

SELF CHECK

I CAN...
. . . look for a job in the paper or on a website.
. . . look for a flat or a house.
. . . talk about more than one person or thing.
. . . say *these/those*.
. . . talk about two people or things.

10 ماذا تعمل؟

maadhaa ta:mal?

What do you do?

In this unit you will learn how to:
► *say what you do every day*
► *talk about your interests*
► *say what you like or dislike*
► *say what you will do in the future.*
► *use different words for* not

CEFR: (A2–B1) *Can talk about likes and dislikes, express opinions and intentions, talk about daily routines.*

Arabic serial dramas

Television serial dramas مسلسلات are very popular in the Arab world. They are normally an extended drama of about 28 episodes الحلقات. Arabic television stations normally have at least one as an evening feature during the month of Ramadan (this is the reason for the 28-episode formula). There are three main types: historical or religious period drama الدراما التاريخية, which serve not only to entertain but also to educate; modern drama الدراما الحديثة, which often have a romantic or mystery thriller theme; and foreign imported soap operas that have been dubbed into Arabic. These largely come from Turkey and Latin America, which are places with similar family values to Arab countries and therefore their programmes are easier to adapt for local consumption. Egypt is considered the home of production of Arabic serial dramas, but there are also several productions made in Syria, Jordan and Morocco.

Which of the following is a typical Arabic television drama?

a مسلسل من ثمانية وعشرين حلقة   **b** مسلسل من عشر حلقات   **c** مسلسل من ثلاثة حلقات

Vocabulary builder

10.01 Listen to the new expressions and repeat them until you can say them with confidence. Listen again and complete the gaps.

ASKING WHAT OTHERS DO AND SAYING WHAT YOU DO

ماذا تأكل_____؟	*What do you eat in the morning?*
ماذا تعمل بعد الظهر؟	*What do you do in the afternoon?*
هل تقرأ كثيرا؟	*Do you read a lot?*
أذهب إلى _____	*I go to the office.*
آكل الفواكه دائما	*I always eat fruit.*
أشرب قهوة كثيرا	*I drink coffee a lot.*
ألعب تنس/جولف	*I play _____.*
أسبح	*I swim.*

ASKING WHAT OTHERS LIKE AND SAYING WHAT YOU LIKE TO DO

ماذا تحب أن تفعل في أوقات الفراغ؟	*What do you like to do in your free time?*
أحب التلفزيون	*I like _____.*
هي لا تحب كرة القدم	*She doesn't like football.*
نكره برامج الرياضة	*We hate sports programmes.*
تحب أن تفعل	*you like to do (lit. 'you like that you do')*

ESSENTIALS

شرب، يشرب	sháriba, yáshrab [S-I a]	*drink*
تكلم، يتكلم	takállama, yatakállam [S-V]	*speak*
عاش، يعيش	:aasha, ya:íish [My-I]	*live*
عمل، يعمل	:ámila, yá:mal [S-I a]	*do, work*
ذهب، يذهب	dháhaba, yádh-hab [S-I a]	*go*
جلس، يجلس	jálasa, yájlis [S-I i]	*sit*
لعب، يلعب	lá:iba, yál:ab [S-I a]	*play*
جاء، يجيء	jáa'a, yajíi' [My-I]	*come*
تقرير، تقارير	taqríir, taqaaríir*	*report*
تجارة	tijáarah	*trade, commerce*
برنامج، برامج	barnáamij, baráamij*	*programme*

Conversation 1

ماذا تعمل كل يوم؟ maadhaa ta:mal kull yawm? *WHAT DO YOU DO EVERY DAY?*

أكل، يأكل	**ákala, yá'kul [S-I u]**	*eat*
فاكهة، فواكه	**fáakihah, fawáakih***	*fruit*
جبنة	**júbnah**	*cheese*
سائق، ـون	**sáa'iq, -úun**	*driver*
وصل، يوصل	**wáSSala, yuwáSSil [S-II]**	*connect, transport*
خبر، أخبار	**khábar, akhbáar**	*news*
طبع، يطبع	**Tába:a, yáTba: [S-I a]**	*print, type*
قرأ، يقرأ	**qára'a, yáqra' [S-I a]**	*read*
مالي	**máalii**	*financial*
استغرق، يستغرق	**istághraqa, yastághriq [S-X]**	*take, use up, occupy (of time)*
استخدم، يستخدم	**istákhdama, yastákhdim [S-X]**	*use*
تعلم	**ta:állama, yata:állam [S-V]**	*learn*
استخدام	**istikhdáam**	*use, employment*
كلية، ـات	**kullíyyah, -aat**	*college, faculty*
عام	**:aamm**	*general*
ناقش، يناقش	**náaqasha, yunáaqish [S-III]**	*discuss*
شأن، شؤون	**sha'n, shu'úun**	*matter, affair*

> **LANGUAGE TIP**
>
> أكل **aakul** *I eat*. Note the spelling of this. This sign over the **alif** (called **maddah**) is always used when (theoretically) two **hamzahs** come together or a **hamzah** is followed by a long **a**-vowel (e.g. in the word for *computer* in the next tip).

A women's magazine has sent Fawzia to interview Kamal, the sales manager of a local business. She asks him about what he does during the day.

1 What does Kamal always eat in the morning?

فوزية	ماذا تأكل الصبح؟
كمال	آكل الفواكه دائما، وأحيانا خبزا وجبنة وأشرب قهوة. وعادة أتكلم مع ابني بالتلفون. هو يعيش في أمريكا.
فوزية	وماذا تعمل بعد ذلك؟
كمال	أذهب إلى المكتب. السائق يوصلني الساعة ٨:٣٠ وأتكلم معه في السيارة عن أخبار اليوم.
فوزية	وبعد ذلك؟
كمال	السكرتيرة تطبع لي رسائل وأنا أقرأ التقارير المالية. هذا يستغرق ساعتين، ثلاث ساعات.
فوزية	هل تستخدم الآلة الحاسبة؟
كمال	نعم، طبعا. تعلمت استخدام الآلة الحاسبة في كلية التجارة.
فوزية	وماذا تعمل بعد الظهر؟
كمال	بعد الظهر أجلس مع المدير العام ونناقش شؤون الشركة، وأحضر اجتماعات يومية مع الموظفين.

> **LANGUAGE TIP**
>
> آلة حاسبة **aalah Haasibah** *computer*. This usage – literally meaning 'counting machine' – is generally accepted, although كمبيوتر **kambyuutir** is also common.

2 Answer the questions.

  a Who does he telephone?

   1 his son   **2** his daughter   **3** his mother

  b How long does he read reports for?

   1 2–3 hours **2** 3–4 hours   **3** 4–5 hours

  c Where did he learn to use a computer?

   1 at school   **2** at college   **3** at work

  d With whom does he sit in the afternoon?

  e How often does he meet the employees?

3 Now read the interview again. Match the English phrases with the corresponding Arabic expressions.

a	I drink coffee.	هو يعيش في أمريكا.	**١**
b	He lives in America.	نناقش شؤون الشركة.	**٢**
c	I talk with him in the car.	أشرب قهوة.	**٣**
d	And what do you do in the afternoon?	وماذا تعمل بعد الظهر؟	**٤**
e	We'll discuss company affairs.	أتكلم معه في السيارة.	**٥**

Conversation 2

ماذا تعمل في أوقات الفراغ؟ maadhaa ta:mal fii awqaat al-faraagh?
WHAT DO YOU DO IN YOUR FREE TIME?

فعل، يفعل	fá:ala, yáf:al [S-I a]	do
أوقات الفراغ	áwqaat al-faráagh	free time
عائش	:áa'ish	living
كذلك	ka-dháalik	also, too (lit. 'like that')
شعر	shi:r	poetry
حديث	Hadíith	new, modern
أحب، يحب	aHábba, yuHíbb [D-IV]	like, love
فضل، يفضل	fáDDala, yufáDDil [S-II]	prefer
رواية، ــات	riwáayah, -áat	novel, story
تفرج، يتفرج على	tafárraja, yatafárraj :ala [S-V]	watch, look at
ولا	wá-laa	and not, nor
كره، يكره	káriha, yákrah [S-I a]	hate
فعلا	fí:lan	really, actually, in fact
ثقافي	thaqáafii	cultural
رياضة	riyáaDah	sport, sports

136

Ruhiyyah and Hisham al-Musallam, on business from Jordan, are discussing with Ali, a Sudanese business contact, what they do in their free time.

1 Who likes to watch Egyptian television serials?

> علي   ماذا تفعل في أوقات الفراغ يا هشام؟
>
> هشام   ألعب الجولف وأسبح. لما كنا عائشين في عمان، كنت ألعب التنس، لكن الآن لا ألعب. أقرأ كثيرا.
>
> علي   أنا أقرأ كثيرا كذلك. أحب الشعر الحديث. هل تحبين الشعر يا روحية؟
>
> روحية   لا، أنا أفضل الروايات. أتفرج على التلفزيون كثيرا، وأحب المسلسلات المصرية.
>
> علي   أنا لا أحبها
>
> هشام   ولا أنا. أكرهها فعلا. أفضل البرامج الثقافية أو الرياضة، لكن روحية لا تحب الرياضة.
>
> روحية   ولكننا نحب السينما نحن الاثنان. سوف نذهب إلى السينما في المساء. ستجيء معنا يا علي؟

2 Answer the questions.

a What does Hisham not play any more? _____

b What do he and Ali have in common?_____

c What does Ruhiyyah invite Ali to do this evening? _____

d Who is the most active?

    1 Hisham   **2** Ruhiyyah   **3** Ali

3 Read the conversation again, then match the English phrases with the appropriate Arabic expressions.

a I used to play tennis.   ١ كنت ألعب التنس.

b Do you like poetry?   ٢ سوف نذهب إلى السينما.

c I prefer novels.   ٣ روحية لا تحب الرياضة.

d Ruhiyyah doesn't like sport.   ٤ هل تحبين الشعر؟

e We are going to the cinema.   ٥ أفضل الروايات.

Language discovery
1 TALKING ABOUT THINGS IN THE PRESENT

This unit contains an overview of the Arabic verb system, placed here for ease of reference. Do not try to absorb all this information at once, as you will have ample opportunity to revise and consolidate your knowledge in future units. The overview should be studied in conjunction with Unit 7, which deals with the past tense and, in particular, with the Verb tables at the end of the course.

How to form the present tense

Look at the present tense column of Table 1 in the Verb tables. You will see that the present tense is formed from a stem (whose short vowels usually differ from those of the past stem), to which are added prefixes for all parts, plus suffixes for certain parts.

With only a few exceptions, the same set of prefixes and suffixes apply to every Arabic verb, so it is obviously important to learn them thoroughly from the beginning.

Here is the present tense of *to write* in transliterated form, without the dual forms, which occur rarely and can be learned later. The stem is underlined:

Singular			Plural		
يكتب	**yaktub**	*he writes, is writing*	يكتبون	**yaktubuun**	*they (m.) write*
تكتب	**taktub**	*she writes*	يكتبن	**yaktubna**	*they (f.) write*
تكتب	**taktub**	*you (m.) write*	تكتبون	**taktubuun**	*you (m) write*
تكتبين	**taktubiin**	*you (f.) write*	تكتبن	**taktubna**	*you (f.) write*
أكتب	**aktub**	*I write*	نكتب	**naktub**	*we write*

Prefixes:

▶ The *you* forms all have the prefix **ta-**, which is similar to the **t** in the pronouns **anta**, **anti**, etc.

▶ All the third person forms have the prefix **ya-** with the exception of the feminine singular.

▶ The *I* form has **a-**; the pronoun is **anaa**.

▶ The *we* form has **na-**; the pronoun is **naHnu**.

Suffixes:

▶ The *you* (f. sing.) has suffix **-iin** to distinguish it from the masculine.

▶ The *they* and *you* (m. pl.) have the external plural suffix **-uun**.

▶ The *they* and *you* (f. pl.) have the suffix **-na**.

Vowelling of the prefixes

In the types of stem that we have marked II, III and IV (see Verb tables), the vowel of all the prefixes changes to **u** (**yu-**, **tu-**, **u-**, etc.)

The present stem

In this unit, both tenses of the verb are given in Arabic script and transliteration in the *he* form, plus the verb type in square brackets [S-III, Mw-I, etc.] to enable you to look them up in the Verb tables.

Example:

	Past	Present	Type	Meaning
فضل، يفضل	faDDala	yufaDDil	[S-II]	*prefer*

In subsequent units, verbs will be given as follows, and you should refer to the appropriate Verb table to identify all the parts of the verb.

Past Ar.	Past trans.	Type	Meaning
فضل	faDDala	[S-II]	*prefer*

Type S-I verbs

Type S-I verbs are the only ones in which the vowel on the middle radical is not predictable. In both tenses, it can be any of the three Arabic short vowels: **a**, **i** or **u**.

Since these vowels are never written in Modern Arabic, they have to be learned. In this book, they are given in the following form:

Past Ar.	Past Trans.	Type	Meaning
كتب	kataba	[S-I u]	*write*

This should be interpreted as follows:

▶ The Arabic gives the three root letters.

▶ The transliterated past identifies the middle radical vowel – here **a** (**kataba**). Note: the vowel on the first radical is always **a** in the past tense and this radical has no vowel in the present.

- The verb type (here, S-I) directs you to the appropriate Verb table.

- The vowel given after the verb type (here, **u**) is the middle radical vowel in the present stem (**kt<u>u</u>b**).

The following scheme of things usually prevails, but there are always exceptions.

Past stem	Vowel on C2	→	Vowel on C2	Present stem
CaCaC	a	→	**u** or **i**	CCuC
kataba *to write*	**ktub**			
CaCiC	i	→	a	CCaC
fahima *to understand*	**fham**			
CaCuC	u	→	u	CCuC
kabura *to be big/grow*	**kbur**			

Most S-I verbs are of the CaCaC → CCu/iC type. There are quite a few CaCiC → CCaC types, but CaCuC → CCuC is rare and usually indicates a state of being or becoming something.

> **LANGUAGE TIP**
>
> You will usually still be understood even if you get these vowels wrong, so don't worry too much about accuracy at this stage.

Function of the present tense

Arabic has only two simple tenses, the past and the present. Just as the past tense serves for *did*, *has done*, the present tense fulfils the functions of *does*, *is doing* and, in questions, *does do*, as in *Does he live here?* Common sense will tell you how to translate from Arabic:

يعيشون في شقة كبيرة في أبو ظبي   *They live in a big apartment in Abu Dhabi.*
they-live in apartment big in Abu Dhabi

تنشر الحكومة الإحصائيات في أول الشهر   *The government publishes the statistics*
     at the beginning of the month.
she-publishes the-government the-statistics
     in first the-month

ماذا تأكل في الصباح؟   *What do you eat in the morning?*
what you-eat in the-morning

The past continuous

The past continuous is what we call a verb phrase such as *was studying, used to study,* and so on.

In Arabic this is expressed with the aid of the verb **kaana** (type Mw-I), in the same way as the *had done* type verb explained in Unit 8, except that the main verb this time is in the present tense.

In all other respects, including agreement and word order, this tense behaves like its sister in Unit 8.

kaana + present tense verb = past continuous *was studying*
kaana + past tense verb = pluperfect *had studied*

كانت فاطمة تدرس في جامعة لندن

Fatimah was studying at the University of London.

she-was Fatimah she-studies in university (of) London

كنا نذهب إلى السوق كل يوم

We used to go to the market every day.

we-were we-go to the-market every day

Talking about what you will do in the future

There is no future tense in Arabic as such. Actions that have not yet happened are expressed by placing the word سوف **sawfa** or the prefix ـسـ **sa-** before a present tense verb. Since it consists of only one Arabic letter, **sa-** is joined to the word that follows it. These are called future markers (noted in literal translations as [future]):

سوف يصل الوزير غدا

The minister will arrive tomorrow.

[future] he-arrives the-minister tomorrow

سأسافر الأسبوع القادم

I shall travel next week.

[future] I-travel the-week the-coming

> **LANGUAGE TIP**
>
> وصل، يصل **wáSala, yáSil** [Fw-I i] means *to arrive*.

2 OTHER WAYS TO SAY *NOT*

Arabic has several ways of expressing *not*, which must be used in different contexts.

Negative	Context	Formation
ليس **laysa***	*is/are* sentences	second noun/adjective, if indefinite, has accusative marker
لا **laa**	present verb	verb takes normal form
ما **maa**	past verb	verb in the past tense
لن **lan**	future verb	**sa-/sawfa** omitted, and verb in the subjunctive**
لم **lam**	past actions	verb in the present jussive** form, but with past meaning***

* Unlike the other negatives, **laysa** is actually a verb and has to be used accordingly. (See Unit 8.)

** For these terms see later in this unit.

*** **maa** + past verb and **lam** + present verb convey exactly the same meaning. In literary Arabic, the latter construction is considered more elegant.

الآن دورك al-'aan dawrak

Put the correct negative word into the sentences.

لم	ليس	ما	لن	لا

a The man is not old.

١ ــــــــــ الرجل كبيرا.

b She did not go to Morocco.

٢ ــــــــــ سافرت إلى المغرب.

c They (m.) don't know French.

٣ ــــــــــ يعرفون اللغة الفرنسية.

d You (f. sing.) will not arrive before noon.

٤ ــــــــــ تصلي قبل الظهر.

e They didn't eat the meat.

٥ ــــــــــ يأكلوا اللحم.

Altered forms of the present verb

If you look carefully at the sentences in the exercise, you will note that the verbs used are slightly different from those you have learned (they have no final ن for example).

Historically, in addition to the normal form, Arabic had two so-called moods of the present (not the past) tense, called the <u>subjunctive</u> and the <u>jussive</u> respectively.

These altered forms must be used after certain words in Arabic. Two of these are **lan**, which requires the subjunctive, and **lam**, which requires the jussive.

Fortunately, for many verbs, the subjunctive and the jussive are identical in writing. They are given in full in Verb table 1 but, for convenience, here are the parts that show a difference. Other parts of the verb remain unchanged.

Verbs which show further deviations will be explained as they occur:

تكتبين **taktubiin** *you write* (f. sing.) → **taktubii** تكتبي

يكتبون **yaktubuun** *they write* (m. pl.) → **yaktubuu** يكتبوا

تكتبون **taktubuun** *you write* (m. pl.) → **taktubuu** تكتبوا

The Arabs call this 'the omission of the **nuun**'.

Remember to use these forms after both **lan** and **lam**.

142

> **LANGUAGE TIP**
>
> An unpronounced **alif** is added at the end. You will remember that the same thing happened in the past tense. In fact, it is a convention that any verb which has a **-uu** suffix adds this redundant letter. Nobody knows why.

3 PREPOSITIONS AND PRONOUN SUFFIXES

Prepositions tell you where something is in relation to something else, such as *on*, *behind*, *in*, etc.

However, in both English and Arabic, they often form an essential part of what are known as <u>phrasal verbs</u>. English examples of phrasal verbs are *call up, call on, call in*, all essentially different meanings derived from the simple verb *call*.

In Arabic, for instance, you don't 'need something', you 'need <u>towards</u> something'.

Here are some examples:

احتاج، يحتاج إلى	**iHtaaja, yaHtaaj ilaa** [Mw-VIII]	*to need something*
احتفل، يحتفل بـ	**iHtafala, yahtafil bi-** [S-VIII]	*to celebrate something*
رغب، يرغب في	**raghiba, yarghab fii** [S-I a]	*to want, desire something*
رحب، يرحب بـ	**raHHaba bi-** [S-II]	*to welcome someone*

Prepositions required after verbs are given in the vocabulary lists.

When prepositions are used with pronouns (*towards <u>him</u>, by <u>her</u>*, and so on), they use the same possessive pronouns suffixes as are used with nouns (see Unit 5):

كتابها	**kitaab-ha**	*her book*
منها	**min-ha**	*from her*

 Pronunciation

10.04 Some Arabic prepositions alter slightly when they are attached to a suffix and some of them affect certain suffixes. Listen and repeat.

a Prepositions ending in **-a** lose the **-a** with the suffix **-ii**, *me*:

ma:a *with* + **-ii** *me* = معي **ma:ii** *with me*

b Prepositions ending in **-n** double this with the suffix **-ii**:

min *from* + **-ii** *me* = مني **minn-ii** *from me*

akhadhuu l-jariidah min-nii أخذوا الجريدة منّي

they-took the-newspaper from-me *They took the newspaper from me.*

(Note: This is different from منّا **min-naa** *from us*, where one **n** belongs to the suffix.)

c After long vowels and **-ay**, **-ii** *me* is pronounced **-ya**:

فيّ **fiiya** (or **fiyya**) *in me*

عليّ: **alayya** *on me*

d After **-i**, **-ii** or **-ay**, **-hu**, **-hum** and **-hunna** change **-u** to **-i** (not visible in the written form):

فيه **fii-hi** *in him*

بهم **bi-him** *with them*

⋮ الآن دورك **al-'aan dawrak**

How do you pronounce فيهم? What does it mean?

e Prepositions ending in long **-aa** written as a **-y** without dots change their endings into **-ay**:

إلى **ilaa** *towards* becomes إليكم **ilay-**: **ilay-kum** *towards you*

على: **alaa** *on* becomes علينا: **alay-**: **alay-naa** *on us*

yaD-Hak :alay-naa يضحك علينا

he-laughs on-us *He's laughing at us.*

f لـ **li-** *to, for* becomes **la-** before all the suffixes except **-ii** (see 'a' above). This change is again not apparent in the written form:

لهم **la-hum** *for them*

سأدفع لها المبلغ المضبوط **sa-adfa: la-haa l-mablagh al-maDbuuT**

(future) I-pay to-her the-sum the-exact *I'll pay her the exact amount.*

li-, as a one letter word (see Arabic script and pronunciation guide) is attached to the word after it. If this has **al-** *the*, the **alif** is omitted:

للولد **li-l-walad** *for the boy*

In addition, if the noun itself begins with **laam**, the doubling sign is used:

للّغة **li-l-lughah** *to the language*

Word discovery

10.05 The word pattern for this unit is C¹uC²aC³áa'*, for example, **wuzaráa'** وزراء *ministers*, which sounds like the English *to a rat* (Cockney/Glaswegian pronunciation of the *t* as a glottal stop).

This shape is mainly used for the plural of certain male human beings that have the singular shape CaCiiC. In fact, it is relatively safe to guess plurals of such nouns using this shape. It does not take the accusative marker:

سفراء **sufaráa'*** from سفير **safíir** *ambassadors*

أمير، أمراء **amíir, umaráa'*** *princes, emirs*

وزير، وزراء **wazíir, wuzaráa'*** *ministers*

مدير، مدراء **mudíir, mudaráa'*** *directors, managers*

It is also used with some adjectives of the same shape:

سعيد، سعداء **sa:íid, su:adáa'*** *happy, joyful*

and some nouns with the singular shape CaaCiC:

شاعر، شعراء **sháa:ir, shu:aráa'*** *poet*

الآن دورك al-'aan dawrak

Based on the patterns above, make the words into plurals:

زميل **d**   رئيس **c**   نظيف **b**   فقير **a**

_____ _____ _____ _____

Practice

لعب، ألعاب	la:b, al:áab	*playing, game*
هواية، ـات	hawáayah, -áat	*hobby*
سباحة	sibáaHah	*swimming*

1 Nafisah plays tennis and enjoys going to the cinema and swimming. She would like to make friends with someone who has the same interests as she does. She sees the following entries on a social media site. Who has most in common with her?

www.kunSadiiq-ii.com

كن صديقي kun Sadiiq-ii! *Be my friend!*

a

اسمي حميد وأنا طالب. هواياتي السينما والتنس والسباحة.

b

أنا سلطان. ألعب كرة، وأحب الألعاب الكمبيوترية والسينما والموسيقى العربية.

c

اسمي خميس. أحب لعب السنوكر والتنس و كرة القدم.

قبيح	qabíiH	*ugly*
الهند	al-hind	*India*

2 Change the sentences into the negative, using one of the words in the box. Use each word only once:

ما	لم	لا	لن	ليست	ليس

١ هذا الجمل قبيح.

٢ البيوت رخيصة في الرياض.

٣ سوف نسافر إلى الهند في الشهر القادم.

٤ ذهبنا إلى المسبح يوم الجمعة.

٥ أختي تعمل في صيدلية.

٦ درس صالح في أمريكا.

3 Complete the sentences using the prepositions from the box:

من	مع	ل	على	إلى

١ المدير يدفع _____ ـها راتبا شهريا.

٢ ستسافر _____ ه في الطائرة.

٣ هل تضحك _____ نا؟

٤ أخذت الجريدة _____ ي.

٥ أهذا كتاب جيد؟ زوجتي تحتاج _____ ـه.

4 Hameed is an active person. Make up complete sentences about him, saying what sports he plays and which he likes and dislikes, using the information in the table. The first one is done for you.

حميد يلعب كرة.   *Hameed plays football.*

يكره	لا يحب	يحب	يلعب
السينما	القراءة	تنس	كرة
التلفزيون	الكتب	السباحة	سكواش

5 Rewrite the sentences, changing the verbs in brackets so they match the English.

١ الأولاد القطريون (يتعلم) اللغة الانجليزية في المدرسة الثانوية.

٢ (يتصل) بأمها كل يوم.

٣ (يشرب) شاي عند رجوعنا من العمل.

٤ (يكتب) رسالة إلى صديقتي نورة.

٥ الموظف يريد أن (يكلمـ ـنا) فورا.

٦ هل (يعرف) ذلك الرجل؟

٧ (يقفل) الصيدليات الساعة ٦.

٨ سوف (يصل) إلى نيو يورك يوم الخميس.

٩ كانت البنات (يلعب) مع أولاد الجيران.

١٠ كان محمود وإخوانه (يكسب) كثيرا في الكويت.

1 Qatari children learn English in secondary school. _____

2 She telephones her mother every day. _____

3 We drink tea on our return from work. _____

4 I am writing a letter to my friend Nourah. _____

5 The official wants to talk to us immediately. _____

6 Do you (f. sing.) know that man? _____

7 The pharmacies close at six o'clock. _____

8 They (f.) will arrive in New York on Thursday. _____

9 The girls used to play with the neighbours' children. _____

10 Mahmoud and his brothers used to earn a lot in Kuwait. _____

مريض، مرضى	**maríiD, márDaa***	*(adj.) ill; (noun) patient*
فحص	**fáHaSa, yáfHaS [S-I a]**	*to examine*

6 Match the English with the Arabic and then change the Arabic verb in (brackets) into the present tense.

a I didn't understand this book.

b The shopkeeper offered us tea.

c He asked his (male) secretary a question.

d The girl carried the coffee to the living room.

e Where did you (m. sing.) go?

f The doctor examined the eyes of the patient.

١ (سأل) سكرتيره سؤالا.

٢ (حملت) البنت القهوة إلى الصالة.

٣ (فحص) الطبيب عيون المريض.

٤ صاحب الدكان (قدم) لنا شاي.

٥ ما (فهمت) هذا الكتاب.

٦ إلى أين (ذهبت)؟

Reading

يقام	**yuqáam**	*is held, takes place (passive verb)*
مهرجان، ـات	**mahrajáan, -áat**	*festival*
تسوق	**tasáwwuq**	*shopping*
استفاد، يستفيد [My-X]	**istafáada, yastafíid [My-X]**	*benefit*
تنزيل، ـات	**tánzíil, -áat**	*lowering, reduction*
سعر، أسعار	**si:r, as:áar**	*price*

بضائع	**baDáa'i:***	*goods, merchandise*
إضافة إلى ذلك	**iDáafatan ílaa dháalik**	*in addition to that*
قدم، يقدم	**qáddama, yuqáddim [S-II]**	*offer, present*
جائزة، جوائز	**jáa'izah, jawáa'iz***	*prize, reward*
قيم	**qáyyim**	*valuable*
سحب، سحوبات	**saHb, suHuubáat**	*lottery*
أيضا	**áyDan**	*also*
فعالية، ـات	**fa:aalíyyah, -aat**	*activity, event*
فني	**fánnii**	*artistic; technical*
مثل	**mithl**	*like*
سباق	**sibáaq**	*racing*
خيل/خيول	**khayl/khuyúul**	*horses (both with plural meaning)*
عرض، عروض	**:arD, :urúuD**	*show, display*
ألعاب نارية	**al:áab naaríyyah**	*fireworks*
فوق	**fawq(a)**	*above, over*

Read the article about the Dubai Shopping Festival and answer the questions:

مهرجان دبي للتسوق

يقام مهرجان دبي للتسوق في شهر مارس ويحضر الناس بالآلاف من الإمارات والعالم كله الى دبي ليستفيدوا من التنزيلات الكبيرة في أسعار البضائع في المراكز التجارية والأسواق. وإضافة إلى ذلك تقدم الشركات جوائز قيمة في سحوبات منها سيارات وكيلو غرامات ذهب وهناك أيضا فعاليات ثقافية، وفنية، ورياضية مثل سباق الخيول وعروض فخمة من الألعاب النارية فوق خور دبي المشهور.

a When does the festival take place? _____

b Why do so many people come to the festival? _____

c Name two of the attractions. _____

d Where is the firework display held? _____

Test yourself

1 Match the Arabic words with the English.

a horse racing

b cultural events

١ الألعاب النارية

٢ سباق الخيول

c	famous		٣ التنزيلات الكبيرة
d	fireworks		٤ فعاليات ثقافية
e	kilos of gold		٥ جوائز قيمة
f	large reductions/discounts		٦ مشهور
g	valuable prizes		٧ كيلو غرامات ذهب

2 Translate the sentences into Arabic.

   a He telephones his father every day. _____

   b They drink coffee on their return from work. _____

   c We are writing a letter to our friend Hakim. _____

   d Do you (m. sing.) know that woman? _____

   e The mall closes at ten o'clock. _____

   f They (m.) will arrive in Oman on Saturday. _____

SELF CHECK

	I CAN...
○	. . . say what I do every day.
○	. . . talk about my interests.
○	. . . say what I like or dislike.
○	. . . say what I will do in the future.
○	. . . use different words for *not*.

11 الأعياد الإسلامية
al-a:yaad al-islaamiyyah

Islamic festivals

In this unit you will learn how to:
▸ *talk about the main Islamic festivals*
▸ *use special greetings for festival days.*
▸ *use the Islamic calendar.*
▸ *ask questions with what?/where?/who?, etc.*
▸ *say to have.*

CEFR: (B1) *Can describe plans, arrangements, habits and routines, past activities and personal experiences; can briefly give reasons and explanations for opinions and plans, and actions; can ask someone to clarify or elaborate what they have just said.*

Muslim festivals

The main religious festivals celebrated by all Muslims are:

:iid al-fiTr عيد الفطر: This is a three-day holiday at the end of Ramadan, a month during which Muslims fast (abstaining from food, drink, smoking and sexual contact) between sunrise and sunset. On the first day there are special prayers in the mosque and then visits to family and friends. Children usually receive money and new clothes.

:iid al-aD-Haa عيد الأضحى *Festival of the Sacrifice*. This is the main feast of Islam. It celebrates the annual **Hajj الحج al-Hajj** *pilgrimage to Mecca* and involves the traditional sacrifice of a sheep, based on the story of the prophet Abraham. Traditionally, a third of the meat is used by the owner, a third is given to friends and family, and the final third is given to the poor. In many countries, the sheep is slaughtered at home and children compete to see who has the best sheep.

mawlid an-nabii مولد النبي *Festival of the Prophet's Birthday*. The Prophet Mohammed's birthday is normally celebrated very simply with prayers and candles.

When would it not be polite to eat and drink in public if you were in a Muslim country?

Vocabulary builder

 11.01 Listen to the new expressions and repeat them until you can say them with confidence.

WHAT TO SAY AT FEAST TIMES AND BIRTHDAYS

The most universal greeting at festival times:

عيد مبارك	:iid mubaarak	*Blessed festival*

The reply:

الله يبارك فيك	Al-laah yubaarik fii-k (fii-ki *to a woman,* fii-kum *to several people*)	*God bless you*

A greeting which can be used for any annual occasion, such as a birthday:

كل عام وأنت بخير	kull :aam w-anta bi-khayr (f. anti, pl. antum)	*Every year and (may) you (be) well, many happy returns.*

The reply:

وأنت بخير	wa anta/anti/antum bi-khayr	*And (may) you (be) well.*

CELEBRATIONS

عيد، أعياد	:iid, a:yáad	*festival, anniversary*
مسلم، ـون	múslim, -uun	*Muslim*
فطر	fiTr	*breaking of a fast*
مناسبة، ـات	munáasabah, -aat	*occasion*
صوم	Sawm	*fast, fasting*
مكّة المكرّمة	mákkah l-mukárramah	*Holy (City of) Mecca*
الكعبة	al-ká:bah	*the Kaabah (Holy Shrine in Mecca)*
احتفل بـ	iHtáfala bi- [S-VIII]	*celebrate*
ذبح	dhábaHa [S-I a]	*slaughter*
ذبيحة، ذبائح	dhabíiHah, dhabáa'iH*	*sacrificial animal*
صلّى الله عليه وسلّم	Sállaa l-Láahu :aláy-hi wa-sállam	*Prayers and Peace be upon Him. (said after mentioning the name of the Prophet)*
عيد الميلاد	:iid al-miiláad	*Christmas*
مسيحي، ـون	masíiHii, -uun	*Christian*

152

Conversation 1

الأعياد الإسلامية al-a:yaad al-islaamiyyah ISLAMIC FESTIVALS

مهم	**muhímm**	*important*
شوال	**shawwáal**	*name of an Islamic month (see Language discovery **)*
عقب	**:áqaba [S-1 u]**	*come after, follow*
كريم، كرام	**karíim, kiráam**	*noble, generous (here used as an honorific adjective for the month of Ramadan, often translated as holy)*
معنى	**má:naa***	*meaning*
نهار	**naháar**	*daytime, hours of daylight*
آخر (f. أخرى	**áakhar*** (f. **úkhraa***)	*other*
آخر	**áakhir**	*last (of something)*
زار	**záara [Mw-I]**	*visit*
خروف، خرفان	**kharúuf, khirfáan**	*sheep*
نهاية	**niháayah**	*end*
عادة، ـات	**:áadah, -aat**	*custom, habit*
إذا	**ídhan**	*so, therefore*
بعض	**ba:D**	*some, part of something*
قطر، أقطار	**quTr, aqTáar**	*region, zone, area*
ثالث	**tháalith**	*third (adj.)*

> **LANGUAGE TIP**
>
> **aakhir** *last* behaves in the same way as **awwal** *first*.

1 How many main festivals do all Muslims celebrate?

جاك   كم عيدا عند المسلمين؟

أحمد   الأعياد المهمّة عندنا اثنان.

فران   وما هما؟

أحمد   الأوّل هو العيد الصغير واسمه عيد الفطر.

جاك   وفي أيّ شهر هو؟

أحمد   العيد الصغير في أوّل يوم من شهر شوال.

فران   وما مناسبته؟

أحمد   مناسبته أنّ شهر شوال يعقب شهر رمضان الكريم، وهو شهر الصوم عند المسلمين.

جاك   وما معنى الصوم عندكم؟

أحمد   الصوم معناه أنّ الناس لا يأكلون ولا يشربون في النهار. هذا هو معنى الصوم.

فران   وما هو العيد الآخر؟

أحمد   هو العيد الكبير أو عيد الأضحى.

جاك   وما مناسبته؟

أحمد   مناسبته الحجّ وهو يبدأ في آخر يوم من أيّام الحج. والحج معناه أنّ الناس يسافرون الى مكّة المكرّمة ويزورون الكعبة.

فران   وكيف يحتفلون بهذا العيد؟

أحمد   هم يذبحون فيه ذبائح.

جاك   وما هي الذبيحة؟

أحمد   الذبيحة هي خروف يذبحونه ويأكلونه في نهاية الحج. وهذا عادة عند المسلمين.

فران   فأعيادكم اثنان فقط إذا؟

أحمد   لا، في بعض الأقطار يحتفلون بعيد ثالث.

جاك   وما هو؟

أحمد   هو مولد النبي، صلّى الله عليه وسلّم، في شهر ربيع الأوّل.

فران   نعم، هذا مثل عيد الميلاد عندنا نحن المسيحيّين.

NOTES

awwal yawm *the first day*. The adjective **awwal** *first* can be used in the normal way, but frequently precedes its noun which then does not have **al-** *the*.

fii-h. The use of prepositions in both English and Arabic is very idiomatic and therefore unpredictable. We would say *on it*, but the Arabs say *in it*. A similar idiosyncracy in English would be: *on Tuesday*, but *in March*.

shahr shawwaal is a possessive construction (the month of **Shawwal**), so the word **shahr** cannot have **al-**.

kharuuf yadhbaHuun-uh *a sheep that they slaughter*. English would supply the word *that*, and ignore the ending **-uh** on the verb. See section on relative clauses in Unit 13.

haadhaa :aadah *this is a custom*. You will recognze *this* as an *is/are* sentence. The **haadhaa** does not agree with the feminine noun, as it refers back to the preceding sentence as a whole.

faqaT *only*. This word always follows what it refers to.

naHnu *we* is for emphasis or contrast here.

muslimiin. The masculine plural ending **-uun** becomes **-iin** after all prepositions (in this case **:ind**) and also when the noun is the possessing item of a possessive construction (see Unit 13). For **:ind** expressing *to have*, see Language discovery.

anna *that* (conjunction), like **inna** (Unit 8), is always followed by a noun showing the accusative marker if applicable, or a pronoun suffix.

معناه **ma:naa-h** *its meaning*. Words ending in **-aa** but written with ى change this to **alif** when anything is added. ى can only exist as the final letter of an Arabic word or word combination, the same as ة (which becomes ت when anything is added).

The verbs *eat* and *drink* are in their full plural agreeing forms because they come after their subject **an-naas** *the people* (see Unit 7).

yazuuruun *they visit*. This kind of verb, called a hollow verb by the Arabs, has two stems for both present and past tenses. This one is vowelled like **kaana**, but there are two other vowel patterns. Study these in Tables **Mw**, **My** and **Ma**, and you can always refer back to them in the future. Like all verbs, these occur usually in the *he* or *she* forms (because of the agreement rules) so are often recognizable from their long **aa** vowel in the past. In the present tense, the long vowel is (order of statistical frequency) **uu**, **ii** or (infrequently) **aa**.

yaHtafiluun *they celebrate*. The verb is plural here, because no subject is stated, it being the *they* implied within the verb.

2 Listen to the audio again and answer these questions.

    a The great festival of the pilgrimage begins:

       1 on the first day   **2** on the last day   **3** in the middle

    b People travel:

       1 to Mecca   **2** to Medina   **3** from Mecca

    c They visit:

       1 the Kaabah   **2** the mosque

    d How do they celebrate the festival?

    e Which Muslim celebration resembles a Christian festival?

3 Read the conversation again and match the English with the Arabic sentences.

a We have two important festivals.	١ في أوّل يوم من شهر شوال.
b Which month is it in?	٢ كيف يحتفلون بهذا العيد؟
c The first day of the month of Shawal.	٣ فأعيادكم اثنان فقط إذاً؟
d What do you mean by fasting?	٤ ما معنى الصوم عندكم؟
e People don't eat or drink in the daytime.	٥ هذا مثل عيد الميلاد عندنا نحن المسيحيّين.
f How do they celebrate this festival?	٦ الأعياد المهمّة عندنا اثنان.
g What is the sacrifice?	٧ هذا عادة عند المسلمين.
h It is a custom among the Muslims.	٨ الناس لا يأكلون ولا يشربون في النهار.
i So you only have two festivals?	٩ ما هي الذبيحة؟
j This is like the Christian Christmas.	١٠ في أيّ شهر هو؟

 Language discovery

1 QUESTION WORDS

These question words differ from the question markers هل **hal** and أ **a** given in Unit 2, which merely turn statements into *yes/no* questions. The words referred to here are more specific.

What?

There are two words for *what*: ما **maa** is used before nouns and subject pronouns:

    ما هو؟   *What (is) it (he)?*

    ما هذا؟   *What (is) this?*

    ما اسمه؟   *What (is) his/its name?*

ماذا **maadhaa** is used before verbs:

ماذا أكلوا؟   *What they ate?*   *What did they eat?*

ماذا يحمل؟   *What he-carries?*   *What is he carrying?*

Note also the common construction in the conversation:

ما هي الذبيحة؟   *What (is) she the-sacrifice-animal?*   *What is a sacrifice animal?*

Who?

من **man** is used before both nouns and verbs. In unvowelled Arabic, this looks identical to **min** *from*. You have to decide from the context, which does not usually present any difficulty:

من هم؟   *Who (are) they?*

من فتح الباب؟   *Who he-opened the-door?*   *Who opened the door?*

Also note:

من هو المدير؟   *Who he (is) the-manager?*   *Who is the manager?*

Which?

أيّ **ayy** (m.), أيّة **ayyah** (f.). This is followed by a singular noun without **al-** and agrees with it in gender:

أيّ رجل؟   *Which man?*

أيّة بنت؟   *Which girl?*

How many?

كم **kam**. This is followed by a singular noun, which requires the accusative marker **-an**, unless it has a feminine ending:

كم عيدا؟   *How many festivals?*

كم سيّارة؟   *How many cars?*

How?

كَيْف kayf(a) is used before nouns and verbs. The final **-a** is often omitted:

كيف سافرت؟	*How you-travelled?*
كيف حالك؟	*How (is) condition-your?* *How are you?* (a very common greeting)

Where?

أَين **ayna**. Note that when **ayna** means *where to?* and *where from?* it is preceded by إلى *to* and مِن *from* respectively:

أين المتحف؟	*Where (is) the-museum?*
إلى أين تذهب؟	*To where you-go?*
من أين حضروا؟	*From where they-came?*

When?

متى **mataa** is usually used with verbs:

متى وصلتم؟	*When you-arrived?*

Why?

لماذا **li-maadhaa** is used before verbs:

لماذا سافرت الى مسقط؟	*Why she-travelled to Muscat?*

2 HOW TO SAY *TO HAVE*

Arabic has no actual verb meaning *to have*, but uses a combination of a preposition and a noun or pronoun.

Three common prepositions are used:

لِ	**li-**	*to, for*
عند	**:ind(a)**	*with* (equivalent of French *chez*)
لدى	**ladaa**	*with*

> **LANGUAGE TIP**
>
> لدى **ladaa** *with* is slightly archaic, though still used. When a pronoun suffix is added, it behaves like **ilaa**. It has not been used much in this book.

So, to say *Mohammed has a new car* we say:

لمحمد سيارة جديدة   *to-muHammad car new*

And to say *I have an excellent book* is:

عندي كتاب ممتاز   *with-me book excellent*

> **LANGUAGE TIP**
>
> ل -li- and عند: -ind are more or less interchangeable. The former is considered more elegant, but
> in spoken Arabic the latter is used almost exclusively. ل- is usually either used to indicate human
> relationships (I have a brother), or ownership of abstract concepts (I have a vision, idea etc.), but not
> really used much for physical possessions.

To say *had*, Arabic uses كان **kaana** *was/were* +- ل **li-** / عند: **ind**:

كانت لمحمد سيارة جديدة   *was to-muHammad car new*

كان عندي كتاب ممتاز   *was with-me book excellent*

In the first example, it is not always necessary for the verb **kaana** to agree with its subject
(here, **sayyaarah**, f.). **kaana** would be just as acceptable.

To say *will have* use **yakuun** (the present tense of **kaana**) + li-/:ind. With this verb the future
marker **sa-** or **sawfa** is optional:

سيكون عندكم ضيف غدا   (future marker) *he-is with-you guest   You will have a guest*

tomorrow   *tomorrow.*

To say *have not* in the present, use the verb ليس **laysa** (see Unit 8) + ل- **li-** / عند:**ind**, and in
the past and future by applying the appropriate words for *not* (see Unit 10).

> **LANGUAGE TIP**
>
> مع is an important preposition expressing *to have* in terms of possession, e.g. 'I have a pen with me now'
> as opposed to 'I own a pen'.

3 THEMATIC SENTENCES

A type of sentence that is often encountered in Arabic is the thematic or topical sentence.

The topic of the sentence, that is, the person or thing the sentence is about, is stated first,
followed by what you want to say about the topic. The part of the sentence that comes
after you have mentioned the topic must be able to stand independently and very often has
a real or implied pronoun, which refers back to that topic.

There are a number of these in the conversation and we have given a few examples with literal translation to help you understand the concept. There is no need to spend a lot of time learning how to use this construction, but the Arabs regard it as elegant, and you will come across it frequently.

> **LANGUAGE TIP**
>
> These are more or less equivalent to English sentences beginning with *as for*, as in *As for Peter, he's rarely at home*. Note that the part of the sentence following the topic (*Peter*) makes complete sense on its own by including the pronoun *he*.

الأول هو العيد الصغير	*the-first he (is) the-festival the-small*
الصوم معناه أن ...	*the-fasting meaning-his (is) that…*

4 THE ORDINAL NUMBERS 1–20

These are adjectives telling you the order things come in. With the exception of *first* and *sixth*, they are easily related to the cardinal numbers, using the root of the number and the word shape CaaCiC (see Unit 2). Apart from *first*, they all form the feminine in the usual way by adding ة -ah:

first	أول **awwal**, f. أولى **uulaa**	
second	ثان، الثاني **thaanin, ath-thaanii**	
third	ثالث **thaalith**	
fourth	رابع **raabi:**	
fifth	خامس **khaamis**	
sixth	سادس **saadis**	
seventh	سابع **saabi:**	
eighth	ثامن **thaamin**	
ninth	تاسع **taasi:**	
tenth	عاشر **:aashir**	
eleventh	حادي عشر **Haadii :ashar** (f. حادية عشرة)	
twelfth	ثاني عشر **thaanii :ashar** (f. ثانية عشرة)	
thirteenth	ثالث عشر **thaalith :ashar** (f. ثالثة عشرة)	

…and so on up to *nineteenth*

twentieth	the cardinal number (عشرون/عشرين) is used for subsequent numbers.

5 THE ISLAMIC CALENDAR

Although nowadays it is only used in most countries for religious purposes (such as festival dates), you should be familiar with the Islamic calendar.

The Islamic date is calculated from the date of the Prophet Mohammed's flight (in Arabic, **hijrah**) from Mecca to Medinah, which took place on 16 July 622 AD. For this reason, Islamic dates are specified as هجري **hijrii**, often abbreviated to هـ. The English abbreviation is AH. Apart from starting more than six centuries later than the Western calendar, the Islamic year consists of 12 lunar months, adding up to only 354 days. Consequently, the years are not synchronized with the solar calendar, so festivals creep forward according to the European dating system. For instance, in 2014 AD (1435–6 هـ) Ramadan started on 28 July.

> **LANGUAGE TIP**
>
> For most secular transactions, Arabic versions of the Western month names are used. The Arabs call the
> AD year ميلادي **miilaadii** *pertaining to the birth* (i.e. of Christ), abbreviated to م.
>
> 2014 م — 1435هـ

Here is a table for the two sets of months. For the reasons given, these do not, of course, correspond except in the order in which they come.

Western calendar	Islamic calendar
يناير yanaayir	محرم muHarram
فبراير fabraayir	صفر Safar
مارس maaris	ربيع الأول rabii: al-awwal
أبريل abriil	ربيع الثاني rabii: ath-thaanii
مايو maayuu	جمادى الأولى jumaada l-uulaa
يونيو yuunyuu	جمادى الآخرة jumaada l-aakhirah

يوليو yuulyuu	رجب rajab
أغسطس aghusTus	شَعْبان sha:baan
سبتمبر sabtambar	رمضان ramaDaan
أكتوبر uktuubir	شوال shawwaal
نوفمبر nuufambar	ذو القعدة dhuu l-qa:dah
ديسمبر diisambar	ذو الحجة dhuu l-Hijjah

LANGUAGE TIP

There is a third set of month names, starting, surprisingly, with **kaanuun ath-thaani** *the second Kanoon*,

used mainly in the Syria–Iraq region, and you should try to learn these if you are going to that area.

Word discovery

 11.03 The word pattern for this unit is C¹aC²aa'iC³*, for example, **jaraa'id** جرائد

newspapers, which sounds like the English *falafel*.

This is another internal plural shape, usually coming from feminine singulars of the shape
CaCiiCah, e.g. جريدة **jariidah**, singular of the above example. It does not show the
accusative marker:

ضرائب from ضريبة **Daríibah, Daráa'ib**   *tax*

حقائب from حقيبة **Haqíibah, Haqáa'ib**   *bag, suitcase*

حدائق from حديقة **Hadíiqah, Hadáa'iq**   *garden, park*

Note that if the singular refers to a female human being, the **-aat** plural is used:

زميلة **zamíilah** (pl. زميلات **zamíiláat**)   *(female) colleague*

: الآن دورك **al-'aan dawrak**
Turn the words into plurals:

رسالة   *letter*   _____

حقيقة   *fact*   _____

نتيجة   *result*   _____

Practice

V   مؤلف، ـون   **mu'állif, -uun**   *author*

شرح   **sháraHa** [S-I a]   *explain*

1 Match the questions with the appropriate answers.

١ ثلاثة: حميد وناصر وسعيد.		a من مؤلف هذا الكتاب؟
٢ سأشرحها لك.		b أين مدينة الاسكندرية؟
٣ في مصر.		c ماذا تعمل الآن؟
٤ هي هدية لك.		d متى رجع من جدة؟
٥ أذهب إلى المكتب.		e كم ولدا عندك؟
٦ نجيب محفوظ.		f لماذا تحب هذه البنت؟
٧ أول بيت على اليمين.		g كيف تلعب هذه اللعبة؟
٨ أقرأ الجرائد.		h أي بيت بيت فريدة؟
٩ يوم الجمعة.		i ما هذا؟
١٠ لأنها جميلة جدا!		j إلى أين تذهبين يا مريم؟

2 Rearrange the months of the year into the correct order.

٧ ديسمبر		١ سبتمبر
٨ مايو		٢ أبريل
٩ نوفمبر		٣ فبراير
١٠ أغسطس		٤ أكتوبر
١١ يونيو		٥ يوليو
١٢ مارس		٦ يناير

V

تلميذ، تلامذة   **tilmíidh, taláamidhah**   *pupil*

فرع، فروع   **far:, furúu:**   *branch (of a tree, company, etc.)*

فستان، فساتين   **fustáan, fasaatíin**   *dress*

3

a Make complete *to have* sentences in the present tense, using either **li-** or **:ind**:

Example: ثلاثة أولاد ← هو له ثلاثة أولاد _____ هو

He _____ three sons. ➜ He has three sons.

٦ نحن _____ سيارة ألمانية.	١ الملك _____ قصور كثيرة.
٧ هم _____ حقائب ثقيلة.	٢ أنت _____ أخت طويلة.
٨ الشركة _____ ٥ فروع.	٣ أنتم _____ أولاد صغار.
٩ محمد _____ شقة واسعة.	٤ أنا _____ آلة حاسبة جديدة.
١٠ سميرة _____ فستان جميل.	٥ المدرس _____ ٥٠ تلميذا.

b Now change the first five sentences into the past tense, using **kaana**.

> **LANGUAGE TIP**
>
> Remember the daily calls to prayer are:
>
> | | | |
> |---|---|---|
> | الفجر | **al-fajr** | *dawn* |
> | الظهر | **aDH-DHuhr** | *midday* |
> | العصر | **al-:aSr** | *mid-afternoon* |
> | المغرب | **al-mághrib** | *sunset* |
> | العشاء | **al-:isháa'** | *late evening* |

4 Prayer times vary according to sunrise and sunset and are always listed in the daily newspapers. Look at the prayer times here from two successive days in the month of April. Which day came first?

a
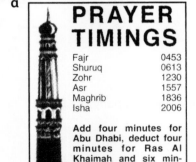

b
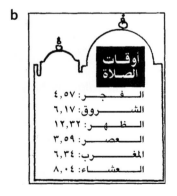

١ اسمي علي. أسكن في الطابق الثالث.

٢ اسمي حمدان. أسكن في الطابق السادس.

٣ اسمي سهام. أسكن في الطابق الثاني.

٤ اسمي مصطفى. أسكن في الطابق التاسع.

٥ اسمي عبد الله. أسكن في الطابق الثامن.

٦ اسمي نورة. أسكن في الطابق العاشر.

٧ اسمي حميد. أسكن في الطابق الأول.

6 Abdullah takes his family shopping to a large superstore out of town. Everyone is looking for something particular and the store is so big that they have to ask at the information desk where to go.

Look at the store guide and say which aisle each of them needs to go to.

1	Household linen	مفارش منزلية ١
2	Men's clothing	ملابس رجالية ٢
3	Women's clothing	ملابس نسائية ٣
4	Children's clothing & shoes	ملابس وأحذية أطفال ٤
5	Men's & women's shoes	أحذية رجالية ونسائية ٥
6	Baby garments	ملابس حديثي الولادة ٦
7	Bicycles	دراجات ٧
8	Toys	لعب ٨
9	Games/sports accessories	ألعاب / مستلزمات رياضية ٩
10	Stationery	قرطاسية ١٠
11	Books/greeting cards	كتب / بطاقات معايدة ١١
12	Hardware/batteries	أدوات / بطاريات ١٢
13	Tables/chairs	موائد / كراسي ١٣
14	Home appliances	أدوات منزلية ١٤
15	DVDs/CDs	أقراص دي في دي/ أقراص مدمجة ١٥
16	Electrical accessories/video games	أدوات كهربائية / ألعاب فيديو ١٦
17	Luggage	حقائب ١٧
18	Computers/software	أجهزة كمبيوتر/ برامج ١٨
19	Phones	هواتف ١٩
20	Cameras/DVD recorders	كاميرات / مسجلات دي في دي ٢٠

Example: Abdullah needs a pair of shoes and a DVD:

يذهب إلى الصف الخامس والصف الخامس عشر.

He goes to the fifth aisle and the 15th aisle.

a Qasim (aged 13) wants a shirt and batteries. _____

b Nadia needs a greetings card for a friend, some coloured pens and a DVD. _____

c Miriam (17) wants a hair dryer, jeans and a new game. _____

d Ali (18) wants a T-shirt, a CD and a computer. _____

e Sarah wants towels, some chairs for the balcony and clothes for the baby. _____

? Test yourself

1 Give the correct responses to these greetings.

a عيد مبارك _____ (singular); _____ (plural)

b كل عام وأنت بخير _____ (singular); _____ (plural)

2 Translate the sentences into Arabic.

a I live on the tenth floor. _____

b Mohammed has a big suitcase. _____

c I had a new dress. _____

d Where did they come from? _____

e Who are they? _____

SELF CHECK

I CAN. . .
. . . talk about the main Islamic festivals.
. . . use special greetings for festival days.
. . . use the Islamic calendar.
. . . ask questions with *what?/where?/who?*, etc.
. . . say *to have*.

12 الخليج العربي
al-khaliij al-:arabi
The Arabian Gulf

In this unit you will learn how to:
▶ *describe places in more detail*
▶ *use the relative pronouns* who, which, that, *etc*
▶ *use passive verbs.*

CEFR: (B1) *Can scan longer text in order to locate desired information in everyday material, such as letters, brochures and short official documents; can write about everyday aspects of his environment (people, places, job).*

Focus on Sharjah

The United Arab Emirates (UAE) الإمارات العربية المتحدة **al-imaaráat al-:arabíyyah al-muttáHidah** was formed in December 1971 as a federation of seven sheikhdoms, of which Sharjah ranks third in size and wealth. The literary Arabic form of the name *Sharjah* is الشّارقة **ash-shaariqah**. The English version omits the Arabic definite article and the **j** comes from a local pronunciation of the Arabic letter ق **q**.

Although their economies are ultimately based on oil production, all the Emirates have made efforts to diversify. Sharjah is relatively small with a population of about 1 million. It has concentrated on promoting and encouraging social, educational and cultural projects, resulting in its being named Arab City of Culture in 1998. It also hosts one of the most influential international book fairs every November, welcoming writers not only from across the Arab world, but also from around the rest of the world.

Do you know what the two largest Emirates are?

Vocabulary builder

12.01 Listen to the new expressions and repeat them until you can say them with confidence.

NEW EXPRESSIONS

دولة، دول	dáwlah, dúwal	country, state
الخليج العربي	al-khalíij al-:árabii	the Arabian Gulf
موقع، مواقع	máwqi:, mawáaqi:*	site, situation, place
ساكن، سكان	sáakin, sukkáan	inhabitant, resident
زائر، زوار	záa'ir, zuwwáar	visitor
إحصاء، ـات	iHSáa', -áat	count, census
نسمة	násamah	individual (used in population counts only)
دائرة، دوائر	dáa'irah, dawáa'ir*	department, directorate (government)
مركز، مراكز	márkaz, maráakiz*	centre
جغرافي	jughráafii	geographical
تجاري	tijáarii	commercial
تاريخي	taaríikhii	historical
ثقافي	thaqáafii	cultural
تعليمي	ta:líimii	educational
أقام	aqáama [Mw-IV]	to hold (of an event)

USEFUL PHRASES

على امتداد العصور	:ala imtidáad al-:uSúur	over the ages
يقدر	yuqáddar [passive of S-II]	is estimated
حسب	Hasb	according to
توصف ... بأَنها	túuSaf ... bi-ánna-haa...	is described as
أجريت	újriyat [passive of Ly-IV]	was carried out
الذي	alládhii (f. التي allátii)	who, which, that
كـ	ka-	as, like
نِصف، أَنصاف	niSf, anSáaf	half
أَي	ay	that is
الكثير من...	al-kathíir min...	many, a great number of...
أهم	ahámm	more/most important

📖 Reading

 ابتسم، أنت في الشارقة! *SMILE, YOU'RE IN SHARJAH!*

ابتسم	**ibtásama** [S-VIII]	*smile*
عبارة، ـات	**:abáarah, -áat**	*phrase, expression*
ترحيبي	**tarHíibii**	*welcoming*
أفاض ب	**afáaDa bi-** [My-IV]	*flood, overflow with*
مشاعر	**masháa:ir***	*feelings, sentiments*
ود	**wadd**	*love, friendship*
صادق	**Sáadiq**	*truthful, true*
استقبل	**istáqbala** [S-X]	*receive, meet*
احتل	**iHtálla** [D-VIII]	*occupy (a place or position)*
متميز	**mutamáyyiz**	*distinctive, prominent*
جعل	**já:ala** [S-I a]	*cause, make do something*
تمتع ب	**tamátta:a bi-** [S-V]	*enjoy*
دور، أدوار	**dawr, adwáar**	*role, turn*
قيادي	**qiyáadii**	*leading*
بين	**báyna**	*among, between*
نشاط	**nasháaT**	*activity*
عدد، أعداد	**:ádad, a:dáad**	*number*
أحدث	**áHdath**	*newest, latest*
كثافة	**katháafah**	*density*
مربع	**murábba:**	*square*
خاص	**khaaSS**	*special; private*
رعى	**rá:aa** [Lh-I]	*take care of, look after*
تنفيذ	**tanfíidh**	*implementation, execution*
إرسال	**irsáal**	*transmission, sending*
أذاع	**adháa:a** [My-IV]	*broadcast*

12.02 *Look at the transcript from a radio advert about Sharjah, describing its role in the Emirates.*

1 Where is Sharjah's geographical location?

ابتسم أنت في الشارقة!

بهذه العبارة الترحيبية التي تفيض بكل مشاعر الود الصادق تستقبل الشارقة ضيوفها. وإمارة الشارقة هي إحدى إمارات دولة الإمارات العربية المتحدة التي تحتل موقعا جغرافيا متميزا على الخليج العربي. وهو موقع جعل الشارقة تتمتع على امتداد العصور بدور قيادي بين بلدان الخليج العربي كمركز من أهم مراكز النشاط التجاري.

ويقدر عدد السكان حسب أحدث الإحصاءات التي أجريت عام ٢٠١٣ بحوالي مليون نسمة أي بكثافة تقدر بحوالي ٣٨٦ نسمة للكيلومتر المربع. وتوصف الشارقة بأنها العاصمة الثقافية لدولة الإمارات، وهناك دائرة خاصة ترعى تنفيذ الأنشطة الثقافية بالإمارة، كما تضم الإمارة عددا من المتاحف العلمية والتاريخية الفخمة ومحطة من أحدث محطات الإرسال التلفزيوني تذيع الكثير من البرامج الثقافية والتعليمية.

2 Answer the questions.

    a What kind of activity is Sharjah a centre for? _____

    b How many inhabitants did Sharjah have at the last census? _____

    c Sharjah considered to be the capital of what in the Emirates? _____

    d What does Sharjah have a number of? _____

    e What type of programmes are transmitted from the television station? _____

 3 There are seven relative clauses in the transcript, three definite and four indefinite. Can you spot them?

4 Match the English phrases with the Arabic expressions.

    a which expresses the feelings of true friendship

    b the latest census which was carried out

    c which looks after the implementation of cultural activities

d a number of magnificent scientific and historical museums

e Sharjah is described as the cultural capital

f 386 people to the square kilometre

g one of the most important centres for commercial activity

h many cultural and educational programmes

١   التي تفيض بكل مشاعر الود _____

٢   عددا من المتاحف العلمية والتاريخية الفخمة _____

٣   ٣٨٦ نسمة للكيلومتر المربع _____

٤   الكثير من البرامج الثقافية والتعليمية _____

٥   أحدث الإحصاءات التي أجريت _____

٦   من أهم مراكز النشاط التجاري _____

٧   ترعى تنفيذ الأنشطة الثقافية _____

٨   توصف الشارقة بأنها العاصمة الثقافية _____

 # Language discovery

1 RELATIVE CLAUSES

Relative clauses in English are the second half of sentences such as:

I replied to the letter <u>which arrived last week</u>.

They are usually introduced by linking words such as *which, who, whom, whose, that,* called <u>relative pronouns</u>. The person or thing which the relative clause describes (here *letter*) is called the <u>antecedent</u>.

There are two important things to decide in Arabic:

   a Whether the antecedent is:

▶ definite (with *the* or the name of a person or place):

▶ indefinite (usually with *a*):

Arabic has two different structures, according to the indefinite/definite status of the antecedent.

   b The antecedent's role in the first part of the sentence, i.e. whether:

▶ it is doing something (subject);

▶ something is being done to it (object);

▶ it belongs to someone or something (possessive).

English makes slight alterations to some of the relative pronouns:

▶ *who* shows that the antecedent is the subject;

▶ *whom* shows that the antecedent is the object, or having something done to it;

▶ *whose* shows a possessive relationship.

Sometimes the relative pronoun is omitted in informal speech:

The woman (whom) I love …   *The films (that) I like …*

Forming relative clauses in Arabic

▶ Relative clauses with definite antecedents require the use of relative pronouns (the equivalents of *who, which, whom,* etc.)

▶ Relative clauses with indefinite antecedents do not use relative pronouns.

Otherwise, the methods of forming both types are identical.

ARABIC RELATIVE PRONOUNS

Form	Arabic pronoun	Used with antecedent types
m. sing.	الّذي **alládhii**	one male/one object of m. gender
f. sing.	الّتي **allátii**	one female/one object of f. gender/plural objects of either gender
m. plur.	الّذين **alladhíina**	plural males only
f. plur.	اللّاتي **alláatii**	plural females only
dual (m.)	اللذان **alladháani**	two men/objects
dual (f.)	اللتان **allatáani**	two women/objects

> **LANGUAGE TIP**
>
> Duals change their endings to ـين **-ayni** when they are governed by another word.

> **LANGUAGE TIP**
>
> In most varieties of spoken Arabic, all the above are reduced to **illi**.

There is no distinction in Arabic between *who, whom* or *which* as there is in English. The relative pronouns agree only in number and gender with the antecedent.

As well as deciding whether to put the relative pronoun in or not, the Arabic relative clause differs from that of English in two ways:

▶ it must constitute a complete and independent sentence on its own. English ones do not; *which I bought yesterday* does not make independent sense.

▶ it must contain some stated or implied pronoun that refers back to the antecedent. This pronoun is called the <u>referent</u>.

Definite antecedent

English: *The film that I saw…*

Arabic: *The film* (m. sing.) + *that* (antecedent is definite, so relative pronoun required; select from table) + *I saw* (referent required to show that what you saw refers to the film).

This gives the model:
The film – that – I saw it

Because *film* is masculine in Arabic, it requires the appropriate masculine relative and it is expressed by masculine **-uh** *him*.

So in Arabic we say:

الفيلم – الذي – شاهدته

In both English and Arabic, the relative clause makes independent sense. The relative pronoun is simply a joining word.

Indefinite antecedent

For indefinite antecedents the process is identical, except that there is no relative pronoun:

A film which I saw   *A film – I saw it (him)*   فيلم — شاهدته

Relationship between verb and antecendent

In the above examples, the antecedent film is the object of the verb, i.e. the action of the verb is being applied to it. There are three other possible common relationships between the antecedent and the verb:

a **Subject.** The antecedent is performing the action of the verb.

The official who works in customs ➜ *The official – who – he-works in the customs*
                                   (definite, so needs relative pronoun)

الموظف – الذي – يعمل في الجمارك

An official who works in the ➜ *(an) official – he-works in the customs* (indef. – no
  customs…   relative pronoun)

موظف – يعمل في الجمارك

b Possessive. This is almost always expressed with the relative pronoun *whose* in English.

Maryam, whose sister lives in London → *Maryam – who – her sister lives in London* (relative pronoun required after proper name, in this case feminine)

مريم – التي – تسكن أختها في لندن

A girl whose sister lives in London → *(a) girl – her sister lives in London*

بنت – تسكن أختها في لندن

c Prepositional phrases.

The contractors to whom I paid a → *The contractors – who – I-paid to-them a large sum*
*   large sum

المقاولون – الذين – دفعت لهم مبلغا كبيرا

Contractors to whom I paid a large sum → *Contractors – I-paid to-them a large sum*

مقاولون – دفعت لهم مبلغا كبيرا

All these examples have verb sentences as the relative clause, but similar combinations are possible with *is/are* verbless sentences. The same rules regarding inclusion or omission of the relative pronoun apply.

The manager, whose name is Qasim… → *The manager – who – his-name Qasim*

المدير – الذي – اسمه قاسم

An official whose name is Muhsin → *Official – his-name Muhsin*

موظف – اسمه محسن

Here are some more examples:

قابلت رجلا يعمل في مصنع الأجهزة الكهربائية

I-met a-man he-works in factory (of) the-appliances the-electrical

I met a man who works in the electrical appliances factory

الصديق الذي زرته أمس يسكن في تونس

the-friend who I-visited-him yesterday he-lives in Tunisia

The friend whom I visited yesterday lives Tunisia

الضابط الذي سيارته هناك جالس في المقهى

the-officer who his-car (is) there (is)

    sitting in the-café

The officer whose car is there is sitting in

    the café

البذلة الجديدة التي اشتريتها مصنوعة في الصين

the-suit the-new which I-bought-it (is)

    manufactured in the-China

The new suit which I bought is made

    in China

2 PASSIVE VERBS

A <u>passive verb</u> is one whose subject suffers the action, rather than carries it out (known as an <u>active verb</u>). English uses the auxiliary verb *to be* for the passive:

Active:	*A bolt of lightning struck the tree.*
Passive:	*The tree was struck by a bolt of lightning.*

The use of the passive is much more restricted in Arabic than in English. In many verbs, it is identical in writing to the active, as the only changes are in the vowelling, which is not shown.

The rules for forming it for the various verb types are given in the Verb tables.

There are four examples in the transcript. Two of these look identical to the active forms, but differ in (unseen) vowelling:

يقدر **yuqaddar** (*active:* **yuqaddir**) *is estimated and its feminine* تقدر **tuqaddar** [S-II verb]

تعتبر **tu:tabar** (*active:* **tu:tabir**) *is considered (f. form)* [S-VIII]

أجريت **ujriyat** (*active* أجرت **ajrat**) *was carried out (f. form)* [Ly-IV]

توصف **tuuSaf** (*active* تصف **taSif**) *is described (f. form)* [Fw-I]

> **LANGUAGE TIP**
>
> Some of these verbs are among the most frequently used passive forms in Arabic newspapers, so look out for them. In the case of those that are identical to the active in spelling, your only guideline is the context. For instance (after you have looked up all the words), the subject of the first example in the transcript is عدد **:adad** *number*. Since numbers can not carry out estimations, the verb must be passive.

Word discovery

12.03 The word pattern for this unit is maC¹aaC²iC³*, for example, **maraakiz** مراكز *centres*, which sounds like the English *maracas*.

This is a plural form for many words in Arabic which begin with the prefix **ma-** or (less commonly) **mi-**, some of which have the feminine ending ة.

> **LANGUAGE TIP**
>
> One of the few mainly reliable rules for forming internal plurals is that, if the vowel after the middle radical of the root is short, then they will almost invariably take this plural shape, e.g. **maraakiz** is the plural of مركز **markaz** (short **a** after middle radical **k**).

This word pattern does not take the accusative marker.

1 Can you find another example from the reading?

Here are a few more common ones.

2 Complete the English translations, thinking about the root of the word:

مدارس **madaaris***	_____		مدرسة **madrasah**	
مصانع **maSaani:***	*factories*		مصنع **maSna:**	
مناطق **manaaTiq***	*regions*		منطقة **minTaqah**	
مكاتب **makaatib***	_____		مكتب **maktab**	

الآن دورك al-'aan dawrak

3 Based on this pattern, what is the plural of this word?

_____ *residences/houses*   منزل **manzil**

Practice

استأجر	**istá'jara** [S-X]	*rent, be a tenant of*
عيادة، ـات	**:iyáadah, -aat**	*clinic*
باع	**báa:a** [My-I]	*sell*
مغنية	**mughánniyyah**	*(female) singer*

1 Rewrite the sentences, supplying the correct relative pronouns (if any).

١ هذا هو البيت ———— سنستأجره.

٢ زارني عامل ———— يعمل في مصنع.

٣ شاهدت الطبيب ———— عيادته في وسط المدينة.

٤ خالد ———— قرأت كتابه يدرس في المدرسة الثانوية.

٥ كان الكرسي ———— جلست عليه مكسورا.

٦ الطلبة ———— يدرسون في الجامعة من الإمارات.

٧ رسالة ———— كتبها الأسبوع الماضي وصلت اليوم.

٨ القمصان ———— يبيعونها في السوق مصنوعة في الصين.

٩ مغنية ———— كانت مشهورة قبل سنوات كثيرة ستزور سورية.

١٠ ابني له صديق ———— أصله اسكتلندي.

2 Match these translations with the sentences in the previous exercise.

a I saw the doctor whose clinic is in the middle of town. ——————

b An employee who works in a factory visited me. ——————

c My son has a friend who is originally (his origin is) Scottish ——————

d The chair that she sat on was broken. ——————

e Khalid, whose book I read, teaches at the secondary school. ——————

f The students who study at the university are from the Emirates. ——————

g A letter that he sent last week arrived today. ——————

h This is the house that we are going to rent. ——————

i A singer (f.) who was famous many years ago will be visiting Syria. ——————

j The shirts that they sell in the souk are made in China. ——————

أعاد	**a:áada** [Mw-IV]	*to repeat, renew*
بناء	**bináa'**	*building, construction*
كائن	**káa'in**	*being, existing, situated*
أمكن	**ámkana** [S-IV]	*to be possible*
مشاهدة	**musháahadah**	*seeing, viewing*
شكل، أشكال	**shakl, ashkáal**	*kind, type, form*
هواء	**hawáa'**	*air*
برجيل، براجيل	**barjíil, baráajiil**	*traditional wind tower*
تبريد	**tabríid**	*cooling*

جدد	**jáddada** [D-II]	*renew, restore*
قلعة، قلاع	**qál:ah, qiláa:**	*fort, fortress, citadel*
شيد	**sháyyada** [My-II]	*erect, construct*
قرن، قرون	**qarn, qurúun**	*century*
ضيق	**Dáyyiq**	*narrow*
تابل، توابل	**táabil, tawáabil**	*spice*
رائحة، روائح	**ráa'iHah, rawáa'iH***	*smell, scent, perfume*
قرنفل	**qurúnful**	*cloves*
هال	**haal**	*cardamom*
قرفة	**qírfah**	*cinnamon*
كيس، أكياس	**kiis, akyáas**	*bag, sack*
أحاط	**aHáaTa** [Mw-IV]	*surround*
متجر، متاجر	**mátjar, matáajir***	*trading place, shop, stall*
سباق، ـات	**sibáaq, -aat**	*race*
هجين، هجن	**hajíin, hújun**	*racing camel*
شعبي	**shá:bii**	*folk (adj.), popular*
شتاء	**shitáa'***	*winter*

3 Read the excerpts from a Gulf tourist brochure and find all the passive verbs and relative clauses.

١- لقد أعيد بناء منزل الشيخ صقر الكائن في هذه المنطقة.

٢- في هذه المنطقة يمكن مشاهدة أول أشكال تكييف الهواء، البرجيل، الذي كان يستخدم لتبريد البيوت في الخليج. جددت القلعة التي شيدت في القرن الماضي، وحولت إلى متحف.

٣- الطرق الضيقة تأخذ الزائر إلى سوق التوابل التي تنبعث منها روائح أنواع التوابل كلها مثل القرنفل والهال والقرفة التي تباع إلى الزوار من الأكياس التي تحيط المتاجر.

٤- سباقات الهجن رياضة شعبية تقام أيام الجمعة أثناء أشهر الشتاء.

البتراء	al-batráa'	Petra
اكتشف	iktáshafa [S-VIII]	discover (passive here)
فرعوني	far:úunii	pharaonic
دمشق*	dimáshq*	Damascus

4 Link the two sentences together using a relative clause:

١ عمر الشريف ممثل مصري. لعب أدوارا مشهورة كثيرة.

٢ ذهبنا إلى مدينة البتراء القديمة. اكتشفت في سنة ١٨١٢.

٣ في مصر آثار فرعونية مهمة. يزورها سواح كثيرون.

٤ يعمل زوجي في الشارقة. تقع الشارقة في الخليج العربي.

٥ نستأجر شقة في دمشق. يسكن صاحبها في الرياض.

٦ سافروا إلى عدن بطائرة الصبح. وصلت الطائرة الظهر.

5 Many adjectives in Arabic are derived from nouns, and there are several examples of them in the transcript. Find the nouns in the wordsnake and write the order in which they appear.

جغرافيا geography	تاريخ history	تجارة commerce	علم science
سياحة tourism	زراعة agriculture	ثقافة culture	اقتصاد economy
اجتماع meeting, sociology	رياضة sports	تعليم education	

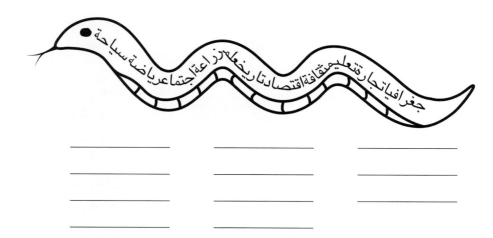

_____   _____   _____

_____   _____   _____

_____   _____

❓ Test yourself

1 Put the words into the correct order to make phrases.

١   الموظف يعمل في الجمارك الذي ─────────

٢   أمينة-تسكن أختها في لندن-التي ─────────

٣   دفع لهم مبلغا كبيرا-مقاولون ─────────

٤   المدير-اسمه ميلود الذي ─────────

2 Match the English sentences with the Arabic sentences.

   a The perfumes that they sell in the market are made in Egypt.

   b Marwa whose book I read works at the hospital.

   c This is the car that we are going to rent.

   d My daughter has a friend who is originally [his origin is] Moroccan.

١   هذه هي السيارة التي سنستأجرها . ─────────

٢   مروة التي كتاب قرأت أعمال في المستشفى . ─────────

٣   ابنتي لديها الصديق الذي هو في الأصل المغربي . ─────────

٤   الروائح التي يبيعونها في السوق مصنوعة في مصر . ─────────

SELF CHECK	
I CAN. . .	
⚪	. . . describe places in more detail.
⚪	. . . use the relative pronouns *who, which, that*, etc.
⚫	. . . use passive verbs.

 **١٣** السمع والطاعة

as-sam: wa T-Taa:ah

*Hearing is obeying**

In this unit you will learn how to:
▶ *follow a recipe*
▶ *tell people to do something*
▶ *address people or attract their attention*
▶ *use duals and masculine plurals in possessive constructions.*

CEFR: (A2/B1) *Can give simple descriptions or presentations as a short series of simple phrases and sentences linked into a list; can establish social contact; can make and respond to invitations, suggestions and apologies.*

Arabic cuisine

Although all Arab countries have their delicacies, the most highly regarded are those of the Lebanon and Syria. These countries excel in **meze** (*appetizers*) and salad dishes as they traditionally had settled populations growing salad and vegetable crops.

In areas with more recent links to their Bedouin heritage, many dishes are based on rice, which was easy to transport. These include **makloube** (*'upside down'*) in the Levant, with meat, cauliflower and aubergine, and **mansef** in Jordan, lamb cooked with yoghurt and rice or **kabsa**. Cookery in the Gulf is much influenced by Indian cuisine, with extensive use of spices.

North Africa has many tasty dishes, but traditionally does not use rice. There are tagines eaten with **couscous**, which is known in the Middle East as **maftoul**. In countries in the Gulf and bordering the Mediterranean there is also a wonderful selection of freshly caught fish and shellfish available. The recipe given in this unit is for **koshari**, a simple vegetarian dish from Egypt.

 Match the words with the dishes mentioned in the text above:

_____ كسكس _____ كشرى _____ مقلوبة _____ منسف _____ كبسة

_____

* The title of this unit is linked to a quote from the *Arabian Nights*.

Vocabulary builder

13.01 **Listen to the new expressions and repeat them until you can say them with confidence. Listen again and complete the gaps.**

QUANTITIES

ملعقة طعام	mil:aqat Ta:aam	*tablespoon*
ملعقة شاي	mil:aqat shaay	*teaspoon*
كوب	kuub	*glass, cup (in recipes)*
مائة غرام	mi'at ghraam	*100 grams*
ليتر	liitir	_____

SOME INGREDIENTS

أرز	arúzz	*rice*
عدس	ads:	*lentils*
ماء	maa'*	*water*
زيت	zayt	*(edible) oil*
ملح	milH	*salt*
معكرونة	ma:karúunah	_____
طماطم	TamáaTim*	_____

PREPARATION METHODS

مقطع	muqáTTa:	*chopped*
مقشر	muqáshshar	*peeled, skinned*
مفروم	mafrúum	*minced, ground*
مطحون	maT-Húun	*ground, milled*

INSTRUCTIONS/IMPERATIVES

f.		**m.**		
انقعي	inqa:ii	انقع	inqa:	*soak*
صفي	Saffii	صفي	Saffii	*strain*
اخلطي	ikhliTii	اخلط	ikhliT	*mix*
حمري	Hammirii	حمر	Hammir	*brown, fry*
اسلقي	usluqii	اسلق	usluq	*boil*
ارفعي	irfa:ii	ارفع	irfa:	*lift*
اتركي	utrukii	اترك	utruk	*leave*
اسكبي	uskubii	اسكب	uskub	*pour*
أضيفي	aDiifii	أضف	aDiif	*add*
رشي	rushshii	رشَ	rushsh	*sprinkle*
غطي	ghaTTii	غط	ghaTT	*cover*
قدمي	qaddimii	قدم	qaddim	*serve*

Reading

الكشري KOSHARI

كمية، ـات	kammíyyah, -aat	amount
كفى	káfaa [Ly-I]	suffice, be sufficient for
شخص، أشخاص	shakhS, ashkháaS	person
مقدار، مقادير	miqdáar, maqáadiir*	quantity, measure
أسود	áswad*	black (here meaning brown (lentils))
رغبة، ـات	rághbah, -áat	desire, wish
سلق	salq	boiling, the action of boiling something
ملعقة، ملاعق	mil:áqah, maláa:iq*	spoon, spoonful
طعام	Ta:áam	food
بصل	báSal	onions
شريحة، شرائح	sharíiHah, sharáa'iH*	slice
صلصة	SálSah	sauce
سمن	sámn	ghee, clarified butter
حبة. ـات	Hábbah, -áat	grain, seed (also used for counting units of certain fruits and vegetables)
فلفل	fúlful/fílfil	pepper
أحمر	áHmar*	red
حار	Haarr	hot
معجون	ma:júun	paste
طريقة، طرائق	Taríiqah, Taráa'iq*	method, way
حتى	Háttaa	until
غلى	ghálaa [Ly-I]	boil, come to the boil
نار	naar	fire (f.)
هادئ	háadi'	gentle, quiet
أثناء	athnáa'(a)	during, while
وضع	wáDa:a [Fw-I a]	put, place
خليط	khalíiT	mixture
طبقة، ـات	Tábaqah, -áat	layer

184

جانب، جوانب*	jáanib, jawáanib*	side
طبق، أطباق	Tábaq, aTbáaq	plate

13.02 *Koshari is a popular Egyptian vegetarian dish of lentils and rice, often sold from carts in the streets.*

1 How many people does this koshari recipe serve?

(الكمية تكفي ٦ أشخاص)

المقادير

- ٤ أكواب ونصف أرز، يغسل ويصفى
- كوب عدس أسود
- نصف كوب زيت
- ملح حسب الرغبة
- ٧ أكواب ونصف الكوب ماء للأرز
- ١٠ أكواب ماء لسلق المعكرونة
- كوبا معكرونة
- ملعقتا طعام زيت للمعكرونة
- ٦ بصلات مقطعة إلى شرائح طويلة

الصلصة

- ملعقتا طعام سمن
- ٦ حبات طماطم مقشرة ومفرومة
- ملعقة صغيرة فلفل أحمر حار مطحون
- ملعقتا طعام من معجون الطماطم
- ملح حسب الرغبة

الطريقة

١ انقعي العدس بالماء لمدة ٦ ساعات وصفيه.

٢ حمري البصل بالزيت ثم ارفعيه واتركيه جانبا. اسكبي الماء فوقه واتركيه حتى يغلي قليلا، ثم أضيفي الأرز والعدس واتركيه على نار هادئة لمدة ٤٠ دقيقة.

٣ اسلقي المعكرونة بالماء ثم أضيفي الزيت.

٤ حمري الطماطم في الزيت، ثم أضيفي الفلفل ومعجون الطماطم والملح.

٥ أثناء التقديم ضعي خليط الأرز والعدس أولا، ثم طبقة من المعكرونة ثم طبقة من البصل، ورشي فوقه الصلصة الحارة أو قدميها إلى جانب الطبق.

2 Answer the questions.

a What proportion of rice is used to lentils? _____

b How long must the lentils be soaked? _____

c How long do they cook with the rice? _____

d What else is layered with the rice, lentils and macaroni? _____

e What is added to the dish before it is served? _____

3 Match the English phrases with the Arabic.

    a fry the onions in the oil

    b leave them on a low heat

    c add the pepper and the tomato paste

    d then add the rice and lentils

    e pour the hot sauce over it

١ أضيفي الفلفل ومعجون الطماطم

٢ رشي فوقه الصلصة الحارة

٣ ثم أضيفي الأرز والعدس

٤ حمري البصل بالزيت

٥ اتركيه على نار هادئة

 # Language discovery

1 GIVING INSTRUCTIONS AND DIRECTIONS

The type of verb used for giving someone instructions or directions is called the <u>imperative</u>.
In English, this does not usually differ from the ordinary present tense verb:

Present tense: *You work hard*

Imperative: *Work hard!*

Arabic uses a special adaptation of the variant form of the present tense called the <u>jussive</u>, which you can find in the Verb tables at the end of the course.

Forming the imperative

This is simply constructed as follows:

    a Look up in the Verb tables the *you* form, or 2nd person singular, jussive form of the present tense, e.g.:

        تقدم **tuqaddim**   *you present, serve*

    b Remove the prefix **ta-** or **tu-**, to get قدم **qaddim**.

    c If the result, as in the above example, begins with:

▶ a consonant followed by any of the vowels, you have formed the imperative masculine singular (قدم **qaddim** *serve!*)

▶ two consonants (Arabic letters **dh** (ذ), **kh** (خ), etc. counting as only one consonant), supply an **alif** at the beginning and pronounce it in most cases as the vowel **i**.

    تستعلم **tasta:lim** *you enquire* → ستعلم **sta:lim** → استعلم **ista:lim** *enquire!*

    d Form I verbs, as usual, show vowel variation. With sound Form I verbs (see Verb table S-I), removing the prefix always results in a two-consonant beginning, so an **alif** must be prefixed. Note the vowel following the second consonant, which can be **a, i** or **u**.

▶ If it is **a** or **i**, the above rules for two consonants apply:

تغسل **taghsil** *you wash* → غسل **ghsil** → اغسل **ighsil** *Wash!*

▶ If it is **u**, the **alif** must also be given a **u**-vowel:

تترك **tatruk** *you leave (aside)* → ترك **truk** → اترك **utruk** *Leave!*

In practice, this is not too important, as these vowels are very often elided unless the imperative comes at the beginning of a sentence.

الآن دورك al-'aan dawrak

1 Based on the rules given, provide the imperatives for these verbs.

أنت تصب _____ أنت تقف _____ أنت تقرأ _____

> **LANGUAGE TIP**
>
> The one exception to these rules is the Form IV verb (all types; see tables). In these verbs, an **alif** with an **a** vowel is always prefixed to the shortened jussive form, whether this begins with two consonants or not. This initial **a** vowel is never elided, and is often written with a **hamzah**:
>
> ترسل **tursil** (from أرسل [S-IV] *to send*) → رسل **rsil** → أرسل **arsil** *Send!*
>
> تضيفي **tuDiifii** (f. sing. from أضاف[My-IV] *to add*) → ضيفي **Diifii** → أضيفي **a Diifii** *Add!* (f. sing.).

The *alif* is added even though the shortened jussive begins with a consonant followed by a vowel.

Irregular imperatives

The following irregular imperatives occur very frequently:

تعال	**ta:aal**	*Come!* (no phonetic relation to the verb جاء **jaa'a**)
خذ	**khudh**	*Take!* (from أخذ **akhadha** *to take*)
هات	**haat**	*Give!* (probably from the verb أتى **ataa**)
كل	**kul**	*Eat!* (from أكل **akala** *to eat*)

الآن دورك al-'aan dawrak

2 Match the Arabic with the English equivalent.

a تعال بسرعة	**1** Take it away!
b خذه بعيدا!	**2** Give me your hand
c كل اللحوم	**3** Eat the meat
d هاتي يدك	**4** Come quickly!

Feminine and plural imperatives

Feminine and plural imperatives obey the rules above, using the relevant parts of the jussive:

ـي **-ii**	f. sing. (addressed to one female)
ـوا **-uu**	m. pl.
ـن **-na**	f. pl.

For *Come!* these same endings are added to تعال *giving* تعالي، تعالوا etc. The same is true for the other irregular imperatives listed.

> **LANGUAGE TIP**
>
> The dual imperatives for addressing two people occur rarely and have been omitted from this section.
>
> However, they can be deduced from the jussive form in exactly the same way.

Negative imperatives

Use the negative word لا **laa** *not* followed by the appropriate part of the jussive, retaining its prefix:

لا تترك	**laa tatruk**	*don't leave (to a man)*
لا تغسلي	**laa taghsilii**	*don't wash (to a woman)*
لا تستعلموا	**laa tasta:limuu**	*don't enquire (to several men)*

You often see imperatives on road signs telling you to do something (*slow down, stop*, etc.)

Many common signs are expressed in a different way, for instance with the word الرجاء **ar-rajaa'** which means *the request*, i.e. *it is requested, please do/don't do something*. This is followed by a noun indicating the action requested. Such signs often feature the word عدم

:adam *lack of, absence of* when the request is a negative one, i.e. not to do something.

الرجاء عدم الازعاج
Please do not disturb

الرجاء ايقاظي لتناول وجبة الطعام
Please wake me for meals

2 MORE WAYS TO ADDRESS PEOPLE

As we have already seen, all forms of Arabic use the vocative particle يا **yaa** when addressing people or attracting attention:

يا سامي!	**yaa saamii**	*Sami!*

A slightly different form is used when the person addressed has the definite article:

يا أيها الأمير!	*O Emir!*

This construction is commonly found in political and other emotive speeches with a plural noun:

يا أيها الإخوة العرب!	*O Arab brothers!*
يا أيتها السيدات!	*Ladies!*

3 MASCULINE PLURALS AND DUALS IN POSSESSIVE CONSTRUCTIONS

As you know, these endings all end in the letter **nuun** ن:

Masculine plural

ـون **-uun** (subject)

ـين **-iin** (object, possessives and after all prepositions)

Dual

ـان **-aan** (f. ـتان **-ataan**) (subject)

ـين **-ayn** (f. ـتين **-atayn**) (object, possessives and after all prepositions)

However, when any of these types of word form the first part of a possessive construction, the final letter **nuun** is dropped. There are several examples of such duals in the recipe:

| كوبا معكرونة | two cups of macaroni |
| ملعقتا طعام زيت | two tablespoons of oil (this is a double possessive, the Arabic literally reading two-spoons (of) food (of) oil) |

Examples of the masculine plural are:

| حضر موظفو الحكومة | The officials of the government attended. |
| تطلب الشركة مندوبي مبيعات | The company is seeking sales representatives. |

Word discovery

13.03 The word pattern for this unit is istiC^{1}C^{2}aaC^3, for example, **istinkaar** استنكار *rejection*, which sounds like the English *(m)ist in car* (omitting first letter).

This is the verbal noun of S-X verbs. Here are some examples.

استخدام	**istikhdaam**	*using, usage, use*
استعمال	**isti:maal**	*same meaning as above*
استعلام	**isti:laam**	*enquiring, enquiry*
استقبال	**istiqbaal**	*reception (of guests, etc.)*
استثناء	**istithnaa'**	*excepting, exception*

Practice

1 You are on a plane and are served a meal. Match each of these packs of food and seasoning with the appropriate English word.

a

سكر
الوزن الصافي ٧ غرام

b

زبدة

c

دوكروس
فلفل

d

ملح

e

ماء

```
1 salt    2 pepper    3 sugar
   4 butter    5 water
```

2 Look at these road signs and match them with the English.

a (خفف السرعة)   b (لف شمال)

c (لف يمين)   d (قف)

| 1 Turn left 2 Stop |
| 3 Slow down 4 Turn right |

عمري ما...	:úmrii maa...	I have never...
جرب	járraba [S-II]	try out, taste
رد إلى	rádda [D-i u]	return something to someone
جرى	járaa [Ly-I]	run
نام	náama [Ma-I]	sleep

3 Match an appropriate response with the cues in the right-hand column. (Note: Some of these are in the feminine singular.)

١ جربه، هو لذيذ	a أنا جوعان
٢ هات واحد جديد	b أنا تعبانة
٣ رده إليه	c تاكسي! تاكسي
٤ كل شيئًا!	d هذا الكوب مكسور
٥ خذها إلى المستشفى	e عمري ما أكلت الكسكس
٦ اجري!	f هذا الكتاب لأحمد
٧ المحطة	g أختي مريضة
٨ نامي	h تأخرت!

4 Read the conversation between Fawzi and his assistant Karim.

كريم   أفتح هذه الرسالة؟

فوزي   نعم، افتحها .

> **LANGUAGE TIP**
>
> Note that where English says *shall I…*, Arabic uses the simple present tense.

Now instruct Karim to do what he offers to do, using an imperative verb (with suffix pronoun if necessary):

١ أرسل الفاكس الآن؟

٢ أكتب الرسالة فورا؟

٣ اتصل بالمكتب؟

5 Fatimah's new maid is helping her with the lunch. Tell her to do what she is offering.

١ أضع الماء على الطاولة؟

٢ أترك الأرز في المطبخ؟

٣ أغسل الصحون؟

 Reading

تعرفة	ta:rífah	*tariff*
رسومٍ	rusúum	*fees*
مجاناً	majáanan	*free, gratis*
دفع	daf:	*payment*
نقود معدنية	nuqúud ma:daníyyah	*coins*
اضغط	íDghaT	*press!*
للحصول على	li-l-HuSúul :ála	*(in order) to obtain*
بطاقة	biTáaqah	*card*
للإلغاء	li-l-ilgháa'	*(in order) to cancel*

192

You are in a car park in Dubai and have to pay the parking fee. Read the instructions on the ticket machine and answer the questions.

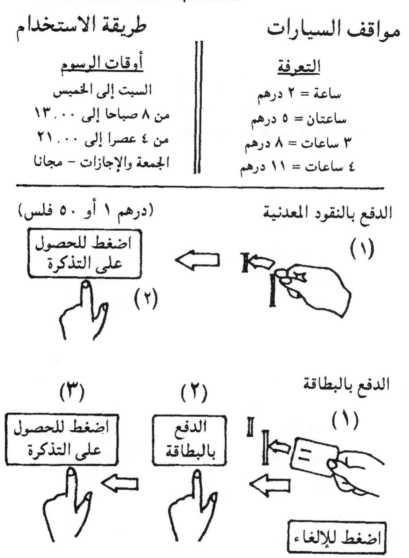

طريقة الاستخدام | مواقف السيارات

أوقات الرسوم | التعرفة

السبت إلى الخميس | ساعة = ٢ درهم

من ٨ صباحا إلى ١٣٫٠٠ | ساعتان = ٥ درهم

من ٤ عصرا إلى ٢١٫٠٠ | ٣ ساعات = ٨ درهم

الجمعة والإجازات – مجانا | ٤ ساعات = ١١ درهم

(درهم ١ أو ٥٠ فلس) | الدفع بالنقود المعدنية

اضغط للحصول على التذكرة

(١)

(٢)

الدفع بالبطاقة

(٣) | (٢) | (١)

اضغط للحصول على التذكرة | الدفع بالبطاقة

اضغط للإلغاء

1 Match the English with the Arabic:

  a Payment by coins

  b Payment by card

١ الدفع بالبطاقة

٢ الدفع بالنقود المعدنية

2 Which coins can you use?

3 On what days do you not need to pay a fee?

4 What is the longest time you can park?

5 How much does it cost to park for two hours?

6 Find the word for *press*.

Listen and understand

قسـم، أقسـام	**qism, aqsáam**	*section, division*
مذهل	**múdh-hil**	*amazing*
غنم	**ghánam**	*sheep (collective)*
جبنة	**jubnah**	*cheese*
طبخ	**Tabakh(a) [S1 u]**	*cook*
تشكيلة، ـات	**tashkíilah, -áat**	*selection*
وجبة، ـات	**wájabah, -áat**	*meal*
جبنة الحلوم	**júbnat al-Hallúum**	Halloumi *cheese*
فورا	**fáwran**	*immediately*

13.04 *A local supermarket has special offers on some food items that are announced over the loudspeaker.*

1 Listen to the audio and answer the questions.

  a How much is the minced lamb per kilo? _____

  b What do they want you to see? _____

  c What do they suggest you make for a meal? _____

  d How long does the cheese offer last? _____

2 Listen to the audio again, and select an appropriate word from the box to complete the text (using the imperative form).

| تعالوا | اطبخوا | اشتروا | شاهدوا | جربوا |

ـــــــــ إلى قسم اللحوم! ـــــــــ بأسعار مذهلة تنزيلات في لحم الغنم المفروم الكيلو بـ ٨ دراهم.

ـــــــــ تشكيلة الجبن من فرنسا وإيطاليا . ـــــــــ وجبة معكرونة للعائلة اليوم.

ـــــــــ جبنة الحلوم اللذيذة. أسعار خاصة لليوم فقط.

Test yourself

1 Match the English with the Arabic.

a Add some sugar to the lemon juice.

b Serve on a large plate with hot bread.

c Pour boiling water into the coffee cup.

d Soak the rice in water for ten minutes.

e Brown some onions in a pan.

f Mix the tomatoes with the
cucumber and olives in a bowl.

١ انقعي الأرز في الماء لمدة عشر دقائق.

٢ حمري بعض البصل في مقلاة.

٣ اسكبي الماء المغلي في كوب القهوة.

٤ اخلطي الطماطم مع الخيار والزيتون في وعاء.

٥ أضيفي بعض السكر إلى عصير الليمون.

٦ قدمي في لوحة كبيرة مع الخبز الساخن.

SELF CHECK

I CAN. . .
. . . follow a recipe.
. . . tell people to do something.
. . . address people or attract their attention.
. . . use duals and masculine plurals in possessive constructions.

14 العرب في هوليوود
al-:arab fii ḥuuliiwuud
Arabs in Hollywood

In this unit you will learn how to:
▸ *make comparisons*
▸ *give biographical information*
▸ *talk about the film industry*
▸ *say how things are done*
▸ *talk about shopping.*

CEFR: (B1) *Can use a series of phrases and sentences to describe family, other people, living conditions, daily routines, educational background and present or most recent job; can read straightforward factual texts on subjects related to his field and interest with a satisfactory level of comprehension.*

The Arabic film industry

In most Arab countries there is no large-scale film industry since cinemas are not widely available. This means that Arab actors and directors often have to find work abroad. However, there are several successful Arab film festivals. These include the Cairo International Film Festival مهرجان القاهرة السينمائي الدولي which was one of the first; the Abu Dhabi Film Festival مهرجان أبو ظبي السينمائي; the Dubai Film Festival مهرجان دبي السينمائي الدولي and the Marrakech International Film Festival المهرجان الدولي للفيلم بمراكش. Some specialize in promoting international films, while others support small independent Arab film production companies and nurture local Arab talent. The best-known Arab actor to have achieved stardom in Western cinema was the Egyptian-born Omar Sharif, famous for his celebrated roles in the films *Lawrence of Arabia* and *Dr Zhivago*.

If you are interested in finding out more about Arabic films stars and directors, the following are a good place to start: Adel Emam عادل إمام, Fatan Hamama فاتن حمامة, Hiam Abbas هيام عباس and the married couple Tahar Rahim طاهر رحيم and Leila Bekhti ليلى بختي.

Vocabulary builder

14.01 Listen to the new expressions and repeat them until you can say them with confidence.

THE FILM INDUSTRY

نجمة، ـات	nájmah, -áat	star, (female) film star
ملامح	maláamiH*	features
بطولات	buTúulaat	leading roles
أسطورة، أساطير	usTúurah, asáaTiir*	legend
منتج، ـون	múntij, -úun	producer
وجه، وجوه	wajh, wujúuh	face, (media) personality
إنتاج	intáaj	production
عقد	:aqd	contract
انتشار	intisháar	spread, currency; (here) popularity
شهير	shahíir	famous

USEFUL PHRASES

سرعان ما	sur:áan maa	quickly, before long
مؤخرا	mu'ákhkharan	recently, lately
غير	ghayr	other than
إذا	ídhaa	if
نفس، نفوس	nafs, nufúus	self; soul (f.)
قائمة، قوائم	qáa'imah, qawáa'im	list
مهاجر، ـون	muháajir, -úun	emigrant
أصل، أصول	aSl, uSúul	origin, basis
اهتمام	ihtimáam	attention, concern, interest
أعطى	á:Taa [Ly-IV]	give
اشترك	ishtáraka [S-VIII]	participate, subscribe
جلب	jálaba [S-I i]	attract, bring

Reading

العرب في هوليوود al-:arab fii huuliiwuud *THE ARABS IN HOLLYWOOD*

قهر	**qáhara** [S-1 a]	conquer
اعتبر	**i:tábara** [S-VIII]	consider, regard
استطاع	**istaTáa:a** [Mw-X]	be able
اخترق	**ikhtáraqa** [S-VIII]	breach (wall, defences, etc.)
سور، أسوار	**suur, aswáar**	wall, fence
فرض	**fáraDa** [S-I i]	impose
أعلى	**á:laa**	highest; the highest point, top
رمز، رموز	**ramz, rumúuz**	symbol, code
سحر	**siHr**	magic
غاية	**gháayah**	extreme, most
ناظر	**náaDHara** [S-III]	equal, compete with
مفضل	**mufáDDil**	preferring
زاحم	**záaHama** [S-III]	jockey for position with
ابنة، بنات	**íbnah, banáat**	daughter (alternative to **bint**)
مقيم	**muqíim**	residing; resident
المكسيك	**al-maksíik**	Mexico
اسباني	**isbáanii**	Spanish
ثمرة	**thámrah**	fruit
حلاوة	**Haláawah**	sweetness; beauty
رصد	**ráSada** [S-I u]	observe, watch, monitor
عين، عيون	**:ayn, :uyúun**	eye; spring (of water) (f.)
اختار	**ikhtáara** [My-VIII]	choose
مذاق	**madháaq**	flavour
الكبرى	**al-kúbraa**	the largest
مفترض	**muftáraD**	assumed, supposed
أسند ل	**ásnada** [S-IV]	entrust to, vest in
أكيد	**akíid**	certain
انطلاقة	**inTiláaqah**	eminence, brightness
قوة، ات	**qúwwah, -áat**	force, power, strength

> **LANGUAGE TIP**
>
> **ibnah** is used for *daughter* in isolation. If you say *daughter of Rashid*, the form is **bint**,
>
> which also means *girl*.

14.02 *Read the magazine article about actress Salma Hayek, looking carefully through the new vocabulary.*

1 What was Salma Hayek the first Arab woman to do?

هوليوود

في الشرق نعتبرها سفيرة الجمال العربي التي استطاعت ان تكون أول امرأة تخترق أسوار هوليوود وتفرض نفسها على أعلى قائمة نجمات السينما.

وفي الغرب يعتبرونها رمزا لسحر الشرق بما تحمله من ملامح شرقية غاية في الجمال الذي يناظر السحر. ولهذا أعطوها البطولات في أكبر أفلامهم مفضلينها على أكثر نجمات هوليوود جمالا.

وإذا سلمى الحايك اليوم تزاحم أنجلينا جولي وبينيلوبي كروز وغيرهما من نجمات هوليوود.

وسلمى الحايك، أو أسطورة الشرق في الغرب، المولودة سنة ١٩٦٦، هي ابنة مهاجر لبناني مقيم بالمكسيك ووالدتها اسبانية الأصل.

وإذا اجتمع الجمال اللبناني والاسباني تكون الثمرة في حلاوة سلمى الحايك. ولأنها جميلة جدا فقد رصدتها عين المنتجين وهي في الثالثة عشر من عمرها واختيرت وقتها كأجمل الوجوه التلفزيونية.

ثم أخذها المنتج تارانتينو إلى لوس أنجليس لتشترك في الفيلم «ديسبيرادو» الى جانب أنطونيو بانديراس وأعطت للفيلم مذاقا خاصا جدا جلب لها اهتمام شركات الإنتاج الكبرى وقدموا لها العقود الكثيرة.

ومنذ ذلك الحين لعبت دور البطولة في العديد من الأفلام مثل «فريد» والآن أصبحت تنتج أفلاما.

NOTES

an takuun. Although no verb *to be* is used in simple statements equating to *is/are*, certain conjunctions, including أنّ *that*, require the present subjunctive after them.

bi-maa is a common conjunction, usually translated as *for, in that, as, because*.

ghayr-humaa lit., *and other than them-two*. The dual suffix is used because two people (Jolie and Cruz) have been named.

takuun *will/would be*. When the present tense of **kaana** is used, it implies future or uncertainty instead of straight fact.

fa-qad. This is **fa-** *so* with the past marker **qad** (see Unit 8)

2 Answer the questions.

    a What aspect of her beauty appeals particularly to the West? _____

    b Which stars does she compete with in Hollywood? _____

    c When was she born? _____

    d Where does her mother come from originally? _____

    e How old was she when she was spotted by producers? _____

    f What film did she work in with Quentin Tarantino? _____

    g How has her career progressed recently? _____

3 Match the English phrases with the Arabic expressions:

a the first woman	١ أكثر نجمات هوليوود جمالا
b the leads in their greatest films	٢ أول امرأة
c most of the stars of Hollywood in terms of beauty	٣ أجمل الوجوه التلفزيونية
d the most beautiful television personality	٤ البطولات في أكبر أفلامهم

> **LANGUAGE TIP**
>
> أول امرأة *the first woman*. أول *first* is treated in Arabic as a superlative adjective. امرأة *woman* is an irregular noun:
>
> ▶ When it has the definite article, it drops both the initial **alif** (المرأة) and the vowel after the **r** and is pronounced **al-mar'ah**.
>
> ▶ It has the phonetically-unrelated plural **nisaa'**, also with the variant **niswaan** (نساء، نسوان).

Language discovery

1 COMPARATIVES AND SUPERLATIVES

Forming comparatives

Because they involve internal changes, true comparatives in Arabic can only be formed from simple adjectives with three root consonants, often plus a long vowel (usually **aa**, **ii**, e.g. **waasi:**, **kabiir**). The comparative of such adjectives can be constructed taking the following steps:

a Identify the three root consonants, e.g.: **kabiir → k-b-r**

b Prefix an **alif** (pronounced **a**) and re-vowel the root letters as follows:

1st radical – no vowel

2nd radical – an **a**-vowel.

e.g. كبير ← radicals ← أكبر ك–ب–ر **akbar**

> **LANGUAGE TIP**
>
> Although it is not always written, the prefixed **alif** technically has a **hamzah** on it (أ), so the **a** vowel is never elided.

This form does not change and is used for all genders and numbers.

الآن دورك al-'aan dawrak

Write the comparative and superlative adjectives, then translate the sentences:

١ محمد هو [طويل] من صالح _____

٢ إنه الامتحان [صعب] _____

٣ وكانت [أول] امرأة تطير طائرة إيرباص _____

٤ إنها [جميل] مدينة _____

The word for *than* is من **min**:

الفيل أكبر من الفأر   *The elephant is bigger than the mouse.*

Look at these common adjectives and their comparatives:

طويل *tall*		أطول *taller*	
قصير *short*		أقصر *shorter*	
كبير *big*		أكبر *bigger/older (humans)*	
صغير *small*		أصغر *smaller/younger (humans)*	
قديم *old*		أقدم *older (things)*	
رخيص *cheap*		أرخص *cheaper*	
جميل *beautiful*		أجمل *more beautiful*	

طـارق سليم

أمي   اختي

سليم أطول من طارق

اختي اقصر من أمي

Salim is taller than Tariq.

My sister is shorter than my mother.

PRONUNCIATION NOTES

▶ If the adjective has the same second and third root letters, the **a**-vowel is shifted back from the second radical to the first and the second and third radicals are written as one (technically with the doubling sign **shaddah**, but this is usually omitted):

شديد *strong, violent* ➔ radicals ش–د–د ➔ أشد **ashadd**

هام *important* ➔ radicals هـ–م–م ➔ أهم **ahamm**

▶ If it ends in one of the weak letters و or ي, this becomes a long **aa** (written ى) in the comparative:

حلو *sweet, beautiful* ➔ radicals ح–ل–و ➔ أحلى **aHlaa**

الغالي ** *expensive* ➔ radicals غ–ل–ي ➔ أغلى **aghlaa**

> **LANGUAGE TIP**
>
> ** given here with the definite article, as indefinites of this type have an irregular spelling (see Unit 16)

▶ For polysyllabic words that cannot conform to the above system, Arabic uses أكثر *more* and أقل *less* followed by an adverbial accusative, ending in a marked or unmarked **-an**.

Forming superlatives

Superlatives are formed in exactly the same way as comparatives, but take different sentence structures. All of the following examples are taken from the article above.

1 Superlative + indefinite singular noun (technically in the genitive)

أول امرأة   *the first woman*

First is regarded as a superlative.

2 Superlative + definite plural noun

أجمل الوجوه التلفزيونية   *the most beautiful television personality*

This equates with the English parallel *the most beautiful of (the) television personalities*.

3 Definite noun + definite superlative

شركات الإنتاج الكبرى   *the biggest production companies*

In the last example, the first word شركات is definite because it is the first term in a possessive (see Unit 6).

This is actually more of an intensive than a superlative, probably better translated as *the great production companies*.

A few common adjectives have a feminine form when required by agreement (here for a neuter plural). This is derived from the three root letters and vowelled and spelled as in كبرى. This is the least common of the three constructions, but is often encountered in set phrases, e.g.:

الشرق الأوسط   *the Middle East* (m.)

بريطانيا العظمى   *Great Britain* (f., from عظيم *mighty*)

Note also that أول *first* functions exactly as a superlative. When used after the noun, as in construction 3, it takes the feminine form أولى, e.g. أول مرة but المرة الأولى *(for) the first time*.

> **LANGUAGE TIP**
>
> Note that none of these comparatives or superlatives takes the **alif** accusative marker.

2 THE ADVERBIAL ACCUSATIVE

The adverbial accusative is often associated with the comparative or superlative, and there are several examples in the article above. We will look at adverbs themselves in more detail in Unit 15.

Use of the adverbial accusative

The adverbial accusative tells us to what respect or characteristic the comparative refers. In English we might say:

He is better off than me in terms of/as regards possessions, but he is worse off for money.

Modern colloquial English often uses the suffix -*wise*:

She has done less well career-wise, but her personal life is more satisfying.

Formation

The adverbial accusative is always indefinite and is formed from a noun or adjective with the ending **-an** (marked by an **alif** on most masculines; unmarked in the feminine). This ending is usually pronounced, even in informal spoken Arabic.

Therefore, you need only remember to put in the **alif** when required. Examples from the passage are:

أكثر نجمات هوليوود جمالا   lit. *the greatest of the Hollywood stars in terms of beauty*
(marked accusative جمالا)

انطلاقة أكثر قوة وانتشارا   *prominence greater in terms of strength and popularity*
(unmarked قوة, marked انتشارا)

This construction is frequently used with the two words أكثر *more* and أقل *less* to form comparatives and superlatives where the adjective is too long or complex to use the direct formation. In this case, the equivalent noun of the adjective is used. This takes experience, but here are two examples:

▶ The adjective مجتهد *hard-working* has far too many letters to form a direct comparative. The equivalent noun is اجتهاد *diligence*. Adding the accusative ending, we get:

أكثر اجتهادا   *more hard-working* (lit. *more in terms of diligence*)

▶ The adjective مفيد *beneficial* comes from the noun إفادة *benefit*:

أقل إفادة   *less beneficial, of less benefit*

Here the noun has a feminine ending, so there is no **alif**.

3 CONJUNCTIONS

Conjunctions join parts of sentences, explaining the relationship of one part to another. Common examples are *and* expressing a direct link and *or*, which expresses an alternative. These are used in much the same way as their English equivalents. Others express a more complex link, for instance, purpose, reason and so on.

These last few conjunctions fall into two distinct categories in Arabic, depending on the type of word that comes after them. Here are some examples of the most commonly encountered conjunctions from the interview above:

Conjunctions followed by verbs

أن *that*. The verb following is usually in the present subjunctive (see Verb tables):

استطاعت أن تكون أول امرأة

(lit. *she was able that she be…*)   she was able to be the first woman…

كان من المفترض أن يسند لمغنية شهيرة

(lit. *…was of the supposed that it*   *…should have been entrusted to a*

   be entrusted)   *famous singer*

لـ *to, in order that*. The verb following is always in the subjunctive:

لتشترك في الفيلم   *(in order) to take part in the film*

> **LANGUAGE TIP**
>
> Note that this لـ should be distinguished from the identical word meaning *to*, for use with nouns, which is a preposition, not a conjunction.

Conjunctions followed by nouns or pronouns

These are technically in the accusative.

أن *that*:

ومن الأكيد أن هذا الفيلم   *and it is certain that this film…*

(followed by a noun with the demonstrative pronoun)

لأن *because*:

ولأنها جميلة جدا   *and because she is very beautiful*

(followed by the suffix – i.e. accusative – pronoun)

ولكن، لكن *but* (no difference in meaning):

ولكن منتجي هوليوود…   *but the Hollywood producers…*

(lit. *producers of Hollywood*) showing accusative masculine plural noun with final **nuun** dropped (see Unit 13)

> **LANGUAGE TIP**
>
> Although not really a conjunction, the slightly emphatic particle إِنَّ also belongs to this category (see Unit 8).

Word discovery

14.03 The word pattern for this unit is C¹aC²aaC³iiC⁴*, for example, **maqaadíir** مقادير *quantities*, which sounds like the English *magazine* (accent on last syllable).

مقدار **miqdaar** *amount, quantity* ➔ مقادير **maqaadiir***

This is another internal plural shape. This one derives from singulars that have four consonants, with a long vowel between the third and the fourth. The accent is always on the last syllable. Presence of the feminine suffix ة **-ah** makes no difference.

This is a pretty safe bet for any such word, but there are a few exceptions. These plurals do not take the accusative marker. In the reading for this unit we have:

أسطورة، أساطير **usTuurah, asaaTiir*** *legend* (the **hamzah** counts as a radical)

Here are some other examples. Watch for the long vowels (any of them) between the third and the fourth radicals:

مفتاح **miftaaH** *key* ➔ مفاتيح **mafaatiiH***

منديل **mandiil** *handkerchief* ➔ مناديل **manaadiil***

عصفور :**uSfuur** *sparrow, small bird* ➔ عصافير :**aSaafiir***

⋮ الآن دورك **al-'aan dawrak**

⋮ **How would you transform the word صندوق** *box, chest*?

There are not many exceptions to this rule. Some adjectives take the ـون -uun ending, and note the following nouns:

أستاذ، أساتذة	**ustaadh, asaatidhah**	*professor*
تلميذ، تلامذة	**tilmiidh, talaamidhah**	*pupil* (but also تلاميذ **talaamiidh**)

Practice

ربح	**rábaHa** [S-I a]	*win, gain, profit*
فاضل	**fáaDil**	*favourable, good*
عرض، عروض	**:arD, :urúuD**	*offer, deal*
زبون، زبائن	**zabúun, zabáa'in***	*customer, client*
نقد، نقود	**naqd, nuqúud**	*cash, money*
مكان، أمكنة	**makáan, ámkinah**	*place*
حسم	**Hasm**	*discount*
امتياز	**imtiyáaz**	*distinction, privilege*

1 The following adverts all offer bargains to the shopper. Look at the ads and answer the questions about each one.

a

b

What do you have to do to win a prize?   How long has the Co-op been serving its customers?

c

What do you get free if you buy the oil?

d

What are the two main prizes to be won?

e

What does Western Union promise you?

f

How do you obtain the discount offered at Bou Khalil?

حسن	good
رخيص	cheap
سريع	fast
شاشة	screen
نظام التشغيل	operating system
ذاكرة	memory
قرص ثابت	hard disk

2 You are thinking of buying a laptop, and have narrowed the choice down to two possibilities. Look at the two specifications.

B

A

شاشة ١٣ بوصة

مشغل القرص الثابت ٢٥٠ غيغابيت

نظام التشغيل :DOS

ذاكرة وصول عشوائي ٤ غيغابيت

٢٥٩٩ درهم

شاشة ١٥ بوصة

مشغل القرص الثابت ٥٠٠ غيغابيت

نظام التشغيل :Windows 10

ذاكرة وصول عشوائي ٨ غيغابيت

٣٨٤٩ درهم

Select appropriate adjectives from the specifications, changing them to the comparative form, to complete the sentences.

١ هذا الكمبيوتر له شاشة ــــــــ.

٢ له ذاكرة ــــــــ.

٣ له قرص ثابت ــــــــ.

٤ هو ــــــــ استعمالا.

٥ هو ــــــــ.

Test yourself

1 Match the Arabic sentences with their English equivalents.

١ محمود أطول من ناصر   **a** She is the most beautiful woman in Hollywood.

٢ هذه هي المشكلة الأصعب   **b** Mahmoud is taller than Nasir.

٣ هل شاهدت البرنامج الأول؟   **c** Did you see the first programme?

٤ هي أجمل امرأة في هوليوود   **d** This is the hardest problem.

2 Translate into English.

١ هي سافرت إلى فرنسا لتشترك في الفيلم. _____

٢ ولد في حلب. _____

٣ انهم ذاهبون الى مهرجان دبي السينمائي الشهر المقبل. _____

٤ مهرجان هذا العام هو أفضل من مهرجان العام الماضي. _____

٥ كم هو الحسم؟ _____

SELF CHECK

	I CAN...
○	...make comparisons.
○	...give biographical information.
○	...talk about the film industry.
○	...say how things are done.
○	...talk about shopping.

15 صفحة الرياضة
SafHat ar-riyaaDah
Sports page

In this unit you will learn how to:
▶ *discuss sports and leisure activities*
▶ *talk about clothing*
▶ *talk about colours*
▶ *describe how or when you have done something.*

CEFR: (B1) *Can describe plans, arrangements, habits and routines, past activities and personal experiences; can write a description of an event – real or imaginary.*

Foreign loan words in Arabic

Some of the sports mentioned in this unit are transliterations into Arabic of English terms. If these contain the letter **g**, which Arabic does not have, various spellings arise. جولف *golf* is written with a ج. Most Egyptians pronounce ج as a hard **g** and this spelling is fairly general. However, in بولينغ *bowling* we have a spelling with the nearest Arabic sound غ **gh**.

There are, unfortunately, no hard and fast rules. It seems to be down to the whim of the writer. In fact, you often even see the same word spelled in two different ways (ج and غ) in the same document. More rarely, ق is used, as this is pronounced hard **g** in the spoken dialects of many Arab countries, including nearly the whole of the Arabian Peninsula.

The other (main) letters which Arabic lacks, **p** and **v**, are usually transcribed as ب **b** and ف **f**, respectively. Occasionally you will see the adopted Persian letters پ **p** and ڤ **v** with three dots, but this is not very common. Foreign words in Arabic often have a liberal sprinkling of long vowels, as their word shapes do not conform to the usual guidelines.

What are these loan words?

e رجبي   **d** سينما   **c** راديو   **b** سندويتش   **a** باص

Vocabulary builder

15.01 Listen to the new expressions and repeat them until you can say them with confidence. Listen again and complete the gaps.

SPORT

كرة، ـات	kúrah, -áat	*ball*
فريق، فِرق	faríiq, fíraq	*team*
متفرج، ـون	mutafárrij, -úun	*spectator*
فوز	fawz	*victory*
هدف، أهداف	hádaf, ahdáaf	*goal, target, aim*
مباراة، مباريات	mubáaraah, mubaarayáat	*match*
مسابقة، ـات	musáabaqah, -áat	*competition*
كأس، كؤوس	ka's, ku'úus	*cup, trophy*
لاعب، ـون	láa:ib, -úun	*player*
لاعب وسط	láa:ib wasT	*midfield player (football)*
تسديدة، ـات	tasdíidah, -áat	*shot (football)*
تسجيل	tasjíil	*registration, scoring*
منطقة، مناطق	mínTaqah, manáaTiq*	*area (football: penalty area)*
حارس، حراس	Háaris, Hurráas	*guard (football: goalkeeper)*
نتيجة، نتائج	natíijah, natáa'ij*	*result, outcome*
ركن، أركان	rukn, arkáan	*corner*
مرمى	mármaa	*goal, goalmouth*
تعادل	ta:áadul	*balance, equality (football: draw, equal score)*
حكم، حكام	Hákam, Hukkáam	*referee, umpire*
ركلة، ـات	ráklah, -áat	*kick*
شبكة، شباك	shábaka, shibáak	*net, netting*
مدافع، ـون	mudáafi:, -úun	*defender*
شوط، أشواط	shawT, ashwáaT	*half (football), heat (athletics, etc.), race*
سجل	sájjala [S-II]	*score, register*
طرد	Tárada [S-I u]	*banish, drive away (football: send off)*
سدد	sáddada [S-II]	*aim (football: shoot)*

> **LANGUAGE TIP**
>
> كرة، ـات **kúrah, -áat** is also used as a shortened form of كرة القدم **kúrat al-qádam** *football*.

USEFUL PHRASES

السيارة الحمراء	as-sayyaarah l-Hamraa'	the _____ car
قميص أزرق	qamiiS azraq	a _____ shirt
زهرة صفراء	zahrah Safraa'	a yellow flower
الجبل الأخضر	al-jabal al-akhDar	the green mountain

Reading

al-laylah s-sawdaa' الليلة السوداء *THE BLACK NIGHT*

ليلة، ــات، ليال	**láyla, -áat, layáalin**	night
أسود، سوداء	**áswad*, f. sawdáa'***	black
مغربي، مغاربة	**mághribii, magháaribah**	Moroccan
تأهل	**ta'áhhala** [S-V]	qualify (لـ li- for)
نهائي	**niháa'ii**	final
قاد	**qáada** [Mw-I]	lead
وحده	**wáHd-uh**	himself
انتهى	**intáhaa** [Ly-VIII]	come to an end, finish
افتتح	**iftátaHa** [S-VIII]	commence, open
عن طريق	**:an Taríiq**	by way of
رائع	**ráa'i:**	splendid, brilliant, marvellous
خدع	**kháda:a** [S-I a]	deceive
فرصة، فرص	**fúrSah, fúraS**	chance, opportunity
وحيد	**waHíid**	sole, only, singular
عندما	**:índamaa**	when
قوسي	**qáwsii**	curved, bowed
دخل	**dákhala** [S-I u]	enter
أدرك	**ádraka** [S-IV]	attain, achieve
بدا	**bádaa** [Lw-I]	appear, seem, show
رفع	**rafa:(a)** [S1 a]	raise, hoist
راية، ــات	**ráayah, -áat**	flag, banner
أبيض، بيضاء	**ábyaD*, f. bayDáa'***	white
سيطر على	**sáyTara :álaa** [Q-I]	dominate
سيطرة	**sáyTarah**	domination
تام	**taamm**	complete
سرعة	**súr:ah**	speed

أودع	**áwda:a** [Fw-IV]	*place*
مرة، ـات	**márrah, -áat**	*time, occasion*
احتسب	**iHtásaba** [S-VIII]	*award, grant*
ركني	**rúknii**	*corner* (adj.)
أصفر، صفراء	**áSfar*, f. Safráa'***	*yellow*

> **LANGUAGE TIP**
>
> بعد ما **ba:d maa** *after*. When **ba:d**, **qabl** *before* and certain other words relating to time are followed by a verb, it is necessary to interpose this (meaningless) **maa**.

 15.02 *Listen to this report of a football match between Morocco and Tunisia.*

1 For which side is it a black night?

ليلة سوداء للكرة المغربية

تأهل الفريق التونسي للدور النهائي من مسابقة كأس العرب لكرة القدم في ليلة سوداء للكرة المغربية. وعلى ملعب الزمالك في القاهرة أمس، وأمام ٤٢ ألف متفرج قاد محمود التركي الفريق التونسي إلى الفوز. وسجل التركي شخصيا ثلاثة أهداف في المباراة التي انتهت ٥_١.

وافتتح الفريق التونسي التسجيل عن طريق لاعب وسطه جعفر أبو عادل بتسديدة رائعة من خارج المنطقة خدعت الحارس المغربي في الدقيقة التاسعة من المباراة. وكانت نتيجة الفرصة الأولى للفريق المغربي هدفهم الوحيد في آخر الشوط الأول عندما سدد طارق الأحمر كرة قوسية دخلت ركن المرمى التونسي وأدرك التعادل.

ولكنه بدا أن اللاعبين المغاربة قد رفعوا الراية البيضاء في الشوط الثاني وسيطر التونسيون على اللعب سيطرة كاملة. وجاءت الأهداف بسرعة فظيعة، آخرها في الدقيقة الأخيرة من المباراة عندما أودع القائد التونسي الكرة في الشبكة المغربية للمرة الثالثة بعد ما احتسب الحكم ركلة ركنية وطرد المدافع المغربي سليمان الفاسي لنيله البطاقة الصفراء الثانية.

2 Answer the questions.

a Which round of the competition is it?

  1 the first   **2** the fourth   **3** the final

b Where did the match take place?

c How many spectators were there?

3 Listen to the audio again and answer these questions.

a By how many goals did Tunisia win?

b Which side scored first?

c Who scored at the end of the first half?

4 Listen to the audio one more time.

a When was the last goal scored?

b What happened to Suleiman al-Fasi?

c Which team was he playing for?

> **LANGUAGE TIP**
>
> نيل *getting, receiving, obtaining* here is a verbal noun, and the phrase لنيل can be paraphrased *because of his getting, for getting*. This type of construction is quite common in Arabic.

5 Match the English phrases with the Arabic expressions.

a a black night for Moroccan football	١	اللاعبين المغاربة قد رفعوا الراية البيضاء
b al-Turki himself scored three goals	٢	للمرة الثالثة
c the Moroccan players raised the white flag	٣	لنيله البطاقة الصفراء الثانية
d for the third time	٤	ليلة سوداء للكرة المغربية
e the referee awarded a corner kick	٥	احتسب الحكم ركلة ركنية
f for getting his second yellow card	٦	سجل التركي وحده ثلاثة أهداف

> **LANGUAGE TIP**
>
> **akhiir** and **aakhir** both mean *last*, but they are used differently:
>
> **akhiir** is a normal adjective coming after the noun:
>
> الفصل الأخير   **al-fasl al-akhiir**   *the last section*
>
> **aakhir** is a noun meaning *the last part of something* and is usually used as the first term of a possessive construction:
>
> آخرها   **aakhir-haa**   *the last of them (i.e. the goals)*

Language discovery

1 IRREGULAR ADJECTIVES

As you learned in Unit 3, most Arabic adjectives form their feminine by adding ة -ah to the masculine form.

There is an important set of adjectives that behave differently. The most common of these refer to the basic colours, and some physical disabilities.

These adjectives have three forms:

▶ Masculine singular

Identical in all respects to the comparative adjective (see Unit 14) and following the same rules regarding doubled and weak radicals.

Does not take the **alif** accusative marker.

▶ Feminine singular

The first radical takes an **a** vowel, the second no vowel and the suffix ء‍ا -aa' is added after the third radical.

Again this does not take the accusative marker.

▶ Plural form

Used only when referring to several human beings. The first radical takes **u-** and the second no vowel.

This form does take the accusative marker when required.

English	Masculine	Feminine	Plural
black	أسود aswad	سوداء sawdaa'	سود suud
white	أبيض abyaD	بيضاء bayDaa'	بيض biiD[1]
red	أحمر aHmar	حمراء Hamraa'	حمر Humr
green	أخضر akhDar	خضراء khaDraa'	خضر khuDr
yellow	أصفر aSfar	صفراء Safraa'	صفر Sufr
blue	أزرق azraq	زرقاء zarqaa'	زرق zurq
lame	أعرج a:raj	عرجاء :arjaa'	عرج :urj
blind	أعمى a:maa[2]	عمياء :amyaa'	عميان :umyaan[3]

216

[1] Arabic will not accept the combination **uy** so the vowel changes to **ii**.

[2] Root ends with ى (See rules for comparatives in Unit 14.)

[3] An alternative form, usually used with this adjective.

2 OTHER COLOURS

The above rules apply only to what Arabic regards as the basic colours. Other colours are formed from nouns with the adjectival ending ـي **-ii** (see Unit 11) and behave normally:

Noun	Adjective
برتقال **burtuqaal** *orange*	برتقالي *orange*
بن **bunn** *coffee beans*	بني *brown*
بنفسج **banafsaj** *violet*	بنفسجي *violet*
ورد **ward** *roses*	وردي *pink*

Examples from the reading are:

ليلة سوداء	*a black night*
الراية البيضاء	*the white flag*
البطاقة الصفراء	*the yellow card*
طارق الأحمر	*Taariq al-aHmar (here used as a proper name)*

الآن دورك al-'aan dawrak
How do you say *the red card* and *the blue team*?

3 ADVERBS

Adverbs describe how, when or where the action of a verb is performed. In both English and Arabic, there are two ways to form them.

Accusative marker

In English, we add the suffix *-ly* to the adjective: *She sings beautiful<u>ly</u>*. The Arabic equivalent of this is to add the accusative marker to an adjective or sometimes a noun. This is written with an **alif** unless the word has the feminine ending and is always pronounced **-an**. Such common words as *very, always, never* are also formed in this way.

So we have شخصيا *personally*, from شخصي *personal*, which is itself derived from شخص *person*.

Here are some other common examples:

From adjectives	From nouns
كثيرا *frequently, a lot, often*	عادة *usually*
نادرا *rarely*	فجأة *suddenly*
قريبا *promptly, soon*	صدفة *by chance, fortuitously*
سريعا *quickly*	أبدا *never*
يوميا *daily*	أحيانا *sometimes*
شهريا *monthly*	فورا *immediately*
أولا *first*	مباشرة *directly*
	حقا *really, truly, in fact*

(also the other ordinal numerals:)

ثانيا	*second*
ثالثا	*third*, etc.
أخيرا	*lastly, at last*
دائما	*always*
رسميا	*officially*

Prepositional

The second way to form adverbs in English is to use a preposition (usually *with*, *in* or *by*) plus a noun: *I am writing this in haste*.

The same applies to Arabic, the usual preposition being **bi-**: بالضبط **bi-DH-DHabT** *with exactness, exactly*.

In Arabic, as in English, both methods can be used, often with a slight change in meaning – *hastily/in haste*. سريعا *quickly* can also be expressed as بسرعة *with speed*.

Common examples of this type are:

ببطء	*slowly*
بجد	*seriously*
بوضوح	*clearly*

Verbal nouns

A common adverbial construction in Arabic is verb + its verbal noun (accusative) + an adjective (also accusative) qualifying the verbal noun.

There is one example in the reading:

سيطر التونسيون على اللعب سيطرة تامة   *The Tunisians dominated the play completely*

(lit. *a complete domination*).

Word discovery

15.03 The word pattern for this unit is C¹aC²C³aC⁴ah, for example, بربرة *barbarism*, which sounds like the English *Barbara*.

This is the verbal noun shape from QI-verbs (see Verb tables).

1 You met one example in the reading. What is it?

Here are a few more examples:

ترجم Q-I ← ترجمة	*translating, translation*
فلسف Q-I ← فلسفة	*philosophizing, philosophy*
زلزل Q-I ← زلزلة	*quaking, earthquake* (also sometimes زلزال)
تلفز Q-I ← تلفزة	*televizing, television*

الآن دورك al-'aan dawrak

2 Give the correct Arabic words.

هندس Q-I ← _____ *engineering, engineering*

سيطر Q-I ← _____ *controlling, control*

Practice

ثلج	**thalj**	*ice*
زورق، زوارق	**záwraq, zawáariq***	*boat*

1 Match these sports with the pictures.

٧	التزلج على الثلج	————		١	ايروبيك	————
٨	بولينغ	————		٢	تنس الطاولة	————
٩	الغوص بالسكوبا	————		٣	كرة الطائرة	————
١٠	صيد السمك	————		٤	كرة القدم	————
١١	التزلج على الماء	————		٥	جولف	————
١٢	الزوارق الشراعية	————		٦	باليه	————

2 Complete the sentences with an adverb from the box. You may only use each adverb once.

جدا	مباشرة	بهدوء	بسرعة	فجأة	صدفة

١ افتح الباب ———— عندنا ضيف.

٢ ذهبت إلى السوق وقابلت أحمد هناك ————.

٣ كان ذلك البرنامج مهما ————.

٤ كنا جالسين في البيت، وقام زيد ———— وخرج.

٥ تسافر هذه الطائرة إلى الرياض ————.

٦ يا أولاد، العبوا ————، الوالد نائم.

3 **You are shopping for clothes with some Arabic-speaking friends. How would you say what they are looking for? Make up complete sentences like this one, using the vocabulary given:**

Yunis – blue coat   →   يحتاج يونس إلى معطف أزرق

- **٥** Faridah – red trousers _____
- **١** Ali – black boots _____
- **٦** Hamed – brown belt _____
- **٢** Sonia – yellow dress _____
- **٧** Anisa – pink handbag _____
- **٣** Saeed – green shirt _____
- **٤** Khalid – white socks _____

حزام   قميص   جوارب

معطف   جزمة   بنطلون   حقيبة   فستان

Reading

نادي، أندية	naadii, andiyah	club (social)
فتاة، فتيات	fataah, fatayaat	young woman
عضوية	:uDuwiyyah	membership
كافة	kaafat	all
أما	ammaa	as for, with regard to
ذكور	dhukuur	males
فقط	faqaT	only

فرديٍ	fardii	single
سنوياا	sanawiyyan	annually
عائلي	:aa'ilii	family (adj.)
يومي	yawmii	daily
كبار	kibaar	adults
تسهيل ـات	tas-hiil, -aat	facilities
حجرة الألعاب الرياضية	Hujrat al-al:aab ar-riyaaDiyyah	sports/games room
منتجع الصحة	muntaja: aS-SiHHah	fitness centre
قاعة التزلج	qaa:at at-tazalluj	ice rink
مركز الفن	markaz al-fann	art/craft centre
ملاعب التنس	malaa:ib at-tanis	tennis courts
استخدام	istikhdaam	use (noun)
عضوة ـات	:uDuwwah, -aat	(female) member
طوال اليوم	Tiwaal al-yawm	all day
الجنسيات	al-jinsiyyaat	(the) nationalities

Read the prospectus for this women's club and answer the questions.

نادي الفتيات

العضوية في النادي مفتوحة لكافة جنسيات السيدات والأطفال.

(البنات من جميع الأعمار أما الأولاد الذكور حتى ١٠ سنوات فقط)

عضوية نادي الفتيات:

عضوية فردية .... ٧٢٠٠ درهم سنويا
عضوية عائلية (الأم + ٣ أبناء) .... ٧٣٠٠ درهم سنويا
عضوية المكتبة .... ٦٢٠ درهم شهريا

عضوية يومية للزوار

الكبار (أكثر من ١٣ سنة)................................ ٥٠ درهم

الصغار (حتى ١٢ سنة)................................ ٢٠ درهم

تسهيلات النادي:

- حجرة الألعاب الرياضية
- سونا
- الأيروبيك*
- المسبح*
- المكتبة*

- منتجع الصحة*
- قاعة التزلج*
- كافتريا*
- مركز الفن
- ملاعب التنس

* الاستخدام للعضوات مجانا

النادي مفتوح طوال اليوم من الساعة ٩ صباحا حتى الساعة ١٠ مساء.

a How much does annual membership cost? _____

b Up to how many children may accompany a mother for free? _____

c Until what age are boys allowed to accompany their mothers? _____

d The club is open from:

    1 9 a.m.   **2** 10 a.m.

e The club closes at:

    1 9 p.m.   **2** 10 p.m.

f How much does monthly membership of the library cost? _____

g Name three facilities which are free for members. _____

Listen and understand

مارس	**máarasa** [S-III]	*practise, carry out, perform*
سؤال		*question*
جواب		*answer*

15.04 Listen to five people talking about how often they take part in sporting activities. Who likes to do what and how often? The first one has been done for you.

سؤال   ماذا تحب من الرياضات؟
جواب   ألعب كرة القدم كثيرا

	Daily	Frequently	Sometimes	Rarely	Never
Example		football			
1					
2					
3					
4					
5					

Test yourself

1 Match the English sentences with the Arabic.

a Taha Hussein, the famous writer, was blind. _____

b The visitor centre is open all day. _____

c Randa plays tennis daily. _____

d Algeria has lots of earthquakes. _____

e Riyad Mahrez scored three goals himself. _____

f Ayman needs white boots. _____

١ سجل رياض محرز وحده ثلاثة أهداف.
٢ كان طه حسين الكاتب الشهير أعمى.
٣ الجزائر لديها زلازل كثيرة.
٤ مركز الزوار مفتوح طوال اليوم.
٥ رندة تلعب التنس يوميا.
٦ يحتاج أيمن إلى جزمة بيضاء.

2 Find the odd one out (and say why).

a 1 متفرجٍ 2 حكم 3 لاعب 4 كأس   _____

b 1 سنوياً 2 بجد 3 يومي 4 شهرياً   _____

c 1 زورق 2 فستان 3 حزام 4 جوارب   _____

d 1 دخل 2 سجل 3 ترجم 4 قاد   _____

SELF CHECK

I CAN. . .
○ . . . discuss sports and leisure activities.
○ . . . talk about colours.
○ . . . talk about clothing.
○ . . . describe how or when you have done something.

16 من كل بلد خبر
min kull balad khabar

News from every country

In this unit you will learn how to:
▶ *say* each, every, all *and* some
▶ *use some irregular nouns and adjectives*
▶ *recognize some common Arabic loan words*
▶ *talk about the media.*

CEFR: (B1) *Can describe experiences and events, dreams, hopes and ambitions and briefly give reasons and explanations for opinions and plans; can identify the main conclusions in clearly signalled argumentative texts.*

Arabic loan words

From their historical role as merchants, traders and travellers to that of modern broadcasters of news and media programmes via satellite channels, Arabs have long been at the centre of the international cultural crossroads. It is hardly surprising then that quite a few Arabic words have entered the English language, often via Spanish and French (the Arabs ruled most of Spain for about 500 years).

Magazine – originally in the military sense – is one of them. It comes from مخازن, plural of مخزن storehouse. Here are a few others: *calibre* derives from قالب mould (for bullets); *algorithm* derives from the name of a famous Arab philosopher الخوارزمي al-khawaarizmii; *algebra* is from Arabic الجبر; both *zero* and *cipher* ultimately derive from صفر zero, the concept of which the Arabs passed to the West; more subtle is *arsenal* from دار الصناعة; *admiral* from أمير البحر (with the last word omitted); *mattress* comes from مطرح, a large cushion or rug for lying on – this has evolved out of the sense something thrown down from the Arabic root طرح to throw; and *adobe* comes from الطوب meaning a brick.

What English words come from the following?

١ غزال   ٢ ليمون   ٣ سكّر

Vocabulary builder

16.01 Listen to the new expressions and repeat them until you can say them with confidence. Listen again and complete the gaps.

HISTORY

أثر، آثار	áthar, aatháar	(sing.) *track, trace*, (pl. also) *archaeological remains, antiquities*
أبو الهول	abuu l-hawl	*the Sphinx* (lit., 'Father of Terror')
قطعة، قطع	qiT:ah, qiTa:	*piece*
حجر، أحجار	Hájar, aHjáar	*stone*
قرن، قرون	qarn, qurúun	*century*
أثري	átharii	*archaeological*
موجود	mawjúud	*found, situated, existing*
تاريخي	taaríikhii	*historical; historic*

PLACES

الخارج	al-kháarij	*abroad, the outside*
أمة، أمم	úmmah, úmam	*nation*
اليمن	al-yáman	_____
رشيد	rashíid	*Rosetta (a town in Egypt); Rashid (a man's name)*
عدن	:ádan	*Aden*
ميناء، المواني	miináa', al-mawáanii (sometimes f.)	*harbour, port*
ولاية، ـات	wiláayah, -aat	*administrative division of a country, here: state*
مكان، أمكنة	makáan, amkínah	*place*
أبو ظبي	abuu Dhábi	_____

PEOPLE

سائح، سواح	sáa'iH, suwwáaH	*tourist*
مليونير	malyoonáyr	_____
فتاة، فتيات	fatáah, fatayáat	*girl, young woman*
مطربة، ـات	múTribah, -aat	*(female) singer, musician*
شاعر، شعراء	sháa:ir, shu:aráa'*	*poet*
أوروبي، ـون	urúubii	_____
ألماني	almáanii	*German (adjective)*
عراقي	:iráaqii	*Iraqi (adjective)*

USEFUL PHRASES

كل عام وأنت بخير	kull :aam wa-anta/anti bi-kahyr	*Happy Birthday/Eid, etc.*
خلال	khaláal	*during*

Reading 1

EGYPT مصر

أعرب عن	á:raba :an [S-IV]	*state, express (requires the preposition* عن*)*
ترحيب	tarHíib	*welcome; welcoming*
قرار، ـات	qaráar, -áat	*decision, resolution*
جمعية، ـات	jam:íyyah, -áat	*group, assembly, society*
عمومي	:umúumii	*general*
متحد	muttáHid	*united*
سماح	samáaH	*permission (requires bi-)*
مهرب	muhárrab	*smuggled*
استرداد	istirdáad	*getting back, reclaiming*
مسروق	masrúuq	*stolen*
أشهر	ásh-har	*more/most famous*
ذقن، ذقون	dhaqn, dhuqúun (f.)	*beard*

> **LANGUAGE TIP**
>
> أشهر is the comparative/superlative of مشهور. This is an irregular formation, actually taken from another word. (See Unit 14.)

 16.02 *Listen to the recording about Egypt.*

1 What has been smuggled abroad?

الآثار المصرية في الخارج

أعرب رئيس دائرة الآثار المصرية أمس عن ترحيبه بقرار الجمعية العمومية للأمم المتحدة بالسماح للدول التي لها آثار مهربة في الخارج باستردادها. وقال إنه هناك حوالي ٢١ مليون قطعة أثرية مصرية مسروقة في الغرب أشهرها ذقن أبو الهول وحجر رشيد الموجودان في المتحف البريطاني في لندن.

2 Answer the questions.

   a Who made a statement welcoming the UN resolution?

   b Which famous Egyptian pieces are in the British Museum?

3 Now find the Arabic for these expressions:

   a the head of the Department of Egyptian Antiquities

   b approximately 21 million

   c the beard of the Sphinx

   d the Rosetta Stone

> **LANGUAGE TIP**
>
> الموجودان The adjective here is in the dual as it refers to two objects (the Sphinx's beard and the Rosetta Stone).

Reading 2

اليمن *THE YEMEN*

سفينة، سفن	**safíinah, súfun**	*ship*
سياحي	**siyáaHii**	*tourist (adj.), touristic*

16.03 *Listen to the piece about Yemen.*

1 What do the tourists hope to visit?

www.touristinformation.com

٤٥٠ سائح أوروبي في عدن

استقبل ميناء عدن أمس الأول سفينة سياحية ألمانية تحمل أكثر من ٤٠٠ سائح وسائحة من مختلف الجنسيات الأوروبية. وسيزور هؤلاء السواح بعض المدن اليمنية التاريخية.

2 Answer the questions.

   a What arrived in the port of Aden?

   b Who was it carrying?

3 Find the Arabic for the English expressions:

   a of various nationalities

   b the tourists will visit some Yemeni towns

> **LANGUAGE TIP**
>
> أول الأمس (lit., *yesterday the-first*). Also occurs in the form أمس الأول, both meaning
>
> *the day before yesterday.*

> **LANGUAGE TIP**
>
> مختلف *various* when used as the first part of a possessive construction.
>
> When used as an ordinary adjective, it means *different.*

Reading 3

أمريكا   *AMERICA*

أعلن	**á:lana** [S-IV]	*announce, state*
تزوج	**tazáwwaja** [Mw-V]	*marry*
احتفال، ـات	**iHtifáal, -áat**	*celebration* (requires **bi-**)
منظم، ـات	**munáDHDHim, -áat**	*regulator*
ضربة، ـات	**Dárbah, Darabáat**	*beat, blow*
قلب، قلوب	**qalb, qulúub**	*heart*
تنقل	**tanáqqala** [S-V]	*be transported*
كرسي، كراسي	**kúrsii, karáasii**	*chair*
عجلة، ـات	**:ájalah, -áat**	*wheel*
بادل	**báadala** [S-III]	*return, reciprocate to someone*

16.04 *Read the article about a millionaire while listening to the audio.*

1 How old is the millionaire?

مليونير أمريكي

أعلن مليونير أمريكي من ولاية كاليفورنيا في الأسبوع الماضي أنه سيتزوج فتاة في الخامسة والعشرين من عمرها. وهذا بعد احتفاله بعيد ميلاده المئوي بأيام قليلة. وهو يستخدم منظما لضربات القلب ويتنقل على كرسي بعجلات. وقال إنه يحبها من كل قلبه وهي تبادله الحب.

2 Answer the questions.

    a What aids does the millionaire need? _____

    b How old is his prospective bride? _____

    c How much does he love his fiancée? _____

3 Find the Arabic for the English expressions:

   a he will marry a girl _____

   b he said that he loves her _____

   c with all his heart _____

> **LANGUAGE TIP**
>
> منظماً لضربات القلب *regulator for beats of the heart, i.e. pacemaker*

> **LANGUAGE TIP**
>
> تبادله *she reciprocates (to him). Many of such Form III verbs take a direct object, where in English a*
>
> *preposition is required. See Verb tables.*

> **LANGUAGE TIP**
>
> **mi'awii** *hundredth. This is not a true ordinal number, rather an adjective meaning centennial from*
>
> مئة **mi'ah** *– irregular but most common spelling – or* مائة *hundred.*

Reading 4

أبو ظبي **ABU DHABI**

16.05 Listen to this radio programme about What's on.

1 Who is Majida Roumi?

ماجدة الرومي
وصلت إلى الإمارات اليوم المطربة
اللبنانية المشهورة ماجدة الرومي في
زيارة خاصة، ستزور خلالها عائلتها
التي تقيم في أبو ظبي. وخلال الزيارة
التي قامت بها، قالت إنها سوف تؤدي
في الحفلة الخيرية التي من المقرر
أن تجرى يوم الجمعة في المركز الثقافي.
وسوف تذهب عائدات الحفل لتوفير
الحماية للأطفال اللاجئين في جميع
أنحاء العالم وضمان مستقبل أفضل لهم.
ولا تزال هناك تذاكر متاحة من شباك
التذاكر وعلى الانترنت.

2 Answer the questions.

   a Why is Majida in Abu Dhabi? _____

   b What two things is she doing during her visit? _____

3 Now find the Arabic for the English expressions:

   a She arrived in the Emirates today. _____

   b She will visit her family. _____

Reading 5

 NEW YORK نيو يورك

أقام	**aqáama** [Mw-IV]	*reside*
منظمة، ـات	**munáDHDHamah, -áat**	*organization*
شعر	**shi:r**	*poetry*
رحب بـ	**ráHHaba** [S-II]	*to welcome* (requires bi-)
مؤمن، ـون	**mú'min, -úun**	*believing; believer (in something)*
إيمان	**iimáan**	*belief, faith*
حد، حدود	**Hadd, Hudúud**	*limit, border*
زمان، أزمنة	**zamáan, azmínah**	*time*
اتساع	**ittisáa:**	*extent, compass*
مالئ	**máali'**	*filling, filler*
لحظة، ـات	**láHDHah, laHaDHáat**	*moment*
فصل، فصول	**faSl, fuSúul**	*section, season (of the year)*
معنى، المعاني	**má:naa, al-ma:áanii**	*meaning*

16.06 *Listen to the magazine radio programme.*

1 What special day has UNESCO chosen to commemorate on 21 March?

يوم عالمي للشعر

لا حدود له أن الشعر أكبر من الزمان
كله، وأكثر اتساعا من الأمكنة جميعا. إنه
مالئ اللحظات والفصول والقرون بجمال
المعنى ومعنى الجمال».

اختارت منظمة اليونسكو يوم ٢١ مارس
يوما عالميا للشعر. ورحب الشعراء
العرب بهذا، بينهم الشاعر العراقي علي
جعفر العلاق الذي قال إنه «مؤمن إيمانا

2 Answer the questions.

  a Who is Ali al-Allaq? _____

  b What is poetry greater than? _____

3 Find the Arabic for the English expressions:

  a Arab poets welcomed this. _____

  b Poetry is greater than all time. _____

  c It fills the moments … with the beauty of meaning. _____

LANGUAGE TIP

يوما عالميا *as a world day.* Adverbial accusative of respect. (See Unit 14.)

LANGUAGE TIP

اتساعا *in extent* and جميعا *all together* are examples of the adverbial accusative.

Language discovery

1 EACH, EVERY AND ALL

All these English words are expressed using the Arabic كل, but with different constructions according to the specific meaning required.

each, every	كل + indefinite singular
all	كل + definite plural
	def. plural + كل + suffix pronoun

الآن دورك al-'aan dawrak

Which phrases would you translate using *each/every* and which would you translate using *all*?

١ كل يوم   ٢ كل الأيام ٣ كل الأشخاص ٤ كل شخص

خير	**khayr**	(state of) well-being
مشكلة، مشاكل	**múshkilah, masháakil***	problem
حل، حلول	**Hall, Hulúul**	solution

Each, every

The construction used for both of these is the same: كل followed by an indefinite singular noun (without the definite article **al-**):

من كل بلد خبر	*from every country news*
كل عام وأنت بخير	*(lit. 'every year and you in well-being')*
كل مشكلة لها حل	*every problem has a solution (lit. 'every problem for it a solution')*

LANGUAGE TIP

The Arabic congratulatory phrase in the second example is used in connection with all anniversaries, particularly birthdays.

عسكري، عساكر	:askárii, :asáakir	soldier
سلاح، أسلحة	siláaH, aslíHah	weapon, arm
حاضر	HáaDir	present, here

All

a كل followed by a noun with the definite article, usually plural. This is a possessive construction and obeys the rules given in Unit 6.

كل المتاحف مقفولة يوم الجمعة	all (of) the museums are closed on Friday
كان كل العساكر يحملون أسلحة	all (of) the soldiers were carrying arms
كل البنات حاضرات	all (of) the girls are present

The noun can be replaced by a suffix pronoun:

كلهم أخذوا قطعة كعك   all of them (they all) took a piece of cake

b A plural noun with the definite article, followed by كل with a suffix pronoun agreeing with the noun. This construction is slightly more common. To make it clear, here are the same examples as above in the new format. The meaning is exactly the same.

المتاحف كلها مقفولة يوم الجمعة	the museums all-of-them are closed on Friday
كان العساكر كلهم يحملون أسلحة	the soldiers all-of-them were carrying arms
البنات كلهن حاضرات	the girls all-of-them are present

When used with a singular noun or pronoun suffix, the translation can be *all* or *the whole*, e.g. from the text:

| الزمان كله | all time, the whole of time |
| أكلت الكعك كله | She ate all the cake, the whole cake. |

234

An alternative word for *all* is جميع **jamii:**, used either with a plural in the same way as كل or, as we have in the text, with the accusative marker as an adverb (see Unit 15):

وأكثر اتساعا من الأمكنة جميعا   *and greater in compass than all places*

Some

The word for *some* is بعض, a noun meaning *a part* of something. This is used in the same way as كل when it means *all* as explained above:

بعض المدن اليمنية التاريخية   *some of the historic Yemeni towns*

بعضهم عرب وبعضهم إنجليز   *some of them are Arabs, and some English*

Summary

كل is a noun meaning *the whole, totality* of something.

بعض is a noun meaning *a part* of something. They are both sometimes used independently:

قال البعض إنها مجنونة   *some said that she was mad*

من كل قلبه   *with all his heart*

> **LANGUAGE TIP**
>
> مجنون، مجانين **majnúun, majaaníin*** *mad*

2 IRREGULAR NOUNS

There are two classes of irregular nouns and adjectives which must be mentioned as the variations in their endings show up in print, i.e. they do not consist entirely of unmarked vowel endings.

> **LANGUAGE TIP**
>
> Remember that literary Arabic recognizes three cases of the noun/adjective, depending on its function in the sentence:
>
> <u>Nominative</u>, used for the subject of all sentences and the complement of verbless sentences; also for the complement of **inna**-type sentences (see Unit 8).
>
> <u>Accusative</u>, used for the object of verb sentences, the subject of **inna**, the complement of **kaana** sentences (Unit 8) and for many adverbial expressions (Unit 15).
>
> <u>Genitive</u>, used for the second part of possessive constructions (i.e. for the possessor) and after all prepositions.

Two common nouns behave differently when they form the first part of a possessive phrase, either with another noun or a pronoun suffix:

أب، آباء	**ab, aabaa'**	*father*
أخ، إخوان\إخوة	**akh, ikhwaan** or **ikhwah**	*brother*

These behave normally when they do not form the first part of a possessive:

له أخ واحد   *he has one brother*

In possessives, they show the nominative case with a و, the accusative with an ١, and the genitive with a ي.

For example, take *her brother/father*, using the possessive suffix **-haa**.

Case	her father	her brother
Nominative	أبوها **abuu-haa**	أخوها **akhuu-haa**
Accusative	أباها **abaa-haa**	أخاها **akhaa-haa**
Genitive	أبيها **abii-haa**	أخيها **akhii-haa**

Examples of the three cases are:

يعمل أبوهم في شركة كبيرة	*their father works in a big company* (nominative, subject of a verb)
ستزور خلالها أباها	*during which she will visit her father* (accusative, object of a verb)
نسكن مع أبينا	*we live with our father* (genitive after a preposition)

> **LANGUAGE TIP**
>
> When the suffix ‍ـي **-ii** *my* is added to these words, the various long vowel endings are omitted and all cases are أبي **ab-ii** and أخي **akh-ii**.

> **LANGUAGE TIP**
>
> Technically, in formal Standard Arabic, the same varying forms should be used before another noun, but this seems to be dropping out of modern press Arabic and the nominative **-uu** form is used in all contexts. This is important, as أبو especially, occurs in many personal and place names. For instance, in the reading we have في أبو ظبي *in Abu Dhabi*, which should technically be أبي **abii** after the preposition في **in**.

You can avoid using **abuu**, etc. in many situations by substituting the regular noun والد

waalid, which also means *father*, but this is not permissible in proper names. You can't do

anything about **akh**, though.

3 DEFECTIVE NOUNS AND ADJECTIVES

Another class of irregular words are the so-called defective nouns and adjectives. The defect

is that, in certain cases as explained, they lose their final letter, which is always ي. These are

perfectly regular in the definite, but the indefinite works as follows, using the word قاضي

judge as a model:

Definite	all cases:	القاضي **al-qaaDii**
Indefinite	Nominative	قاض **qaaDin**
	Accusative:	قاضيا **qaaDiyan**
	Genitive:	قاض **qaaDin**

The class also includes adjectives such as الماضي، ماض، ماضيا **al-maaDii, maaDin,**

maaDiyan *past, former.*

Important note: To save confusion, and because they look peculiar in isolation in their truncated form, words of this class have been given in the vocabularies and glossaries with the definite article, e.g.:

| القاضي، قضاة | **al-qaaDii, quDaah** | *judge* |
| الماضي | **al-maaDii** | *past* (adj.) |

Note that it can be the singular which is defective, as in the examples above, or the plural as in the following examples:

معنى، المعاني	**ma:naa, al-ma:aanii**	*meaning*
ميناء، المواني	**miinaa', al-mawaanii**	*harbour*
ماء، مياه	**maa, miyaah**	*water*
الصافي	**aS-Saafii**	*pure, clear*
سد، سدود	**sadd, suduud**	*dam*
العالي	**al-: aalii**	*high*

Here are another couple of common defective adjectives:

| ماء صاف | **maa' Saafin** | *pure water* |
| السد العالي | **as-sadd al-:aali** | *the High Dam (in Egypt)* |

Practice

1 Find the odd one out:

١ أخي – عمي – أمي – أبي

٢ أب – مطرب – مدير – شاعر

٣ أبو صالح – أبو ظبي – أبو الهول

٤ كرسي – طاولة – غسالة – رئيس

٥ ميناء – قلب – سفينة – ماء

قبل	qábila [S-I a]	accept
بطاقة التسليف	biTáaqat at-tasliif	credit card
تكييف	takyíif	air conditioning
صالون تجميل	Sáaluun tajmíil	beauty salon
خدمة، ـات	khídmah, -áat	service
تنظيف	tanDHíif	cleaning
ملابس	maláabis	clothes
لاسلكي	laasilki	WiFi

2 Here is part of a hotel guide for Algiers. Look at the key to the hotel facilities and decide whether these statements referring to the four hotels described are true or false.

١ كل غرفة في فندق الخليج فيها تلفزيون ولاسلكي وعرض أفلام. ───────────

٢ بعض الفنادق فيها ملعب تنس. ───────────

٣ كل الفنادق تقبل بطاقات التسليف. ───────────

٤ بعض الفنادق لها مواقف سيارات. ───────────

٥ كل فندق فيه تكييف. ───────────

٦ كل الفنادق فيها صالون تجميل. ───────────

٧ كلها فيها مسبح. ───────────

٨ بعض الغرف في فندق «اللؤلؤة» فيها حمام. ───────────

٩ في كل فندق خدمة تنظيف الملابس. ───────────

١٠ ليس في كل الغرف في فندق «سبلنديد» هاتف. ───────────

دليلك المفضل إلى... **الفنادق**

🖼 مكيف هواء	⊶ مجموع عدد الغرف
🖼 خدمة تنظيف الملابس	P موقف سيارات
🍽 مطاعم	🖼 بطاقات التسليف مقبولة
✂ صالون تجميل	🎾 ملاعب تنس
🛁 حمام في الغرفة	🏊 بركة سباحة خارجية
☎ هاتف في كل غرفة	📶 لاسلكي في كل غرفة
TV تلفزيون في كل غرفة	🎬 عرض أفلام في الغرفة

فندق سبلنديد **** ⊶ ٣١٦ 🖼 🖼 🎬 📶 TV ✂ 🛁
P 🖼 🍽 ✂ 🎾 🏊

فندق مريديان **** ⊶ ٢٥٠ 🖼 🖼 🎬 📶 TV ✂ 🛁
P 🖼 🍽 ✂ 🎾 🏊

فندق الخليج *** ⊶ ١٧٤ 🏊 🖼 🖼 📶 TV ☎ 🛁
P 🖼 🍽

فندق اللؤلؤة * ⊶ ٢٥ ١٢ 🖼 🎬 TV 🖼 P

---

3 Match the Arabic with the English sentences.

a I put the books on the shelf.

b The students studied for their examinations.

c The shops open in the evening.

d His sisters met him in at the airport.

e The employees welcomed the director's report.

f The tourists arrived from Germany.

١ درس الطلبة للامتحانات.

٢ وصل السواح من ألمانيا.

٣ تفتح الدكاكين في المساء.

٤ رحب الموظفون بتقرير المدير.

٥ استقبلته أخواته في المطار.

٦ وضعت الكتب على الرف.

4 Add the word *all* to the plural nouns (highlighted) in the sentences in Exercise 3, using كل with a suffix pronoun agreeing with the noun.

Example:

لعب الأولاد في الحديقة   *The children played in the garden.*

لعب الأولاد كلهم في الحديقة   *All the children played in the garden.*

Test yourself

16.07 The following is a revision exercise, covering the word shapes given in all the previous units. You are given an Arabic root, along with its basic meaning. Refer back to the relevant unit and create the required word shape. The answers, along with their meanings, are given in the key and on the audio:

Unit 1	و–ح–د	*to be one, unique*
Unit 2	ب–ر–د	*being cold*
Unit 3	ض–ب–ط	*being exact, accurate*
Unit 4	ل–ع–ب	*playing*
Unit 5	ف–ط–ر	*breaking one's fast*
Unit 6	ط–ب–ع	*printing, typing*
	ف–س–ر	*explaining, elucidating*
Unit 7	ف–ه–م	*understanding*
Unit 8	ر–س–م	*drawing*
Unit 9	ع–ل–م	*knowing*
Unit 10	ع–ل–م	*knowing*
Unit 11	ف–ض–ل	*being preferable, good, excellent*
Unit 12	ن–ظ–ر	*seeing, looking at*
Unit 13	ك–ش–ف	*uncovering, discovering*
Unit 14	ف–ت–ح	*opening*
Unit 15	ل–خ–ب–ط	*being mixed up, in a mess*

SELF CHECK	
I CAN...	
⊙	...say *each, every, all* and *some*.
⊙	...use some irregular nouns and adjectives.
⊙	...recognize some common Arabic loan words.
⊙	...talk about the media.

Answer key

ARABIC SCRIPT AND PRONUNCIATION GUIDE

1 Volvo, Honda, Jeep, Toyota, Chrysler, IKEA **2** Autolease

Practice a فيلم **e** سينما **d** طبيب **c** شجرة **b** أمير

UNIT 1

Greetings a

Vocabulary builder woman; woman; man; woman

Conversation 1

1 السلام عليكم

Conversation 2

1 morning

2 الخير **b** صباح **c** مساء **d** النور **a**

3 صباح الخير **b** مساء النور **c** السلام عليكم **d** عليكم السلام **e** **a**

4 صباح اِلخير SabáaH al-kháyr

Conversation 3

1 fine

2 And you, how are you?

Language discovery

1 Sun: a, c, d, e, g Moon: b, f

2 a ٣ **b** ١ **c** ٢ **d** ٤

3 الهرم الكبير al-háram al-kabíir

Word discovery

1 سندويتش sandawíitsh, because it is a foreign loan word

2 a 3 **b** 2 **c** 4 **d** 1

3 a S-gh-r ص–غ–ر **b** T-w-l ط–و–ل **c** b-:-d ب–ع–د **d** q-r-b ق–د–م **e** j-d-d ص–ح–ح **f** q-d-m ج–د–د **g** j-m-l ج–م–ل **h** l-T-f ل–ط–ف **i** k-r-m ك–ر–م **j** S-H-H

Listen and understand

1 a 3 **b** 2 **c** 1

2 a 3 **b** 2 **c** 1

3 a شاي بسكر **b** المصباح **c** الأهرام **d** سندوتش

Practice

1 a 4 **b** 2 **c** 5 **d** 3 **e** 1

2 a coffee **b** lemon **c** small Coca-Cola **d** chocolate ice cream

3 please

4 a the cinema **b** the bank

5 a 7 **b** 6 **c** 4 **d** 2 **e** 5 **f** 8 **g** 1 **h** 3

6 البيت الكبير الواسع **e** فيلم طويل **d** كتاب جميل **c** بنت صغيرة **b** السينما الجديدة **a**

7 كيف حالك؟ káyfa Háal-ak

الحمد لله وأنت؟ al-Hámdu lil-láah wa ánta?

أهلا بك áhlan bi-k أهلا وسهلا áhlan wa-sáhlan

8 كيف حالكم؟

9 أهلا وسهلا

Test yourself

1 a صباح الخير SabaH al-khayr **b** الحمد لله al-Hamdu lil-láah **c** كيف حالك؟

káyfa Haal-ak? **d** السلام عليكم as-saláamu :aláy-kum **e** مساء الخير masáa' al-kháyr

2 a as-sandawíitsh **b** at-tilifúun **c** al-bayt **d** aT-TamáaTim **e** as-síinima **f** al-bíirah

aS-Saghíirah **g** al-bárgar al-kabíir **h** ar-ráadyo al-jadíid

UNIT 2

Arabic names أم مصطفى Umm Mustapha

Vocabulary builder Egypt, Alexandria, Cairo, Dubai, London, Manchester, Sudan, France

Conversation 1

1 Michael

2 a Manchester **b** Alexandria

3 أنا من مانشستر **b** أنا من الإسكندرية **a**

4 Arabic doesn't have a word for *to be*. Instead it is generated by putting a definite and indefinite word next to each other.

Conversation 2

1 that it is big, beautiful and very old

2 a in Tahrir Square **b** an excellent restaurant

3 هناك فندق ممتاز في المدينة

Conversation 3

1 They are written from left to right (the opposite direction to the script)

2 6215500; 6207589

3 رقم تلفون

4 رقم تلفوني ٣٣٠٧٥

5 b

Language discovery

1 كم؟ kam? How many/much?, من أين؟ min áyna? Where?, ما؟ maa? what?,

كيف؟ kayfa? how?

Word discovery 1

1 By adding an ا alif after the first letter of the root

2 a ع‑د‑ل b ل‑ز‑م c م‑ش‑ن d ك‑م‑ل e ن‑ف‑ع f ع‑ح‑ص g م‑ل‑س

Practice

1 a أنا من مصر b أنا من روسيا c أنا من أمريكا d أنا من إسكتلندا

e أنا من اليابان f أنا من أستراليا

2 a البيت الصغير b السيارة الجميلة c الولد الطويل d السكرتير الجديد e المدير المشغول

3 a البيت صغير b السيارة جميلة c الولد طويل d السكرتير جديد e المدير مشغول

4 a هو صغير b هي جميلة c هو طويل d هو جديد e هو مشغول

5 a أأنت من مصر؟ b هل محمد في دبي؟ c أهي أمريكية؟

d هل الكتاب جديد؟ e هل يتكلم عربي؟

6 a السيارة جديدة b هي مشغولة c الفندق قريب من الأهرام d محمد هنا e هو مشغول

7 a Tunis b Lebanon c Paris d Scotland e Abu Dhabi f Italy

8 a 2 Dubai b 4 Ras al-Khaimah c 1 Abu Dhabi

9 a 973 ٩٧٣ b 20 ٢٠ c 1 ١ d 974 ٩٧٤ e 966 ٩٦٦ f 39 ٣٩

Test yourself

1 a ما اسمك؟ b من أين أنت؟ c رقم تلفونك كم؟ d اسمي... e أنا من لندن

f هل السيارة صغيرة؟

2 a ٢ b واحد ١ c ١ d 1 e خمسة f khámsah g ٥ h 20456 i ٩٣٨٧

UNIT 3

Arabic professions hotel manager

Vocabulary builder England, كثير, English, قليلة, عربي/العربية, Arabic

Conversation 1

1 أين طنطا؟ **2** a Sudanese b Khartoum **3** أنا **4** a Egypt b England

c Australia d Lebanon e France

Conversation 2

1 speaks Arabic, not English **2** a هل تتكلم إنجليزي/الإنجليزية؟ b قليلة **3** true

Conversation 3

1 student   **2** in Amman   **3 a** ما عملك؟   **b** أنا طبيب

Conversation 4

1 museums/bridges/shops   **2** university

Language discovery

1 To form a masculine adjective, add ـِي -ii to the name of the place. To form a feminine adjective, add ـِيّة -íyyah

2 I, you (m.), you (f.), he, she

Word discovery

1   فرض f   بسط e   منع d   سمح c   كتب b   كتم a

Practice

1 a 4 Morocco   **b** 2 Jordan   **c** 1 Oman   **d** 5 Bahrain   **e** 3 Kuwait

2 a 4E   **b** 7C   **c** 6A   **d** 2G   **e** 1B   **f** 3D   **g** 5F

3 a Salma   **b** Damascus, Syria   **c** هي مدرسة   **d** تتكلم اللغة العربية

4   قليل d   أنا طالب c   أمريكي b   اسمي مارتن رومانو a
بطلاقة ... اللغة الإيطالية، نعم f   !نعم، طبعا e

5   نافعة، الإنجليزية 6 جديدة 5 أمريكية، الكبيرة 4 جديد 3 مشهورة، المصرية 2 مشغولة 1
سعيدة 9 واحدة 8 كثيرة، جديدة 7

6   هي طبيبة f   هي طالبة e   هي مديرة d   هو مهندس c   هو طالب b   هي مدرسة a

Test yourself

1   هل تتكلم/تتكلمين عربي؟ b   أنت سوداني؟/ أنت سودانية؟ a
هو طبيب. f   أين المتحف؟ e   ما عملك؟ d   هل مكة مدينة كبيرة؟ c

2   وسط d   أين c   كبيرة b   مدينة a

UNIT 4

Telling the time nine o'clock in the morning; seven o'clock at night

Vocabulary builder open/close, seven, بعد, tomorrow, أيام, Monday, Thursday, بكم, five

Conversation 1

1 The Old Town/City   **2 a** It's too far   **b** The Fort Museum   **3 a** ٤   **b** ٢   **c** ٣   **d** ١

Conversation 2

1 10:15 a.m.   **2 a** 1 p.m.   **b** 4 p.m.   **c** a brochure   **3 a** ٤   **b** ١   **c** ٦   **d** ٢   **e** ٥   **f** ٣

Conversation 3

1 Dhs.3   **2 a** Dhs.6   **b** Dhs.18   **3 a** ٤   **b** ١   **c** ٢   **d** ٣

Language discovery

1 There is no difference between masculine and feminine in the plural words for *these* and *those*.

Word discovery

1 a place where the action of the root takes place

2 entrance, exit, playing field, swimming pool

Practice

1 a 1:30 **b** 6:55 **c** 10:15 **d** 5:00 **e** 9 a.m.

2 a الساعة تاسعة as-sáa:ah tis:ah **b** الساعة ثلاثة و نصف as-sáa:ah thalaatha wa-niSf **c** الساعة اثنا عشر الا ربع as-sáa:ah ithna:shar illaa rub: **d** الساعة أربعة وثالث as-sáa:ah arba:ah wa thulth **e** الساعة الثانية عشرة و عشرة as-sáa:ah ithna:shar wa-:asharah **f** الساعة الثانية إلا خمس as-sáa:ah ithnayhn illa khamsah

3 ١ يوم ٢ يوم الأربعاء ٣ أمس ٤ يوم الأحد ٥ بعد غد ٦ يوم الجمعة

4 ١هذا ٢ هذه ٣ أولائك ٤ هذه ٥ أولائك ٦ تلك

5 a 3/12/1952 **b** 19/11/1967 **c** 1/1/2000 **d** 28/2/1990 **e** 17/4/1836

6 a الساعة الثانية والنصف وخمسة b الساعة الثامنة وعشر دقائق c الساعة التاسعة ونصف إلا خمسة d الساعة السابعة e الساعة الرابعة إلا الربع f الساعة الخامسة والنصف g الساعة الواحدة والربع h الساعة الواحدة إلا خمسة i الساعة الثالثة والثلث j الساعة العاشرة وخمس دقائق

Reading a Wednesday evenings **b** Monday **c** 8:30 p.m. **d** 9 a.m. **e** Friday (Monday also possible) **f** five

Speaking 1 a مساء الخير b التذكرة بكم؟ c أربع تذاكر من فضلك d تفضل e المسرح يفتح الساعة كم؟ f شكرا

2 a 4 dinars **b** 7 o'clock **c** half past seven

Test yourself

1 a الساعة كم؟ b يفتح الساعة كم؟ c يفتح الساعة عشرة ونصف d التذكرة بكم، من فضلك؟ e هذا هو محمد.

2 a يوم الأحد b يوم الثلاثاء c Wednesday d يوم الجمعة e Saturday

UNIT 5

Segregated social events Don't ask about his wife or other female relatives.

Vocabulary builder eight, wife, aunt (father's/mother's side), grandfather, bint :amm/khaal

Conversation

1 The endings are different. Hamed uses the singular سنة ١٢ because all of his family is older than ten, but Tom has children under ten so uses the plural noun سنوات، ٥

2 a his wife, Salma **b** 15 **c** 21

3 a هذا والدي b تفضل اجلس c هذا ابننا d أولادك أنت، كم عمرهم؟
e بنتنا عمرها ٣ سنوات

Language discovery

1 20 ishríin 33 thaláathah wa-thalaathíin 40 ٤٠ 44 árba:ah wa-arba:íin 57 sáb:ah wa-khamsíin 68 thamáanyah wa-sittíin 76 síttah wa-sab:íin 85 khámsah wa-thamaaníin 99 tís:ah wa-tis:íin

2 her car

Word discovery

1 a جيوب b صحون c جسور d عبور e جلوس

Practice

1 ١٤ ٢٤ ٢٨ ٣١ ٤٢ ٥٣ ٥٨ ٦٧ ٨٨ ٩٦

2 a Lantern Dhs.99 **b** Barbecue Dhs.89 **c** Lounger Dhs.65 **d** Tow rope Dhs.50
e Sleeping bag Dhs.42 **f** Ice chest Dhs.79 **g** Charcoal Dhs.25

3 a ٤ **b** ١ **c** ٣ **d** ٦ **e** ٥ **f** ٢

4 ٢ والدتي إيطالية ٣ هرمي هو الكبير ٤ هذه أختي مريم ٥ ليست هذه السيارة سيارتي
٦ أهذا مكتبه الجديد؟ ٧ جدهم من تونس ٨ أين حقائبنا ؟

5 a ٣ **b** ٢ **c** ١ **d** ٨ **e** ٦ **f** ٧ **g** ٥ **h** ٤

6 a ١خالد ٢مريم ٣سلمان،وفهد،وخميس b١ابنه ٢بنته ٣والده ٤أخته
c١بنت عمته ٢زوج عمته ٣جدهم

Test yourself

1 a أهذا بيتك؟ b أولادك أنت، كم عمرهم؟ c أنا بخير الحمد لله
d لا ، ليست هذه سيارتها e هذه هدية لك

2 a 21/٢١ **b** واحد وخمسون **c** ثلاثة وعشرين **d** 84/٨٤ **e** ثلاثة وستون
f 76/٧٦ **g** 100/١٠٠

UNIT 6

Arabic place names and compass points b وسط

Vocabulary builder metre, right, go straight ahead, behind, after

Conversation

1 عن اذنك! اذنك

2 **a** 1   **b** left   **c** 100m   **d** petrol station   **e** 3

3 **a** ٧   **b** ٢   **c** ٥   **d** ٣   **e** ٦   **f** ١   **g** ٤

Language discovery

1 **a** مصري   **b** يابانية   **c** تاريخية   **d** رجولي

Word discovery

1 the place in which the person operates

2 أمير amíir prince

Listen and understand

2 **a** hotel   **b** mosque   **c** fish market   **d** post office   **e** park   **f** old fort

Practice

1 **a** منطقة زراعية   **b** قمر صناعي   **c** البنك الوطني   **d** الشؤون الخارجية   **e** منطقة عسكرية   **f** الآثار التاريخية   **g** الدراسات الأدبية   **h** العلوم الطبيعية   **i** القصر الملكي   **j** المستشفى المركزي   **k** بريد داخلي   **l** المعدات الكهربائية

2 **a** 4   **b** 5   **c** 7   **d** 2   **e** 3   **f** 1   **g** 6

3 **a** أين البلدية؟   **b** أين مركز الشرطة؟   **c** أين مركز التسوق البستان؟   **d** أين شارع الملك فيصل؟   **e** أين مطعم شهرزاد؟

4 **a** على شمال الميدان، أمام سوق السمك   **b** وراء الميدان، بين سوق السمك و البنك   **c** أمام برج الاتصالات على شمال الصيدلية   **d** بين الكورنيش وشارع جمال عبد الناصر   **e** وراء مركز الشرطة بين سوق الذهب والفندق

5 **a** مدير البنك   **b** مركز المدينة   **c** عاصمة البلاد   **d** مكتب الشركة   **e** أخت رشيد

6 **a** شوارع أبوظبي عريضة   **b** حدائق القصر جميلة   **c** غرف الشقة واسعة   **d** طبيخ المغرب لذيذ   **e** دكاكين السوق صغيرة

Test yourself

1 **a** جامعة القاهرة كبيرة   **b** عاصمة البلاد   **c** وزارة العدل قريبة من الميدان   **d** أين هي السفارة المغربية؟   **e** هل هناك مركز الشرطة ؟

2 **a** منطقة صناعة   **b** الطبخ العربي   **c** المتحف الشعبي   **d** القنصلية الأمريكية   **e** الإدارة البلدية

UNIT 7

Arab travellers and their influence **a** 1 C   **b** 4 E   **c** 5 B   **d** 3 A   **e** 2 D

Vocabulary builder bus, taxi

Reading

1 September

2 a True   **b** False

3 a ٣   **b** ١   **c** ٢

Conversation 2

1 She visited Ahmed

2 a 2   **b** 1   **c** 2   **d** 3   **e** 1   **f** 3

3 a ٤   **b** ١   **c** ٥   **d** ٢   **e** ٣

Language discovery

1   وصلوا من الرباط الأسبوع الماضي

2 a ما تأخرت الطائرة The aeroplane wasn't late   **b** ما كلم العمال الرئيس The workmen
didn't speak to the boss   **c** ما أكلت الخبز I didn't eat the bread

Word discovery a

Practice

1 a ٥   **b** ١   **c** ٢   **d** ٣   **e** ٤

2 a ٨   **b** ٣   **c** ١   **d** ٦   **e** ٧   **f** ٥   **g** ٢   **h** ٤

3   **a** سافروا **b** فتحت **c** تفرجت **d** وصلت **e** طبخت، أكلنا

4 a ٢   **b** ٥   **c** ٦   **d** ١   **e** ٤   **f** ٣

5   **a** لعبت **b** قابلت **c** جلست **d** ركبت **e** شربت **f** ذهبت

6   ١ كتبتها ٢ أكلتها ٣ كلمهم ٤ سألته ٥ غسلنها ٦ قابلها

7 a ٣   **b** ٤   **c** ١   **d** ٥   **e** ٢

8   سافر بيل وميري والأولاد من لندن ووصلوا إلى دبي في شهر مارس سنة 2010.
قعدوا هناك لمدة أسبوع. سكنوا في شقة كبيرة قريبة من البحر، وقابلوا ناسا كثيرين
من الإمارات. يوم الاثنين لعب بيل تنس، وذهبت ميري إلى الشاطئ. يوم الثلاثاء ذهبوا
إلى بيت صديقهم منصور، وطبخت لهم زوجته طعاما عربيا.

Translation: Bill and Mary and the children travelled from London and arrived in Dubai in
March 2010. They stayed there for a week. They lived in a big flat near the sea and met
many people from the Emirates. On Monday Bill played tennis and Mary went to the
beach. On Tuesday they went to the house of their friend Mansour, and his wife cooked
Arabic food for them.

9   ١ محمد سافر إلى القاهرة   ٢ الأولاد رجعوا من المدرسة   ٣ المهندسون حضروا
المؤتمر   ٤ البنات طبخن طعاما عربيا   ٥ الصحون وقعت من المائدة

Test yourself

1 How did you go there?

2 I went by taxi.

3 The student read the book in the university library.

4 He lived with my uncle.

5 The secretaries drank coffee every day.

6 I found the letter in my pocket.

7 He lived in Bahrain.

8 They (m. pl.) came out of the room.

UNIT 8

Storytelling ليلة

Vocabulary builder كان, جيبه, الفندق, من قبل

Reading 1

1 b

2 **a** to a merchant's house in the market   **b** he was tired and thirsty   **c** 2   **d** Whose palace is this?

3 a ٥   b ٦   c ١   d ٣   e ٢   f ٤

Reading 2

1 b

2 **a** because Hindbad hadn't heard of Sindbad the Sailor   **b** 1   **c** 3   **d** 2   **e** deliver the load to the merchant

3 a ٦   b ٤   c ٢   d ٨   e ١   f ٧   g ٣   h ٥

Language discovery كانت الممثلة مشهورة The actress was famous

كانت البيوت قديمة The houses were old

Word discovery خياطة khayyaaTah

Practice

1 ١ كانت ٢ كانت ٣ كانوا ٤ كان

2 ١ كان ذلك الطعام لذيذا ٢ كانت حدائق الفندق واسعة ٣ كانت شركتنا مشهورة في الخليج ٤ كان عمر الشريف ممثلا مصريا ٥ كان الأولاد سعداء

3 ١ لا، ليست الساعة ١٠:٣٠ الصبح. ٢ لا، ليس محمود في البهو. ٣ لا، ليست في مطعم البستان. ٤ لا، لسن في المسبح. ٥ نعم، هو في مركز الأعمال. ٦ نعم، هي في ملعب الجولف. ٧ لا، ليست أرقام الغرف ٥١١و ٥١٢و٥١٣. ٨ نعم، هم في ملعب التنس.

4 ليس الفهد مخططًا وليس النمر منقطا

١ ليس علي طالبا كسلانا ٢ لست تعبانا بعد رحلتي ٣ ليست الفنادق الكبيرة في وسط 5
المدينة ٤ ليست مشهورة جدا ٥ ليس الطبيب مشغولا في المستشفى
٦ ليست هذه القصة من ألف ليلة وليلة طويلة جدا
١ كانت شهرزاد قد روت قصة جديدة كل ليلة. ٢ كان البحري خبر الحمال عن رحلاته العجيبة. 6
٣ كان الضيف قد وصل في الفنادق الكبيرة في وسط المدينة
٤ كانت الخادمات قد تبعنه الى داخل القصر. ٥ كان الناس قد أكلوا الأكل اللذيذ.

Test yourself

1 a We were in كنا في بيروت في الصيف **b** The porter was busy كان الحمال مشغولا
Beirut in the summer

2 a٣ **b**١ **c**٢ **d**٤

UNIT 9

Classified ads بيع
Vocabulary builder للإيجار، مطلوب, villa, bathroom, shower

Conversation 1

1 Arabic and English

2

١ جون باركر
٢ ٣٢ سنة
٣ إنجليزي
٤ متزوج
٥ ص ب ٥٦٧
٦ أ بوظبي ١٢٣٤٥٦
٧ الإنجليزية، العربية
٨ نعم
٩ نعم
١٠ ٥ سنوات

Conversation 2

1 one, Saliha has two bathrooms

2

aصالحة **b**مجيد **c**حليم **d**فرح

Word discovery

1 teacher

2 مدرسة mudárrisah astrologer

Reading

1 c

2 1c 2a 3b

3 b 1 c 2 3 a 8 b 3 c 7 d 1 e 10 f 5 g 4 h 2

4 a 2, 4, 6, 7, 9 b 4, 6 c 4, 7, 9, 10

5 three years' experience in UAE food sales; good English; valid residence permit; aged
24–28 years; Emirates' driving licence

Practice

1

١ هؤلاء الأولاد أذكياء

٢ بناتك جميلات

٣ القمصان مخططة

٤ قرأنا الجرائد الإنجليزية

٥ البنوك مقفولة بعد الظهر

٦ الرجال المصريون نشاط

2

١ وجدنا مطاعم جيدة في القاهرة

٢ حضر المدراء الاجتماع

٣ هل أنتم جوعى؟

٤ السكرتيرات مشغولات

٥ بناتها طالبات في الجامعة

٦ هم ممثلون كويتيون

٧ كانت الأفلام طويلة

3

١ وصل العمال الجدد

٢ أين الكتب الفرنسية ؟

٣ وجدته المدرسات على الرف

٤ أصبح الأولاد سمانا

٥ خرج الضيوف من الفنادق

4 ١d ٤c ٢b ٣a

5

١ المكتبان مقفولان

٢ ليس الفنيان حاضرين

٣ الحمامان واسعان

٤ عمل الموظفان في الوزارتين

٥ كلمت المديرتان العاملين

6 a٣ b٤ c١ d٥ e٢

7 a4 b5 c2 d1 e4 f7 g3

Test yourself

1 **1** They became students (f.)   **2** The engineers attended the conference   **3** The books are on the shelf   **4** The boys are active   **5** Those girls are new

2 **1** أنتما ذكيان Both of you are clever   **2** أنتما غريبان Both of you are strange

3 القدمان صغيران The two feet are small

UNIT 10

Arabic serial dramas a (a 28-episode serial/soap opera)

Vocabulary builder المكتب, الصبح, tennis/golf, television

Conversation 1

1 fruit

2 a 2   b 1   c 2   d the general manager   e daily

3 a٣ b١ c٥ d٤ e٢

Conversation 2

1 Ruhiyyah

2 a tennis   b reading a lot   c go to the cinema   d 1

3 a١ b٤ c٥ d٣ e٢

Language discovery

2

١ ليس ٢ ما ٣ لا ٤ لن ٥ لم

Pronunciation fi-him *in them*

Word discovery

a فقراء   b نُظَفاء   c رؤساء   d زملاء

Practice

1 a Hameed

2

١ ليس هذا الجمل قبيحا

٢ ليست البيوت رخيصة في الرياض

٣ لن نسافر إلى الهند في الشهر القادم

٤ ما ذهبنا/لم نذهب إلى المسبح يوم الجمعة

٥ أختي لا تعمل في صيدلية

٦ ما درس/لم يدرس صالح في أمريكا

3

١ لها ٢ معه ٣ علينا ٤ مني ٥ إليه

4

يحب التنس والسباحة. لا يحب القراءة والكتب.   حميد يلعب كرة وسكواش.

5 ١ يتعلمون ٢ تتصل ٣ نشرب ٤ أكتب ٥ يكلمـنا ٦ تعرفين ٧ تقفل ٨ يصلن

٩ يلعبن ١٠ يكسبون

6 ٥ a (لا) أفهم b ٤ يقدم c ١ يسأل d ٢ تحمل e ٦ تذهب

Reading a March **b** price reductions and valuable prizes **c** cultural events/artistic events/
sporting events/horse races/fireworks **d** above the famous Dubai creek

Test yourself

1 a٢ **b**٤ **c**٦ **d**١ **e**٧ **f**٣ **g**٥

2 a يتصل بوالده كل يوم b يشربون القهوة بعد رجوعهم من العمل. c نكتب رسالة الى
صديقنا حكيم. d هل تعرف تلك المرأة؟ e يقفل المركز التجاري الساعة ١٠
f سوف يصل الى عمان يوم السبت

UNIT 11

Muslim festivals During daylight hours in Ramadan

Conversation 1

1 three

2 a 1 **b** 1 **c** 1 **d** they sacrifice a sheep **e** the Prophet's birthday

3 a٦ **b**١٠ **c**١ **d**٤ **e**٨ **f**٢ **g**٩ **h**٧ **i**٣ **j**٥

Word discovery نتائج حقائق رسائل

Practice

1 a٥ **b**١٠ **c**١ **d**٤ **e**٨ **f**٢ **g**٩ **h**٧ **i**٣ **j**٥

2 ٧، ٩، ٤، ١، ١٠، ٥، ١١، ٨، ٢، ١٢، ٣، ٦

3 a ١ الملك له قصور كثيرة

٢ أنت عندك أخت طويلة ٣ أنتم عندكم أولاد صغار ٤ أنا عندي آلة حاسبة جديدة ٥
المدرس عنده ٥٠ تلميذا ٦ نحن عندنا سيارة ألمانية

٧ هم عندهم حقائب ثقيلة ٨ الشركة لها ٥ فروع ٩ محمد عنده شقة واسعة ١٠ سميرة
عندها فستان جميل

b ١ الملك كانت له قصور كثيرة.

٢ أنت كانت عندك أخت طويلة.

٣ أنتم كان عندكم أولاد صغار.

٤ أنا كانت عندي آلة حاسبة جديدة.

٥ المدرس كان عنده ٥٠ تلميذا.

4 b (The days are getting longer)

5 ١ Ali–3rd ٢ Hamdan–6th ٣ Siham–2nd ٤ Mustafa–9th ٥ Abdullah–8th

٦ Noora–10th ٧ Hameed–1st

6

a يذهب إلى الصف الرابع، والصف السادس عشر والصف الثاني عشر

b تذهب إلى الصف الحادي عشر والصف العاشر والصف الخامس عشر

c تذهب إلى الصف السادس عشر والصف الثالث والصف التاسع

d يذهب إلى الصف الثاني والصف الرابع عشر والصف الثامن عشر

e تذهب إلى الصف الأول والصف الثالث عشر والصف السادس

Test yourself

1 a الله يبارك فيك / الله يبارك فيكم b وأنت بخير / وأنتم بخير

2 a أسكن في الطابق العاشر. b محمد عنده حقيبة كبيرة. c أنا كان عندي فستان جديد.

d من أين حضروا؟ e من هم؟

UNIT 12

Focus on Sharjah Abu Dhabi and Dubai

Reading

1 on the Arabian Gulf

2 **a** commercial **b** a million **c** cultural **d** museums **e** cultural and educational

3 definite: .... التي تفيض بكل مشاعر الود.../ التي تحتل موقعا.../ التي أجريت عام

indefinite: دائرة خاصة ....ترعى.../ موقع جعل الشارقة تتمتع.../ بكثافة تقدر

٢٠١٣ بحوالي ٣٨٦ نسمة للكيلومتر المربع.../ تذيع الكثير من البرامج

4 **a** ١ **b** ٥ **c** ٧ **d** ٢ **e** ٨ **f** ٣ **g** ٦ **h** ٤

Word discovery

1 مواقع mawaaqi:* situations موقع mawqi:

2 schools, offices or desks

3 منازل

Practice

1

١ هذا هو البيت الذي سنستأجره.

٢ زارني عامل يعمل في مصنع.

٣ شاهدت الطبيب الذي عيادته في وسط المدينة.

٤ خالد الذي قرأت كتابه يدرس في المدرسة الثانوية.

٥ كان الكرسي الذي جلست عليه مكسورا.

٦ الطلبة الذين يدرسون في الجامعة من الإمارات.

٧ رسالة كتبها الأسبوع الماضي وصلت اليوم.

٨ القمصان التي يبيعونها في السوق مصنوعة في الصين.

٩ مغنية كانت مشهورة قبل سنوات كثيرة ستزور سورية.

١٠ ابني له صديق أصله اسكتلندي.

2 a٣ b٢ c١٠ d٥ e٤ f٦ g٧ h١ i٩ j٨

3

١ لقد أُعيد بناء منزل الشيخ صقر الكائن في هذه المنطقة

٢ في هذه المنطقة يمكن مشاهدة أول أشكال تكييف الهواء، البرجيل، الذي كان يُستخدم لتبريد البيوت في الخليج. جُددت القلعة التي شُيدت في القرن الماضي، وحُولت إلى متحف.

٣ الطرق الضيقة تأخذ الزائر إلى سوق التوابل التي تنبعث منها روائح أنواع التوابل كلها مثل القرنفل والهال والقرفة التي تباع إلى الزوار من الأكياس التي تحيط المتاجر.

٤ سباقات الهجن رياضة شعبية تقام أيام الجمعة أثناء أشهر الشتاء.

4

١ عمر الشريف ممثل مصري لعب أدوارا مشهورة كثيرة.

٢ ذهبنا إلى مدينة البتراء القديمة التي اكتشفت سنة ١٨١٢.

٣ في مصر آثار فرعونية مهمة يزورها سواح كثيرون.

٤ يعمل زوجي في الشارقة التي تقع في الخليج العربي.

٥ نستأجر شقة في دمشق يسكن صاحبها في الرياض.

٦ سافروا إلى عدن بطائرة الصبح التي وصلت الظهر.

5 **1** geography **2** commerce **3** education **4** culture **5** economy **6** history **7** science **8** agriculture **9** meeting, sociology **10** sports **11** tourism

Test yourself

1

١ الموظف الذي يعمل في الجمارك

٢ أمينة التي تسكن أختها في لندن

٣ مقاولون دفع لهم مبلغا كبيرا

٤ المدير الذي اسمه ميلود

2 a٤ b٢ c١ d٣

UNIT 13

Arabic cuisine kabsa, mansef, makloube, koshari, couscous

Vocabulary builder litre, macaroni, tomatoes

Reading

1 six

2 **a** four and a half times as much **b** six hours **c** 40 minutes **d** onions **e** tomato sauce

3 a٤ b٥ c١ d٣ e٢

Language discovery

1   اقرأ توقف سب

2 a 4   b 1   c 3   d 2

Practice

1 a 3   b 4   c 2 d 1   e 5

2 a 3   b 1   c 4   d 2

3   ٦h ٥g ٣f ١e ٢d ٧c ٨b ٤a

4   ١ ارسله ٢ اكتبها ٣ اتصل

5   ١ ضعيه ٢ اتركيه ٣ اغسليها

Reading

1 a ٢ b ١

2 1 dirham, 50 fils

3 Fridays and holidays

4 four hours

5 5 dirhams

6 اضغط

Listen and understand

1 a 8 dirhams   b selection of cheeses   c macaroni   d today only

2   تعالوا، اشتروا، شاهدوا، اطبخوا. جربوا

Test yourself

1 a ٥   b ٦   c ٣   d ١   e ٢   f ٤

UNIT 14

Reading

1 breach the walls of Hollywood

2 a her oriental features   b Angelina Jolie and Penelope Cruz   c 1966   d Spain   e 13

   f Desperado   g She has also become a producer

3 a ٢   b ٤   c ١   d ٣

Language discovery

Mohammed is taller than Saleh أطول ١

It's the most difficult exam الأصعب ٢

She was the first woman to fly an Airbus الأول ٣

It's the most beautiful city أجمل ٤

Word discovery

Practice

1 a spend more than 250 dirhams   **b** more than 20 years   **c** spaghetti   **d** gold and cash

e your money will arrive in minutes   **f** use the Privilege card

2 suggested answers:

١ هذا الكمبيوتر له شاشة أكبر.

٢ له ذاكرة أصغر.

٣ له قرص ثابت أحسن.

٤ هو أسهل استعمالا.

٥ هو أرخص.

Test yourself

1 ١ b ٢ d ٣ c ٤ a

2 ١ She travelled to France to take part in the film ٢ He was born in Aleppo ٣ They are
going to the Dubai Film Festival next month ٤ This year's film festival is better than last
year's festival ٥ How much is the discount?

UNIT 15

Foreign loan words in Arabic a bus   **b** sandwich   **c** radio   **d** cinema   **e** rugby

Vocabulary builder red, blue

Reading

1 Morocco

2 a 3   **b** Cairo   **c** 42,000

3 a four   **b** Tunisia   **c** Tariq al-Ahmar (Morocco)

4 a the last minute of the match   **b** he got a second yellow card and was sent off

c Morocco

5 a ٤   **b** ٦   **c** ١   **d** ٢   **e** ٥   **f** ٣

Language discovery الفريق الأزرق \ البطاقة الحمراء

Word discovery

1 سيطرة domination

2 هندسة سيطرة فلسفة

Practice

1 ١ g   ٢ e   ٣ d   ٤ l   ٥ a   ٦ j   ٧ h   ٨ f   ٩ c   ١٠ k   ١١ b   ١٢ i

2

١ افتح الباب بسرعة. عندنا ضيف.

٢ ذهبت إلى السوق وقابلت أحمد هناك صدفة.

٣ كان ذلك البرنامج مهما جدا.

٤ كنا جالسين في البيت، وقام زيد فجأة وخرج.

٥ تسافر هذه الطائرة إلى الرياض مباشرة.

٦ يا أولاد، العبوا بهدوء، الوالد نائم.

3

١ يحتاج علي إلى جزمة سوداء.

٢ تحتاج سونية إلى فستان أصفر.

٣ يحتاج سعيد إلى قميص أخضر.

٤ يحتاج خالد إلى جوارب بيضاء.

٥ تحتاج فريدة إلى بنطلون أحمر.

٦ يحتاج حامد إلى حزام بني.

٧ تحتاج أنيسة إلى حقيبة وردية.

Reading a Dhs. 2,700 **b** 3 **c** 10yrs **d** 1 **e** 2 **f** Dhs. 260 **g** any three of: gym, aerobics, library, swimming pool, ice-skating, café

Listen and understand

1 golf, frequently; tennis, sometimes

2 gym, daily

3 skating, frequently; swim, rarely

4 swim and sail, sometimes

5 aerobics, frequently; sail, rarely

Test yourself

1 a ٢ **b** ٤ **c** ٥ **d** ٣ **e** ١ **f** ٦

2 a 4 (1–3 are people, 4 is a trophy) **b** 2 (1, 3, 4 are all adverbs of time, 2 is seriously) **c** 1 (2–4 are clothing, 1 is boat/dinghy) **d** 3 (1, 2, 4 are standard verbs, 3 is a quadrilateral verb)

UNIT 16

Arabic loan words

1 gazelle

2 lemon

3 sugar

Vocabulary builder Yemen, Abu Dhabi, millionaire, European

Reading 1

1 antiquities

2 a the head of the Department of Egyptian Antiquities

  b the Sphinx's beard and the Rosetta stone

3 a رئيس دائرة الآثار المصرية b حوالي 21 مليون c ذقن أبو الهول d حجر رشيد

Reading 2

1 some of Yemen's historical towns

2 a German tourist ship **b** more than 400 tourists

3 a من مختلف الجنسيات b سيزور هؤلاء السواح بعض المدن اليمنية

Reading 3

1 100 years old

2 a pacemaker, wheelchair **b** 25 **c** with all his heart

3 a سيتزوج فتاة b قال إنه يحبها c من كل قلبه

Reading 4

1 a Lebanese singer

2 a for a private visit **b** performing at a charity concert and visiting family

3 a وصلت إلى الإمارات اليوم b ستزور عائلتها

Reading 5

1 World Poetry Day

2 a an Iraqi poet **b** all time

3 a رحب الشعراء العرب بهذا b الشعر أكبر من الزمان كله c انه مالئ اللحظات بجمال المعنى

Language discovery 1 each/every: ١، ٤ all: ٢ ٣،

Practice

1 ١ أمي ٢ أب ٣ أبو صالح ٤ رئيس ٥ قلب

2 ١ F ٢ T ٣ T ٤ F ٥ T ٦ T ٧ F ٨ T ٩ T ١٠ F

3 a ٦ **b** ١ **c** ٣ **d** ٥ **e** ٤ **f** ٢

4

١ درس الطلبة كلهم للامتحانات.

٢ وصل السواح كلهم من ألمانيا.

٣ تفتح الدكاكين كلها في المساء.

٤ رحب الموظفون كلهم بتقرير المدير.

٥ استقبلته أخواته كلهن في المطار.

٦ وضعت الكتب كلها على الرف.

Test yourself Unit 1: وحيد waHiid unique **Unit 2:** بارد báarid cold **Unit 3:** مضبوط maDbuuT exact, accurate **Unit 4:** ملعب mál:ab playing field/court/pitch **Unit 5:** فطور fuTuur breakfast **Unit 6:** طباعة Tibaa:ah printing, typing تفسير tafsiir explanation, interpretation **Unit 7:** تفاهم tafaahum (mutual) understanding **Unit 8:** رسام rassaam artist **Unit 9:** معلم mu:allim teacher, instructor, master **Unit 10:** علماء ulamaa' scholars, religious leaders **Unit 11:** فضائل faDaa'il advantages, good points **Unit 12:** مناظر manáaDHir views, sights **Unit 13:** استكشاف istikshaáf discovery, act of trying to discover **Unit 14:** مفتاح miftaaH key **Unit 15:** لخبطة lakhbaTah mix up, mess

Audio transcripts and translations

In many cases the transcripts and/or translations are already in the units. They are only listed here when this is not the case.

UNIT 1
Conversation 1

| Kamal | Hello John! |
| John | Hello Kamal! |

Conversation 2

| Suad | Good morning. |
| Student | Good morning. |

Conversation 3*

Suad	How are you?
Student	Fine (lit. 'Thanks be to God').
Suad	Welcome!
Student	Thanks (lit. 'Welcome to you') How are you?
Suad	Fine (lit. 'Thanks be to God').

* Many of these phrases are formulaic greetings and can only be used in these contexts.

Listen and understand

Conversation one:

| A | Taxi! The pyramids, please. |
| B | Yes, sir. |

Conversation two:

A	The lamp please.
B	My pleasure.
A	Thank you.

Conversation three:

| A | Tea and a sandwich please. |
| B | Tea with sugar? |

A	No, thanks, without sugar. How much is that?
B	Thirty pounds, please.

UNIT 2

Conversation 1

Suad	Hásanan ána ísm-ii su:áad. maa ísm-ak?
Student	ána ísm-ii máaykal.
Suad	áhlan wa-sáhlan ya máaykal min áyna ánta?
Student	ána min mánshastar fii inglátárra. wa ánti?
Suad	ána min al-iskandaríyyah fii miSr.

Suad	Well. My name is Suad. What's your name?
Student	My name is Michael.
Suad	Welcome, Michael. Where are you from?
Student	I am from Manchester, in England. And you?
Suad	I am from Alexandria, in Egypt.

Conversation 2

miSr jamíilah jíddan. al-qáahirah madíinah kabíirah, wa hiya qadíimah jíddan.

al-mátHaf al-míSrii fii maydáan at-taHríir qaríib min fúnduq an-níil.

hunáaka máT:am mumtáaz fii fúnduq an-níil fii maydáan at-taHríir. wa Táb:an hunáaka al-ahráam fii al-jíizah.

Egypt is very beautiful. Cairo is a big city and it is very old. The Egyptian Museum is in Tahrir Square close to the Nile Hotel. There is an excellent restaurant in the Nile Hotel in Tahrir Square. And, of course, there are the pyramids in Giza.

Conversation 3

Zaki	raqm tilifóon-ak kam ya Hamad?
Hamid	raqm tilifóon-i síttah thaláathah árba:ah sáb:ah ithnáyn wáaHid wáaHid wa raqm tilifóon-ak ánta?
Zaki	raqm tilifóon-i síttah ithnáyn wáaHid khámsah khámsah Sifr Sifr. Ya maarii raqm tilifóon-ik kam?
Marie	raqm tilifóon-i síttah ithnáyn Sifr sáb:ah khámsah thamáanyah tís:ah.

Zaki	What's your phone number, Hamid?
Hamid	My phone number is 6347211. And your phone number?
Zaki	My phone number is 6215500. Marie, what's your phone number?
Marie	My phone number is 6207589.

UNIT 3
Conversation 1
Part 1

Husáam	márHaban. 'a-ánta míSrii?
Zaki	laa, ána suudáanii min al-kharTúum. wa-ánta?
Husáam	ána míSrii min TánTaa.
Zaki	áyna TánTaa?
Husáam	TánTaa qaríibah min al-qáahirah.

Husáam	Hello! Are you Egyptian?
Zaki	No, I'm Sudanese, from Khartoum. And you?
Husáam	I'm Egyptian, from Tanta.
Zaki	Where is Tanta?
Husáam	Tanta is near Cairo.

Part 2

Suad	ána miSríyyah, wa-ánta yaa máayk?
Mike	ána inglíizii.
Kylie	ána ustraalíyyah.
Younis	ána lubnáanii. ána min bayrúut.
Marie	ána faransíyyah.

Suad	I am Egyptian, and you, Mike?
Mike	I am English.
Kylie	I am Australian.
Younis	I am Lebanese. I am from Beirut.
Marie	I am French.

Conversation 2

ráakib	:an ídhn-ik. min áyna ánti?
júulii	ána min ingiltárra. wa-ánta?
ráakib	ána min :ammáan. ána úrdunii.
júulii	hal tatakállam inglíizii?
ráakib	laa, má:a l-ásaf, laa atakállam inglíizii. atakállam :árabi fáqaT.
ráakib	tatakallamíin al-:arabíyyah bi-Taláaqah!
júulii	laa, qalíilan fáqaT.

Passenger	Excuse me. Where are you from?
Julie	I am from England. And you?
Passenger	I am from Amman. I am Jordanian.
Julie	Do you speak English?
Passenger	No, I am sorry, I don't speak English. I only speak Arabic.
Passenger	You speak Arabic fluently!
Julie	No, only a little.

Conversation 3

ráakib	maa :ámal-ik?
júulii	ána Táalibah fii jáami:at lándan. wa-anta?
ráakib	ána Tabíib fii :ammáan.

Passenger	What is your occupation?
Julie	I am a student, at London University. And you?
Passenger	I am a doctor in Amman.

Conversation 4

ráakib	hal lándan madíinah kabíirah?
júulii	ná:am híya madíinah kabíirah jíddan. hunáaka matáaHif kabíirah kathíirah wa-jusúur wa-maHalláat.
ráakib	áyna l-jáami:ah?
júulii	híya fii wasT al-madíinah, qaríibah min al-mátHaf al-bríiTáanii.

Passenger	Is London a big city?
Julie	Yes, it is a very big city. There are many big museums and bridges and shops.
Passenger	Where is the university?
Julie	It is in the middle of the town, near the British Museum.

Exercise 3

... ísm-haa sálmaa wa-híya suuríyyah min dimáshq. tatakállam al-lughah al-:arabíyyah wa l-ingliizíyyah wa l-faransíyyah. híya mudárrisah.

... her name is Salma and she is Syrian, from Damascus. She speaks Arabic, English and French. She is a teacher.

Exercise 4

máartin ruumáanuu min amríikaa. huwa Táalib. yatakállam inglíizii, wa-iiTáalii bi-Taláaqah wa :árabi qalíilan.

Martin Romano is American. He is a student. He speaks English, fluent Italian, and a little Arabic.

UNIT 4

Conversation 1

Hassan	This is the map of Sharjah. This is the Old Town and this is the fish market.
Jim	Where are the museums?
Hassan	These are the museums here and here. This is the Art Museum and this is the Natural History Museum, on the airport road.
Bridget	That museum is far away.
Jim	Yes, that's true. Look, the Fort Museum is here, in Tower (Burj) Street. It's an excellent museum, and maybe afterwards we can go to the Old Town.
Bridget	Good. We'll go to the Fort Museum.

Conversation 2

Hassan	Good morning. At what time does the museum close?
Attendant	Good morning. It closes at one o'clock and opens at four o'clock in the afternoon.
Bridget	What is the time now?
Hassan	It's a quarter past ten.
Bridget	Good. We have plenty of time.

Attendant	Welcome, come in. This is a brochure of the museum.
Hassan	Thank you.

Conversation 3

Hassan	Hello!
Attendant	Hello!
Hassan	How much is a ticket, please?
Attendant	Adults are six dirhams and children three dirhams.
Hassan	Three tickets at six dirhams please.
Attendant	Eighteen dirhams please. Thank you. Here are the tickets.
Hassan	Thank you.

Exercise 2

a as-sáa:ah tis:ah **b** as-sáa:ah thalaatha wa-niSf **c** as-sáa:ah ithna:shar illaa rub: **d** as-sáa:ah arba:ah wa-thulth **e** as-sáa:ah ithna:shar wa-:asharah **f** as-sáa:ah ithnayn illa khamsah

Exercise 6

a as-sáa:ah síttah wa-niSf wa-khámsah **b** as-sáa:ah thamáanyah wa-:ásharah **c** as-sáa:ah tís:ah wa-niSfílla khámsah **d** as-sáa:ah sáb:ah **e** as-sáa:ah árba:ah ílla rub: **f** as-sáa:ah khámsah wa-niSf **g** as-sáa:ah wáaHidah wa-rub: **h** as-sáa:ah ithna:shar **i** as-sáa:ah thaláathah wa-thulth **j** as-sáa:ah: ásharah wa-khámsah

UNIT 5

Conversation 1

Hamed	Tom, come in, please.
Tom	Thank you, Hamed.
Hamed	This is my wife, Salma. Salma, this is Tom, from the office.
Tom	Good evening, Salma, how are you?
Salma	I'm well, praise God. Welcome. And how are you?
Tom	Praise God. This is a present for you. (He gives Salma some flowers.)
Salma	Thank you, Tom. This is my father and this is my mother ... and this is our son, Tamiim. Please, sit down.
Tom	How old is Tamiim?
Salma	He is 15 years old and our daughter Farida is 21.

Hamed	How old are your children, Tom?
Tom	Our children are small – our son is 5 and our daughter is 3 years old.

Exercise 2

a tis:ah wa-tis:iin dirham **b** tis:ah wa-thamaaniin dirham **c** khamsah wa-sittiin dirham **d** khamsiin dirham **e** ithnayn wa-arba:iin dirham **f** tis:ah wa-sab:iin dirham **g** khamsah wa-:ishriin dirham

UNIT 6

Conversation 1

Andy	Excuse me, where is the centre of town?
Man	Straight ahead. Where are you going to?
Andy	I'm going to the office of Ali al-Mabrouk. Do you know it? Here is a map of the town. (Andy produces a map of the town.)
Man	Yes, I know it. Let me think. Yes, it's here. (He shows Andy on the map.) After the big mosque, turn left at the traffic lights. This is King Hussein Street. Go straight ahead for about 100 metres.
Andy	Yes, I understand.
Man	The office of Ali al-Mabrouk is on the right, beside the petrol station, opposite the Plaza cinema.
Andy	Oh, yes. Thank you. Is there a car park there?
Man	Yes, there is a big car park behind the office of Ali al-Mabrouk.
Andy	Thank you very much.
Man	You're welcome.

Exercise 3

a أين البلدية؟

b أين مركز الشرطة؟

c أين مركز التسوق «البستان»؟

d أين شارع الملك فيصل؟

e أين مطعم شهرزاد؟

Exercise 4

a على شمال الميدان، أمام سوق السمك

b وراء الميدان، بين سوق السمك والبنك

c أمام برج الاتصالات على شمال الصيدلية

d بين الكورنيش وشارع جمال عبد الناصر

e وراء مركز الشرطة بين سوق الذهب والفندق

UNIT 7

Conversation 1

He travelled to Amman in March and worked in the Jordanian office of his company. He stayed with my uncle. We wrote a letter to him every week. He returned to Kuwait in September.

Conversation 2

Zaki	What did you do yesterday?
Sonya	Yesterday I went to the house of Ahmed.
Zaki	How did you go there?
Sonya	I went by taxi. He and his family live in Zamalek.
Zaki	What did you do?
Sonya	I met his father and his mother and his sisters. His mother cooked lunch. After lunch we drank Arabic coffee.
Zaki	And did you like it?
Sonya	Yes, it is delicious.
Zaki	Did you return by taxi?
Sonya	No, I didn't come back by taxi. Ahmed gave me a lift home in his car.

UNIT 8

Reading 1

In the days of the Caliph Harun al-Rashid there was, in Baghdad, a poor porter whose name was Hindbad. One day this Hindbad was carrying a heavy load to the house of a merchant in the market. And that was in the summer and the heat of the sun was very strong. Hindbad became tired and thirsty. So he stopped in the road at the gate of a magnificent palace to rest from his work. He put his burden on the ground and sat down. And while he was sitting like that, he heard beautiful music emanating from inside the palace. And there was a servant standing in front of the gate of the palace, so Hindbad asked him: Who is the owner of this magnificent palace?

Reading 2

And the servant said to him: Verily it is the palace of Sindbad the Sailor. And the porter said: And who is he? And the servant was astonished and said: You are living in Baghdad and you have not heard of Sindbad the Sailor? Hindbad said: No. The servant said: He is the one who has travelled the seven seas and has seen all the wonders of the world. And the porter became sad and asked himself, saying: Why is this Sindbad rich and I am not rich? And Sindbad heard this from inside the palace and despatched another servant to the gate. This servant came out of the palace gate and said to Hindbad: Come with me. So the porter followed him inside the palace and he saw there a tall man, sitting in the midst of a group of people, and this man was Sindbad. And the Sailor said to the porter: Greetings and welcome. And he seated him next to himself and offered him many kinds of delicious food. And after that he told him about his amazing voyages and Sindbad had already ordered his servants to take Hindbad's load to the merchant's house.

UNIT 9
Conversation 1

Haydir	man huwa jawn parkir?
Imad	jawn parkir ingliizi. u:mruhu ithnáyn wa-thalaathíin sanah. Huwa mutazáwwaj. yatakállam :árabi wa aqaama fi al-imaaráat.
Haydir	maa lahu khabirah?
Imad	lahu khabirah khámsah sanawat fi al-mubii:ayat fi al-imaaráat. ladayh rakhaaSSah siwwaqah.

Haydir	Who is John Parker?
Imad	John Parker is English. He is 32 years old. He is married and speaks Arabic and lives in the Emirates.
Haydir	What is his experience?
Imad	He has five years' experience in sales in the Emirates. He has a driving licence.

Conversation 2

Hamid	Hello Halim. What's your house like?
Halim	I live in a small flat near the centre of town. It has one bedroom, a living room, a bathroom and a kitchen.

Hamid	Hello Farah. What's your house like?
Farah	We live in a new apartment. There are two bedrooms, one for me and my husband and one for the children, and a living room.
Hamid	Hello Saliha. What's your house like?
Saliha	We live in a house near the sea. It is very beautiful. We have four bedrooms, two bathrooms and two living rooms, and there is a kitchen as well.
Hamid	Hello Majid. What's your house like?
Majid	We live in a small house. There are three bedrooms, a living room, a bathroom and a kitchen.

UNIT 10

Conversation 1

Fawzia	What do you eat in the morning?
Kamal	I always eat fruit and sometimes bread and cheese, and I drink coffee. I usually telephone my son. He lives in America.
Fawzia	And then what do you do?
Kamal	I go to the office – my driver takes me at 8.30 and I talk with him in the car about the day's news.
Fawzia	And then?
Kamal	The secretary types letters for me while I read financial reports. This takes two to three hours.
Fawzia	Do you use a computer?
Kamal	Yes, of course. I learned the use of a computer at the College of Commerce.
Fawzia	And what do you do in the afternoon?
Kamal	In the afternoon I sit with the general manager and we discuss company affairs and I attend daily meetings with the employees.

Conversation 2

Ali	What do you do in your leisure time, Hisham?
Hisham	I play golf and I swim. When we lived in Amman I used to play tennis, but I don't play now. I read a lot.
Ali	I read a lot too. I like modern poetry. Do you like poetry, Ruhiyyah?
Ruhiyyah	No, I prefer novels. I watch television a lot and I like the Egyptian serials.

Ali	I don't like them.
Hisham	Me neither. I really hate them. I prefer cultural programmes or sports, but Ruhiyyah doesn't like sport.
Ruhiyyah	But we both like the cinema. We are going to the cinema this evening. Will you come with us, Ali?

UNIT 11
Conversation

Jack	how-many festival with the-Muslims?
Ahmad	the-festivals the-important with-us [are] two
Fran	and-what [are] they-two?
Ahmad	the-first he [is] the-festival the-small and-name-his [is] festival [of] the-fast-breaking
Jack	and in which month he?
Ahmad	festival [of] the-fast-breaking he [is] in first day [of] month [of] Shawal
Fran	and what [is] occasion-his?
Ahmad	occasion-his [is] that [the] month [of] Shawal he-follows [the] month [of] Ramadan the-holy, and-he [the] month [of] the-fasting with the-Muslims
Jack	and what [is] meaning [of] the-fasting with-you?
Ahmad	the-fasting, his-meaning [is] that the-people not they-eat and-not they-drink in the-daytime. This he [is] meaning of the-fasting
Fran	and what [is] he the-festival the-other?
Ahmad	he [is] the-festival the-great or festival [of] the-sacrifice
Jack	and what [is] occasion-his?
Ahmad	occasion-his [is] the-pilgrimage and he-begins in last day of [the] days [of] the pilgrimage. And the-pilgrimage, meaning-his [is] that the-people they-travel to Mecca the-Holy and-they-visit the-Kaabah
Fran	and how they-celebrate [for] this the-festival?
Ahmad	they they-slaughter in-him [i.e. it] sacrifice [animals]
Jack	and what [is] she the-sacrifice[animal]?
Ahmad	the sacrifice [animal] she [is a] sheep [which] they-slaughter-him and-they-eat-him in [the] end [of] the-pilgrimage. And he [i.e. it] [is a] custom with the-Muslims
Fran	so festivals-your two only then?
Ahmad	no, in some [of] the-regions they celebrate [with] festival third

272

Jack	and what [is] he?
Ahmad	he [is] birthday [of] the-prophet PBUH* in [the] month [of] Rabii the-first
Fran	yes, this [is] like [the] festival [of] the-birth with-us we the Christians

* Prayers and peace be upon Him [said after the name of the Prophet]

UNIT 12
Reading

With this the-phrase the-welcoming which overflows with-all the-feelings [of] the-friendship the-true she-greets [the-]Sharjah her-guests. And Emirate [of] the-Sharjah she [is] one [of] emirates [of the] state [of] the-Emirates the-Arab the-United which she-occupies [a] situation geographical prominent on the-Gulf the-Arab. And-he [is a] situation [which] has-caused the-Sharjah she-enjoys [i.e. to enjoy] over [the] extent [of] the-ages [a] role leading among [the] countries [of] the-Gulf the-Arab as [a] centre [of the] most-important [of] centres [of] the-activity the-commercial.

And-he-is-estimated [the] number [of] the-inhabitants according-to [the] latest the-census which was-carried-out [in] year 2013 at-about a million individuals that [is] in-density [which] is-estimated at-about 386 individual to-the-kilometre the-square.

And-Sharjah she-is-described by-that-she [is] the-capital the-cultural for-[the] state [of] the-Emirates, and-there [is a] department special [which] she-looks-after [the] implementation [of] the-activities the-cultural in the-Emirate, also she-comprises the-Emirate [a] number [of] the-museums the-scientific and-the-historical the-magnificent and [a] station from [the] most-modern [of] stations [of] the-transmission the-televisual [which] she-broadcasts the-many of the-programmes the-cultural and-the-educational.

UNIT 13
Reading

The-Koshari

(the-amount she-suffices 6 persons)

The-quantities

four cups and-half rice, it-is-washed and-it-is-strained

Cup [of] lentils black

Half cup [of] oil

Salt according-to the-desire

seven cups and-half [of] the-cup [of] water for-the-rice

ten cups [of] water for-boiling [of] the-macaroni

two-cups [of] macaroni

two spoons [of] food (i.e. tablespoons) [of] oil for-the-macaroni

six onions cut into slices long

The-sauce

two-spoons [of] food [of] ghee

six fruits [of] tomato peeled and-chopped

[a] spoon small [of] pepper red hot ground

two-spoons [of] food of paste [of] the-tomatoes

salt according-to the-desire

The-method

1- soak the-lentils in-the-water for-period [of] six hours and strain-it

2- fry the-onions in-the-oil then lift-them and-leave-them aside. Pour the-water over-them and-leave-them until they-boil a-little, then add the-rice and-the-lentils and-leave-them on fire gentle for-period [of] 40 minute

3- boil the-macaroni in-the-water then add the-oil

4- fry the-tomatoes in-the-oil, then add the pepper and the paste [of] the-tomatoes and the-salt

5- during the-presenting (i.e. serving) place [the] mixture [of] the-rice and-the-lentils firstly, then [a] layer of the-macaroni then [a] layer of the-onions, and-sprinkle over-it the-sauce the-hot or present-it to [the] side [of] the-plate

Listen and understand

Come to the meat section! On sale at amazing prices!

Sales of minced lamb 30 dirhams a kilo.

Look at the cheese selection from France and Italy.

Cook a dish of macaroni for the family today. Try the delicious Halloumi cheese.

Special rates for today only.

UNIT 14

Reading

Salma the-Arab [girl] who she-conquered Hollywood

In the-east we-regard-her [as the] female ambassador [of] the-beauty the-Arab who she-was-able that she-be [the] first woman [who] she-penetrates [the] walls [of] Hollywood and-she-imposes self-her on [the] top [of the] list [of the] stars [of] the-cinema

And-in the-west they-regard-her [as a] symbol of-[the]-magic [of] the-East by-what she-bears-it of features oriental [the] extreme in the-beauty which it-equals the-magic and-for-this they-gave-her the-leads in [the] greatest [of] films-their preferring-her to most [of the] stars [of] Hollywood beauty-wise and-so Salma Hayek today she-competes [with] Angelina Jolie and-Penelope Cruz and-other-[than]-them-two of [the] stars [of] Hollywood

And-Salma al-Hayek, or [the] legend [of] the-East in the-West, the-born [in the] year 1966 she [is the] daughter [of an] emigrant Lebanese residing in-Mexico mother-her Spanish [of] the-origin and-if came-together the-beauty the-Lebanese and-the-Spanish will-be the-fruit in [the] beauty [of] Salma al-Hayek. And-because-she [is] beautiful very so-[past marker] spotted-her [the] eye [of] the-producers and-she in the-thirteenth [year] of age-her and-she-was-chosen at-that-time as-[the]-most-beautiful [of] the-faces the-television. Then he-took-her the-producer Tarantino to-Los Angeles so-she-participated in the-film Desperado at [the] side [of] Antonio Banderas and-she-gave to-the-film [a] flavour special very [which] it-attracted to-her [the] interest [of the] companies [of] the-production the-great and-soon they-offered to-her the-contracts the-many

Since then she has starred in many films such as Frida and in fact even become a producer. One of her most recent film is The Prophet an animation film of the famous book by the Lebanese writer Khalil Gilbran

UNIT 15

Reading

Night black for-the [foot]ball the-Moroccan

Qualified the-team the-Tunisian for the-round the-final of [the]competition [of the] Cup [of] the-Arabs in night black for-the [foot]ball the-Moroccan. And-on [the] pitch of the-Zamalek in the-Cairo yesterday, and-before 42 thousand spectator led Mahmoud al-Turki the-team the-Tunisian to the-victory. And-scored al-Turki personally three goals in the-match which ended 5-1

And-opened the-team the-Tunisian the-scoring by way [of] its-centre Jaafar Abu Adil with [a] shot splendid from outside the-area [which] deceived the-goalkeeper the-Moroccan in the-minute the-ninth of-the-match. And-was [the]-result of-the-opportunity the-first for-the-team the-Moroccan their-goal the-sole in [the] end [of] the-half the-first when shot Tariq al-Ahmar [a] ball curved [which] entered [the] corner [of] the-goal the-Tunisian and gained the-equality

But-it appeared that the-players the-Moroccan [past marker] raised the-flag the-white in the-half the-second and-dominated the-Tunisians [on] the-play domination complete. And-came the-goals with-speed horrific, [the] last-[of]-them in the-minute the-last of-the-match when placed the-captain the-Tunisian the-ball [in] the-net the-Moroccan for-the-time the-third after awarded the-referee kick corner and-sent-off the-defender the-Moroccan Suleiman al-Fasi for-his-getting the-card the-yellow the-second

Listen and understand

Example:

سؤال   ماذا تحب من الرياضات؟

جواب ألعب كرة القدم كثيرا

1 ماذا تلعب يا يونس؟

ألعب تنس أحيانا، لكن ألعب جولف كثيرا

2 وأنت يا سعيد؟

أذهب إلى القاعة الرياضية يوميا

3 هل تمارسين السباحة يا فريدة؟

لا، أمارس السباحة نادرا. أفضل التزلج. أمارس التزلج كثيرا

4 هل تمارس السباحة يا حامد؟

نعم، أسبح أحيانا، وأحيانا أركب الزوارق الشراعية

5 يا سونية، هل ركبت الزوارق الشراعية؟

لا أبدا. أمارس الايروبيك كثيرا

UNIT 16

Reading 1

The-antiquities the-Egyptian in the-abroad

He-stated head [of the] department [of the] antiquities the-Egyptian yesterday about welcoming-his of-resolution [of] the-assembly the-general to-the-Nations the-United to-the-allowing to-the-states which to-them antiquities smuggled in the-abroad for-reclaiming-them. And-he-said that-it there approximately 21 million piece archaeological Egyptian stolen in the-West most-famous-[of]-them beard [of] Father of Terror [i.e. the Sphinx] and stone [of] Rosetta the-situated in the-Museum the-British in London

Reading 2

450 European Tourists in Aden

Received port [of] Aden yesterday the-first [i.e. the day before yesterday] ship touristic German [which] she-carries more than 400 tourist [male] and-tourist [female] from various [of] the-nationalities the-European. And-[future marker]-visit these the-tourists some [of] the-towns the-Yemeni the-historical

Reading 3

Announced millionaire American from state [of] California in the-week the-past that-he [future marker] marry [a] girl in the-fifth and-the-twenty of life-her. And-this after celebrating-his of-anniversary [of] birth-his the-hundredth by-days few. And-he he-uses regulator for-beats [of] the-heart and-he- is transported on chair with-wheels. And-he-said that-he he-loves-her from all [of] his-heart and-she returns-him the-love

Reading 4

Arrived in the UAE today the famous Lebanese singer Majida Roumi on a private visit, during which she will visit her family, who lives in Abu Dhabi. During her visit, she will perform at the charity concert which is scheduled to take place on Friday at the Cultural Center. The proceeds of the concert will go to provide protection for refugee children around the world and ensure a better future for them. Tickets are still available from the box office and on the Internet.

Reading 5

International poetry day

Chose organization [of] the-UNESCO [the] day 21 March [as a] day world-wide for-the-poetry. And-welcomed the-poets the-Arab [with]-this, among-them the-poet the-Iraqi Ali Jaafar al-Allaq who he-said that-he [was] "Believing belief not limits to-it that the-poetry [is] bigger than the-time all-[of]-it, and-more extent-wise than the-places totally. Indeed-it [is] filler [of] the-moments and-the-seasons and-the-centuries with-beauty [of] the-meaning and meaning [of] the-beauty"

Grammar summary

This grammar summary is intended to be used as a reference and does not cover all the language given in the course.

1 Definite and indefinite

In Arabic, all nouns and adjectives are either <u>definite</u> or <u>indefinite</u>.

THE DEFINITE ARTICLE

A definite noun is specific and can be a proper noun (e.g. *Cairo, Mohammed*), a pronoun (e.g. *I, you, they*) or preceded by the word **al-** *the*, called the definite article. **al-** never changes for gender or number and is always attached to the following noun or adjective, e.g. البيت **al-bayt** *the house*.

al- is always the same in written Arabic. In pronunciation, if the preceding word ends in a vowel or **-ah**, the **a** of **al-** is omitted, e.g. القهوة اللذيذة **al-qáhwah l-ladhíidhah** *the delicious coffee*.

If the word begins with one of the following Arabic letters:

t ت **th** ث **d** د **dh** ذ **r** ر **z** ز **s** س **sh** ش **S** ص **D** ض **T** ط **DH** ظ **l** ل **n** ن

the **l** of the **al-** is omitted in pronunciation and the following letter is clearly doubled.

Written	Pronounced after a consonant	Pronounced after a vowel
الرَجُل	**ar-rajul**	**r-rajul** *the man*
الشمس	**ash-shams**	**sh-shams** *the sun*
النور	**an-nuur**	**n-nuur** *the light*

THE INDEFINITE ARTICLE

There is no indefinite article or word for *a* in Arabic. **bayt** in Arabic means *a house*.

2 Nouns

MASCULINE AND FEMININE

In Arabic, all nouns are either masculine or feminine in gender. Nouns ending in **-ah** are usually feminine, but there are a few feminine nouns that do not have this ending, e.g. أم **umm** *mother*, and a handful of masculine nouns end in **-ah**, e.g. خليفة **khaliifah** *caliph*.

SINGULAR AND PLURAL

Arabic plural formations should be learned at the same time as the singular.

The plural in Arabic refers to more than two (2+). For just two of anything, we need to use the <u>dual</u> (see the following section on this).

The <u>external masculine plural</u>, used in words for male human beings, is formed by adding ون **-uun** to the singular noun, e.g. مدرسون ،مدرس mudarris → **mudarrisuun** (m.) *teachers*. (For the accusative form, add ين **-iin** to the singular.)

The <u>external feminine/neuter plural</u>, used for the plural of most females and some other nouns, is formed by dropping the ة **-ah** (if there is one) and adding ات **-aat** to the singular word, e.g. مدرسات ،مدرسة mudarrisah → **mudarrisaat** (f.) *teachers*. (There is no special accusative form.)

The <u>internal plural</u>, used mainly for males and things, is formed by altering the internal vowelling of the word and/or by adding prefixes or suffixes. Although there is no general relationship between the singular word shape and the plural word shape, short words are more likely to take an internal plural, e.g. كتب ،كتاب kitaab → **kutub** *books*.

All plurals of things are regarded in Arabic as feminine singular for the purposes of agreement of adjectives and verbs.

THE DUAL

The <u>dual</u> must be used when talking about two of anything and is mostly regular for both nouns and adjectives. It is formed by adding an external suffix, similar to the masculine external plural, to the majority of nouns and adjectives.

Case	Suffix	Example
Subject	**-aan** ـان	SaaHibaan صاحبان
Other cases	**-ayn** ـين	SaaHibayn صاحبين

If a word has the feminine **-ah** ending, this changes to **-at** (spelled with an ordinary ت), and the suffix **-aan** is added to it.

Adjectives must take the appropriate masculine or feminine dual ending and also agree with the noun in case, e.g. السيارتان كبيرتان **as-sayyaarataan kabiirataan** *the two cars are big*. It is not usually necessary to insert the numeral word.

As with the masculine plural ending ون / ـين **-uun/-iin**, the final ن is omitted if the word has a pronoun suffix or is the first term of a possessive construction, e.g. كوبا ماء **kuubaa maa'** *two cups of water*.

In spoken Arabic, the ending **-ayn** is used in all contexts.

3 Adjectives

AGREEMENT OF ADJECTIVES

Adjectives must agree in number, gender and definiteness with the nouns they describe, e.g.:

الفيلم الممتاز	**al-fiilm al-mumtaz**	*the excellent film*
جريدة جيدة	**jariidah jayyidah**	*a good newspaper*

In most cases, the feminine of an adjective is formed by adding ة **-ah** to the masculine, e.g. طويل، طويلة **Tawiil, Tawiilah** *tall, long*.

If there is more than one adjective, it is added after the first one, agreeing with it and the noun, e.g.:

الفندق الكبير الجديد	**al-funduq al-kabiir al-jadiid**	*the big new hotel*
بنت جميلة صغيرة	**bint jamiilah Saghiirah**	*a beautiful young girl*

ADJECTIVES OF NATIONALITY

Adjectives indicating nationality are formed by adding ي **-ii**/ية **-íyyah** to the name of the country, e.g. مصر **miSr** *Egypt* → مصرية مصري **míSrii/miSríyyah** *Egyptian*.

Where the name of a country ends in **-aa** or **-ah**, this is omitted before the ending is added:

بريطانيا	**briiTáanya**	*Britain*
بريطاني/بريطانية	**briiTáanii/briiTaaníyyah**	*British*

If the Arabic place name has the word **al-** *the* in front of it, this is omitted from the nationality adjective:

المغرب	**al-mághrib**	*Morocco*
مغربي/مغربية	**mághribii/maghribíyyah**	*Moroccan*

SINGULAR AND PLURAL ADJECTIVES

The plurals of Arabic adjectives follow the same rules as nouns, adding the **-uun** (m.) or the **-aat** (f.) ending, or by means of internal plurals, which are given in the vocabulary with their singulars.

All plurals of things are regarded in Arabic as feminine singular, e.g. الكتب الطويلة **al-kútub aT-Tawíilah** *the long books.*

Noun	Adjective
Male human beings	either internal plural if it has one or+ **-uun**
Female human beings	+ **-aat**
Things/abstracts	+ **-ah** (f. sing.)

The primary colours are an exception (see Unit 15).

WORD ORDER

The adjective comes after the noun. In sentences with verbs, the verb usually (but not always) comes first.

4 Pronouns

SUBJECT OR PERSONAL PRONOUNS

Subject pronouns are always definite.

Singular	Plural
أنا **ána** *I*	نحن **náHnu** *we*
أنت **ánta** *you* (m.)	أنتم **ántum** *you* (m. pl.)
أنت **ánti** *you* (f.)	أنتن **antúnna** *you* (f. pl.)
هو **húwa** *he*	هم **hum** *they* (m.)
هي **híya** *she*	هن **húnna** *they* (f. pl.)

The final **alif** of أنا **ana** is pronounced short and the first syllable is accented. Most final **-aa** sounds in informal modern Arabic are pronounced short unless they bear the stress.

The male and female singular you forms are identical in writing, but the context usually makes clear which one is intended.

English *it* is translated into Arabic as *he* or *she*, depending on the gender of the word to which it refers.

POSSESSIVE PRONOUN SUFFIXES

There is no equivalent in Arabic to English *mine*, *yours*, etc. The words *my*, *your*, *his*, etc. are expressed in Arabic as suffixes joined on to the object that is possessed, e.g. بيتهم **báyt-hum** *their house.*

Singular	Plural
ي **-ii** *my*	نا **-na(a)** *our*
ك **-ak** *your* (m.)	كم **-kum** *your* (m.)
ك **-ik** *your* (f.)	كن **-kúnna** *your* (f.)
ه **-uh** *his*	هم **-hum** *their* (m.)
ها **-ha(a)** *her*	هن **-húnna** *their* (f.)

OBJECT PRONOUN SUFFIXES

Arabic uses the same pronoun suffixes as the possessive pronoun suffixes, with the exception of *me*, which is ني **-nii** after verbs.

The suffixes are added to the verb to express the object of the sentence, e.g.:

كلمته أمس	**kallamt-uh ams**	*I spoke to him yesterday*
خبرني ناصر	**khabbar-nii naaSir**	*Nasser told me*

5 Saying *to have*

There is no verb *to have* in Arabic. Instead, this is expressed by using one of the prepositions لـ **li-** *to/for* or عند **:ind(a)** *with* (cf. French *chez*) with a noun or pronoun, e.g. للولد كتاب **li-l-walad kitaab** *the boy has a book.*

The object of the English verb then becomes the subject of the Arabic sentence, e.g. *he has a car* → عنده سيارة **:ind-uh sayyaarah** (lit. *with him (is) a car*).

6 Accusative marker

ARABIC CASES

Formal Arabic has three varying case endings showing the part played by a word in a sentence, most of which are omitted in modern Arabic.

The only case ending appearing in print in contemporary written Arabic – except for a few special types of noun – is the accusative case of indefinite unsuffixed nouns or adjectives. It is written by placing an **alif** after the noun/adjective and pronounced **-an**. This ending is generally ignored in spoken Arabic except in many adverbs and some traditional Arabic greetings, e.g. طبعا **Tab:an** *naturally*, أهلاً وسهلاً **ahlan wa sahlan** *hello, welcome*.

The few unsuffixed nouns and adjectives that do not add the alif include the main colours, some forms of the internal plural and many proper nouns. These are all marked in the vocabulary boxes and the glossaries with an asterisk (*).

كان الكلب أبيض	kaana l-kalb abyaD	*the dog was white*
قرأنا جرائد كثيرة أمس	qara'naa jaraa'id kathiirah ams	*we read many newspapers yesterday*
قابلنا أحمد في السوق	qaabalnaa aHmad fi s-suuq	*we met Ahmed in the souq*

USES OF THE ACCUSATIVE MARKER

In Arabic, the accusative marker is used where the second noun is the object of the sentence: شاهدوا قصراً فخماً **shaahaduu qaSran fakhman** *they saw a magnificent castle*.

It is also used after the verbs كان **kaana** *was, were/to be*, ليس **laysa** *is not, are not/not to be*, أصبح **aSbaHa** *to become* and a few other similar verbs.

It is also used in some common expressions and adverbs (see earlier) and also after certain short words or particles, such as إنّ **inna** and أنّ **anna**.

7 Verbs

IS/ARE SENTENCES

There is no Arabic equivalent to the English *is/are*. Instead, a definite concept is simply followed by an indefinite one, e.g. **al-bayt kabiir** *the house is big*.

PAST TENSE

All Arabic verbs are derived from a root, usually a three-letter one, e.g. ك-ت-ب **k-t-b**, which has the meaning of *writing*. Most verbs are formed from either a past or a present stem, with a standard set of prefixes and suffixes. The same prefixes and suffixes apply to every Arabic verb.

The Arabic past tense is used when the action of the verb is complete. To form the past tense, suffixes are added to the past stem, e.g. **katab**, as follows:

Singular	Plural
kátab-a *he wrote*	**kátab-uu** *they (m.) wrote*
kátab-at *she wrote*	**katáb-na** *they (f.) wrote*
katáb-t(a) *you (m.) wrote*	**katáb-tum** *you (m.) wrote*

katáb-ti *you (f.) wrote*	**katab-túnna** *you (f.) wrote*
katáb-t(u) *I wrote*	**katáb-na(a)** *we wrote*

If the subject is not stated as a noun, it is usually unnecessary to use a subject pronoun, since the suffix distinguishes the subject, e.g. **katabat** *she wrote.*

If the subject is a noun, the normal (but not exclusive) word order in Arabic is V–S–O:

1 Verb   2 Subject   3 Object/the rest

Verbs that come at the beginning of the sentence in Arabic can only have the *he* or *she* form, i.e. always singular, never plural, e.g. زار الوزراء البيوت الجديدة **zaara l-wuzaaraa' al-buyuut al-jadiidah** *the ministers visited the new houses.*

Verb	Subject
he form for ...	1 one male being
	2 two or more male beings
	3 one or two objects (grammatically m.)
she form for ...	1 one female being
	2 two or more female beings
	3 one or two objects (grammatically f.)
	4 more than two of any objects

If the sentence has two verbs, the word order is V1–S–O–V2:

1 1st Verb   2 Subject   3 Object (if any)   4 2nd Verb

The first verb is in the *he/she* form and the second verb follows the subject and agrees fully with it, e.g. ذهب الأولاد إلى السينما وشاهدوا الفيلم **dhahaba l-awlaad ilaa s-siinamaa wa-shaahaduu l-fiilm** *the boys went to the cinema and watched the film.*

A verb that for any reason comes after its subject must agree fully in number and gender.

SAYING *WAS* AND *WERE*

Although there is no verb in Arabic for *is/are*, the verb كان **kaana** is necessary for *was/were*.

The suffix endings are the same past tense ones used on all Arabic verbs.

Singular	Plural
كان **kaan-a** *he was*	كانوا **kaan-uu** *they (m.) were*
كانت **kaan-at** *she was*	كنّ **kun-na** *they (f.) were*
كنت **kun-t(a)** *you (m.) were*	كنتم **kun-tum** *you (m.) were*
كنت **kun-ti** *you (f.) were*	كنتن **kun-tunna** *you (f.) were*
كنت **kun-t(u)** *I was*	كنّا **kun-naa** *we were*

The final vowels in parentheses are omitted in informal speech.

Since the last letter of the root of this verb is -n, the doubling sign is used when the suffix also begins with an **-n**, e.g **kunna** *they* (f.) and **kunnaa** *we*, e.g كنّا في تونس في الصيف **kunnaa fii tuunis fi S-Sayf** *we were in Tunisia in the summer.*

The doubling sign does not usually appear in printed Arabic.

After the verb **kaana** the accusative marker must be used with unsuffixed indefinite nouns or adjectives.

kaana usually comes first in the sentence, e.g كان جمال عبد الناصر قائدا عظيما **kaana jamaal :abd an-naaSir qaa'idan :aDHiiman** *Jamaal Abd al-Nasir was a great leader.*

PRESENT TENSE

The Arabic present tense is used if the action of the verb is incomplete. To form the present tense, prefixes – and suffixes for certain parts – are added to the present tense stem, e.g. **ktub**, as follows:

Singular	Plural
ya-ktub *he writes, is writing*	**ya-ktub-uun** *they (m.) write*
ta-ktub *she writes*	**ya-ktub-na** *they (f.) write*
ta-ktub *you (m.) write*	**ta-ktub-uun** *you (m.) write*
ta-ktub-iin *you (f.) write*	**ta-ktub-na** *you (f.) write*
a-ktub *I write*	**na-ktub** *we write*

A full explanation of how to find the present stem of the verb is given in the Verb tables.

EXPRESSING THE FUTURE

Arabic expresses what you will do in the future by placing the word سوف **sawfa** before the present tense verb or the prefix ـس **sa-**, which is joined to the verb that follows it, e.g. سوف يصل الوزير غدا **sawfa yaSil al-waziir ghadan** *the minister will arrive tomorrow*; سيلعب الأولاد في الشارع **sa-yal:ab al-awlaad fi-sh-shaari:** *the children will play in the street*.

PLUPERFECT TENSE

The pluperfect tense is formed by using the verb كان **kaana** with the past tense.

The word قد **qad** emphasizes that the action is completely over and done with.

The word order is always:

1 **kaana**   2 Subject   3 **qad** (optional)   4 Main verb   5 The rest

The same rules of agreement must be followed as those given above. The pluperfect tense is used to say what you had done, e.g. كان المدير (قد) وصل يوم السبت **kaana al-mudiir (qad) waSal yawm as sabt** *the manager had arrived on Saturday*.

THE PAST CONTINUOUS

The past continuous is formed with **kaana** and the present tense verb. It is used to say what used to happen or what was habitual, e.g. كنا نذهب إلى السوق كل يوم **kunnaa nadhhab ilaa s-suuq kull yawm** *we used to go to the market every day*.

Verb tables

The Arabic verb

The Arabic verb is best considered from three distinct points of view: grammatical, phonetic and stem modification.

1 GRAMMATICAL

The grammatical variations of the verb are there for two main reasons:

▶ to tell us who is carrying or has carried out the action. This is important as, unlike English, Arabic commonly omits the subject pronouns *I*, *you*, *he*, etc. so the verb itself has to carry this information;

▶ to tell us the timing of the action, i.e. when it takes (*has taken/will take*, etc.) place.

Subject markers

The grammatical term for who is responsible for the action of a verb is called <u>person</u>.

Like English, Arabic verbs have three persons:

▶ the person(s) speaking (*I*, *we*), called the <u>first person</u>

▶ the person(s) spoken to (*you*), called the <u>second person</u>

▶ the person(s) spoken about (*he*, *she*, *it*, *they*) called the <u>third person</u>.

However, Arabic makes finer distinctions in some cases:

▶ The second person has to indicate the sex of the person spoken to. This is called <u>gender</u>.

▶ The Arabic verb has a set of parts referring to two people known as the <u>dual</u>. English only distinguishes between *one* and *more than one*.

> **LANGUAGE TIP**
>
> Traditionally, the Arabic verb is tabled in the reverse order of persons, i.e. starting with the third. This is because the third person *he* part is regarded as the simplest, most basic form of the verb. This convention has been employed throughout this book.

	Singular	Dual	Plural
third person	*he*	*they two* (m)	*they* (m.)
	she*	*they two* (f.)	*they* (f.)

second person	you (m.)	you two (m. & f.)	you (m.)
	you (f.)	you (f.)	
first person	I (m. & f.)	we (m. & f.)	

*Since Arabic has no neuter gender, English *it* must be rendered (*he* or *she*) according to the grammatical gender of the Arabic noun.

Tense

The tense of a verb refers to when the action takes/took/will take place. Arabic has only two true tenses, <u>present</u> and <u>past</u>.

Other grammatical characteristics

The present tense – but not the past – of the Arabic verb has three variants called <u>moods</u>. The normal form of the present tense is called the <u>indicative</u> and the other two forms are the <u>subjunctive</u> and the <u>jussive</u>. These are not so important in Modern Arabic, as often all three look identical. However, in some types of verb, the jussive, especially, shows changes in spelling and so all three have been included in the tables. The subjunctive and the jussive are mainly used with certain conjunctions. These are dealt with in the main body of the book.

The imperative is a special form of the jussive, used in issuing commands. This is not included in the tables, as its formation from the jussive is explained in Unit 13.

Another distinction is that technically known as <u>voice</u>. Normal verbs where the subject is responsible for the action are called <u>active</u>: *He ate the cake*. So-called <u>passive</u> verbs are those where the grammatical subject has the action of the verb performed on it: *The cake was eaten*.

For technical reasons, passives are much less important in Arabic than in English, but they have been included for the sake of completeness.

2 PHONETIC

The Arabic verb is relatively regular. Virtually all verbs take the same prefixes and suffixes and those that vary do so in a minor way. There are, for example, no so-called irregular or strong verbs as proliferate in European languages, such as English *go, went, has gone/is, was, has been*, and so on.

However, there are several phonetic factors which affect verbs:

▶ The presence of one of the letters و or ي as a root letter in any position. These letters tend to be elided or smoothed out into vowels.

▶ Verb roots where the third consonant is the same as the second, e.g. **d-l-l**, **m-r-r**, etc. This causes contracted verb forms.

▶ The letter ء **hamzah** causes some spelling difficulties when it occurs in a root. However, these are learned by experience and observation and no tables have been given.

> **LANGUAGE TIP**
>
> Verbs that do not have any of the above features have been termed <u>sound</u> (abbreviation S) in this book.

3 STEM MODIFICATION

The tenses of the Arabic verb are formed by attaching prefixes and suffixes to the 'heart' or 'nucleus' of the verb, called the <u>stem</u>. An approximate English parallel would be to take talk as the stem of that verb. In language instruction, we can then say that, for instance, you add the suffix -s for the *he* form – *he talks* – and -ed to form the past tense – *talked*.

A significant feature of the Arabic verb is <u>stem modification</u>, which means that the stems themselves are modified in a finite number of ways to give different meanings. The nearest we get to this in English is *to fall* and *to fell (a tree)* i.e. *cause it to fall*, but, in Arabic, the phenomenon is very widespread.

Every Arabic verb has the potential to modify its stem in nine different ways, which, by Western (but not Arab) convention are referred to as <u>derived forms</u> and indicated using the Roman numerals I–X, Form I being the base form. It is doubtful if any verb possesses the total of ten derived forms, but it is essential to learn them all, as many basic everyday verbs are up in the high numbers.

TABLE 1: PREFIXES AND SUFFIXES OF THE VERB

This table gives all the prefixes and suffixes which, when applied to the relevant present or past stem, give all the parts of the Arabic verb. It should be studied in conjunction with the following notes.

The table in transliteration follows English order, from left to right:
*Hyphen + letter = suffix (e.g. **-at**)*
*Letter + hyphen = prefix (e.g. **ya-**)*

	Past	Present	Subjunctive/Jussive
Singular			
he	stem-a	ya-stem	no written change in sound verbs except for parts given
she	stem-at	ta-stem	
you (m.)	stem-ta	ta-stem	
you (f.)	stem-ti	ta-stem-iina	ta-stem-ii
I	stem-tu	a-stem	
Dual			
they two (m.)	stem-aa	ya-stem-aani	ya-stem-aa
they two (f.)	stem-ataa	ta-stem-aani	ta-stem-aa
you two (m. & f.)	stem-tumaa	ta-stem-aani	ta-stem-aa
Plural			
they (m.)	stem-uu	ya-stem-uuna	ya-stem-uu
they (f.)	stem-na	ya-stem-na	
you (m.)	stem-tum	ta-stem-uuna	ta-stem-uu
you (f.)	stem-tunna	ta-stem-na	
we	stem-naa	na-stem	

> **LANGUAGE TIP**
>
> Make a habit while learning these verb parts of noting which suffixes begin with a vowel
>
> and which with a consonant.

Here is an Arabic example, using the verb *to write*. In order to highlight the prefixes and suffixes, lengthened ligatures (lines joining the letters) have been used and the vowelling of the past and present stems (كَتَب and كْتُب respectively) has been omitted.

	Past	Present	Subjunctive/Jussive
Singular			
he	كتَبَ	يَـكتب	no written change in sound verbs except for parts given
she	كتَبَتْ	تَـكتب	
you (m.)	كتبْـتَ	تَـكتب	
you (f.)	كتبْـتِ	تَـكتبِـينَ	تَـكتبِي
I	كتبْـتُ	أكتب	
Dual			
they two (m.)	كتبَـا	يَـكتبَـانِ	يَـكتبَـا
they two (f.)	كتبَـتَـا	تَـكتبَـانِ	تَـكتبَـا
you two (m. & f.)	كتبْـتُـمَـا	تَـكتبَـانِ	تَـكتبَـا
Plural			
they (m.)	كتبُـوا	يَـكتبُـونَ	يَـكتبُـوا
they (f.)	كتبْـنَ	يَـكتبْـنَ	
you (m.)	كتبْـتُـمْ	تَـكتبُـونَ	تَـكتبُـوا
you (f.)	كتبْـتُـنَّ	تَـكتبْـنَ	
we	كتبْـنَـا	نَـكتب	

> **LANGUAGE TIP**
>
> The Arabic version of the tip given above is to note which stems end with a **sukuun** (no vowel sign) on the last consonant of the root and which do not.

NOTES:

▶ The above tables give all the prefixes and suffixes which, when applied to the appropriate stems, give all the parts of any Arabic verb, with the following minor exceptions:

  ▷ *with derived stems II, III and IV (see Table S) and all passive stems (Table S) the prefixes of the present tense are vowelled with* **u**, *i.e.* يُـ، تُـ، أُ، نُـ.

- ▷ in certain stems whose final radical is و or ي certain of the endings are slightly modified in pronunciation, but not in writing. These changes are of little importance in practice, but are dealt with in the appropriate tables.
- ▶ Certain short final vowels are habitually omitted in speech:
  - ▷ Past tense: final vowel of he, you (m.) (but not f.), and I in the singular. Any resulting ambiguity is usually cleared up by context.
  - ▷ Present tense: **-i** of the dual forms ending in **-aani**, and **-a** of the second person singular feminine and the plural forms ending in **-uuna** (but not the **-a** of the feminine plural **-na** ending).
- ▶ Note carefully the (unpronounced) **alif** written after plural forms ending in **-uu** in both tenses. This is a spelling convention which applies only to this verb suffix.
- ▶ The moods. Where no written changes are indicated in the table, the unsuffixed parts of the indicative originally ended in **-u**, those of the subjunctive in **-a** and the jussive with no vowel. These are unmarked in Modern Arabic and have thus been ignored in this book, only parts which differ in spelling having been noted. You will note that verb parts ending in **-uuna** and **-aani** lose their ن in the subjunctive and jussive – see also note above. The feminine plural **-na** ending is not affected.

Verb tables

INTRODUCTION

So that you can identify each verb and cross-reference it with the Verb tables, we have devised the following system and tagged all the verbs in the vocabularies and glossaries accordingly.

The verb entries are given as in the following example:

كتب   **kataba** [S-I u]   *to write*

Reading from left to right these represent:

- ▶ كتب The *he* form of the past tense in the Arabic script (see Tip box in section 1 above). This also in most cases constitutes the past stem.
- ▶ **kataba** This is the transliteration of the Arabic script and provides the vowel of the middle radical (especially relevant to Form I verbs).
- ▶ **[S-I u]** This identifies the verb type so that you can look it up in the tables. This example is an S type, Form I [S-I]. The following lowercase letter (here **u**) is the vowel to be used

in the present stem. It is only necessary to give this vowel for Form I verbs as other types show no variation.

▶ *to write* The meaning.

<blockquote>
LANGUAGE TIP

In virtually all Arabic verbs, it is only the stem that changes. Once you have learned the prefixes and suffixes given in the table above, you can apply them to all verbs. So, although there appear to be a lot of tables, you only have to learn between two and four stem parts for each verb. Your task will therefore be much lighter if you spend some time now mastering the prefixes and suffixes thoroughly.
</blockquote>

TABLE S, SOUND VERBS [S-I TO S-X]

'Sound' in this context means 'without weakness'. The definition in relation to the Arabic verb is simple: a sound verb is one which:

▶ does not have و or ي as any of its radicals (root consonants)

▶ does not have the same letter for its middle and last radical (such as ر–د–د, for example).

If a root does not display either of the above two features, it is sound (**S**).

<blockquote>
IMPORTANT NOTE

Since it is impossible to find a verb that occurs in all the derived forms (II–X), we have followed the convention of using the root ف – ع – ل **f-:-l** in the following table. Although not particularly user friendly because of the difficult middle consonant, this has the advantage of being the system that the Arabs use. You will, therefore, be able to seek advice from native speakers.
</blockquote>

Verbs in these categories are marked in the glossaries S-I to S-X (but see special notes on Forms I and IX).

The following table gives the past and present stems. To construct the required verb part, simply add the prefixes and/or suffixes given in Table 1 (above) to the appropriate stem, observing the Form I vowellings where necessary.

Active	Past stem	Present stem
S-I	فَعَل	فْعَل
S-II	فَعَّل	فَعِّل
S-III	فَاعَل	فَاعِل
S-IV	أَفْعَل	فْعِل

	Past stem	Present stem
S-V	تَفَعَّل	تَفَعَّل
S-VI	تَفَاعَل	تَفَاعَل
S-VII	اِنْفَعَل	نْفَعِل
S-VIII	اِفْتَعَل	فْتَعِل
S-IX	see notes	
S-X	اِسْتَفْعَل	سْتَفْعِل

Passive	Past stem	Present stem
S-I	فُعِل	فْعَل
S-II	فُعِّل	فَعَّل
S-III	فُوعِل	فَاعَل
S-IV	أُفْعِل	فْعَل
S-V	تُفُعِّل	تَفَعَّل
S-VI	تُفُوعِل	تَفَاعَل
S-VII	none	
S-VIII	أُفْتُعِل	فْتَعَل
S-IX	see notes	
S-X	أُسْتُفْعِل	سْتَفْعَل

General notes

The passive is given in full for the sake of completeness, but it is not worth devoting a lot of time to learning it as it is much more restricted in use than its English equivalent. Form VII does not have a passive, and in some other forms it is rare.

Form IX. For technical reasons, this comparatively rare form is given along with the Doubled verb (Table D).

Form S-I

This is the only form that has more than one vowel pattern. In the glossaries, the past stem vowelling can be obtained from the transliteration (e.g. **kataba**), while the present stem vowelling is given after the verb type (e.g. S-I u). So the verb فَعَل فْعَل **fa:ala f:al** given in the table would be marked S-I a. As there is no reliable way to predict these vowellings they have to be learned along with their verbs. The vowels in the passive of Form I, however, do not change.

Form S-II

This is formed by doubling the middle radical and vowelling according to the table. It often has a causative meaning, e.g. **fahima** (I) *to understand*, **fahhama** (II) *to make someone understand, explain*. The present tense prefixes take a **u** vowel (see above).

Form S-III

Formed by interposing an **alif** between the first and middle radicals. Again, the present tense prefixes take a **u** vowel.

Form S-IV

Formed by prefixing أ to the root in the perfect. This disappears in the present, which again takes a **u** vowel. Like Form II, this often has a causative meaning.

Form S-V

Formed by prefixing **ta-** and doubling the middle radical. (Note: the past and present stems of Forms V and VI are identical. All the other derived forms above Form I alternate a middle radical vowel of **a** in the past with **i** in the present.)

Form S-VI

Formed by prefixing **ta-** and introducing an **alif** after the first radical. Again, both stems are identical.

Form S-VII

Formed by prefixing انـ **in-** to the stem and following the vowel pattern given. Like all other forms beginning with **alif**, this disappears in the present.

Form S-VIII

Formed by prefixing **alif** and introducing ت after the first radical. Some assimilations occur in this form when certain letters occur as the first radical. These will be pointed out as they occur.

Form S-IX

Because its formation involves the reduplication of the last radical, this behaves like a doubled verb and is therefore given in Table D.

Form S-X

Formed by prefixing اِسْتـ ist- to the root. The **alif** disappears in the present.

> **SUMMARY**
>
> Study this table carefully, as it comprises the bones of the Arabic verb system. Pay attention in particular
>
> to the vowel on the middle radical. Remember that you have only two things to learn:
>
> ▸ the prefixes and suffixes given in Table 1
>
> ▸ the variations in the stem vowel of Form I, i.e. that on the middle radical.

TABLE Q, QUADRILITERAL VERBS [Q-I AND Q-II]

These are verbs that have four consonant roots instead of the usual three consonants. They normally only exist in two derived forms, called I and II although they differ from the normal patterns for those categories).

We use the root **z-l-z-l**, which means *to shake something* in Form I and *to be shaken* in Form II.

Active	Past stem	Present stem
Q-I	زَلْزَل	زَلْزِل
Q-II	تَزَلْزَل	تَزَلْزَل

Although conventionally known as Forms Q-I and Q-II, these actually work like S-II and S-V verbs, respectively. If you remember that the **shaddah** (doubling sign) used on these represents a letter without a vowel followed by one with a vowel (in this case its twin, e.g. **bb**, **kk**, and so on) you will see that the verbs above show the same sequence of unvowelled letter followed by vowelled letter (in the case of our example, **lz**). Q-I and Q-II therefore form exact parallels to SII and SV. QI, uniquely among Form I verbs, shows no variations in vowelling and the present prefix takes a **u** vowel.

TABLE D, DOUBLED VERBS [D-I TO D-X]

Doubled verbs are those whose middle and last root letters are the same (**d-l-l**, **m-r-r** and the like). Because Form IX involves the doubling of this radical, it is included here rather than in Table S.

All doubled verbs (including Form IX) have two stems for each tense (past and present). It will help you to understand this if you think along the lines of suffixes that begin with a vowel as opposed to those that begin with a consonant (prefixes don't matter). These two factors determine the stems used.

To put it another way:

▶ Past tense. All parts except *he*, *she*, *they* (m.) in the past tense use the normal stem (i.e. like the sound verb, Table S).

▶ Present tense. All parts except the (comparatively rare) second and third person feminine plural use the normal stem.

Apart from those verb parts mentioned above, a contracted stem is used, contracted in this context meaning that the middle and final radicals are reduced to one letter and written with the doubling sign **shaddah**. To illustrate this type of verb, we use the root م–د–د **m-d-d**. Form I means *to extend, stretch*. Not all the derived forms given here exist, but the same root is used throughout the table for the sake of uniformity.

> **LANGUAGE TIP**
>
> Forms D-II and D-V behave like sound verbs as the middle radical is doubled and therefore cannot contract.

NS = normal stem (i.e. as in Table S)

CS = contracted stem

Active	Past stem	Present stem
I NS	مَدَد	مْدُد
CS	مَدّ	مُدّ
II	مَدَّد	مَدِّد
III NS	مَادَد	مَادِد
CS	مَادّ	مَادّ
IV NS	أَمْدَد	مْدِد
CS	أَمَدّ	مِدّ
V	تَمَدَّد	تَمَدَّد
VI NS	تَمَادَد	تَمَادَد
CS	تَمَادّ	تَمَادّ
VII NS	انْمَدَد	نْمَدِد
CS	انْمَدّ	نْمَدّ
VIII NS	امْتَدَد	مْتَدِد
CS	امْتَدّ	مْتَدّ

	Past stem	Present stem
X NS	اِسْتَمْدَد	سْتَمْدِد
CS	اِسْتَمَدّ	سْتَمَدّ

The passives are given only for forms that occur reasonably frequently.

Passive	Past stem	Present stem
I NS	مُدِد	مْدَد
CS	مُدّ	مَدّ
IV NS	أُمْدِد	مْدَد
CS	أُمِدّ	مَدّ
VIII NS	اُمْتُدِد	مْتَدَد
CS	اُمْتُدّ	مْتَدّ
X NS	اُسْتُمْدِد	سْتَمْدَد
CS	اُسْتُمِدّ	سْتَمَدّ

Form S-IX

The comparatively rare Form S-IX is not a true doubled verb in terms of root. However, as its construction involves doubling the last radical, it behaves like a doubled verb and has been included here. In Modern Arabic, it is only used with the special adjective roots given in Unit 15 and has no passive. We shall use here **iHmarra** *to become red, to blush*.

Active	Past stem	Present stem
IX NS	اِحْمَرَر	حْمَرَر
CS	اِحْمَرّ	حْمَرّ

Form D-I

Like all Form I verbs, the doubled roots admit various vowellings. These are given in the usual way, e.g. **D-I u** (the vowelling of the example in Table D). However, in the past tense, the contracted stem always takes an **a** vowel and the 'true' vowel only appears in the normal stem. In the present, the vowel given goes on the second radical in the normal stem and the first radical in the contracted stem. Here, for example, are the stems of the **D-I a** verb from the root **DH-l-l**:

Active	Past stem	Present stem
I NS	ظَلِل	ظْلَل
CS	ظَلّ	ظَلّ

Forms II and V

These behave like S verbs, as the doubling of the middle radical inhibits any contraction.

TABLE FW, VERBS WITH FIRST RADICAL W [FW-I TO FW-X]

We use the root **w-S-l** to arrive in Form I as the model for this type of verb.

Active	Past stem	Present stem
I	وَصَل	صِل
IV	أَوْصَل	وصِل
VIII	اتَّصَل	تَّصِل
Passive	**Past stem**	**Present stem**
I	وُصِل	وصَل
IV	أَوْصَل	وصَل
VIII	اتُّصِل	تَّصَل

Forms not given are regular (Table S) or do not occur.

Form I

The main feature of this is that the present stem loses its و altogether. Also, the middle radical of Form I has varying vowels, indicated in the vocabularies by the usual convention. The example verb in the table is **Fw i**.

Form IV

The only slightly unusual feature here is that, in the present, the و combines with the **u** vowel of the prefix to form a long vowel **uu**. So, for instance, **yu- + wSil** is pronounced **yuuSil**.

Form VIII

The و becomes assimilated to the following ت, giving **ittaSala**, **yattaSil**.

> **LANGUAGE TIP**
>
> This is because Arabic will not allow the sequence **iw**. The same goes for **ui**, so if you concoct a verb form –
> or any word for that matter – containing such a sequence, it is going to be wrong (see also Table Fy).

Passive

Again, when the و is preceded by a **u** vowel, the two combine into a long **uu**.

> **LANGUAGE TIP**
>
> Doubled verbs beginning with و do not drop the letter, but behave like normal doubled verbs (see Table D).

TABLE FY, VERBS WITH FIRST RADICAL Y [FY-I TO FY-X]

Such verbs are not common. We use the example **yabisa** *to be or become dry*.

Active	Past stem	Present stem
I	يَبِس	يْبَس
IV	أَيْبَس	وبِس

Passive	Past stem	Present stem
IV	أُيْبَس	وبِس

Forms not given are regular (Table S) or do not occur.

Form I

The ي does not drop out in the present.

Form IV

In the present of IV active and passive, the theoretical combination **ui** is replaced by **uu** (see Table Fw above).

TABLE MW, VERBS WITH MIDDLE RADICAL W [MW-I TO MW-X]

Like the doubled verb, these have two stems for each tense. In this case, it is better to call them long stem (LS) and short stem (SS). The rules for their use are identical in principle to those applying to the doubled verb: LS before a suffix beginning with a vowel and SS before one beginning with a consonant. Please see under doubled verb for a more detailed explanation.

We use the root **q-w-l** *to say* in Form I.

Active	Past stem	Present stem
I LS	قَال	قُول
SS	قُل	قُل
IV LS	أَقَال	قِيل
SS	أَقَل	قِل
VII LS	انْقَال	نْقَال
SS	انْقَل	نْقَل
VIII LS	اقْتَال	قْتَال
SS	اقْتَل	قْتَل
X LS	اسْتَقَال	سْتَقِيل
SS	اسْتَقَل	سْتَقِل

Jussive

In this type of verb, the jussive differs from the normal present tense and the subjunctive. The prefixes and suffixes are given in Table 1 and Table S, but note that in Mw verbs the short stem is used in all parts of the jussive that do not have a vowel in the last radical, e.g. يَقُل، تَقُل **yaqul, taqul** *he, you,* etc. but يَقُولُوا، تَقُولُوا، تَقُولِي **yaquuluu, taquuluu, taquulii** *they, you* pl., *you* f. sing.

Passive

In the passive, the vowelling of the stems is as follows:

Passive	Past stem	Present stem
I LS	قِيل	قَال
SS	قِل	قَل
IV LS	أُقِيل	قَال
SS	أُقِل	قَل
VII	none	

VIII LS	أُقْتيِل	قْتَال
SS	أُقْتَل	قْتَل
X LS	أُسْتُقِيل	سْتَقَال
SS	أُسْتُقِل	سْتَقَل

Derived forms

As usual, the forms not mentioned are regular and behave like sound verbs, the و behaving like a consonant.

TABLE MY, VERBS WITH MIDDLE RADICAL Y [MY-I TO MY-X]

Apart from Form I, these behave in an identical way to Mw verbs in the table. We use the root **S-y-r** *to become*.

Active	Past stem	Present stem
I LS	صَار	صِير
SS	صِر	صِر

Jussive

See Table Mw. The same principle applies here: يَصِر، تَصِر **yaSir**, **taSir** *he, you*, etc. but يَصِيرُوا، تَصِيرُوا، تَصِيرِي **yaSiiruu**, **taSiiruu**, **taSiirii** *they, you* pl., *you* f. sing.

Passive

Same as Table Mw.

Derived forms

See Table Mw. These verbs behave in the same way.

TABLE MA

This is a slight misnomer, in that these verbs actually have either **w** or **y** as the middle radical. However, as the present tense takes an **a** vowel, the code Ma has been used.

This is a small group of verbs, but it includes some very common ones. We use the root **n-w-m** *to sleep*.

Active	Past stem	Present stem
I LS	نَام	نَام
SS	نِم	نَم

Jussive

See Table Mw. The same principle applies here: يَنَم، تَنَم **yanam**, **tanam** *he*, *you*, etc. but يَنَامُوا، تَنَامُوا، تَنَامِي **yanaamuu**, **tanaamuu**, **tanaamii** *they*, *you* pl., *you* f. sing.

Passive

See Table Mw.

Derived forms

See Table Mw. These verbs behave in the same way.

TABLE LW-I, VERBS WITH LAST RADICAL W

> **NOTES**
>
> ▶ This type of verb and those in the following tables do not lend themselves easily to a reduction into a convenient number of stems, so their conjugations are given in a fuller form and are best learned by heart.
>
> ▶ The derived forms are the same for all types, so these are given separately.

We use the root **n-d-w** *to call, invite*.

Active	Past	Present	Subjunctive	Jussive
			as present except parts given	as subj. except parts given
Singular				
he	نَدَا	يَنْدُو		يَنْدُ
she	نَدَتْ	تَنْدُو		تَنْدُ
you (m.)	نَدَوْتَ	تَنْدُو		تَنْدُ
you (f.)	نَدَوْتِ	تَنْدِينَ	تَنْدِي	

	Past	Present	Subjunctive	Jussive
I	نَدَوْتُ	أَنْدُو		أَنْدُ
Plural				
they (m.)	نَدَوْا	يَنْدُونَ	يَنْدُوا	
they (f.)	نَدَوْنَ	يَنْدُونَ		
you (m.)	نَدَوْتُمْ	تَنْدُونَ	تَنْدُوا	
you (f.)	نَدَوْتُنَّ	تَنْدُونَ		
we	نَدَوْنَا	نَنْدُو		نَنْدُ

SUMMARY

There are many phonetic factors at work here, which cause different sorts of elisions and changes. To list all these would defeat the purpose so, as has been suggested, it is better to learn these verbs by heart, spending more time on the most commonly occurring parts.

Active	Past	Present	Subjunctive	Jussive
			as present except parts given	as subj. except parts given
Singular				
he	نُدِيَ	يُنْدَى		يُنْدَ
she	نُدِيَتْ	تُنْدَى		تُنْدَ
you (m.)	نُدِيتَ	تُنْدَى		تُنْدَ
you (f.)	نُدِيتِ	تُنْدَيْنَ	تُنْدَيْ	
I	نُدِيتُ	أُنْدَى		أُنْدَ
Plural				
they (m.)	نُدُوا	يُنْدَوْنَ	يُنْدَوْا	

	Past	Present	Subjunctive	Jussive
they (f.)	نُدِينَ	يُنْدَوْنَ		
you (m.)	نُدِّيتُمْ	تُنْدَوْنَ	تُنْدَوْا	
you (f.)	نُدِّيتُنَّ	تُنْدَيْنَ		
we	نُدِّينَا	نُنْدَى		نُنْدَ

TABLE LY-I, VERBS WITH LAST RADICAL Y

This is by far the most common of this type of verb. We shall use the root **r-m-y** *to throw*, and, again, give the verb in full.

Active	Past	Present	Subjunctive	Jussive
			as present except parts given	as subj. except parts given
Singular				
he	رَمَى	يَرْمِي		يَرْمِ
she	رَمَتْ	تَرْمِي		تَرْمِ
you (m.)	رَمَيْتَ	تَرْمِي		تَرْمِ
you (f.)	رَمَيْتِ	تَرْمِي	تَرْمِينَ	
I	رَمَيْتُ	أَرْمِي		أَرْمِ
Plural				
they (m.)	رَمَوْا	يَرْمُونَ	يَرْمُوا	
they (f.)	رَمَيْنَ	يَرْمِينَ		
you (m.)	رَمَيْتُمْ	تَرْمُونَ	تَرْمُوا	
you (f.)	رَمَيْتُنَّ	تَرْمِينَ		
we	رَمَيْنَا	نَرْمِي		نَرْمِ

306

Passive

Identical to Lw type. See table.

TABLE LA-I

Again, a slight misnomer. These verbs actually have third radical **w** or **y**, but the past has an **i** vowel and the present an **a** vowel on the middle radical. We use the root **l-q-y** *to meet with, find.*

Active	Past	Present	Subjunctive	Jussive
			as present except parts given	as subj. except parts given
Singular				
he	لَقِيَ	يَلْقَى		يَلْقَ
she	لَقِيَتْ	تَلْقَى		تَلْقَ
you (m.)	لَقِيتَ	تَلْقَى		تَلْقَ
you (f.)	لَقِيتِ	تَلْقَيْنَ	تَلْقَي	
I	لَقِيتُ	أَلْقَى		أَلْقَ
Plural				
they (m.)	لَقُوا	يَلْقَوْنَ	يَلْقَوْا	
they (f.)	لَقِينَ	يَلْقَيْنَ		
you (m.)	لَقِيتُمْ	تَلْقَوْنَ	تَلْقَوْا	
you (f.)	لَقِيتُنَّ	تَلْقَيْنَ		
we	لَقِينا	نَلْقَى		نَلْقَ

Passive

Identical to Lw type. See table.

TABLE LH-I

The h here stands for hybrid. A few verbs conjugate like **r-m-y** in the past (Table Ly) and **l-q-y** in the present (Table La). We shall give merely a few sample parts, using the root **s-ʿ-y** *to hurry, make an effort at something.*

Active	Past	Present	Subjunctive	Jussive
			as present except parts given	as subj. except parts given
Singular				
he	سَعَى	يَسْعَى		يَسْعَ
she	سَعَتْ	تَسْعَى		تَسْعَ

Passive

As usual, the same as all the L-type verbs (see tables).

L-TYPE VERBS, DERIVED FORMS [LW/Y/A, ETC. II–X]

The derived forms are the same for all three types of verb with و or ي as the last radical.

Although a table is given, there is a shortcut to learning these:

▶ Forms II, III, IV, VII, VIII and X (there is no Form IX) conjugate like **r-m-y** (Table Ly) in both tenses.

▶ V and VI conjugate like r-m-y (Table Ly) in the past and **l-q-y** (Table La) in the present.

The following table, therefore, only gives two parts (the *he* form of the past and the present). The rest of the parts can be found by referring to the two tables mentioned.

Again we use the root **l-q-y**, which exists in quite a number – but not all – of the derived forms.

Active	Past stem	Present stem
II	لَقَّى	يُلَقِّي
III	لاقَى	يُلاقِي

	Past stem	Present stem
IV	أَلْقَى	يُلْقِي
V	تَلَقَّى	يَتَلَقَّى
VI	تَلاقَى	يَتَلاقَى
VII	انْلَقَى	يَنْلَقِي
VIII	الْتَقَى	يَلْتَقِي

Passive	Past stem	Present stem
X	اسْتَلْقَى	يَسْتَلْقِي
II	لُقِّيَ	يُلَقَّى
III	لُوقِيَ	يُلاقَى
IV	أُلْقِيَ	يُلْقَى
V	تُلُقِّيَ	يُتَلَقَّى
VIII	الْتُقِيَ	يُلْتَقَى
X	اُسْتُلْقِيَ	يُسْتَلْقَى

The forms not given are either non-existent or extremely rare.

SOME IRREGULARITIES

▶ The only really irregular verb in Arabic is لَيْسَ *not to be*, used for negation. This is given in full in Unit 8. It only exists in one tense, which is past in form, but present in meaning.

▶ The verb رَأَى *to see* conjugates in the past like رَمَى (Table Ly), but has the irregular present form يَرَى where the **hamzah** and its supporting **alif** are dropped. This tense is vowelled like the present of La verbs, e.g. يَرَى، تَرَى **yaraa, taraa**, etc.

▶ The verb رَأَى has no imperative, that of the alternative verb نَظَرَ *to look, see* being used instead (اُنْظُر).

▶ Verbs with **hamzah** as one of their radicals are mainly regular, but are sometimes difficult to spell. The rules for this are too complex to be practically useful and it is better to learn by experience.

▶ There are a number of 'doubly weak' verbs, showing the characteristics of two different types. These and certain other phonetic variations – especially of Form VIII verbs – have been noted in the text.

Arabic–English vocabulary

This glossary relates mainly to the texts in the units and the Vocabulary builders. It is arranged according to the order of the Arabic alphabet (see the Arabic script and pronunciation guide) as opposed to the root system used by most dictionaries. This should enable you to find words more easily. The Arabic definite article (the الـ) has been included with words that always have it (e.g. الدنيا **ad-dunyaa** *the world*), but left out where you are more likely to be looking for the word in its non-definite form (e.g. **Sharjah**, الشارقة **ash-shaariqah**). Words that do not take the accusative marker are marked with an asterisk (*).

ا

آلة حاسبة	**aalah Haasibah**	*computer*
أب	**ab**	*father*
أحاط بـ	**aHaaTa bi- [My-IV]**	*surround*
احتفال، ات	**iHtifaal, -aat**	*party, celebration*
ابتسم	**ibtasama [S-VIII]**	*smile*
ابن، أبناء	**ibn, abnaa'***	*son*
ابنة، بنات	**ibnah, banaat**	*daughter*
أبو الهول	**abuu l-hawl**	*the Sphinx*
أبو ظبي	**abuu DHabi**	*Abu Dhabi*
أبيض، بيضاء	**abyaD*, f. bayDaa'***	*white*
أثر، آثار	**athar, aathaar sing.**	*track, trace, pl. also archaeological remains*
أثري	**atharii**	*archaeological*
اتساع	**ittisaa:**	*extent, compass*
اجتمع	**ijtama:a [S-VIII]**	*meet, come together*
أجمل	**ajmal***	*more/most beautiful*
أحب، يحب	**aHabba [D-IV]**	*like, love*
احتسب	**iHtasaba [S-VIII]**	*award*
احتفل ب	**iHtafala bi- [S-VIII]**	*celebrate*
احتل	**iHtalla [D-VIII]**	*occupy*
أحدث	**aHdath**	*newest, latest*

إحصاء، ات	iHSaa', -aat	count, census
أحمر	aHmar*	red
أخ، إخوان/ إخوة	akh, ikhwaan or ikhwah	brother
أخت، أخوات	ukht, akhawaat	sister
اختار	ikhtaara [My-VIII]	choose
اخترق	ikhtaraqa [S-VIII]	breach
أخذ	akhadha [S-I u]	take
آخر	aakhar* (f. أخرى ukhraa)	other
آخر	aakhir	end, last part of something
أخضر	akhDar*	green
أخير	akhiir	last
أدرك	adraka [S-IV]	attain, achieve
إذا	idhaa	if
إذاً	ídhan	so, therefore
أذاع	adhaa:a [My-IV]	broadcast
أذن	udh(u)n (f.)	ear
أربعة	arba:ah	four
أردني	urduni	Jordanian
أرز	aruzz	rice
إرسال	irsaal	transmission, sending
أرسل	arsala [S-IV]	send
أرض	al-arD (f.)	the ground, the earth
اسباني	isbaanii	Spanish
استأجر	ista'jara [S-X]	rent, be a tenant of
استخدام	istikhdaam	use, employment
استخدم	istakhdama [S-X]	use, employ
استرداد	istirdaad	demanding back, reclaiming
استطاع	istaTaa:a [Mw-X]	be able
استعمال	isti:maal	use, usage
استغرق	istaghraqa [S-X]	take, use up, occupy (of time)
استقبل	istaqbala [S-X]	receive, meet

أسطورة، أساطير	usTuurah, asaaTiir*	legend
اسم، أسماء	ism, asmaa'	name
أسند ل	asnada [S-IV]	entrust to, vest in
أسود، سوداء	aswad*, f. sawdaa'*	black
إشارة، ات	ishaarah, -aat (traffic)	signal
اشترك	ishtaraka [S-VIII]	participate, take part
أشكرك	ashkur-ak/ik	thank you (to a man/woman)
أشهر	ash-har*	more/most famous
أصاب	aSaaba	hit, strike
أصبح	aSbaHa [S-IV]	become
أصفر، صفراء	aSfar*, f. Safraa'*	yellow
أصل، أصول	aSl, uSuul	origin, basis
أضاف	aDaafa [My-IV]	add
أعاد	a:aada [Mw-IV]	repeat, renew
اعتبر	i:tabara [S-VIII]	consider, regard
أعرب عن	a:raba :an [S-IV]	state, express
أعزب	a:zab*	bachelor, single
أعطى	a:Taa [Ly-IV]	give
أعلن	a:lana [S-IV]	announce, state
أعلى	a:laa	highest; the highest point, top
أفاض ب	afaaDa bi- [My-IV]	flood, overflow with
افتتح	iftataHa [S-VIII]	commence, open
أقام	aqaama [Mw-IV]	reside; hold (an event, etc.)
اكتشف	iktashafa [S-VIII]	discover
أكثر	akthar*	more/most
أكل	akl	things to eat, food
أكل، يأكل	akala, ya'kul [S-I u]	eat
أكيد	akiid	certain, definite
الـ	al-	the
الآن	al-'aan	now
الإسكندرية	al-iskandariyyah	Alexandria

الإمارات العربية المتحدة	al-imaaraat al-:arabiyyah al-muttaHidah	the United Arab Emirates
الأهرام	al-ahraam	the pyramids
الحمد لله	al-Hamdu li-l-laah	praise God
الحين	al-Hiin	now
الذي	alladhii (f. التي allatii)	who, which, that
السعودية	as-sa:udiyyah	Saudi Arabia
السلام عليكم	as-salaamu-alaykum	hello
العالم	al-:aalam	the world
الغد	al-ghad	tomorrow
ألف، آلاف	alf, aalaaf	thousand
إلا	illaa	except
الله	Al-laah	God, Allah
ألماني	almaanii	German
المغرب	al-maghrib	sunset; Morocco
اليوم	al-yawm	today
أمّا	ammaa	as for
أمة، أمم	ummah, umam	nation
أمام	amaam	in front of
امتياز	imtiyaaz	distinction, privilege
امرأة، نساء	imra'ah, nisaa' (irregular plural)	woman
أمريكا	amriika	America
أمس	ams	yesterday
أمس الأول	ams al-awwal	the day before yesterday
أمكن	amkana [S-IV]	be possible
إن	in	if
أنا	ána	I
انبعث	inba:atha [S-VII]	emanate, be sent out
أنت	anta/anti	you (m./f.)
إنتاج	intaaj	production
انتشار	intishaar	spread, currency; popularity

انتهى	**intahaa [Ly-VIII]**	*come to an end, finish*
إنجلترا	**ingiltarra** (with g as in garden)	*England*
إنجليزي	**ingliizi**	*English*
انسان، ناس	**insaan, naas**	*human being; pl. = people*
إنشاء	**inshaa'**	*foundation, setting up*
انظري	**unDHurii**	*look! (to a woman)*
اهتمام	**ihtimaam**	*attention, concern, interest*
أهلا وسهلا	**ahlan wa-sahlan**	*welcome*
أهم	**ahamm**	*more/most important*
أو	**aw**	*or*
أودع	**awda:a [Fw-IV]**	*place*
أوروبي، ون	**uruubii**	*European*
أول	**awwal**	*first*
أولا	**awwalan**	*first (adv.)*
أي	**ay**	*that is*
أيّ	**ayy**	*which*
أيس كريم	**ays kriim**	*ice cream*
أيضاً	**ayDan**	*also*
إيمان	**iimaan**	*belief, faith*
أين	**ayna**	*where*

ب

بـ	**bi-**	*with*
باب، أبواب	**baab, abwaab**	*gate, door*
بادل	**baadala [S-III]**	*swap, exchange with someone*
بارد	**baarid**	*cold (adj.)*
باع	**baa:a [My-I]**	*sell*
بالغ، ون	**baaligh, baalighuun**	*adult*
بجانب	**bi-jaanib**	*next to, beside*
بحر، بحار	**baHr, biHaar**	*sea, large river*

بدأ	bada' [S-I a]	begin
بدا	badaa [Lw-I]	appear, seem, show
بدون	bi-duun	without
برج، أبراج	burj, abraaj	tower
برجيل، براجيل	barjiil, baraajiil	traditional wind tower
برغر، ات	barghar, -aat	hamburger
برنامج، برامج	barnaamij, baraamij*	programme
بريطانيا العظمى	briiTaanyaa l-:uDHmaa	Great Britain
بريطاني	briiTaanii	British
بصل	baSal	onions
بطاقة، ات	biTaaqah, -aat	card
بطاقة التسليف	biTaaqat at-tasliif	credit card
بطلاقة	bi-Talaaqah	fluently
بطولات	buTuulaat	leading roles
بعد	ba:d	after
بعد الظهر	ba:d aDH-DHuhr	(in the) afternoon
بعد ما	ba:d maa	after (before a verb)
بعض	ba:D	some, part of something
بعيد	ba:iid	far away, distant
بكم	bi-kam	how much
بل	bal	rather; in fact, indeed
بلد، بلاد/بلدان	balad, bilaad/buldaan	country
بناء	binaa'	building, construction
بنت، بنات	bint, banaat	girl, daughter
بنزين	banziin	petrol
بهو	bahw	lobby (hotel)
بنك، بنوك	bank, bunuuk	bank
بيت، بيوت	bayt, buyuut	house
بيرة	biirah	beer
بين	bayna	between, among
بينما	baynamaa	while

تابل، توابل	**taabil, tawaabil**	*spice*
تاجر، تجار	**taajir, tujjaar**	*merchant*
تاريخ	**taariikh**	*history*
تاريخي	**taariikhii**	*historical*
تاكسي	**taaksi**	*taxi*
تاسع	**taasi:**	*ninth*
تام	**taamm**	*complete*
تأهل إلى	**ta'ahhala [S-V]**	*qualify (لـ **ilaa** for)*
تبريد	**tabriid**	*cooling*
تبع	**tabi:a**	*follow*
تجارة	**tijaarah**	*trade, commerce*
تجاري	**tijaarii**	*commercial*
تخصص	**takhaSSaS [S-V]**	*specialize*
تذكرة، تذاكر	**tadhkirah, tadhaakir***	*ticket*
ترحيب	**tarHiib**	*welcome, welcoming (noun)*
ترحيبي	**tarHiibii**	*welcoming (adj.)*
ترك	**taraka [S-I u]**	*leave, let be*
تزوج	**tazawwaja [Mw-V]**	*marry*
تسجيل	**tasjiil**	*registration, scoring*
تسديدة، ات	**tasdiidah, -aat**	*shot (football)*
تسهيلات	**tas-hiilaat**	*facilities*
تسوق	**tasawwuq**	*shopping*
تشكيلة، ات	**tashkiilah, -aat**	*selection*
تصميم	**taSmiim**	*design, designing*
تعادل	**ta:aadul**	*balance, equality (football: draw, equal score)*
تعبان	**ta:baan**	*tired*
تعلم	**ta:allama [S-V]**	*learn*
تعليمي	**ta:liimii**	*educational*
تفاحة، تفاح	**tuffaaHah, tuffaaH**	*apple*
تفرج على	**tafarraja :ala [S-V]**	*watch, look at*

تفضل	tafaDDal	come in (to a man)
تقديم	taqdiim	presentation
تقرير، تقارير	taqriir, taqaariir*	report
تكلم	takallama [S-V]	speak
تكييف	takyiif	air conditioning
تلفون	tilifuun	telephone
تلفزيوني	tilifizyuunii	television (adj.), televisual
تمتع بـ	tamatta:a	[S-V] enjoy
تنس	tanis	tennis
تنظيف	tanDHiif	cleaning
تنفيذ	tanfiidh	implementation, execution
تنقل	tanaqqala [S-V]	be carried, transported

ث

ثالث	thaalith	third (adj.)
ثالثة عشر	thaalithah :ashar	thirteenth
ثقافي	thaqaafii	cultural
ثقيل	thaqiil	heavy
ثلاثة	thalaathah	three
ثلج	thalj	ice
ثم	thumma	then
ثمرة	thamrah	fruit

ج

جاء، يجيء	jaa'a, yajii' [My-I]	come
جار، جيران	jaar, jiiraan	neighbour
(الـ) جاري	al-jaarii	the current
جالس	jaalis	sitting, seated
جامع، جوامع	jaami:, jawaami:*	large mosque
جامعة، ات	jaami:ah	university
جانب، جوانب	jaanib, jawaanib*	side
جانبا	jaaniban	aside, to one side

جبنة	jubnah	cheese
جدا	jíddan	very
جدد	jaddada [D-II]	renew, restore
جديد	jadiid	new
جرب	jarraba [S-II]	try out, taste
جرى	jaraa [Ly-I]	run
جريدة، جرائد*	jariidah, jaraa'id*	newspaper
جسر، جسور	jisr, jusuur	bridge
جعل	ja:ala [S-I a]	cause, make do something; place, put
جغرافي	jughraafii	geographical
جلب	jalaba [S-I i]	attract
جلس	jalasa [S-I i]	sit, sit down
جماعة، ات	jamaa:ah, -aat	group, gathering
جمال	jamaal	beauty
جائزة، جوائز*	jaa'izah, jawaa'iz*	prize, reward
جمرك، جمارك*	jumruk, jamaarik*	customs, excise
جميع	jamii:	all
جمعية، ات	jam:iyyah, -aat	group, assembly, society
جمل، جمال	jamal, jimaal	camel
جميعا	jamii:an	all together
جميل	jamiil	beautiful
جنسية، ات	jinsiyyah, -aat	nationality
جنيه، ات	junayh, -aat	pound (money)
جوعان، جوعى	jaw:aan*, jaw:aa*	hungry
جولف	guulf	golf
جيب، جيوب	jayb, juyuub	pocket
جيد	jayyid	of good quality
(الـ)جيزة	al-jiizah	Giza, a district of Cairo

ح

حار	Haarr	hot
حارس، حراس	Haaris, Hurraas	guard (football: goalkeeper)

حاضر، ون	HaaDir, -uun	present, here
حافظ على	HaafaDHa :alaa [S-III]	keep, preserve
حبة، ات	Habbah, -aat	grain, seed; also used for counting units of certain fruits and vegetables
حتى	Hattaa	until, even
(الـ)حج	al-Hajj	the pilgrimage
حجر، أحجار	Hajar, aHjaar	stone
حجرة	Hujrah	room
حد، حدود	Hadd, Huduud	limit, border
حديث	Hadiith	modern, up-to-date
حديقة، حدائق*	Hadiiqah, Hadaa'iq*	garden, park
حرارة	Haraarah	heat
حزين	Haziin	sad
حسب	Hasb	according to
حسم	Hasm	discount
حسنا	Hasanan	well, right, OK
حصن، حصون	HiSn, HuSuun	fort, fortress
حضر	HaDara [S-I u]	attend
حقيبة، حقائب*	Haqiibah, Haqaa'ib*	bag, suitcase
حكم، حكام	Hakam, Hukkaam	referee, umpire
حل، حلول	Hall, Huluul	solution
حلاوة	Halaawah	sweetness, beauty
حمال، ون	Hammaal, -uun	porter
حمام، ات	Hammaam, -aat	bathroom
حمر	Hammara [S-II]	brown, fry
حمل، أحمال	Himl, aHmaal	load, burden
حمل	Hamala [S-I i]	carry
حوالي	Hawaalii	about, approximately

خ

خادم، خدام	khaadim, khuddaam	servant
خادمة، ات	khaadimah, -aat	(female) servant

(الـ)خارج	al-khaarij	the outside, abroad
خارج	khaarij	outside
خاص	khaaSS	special; private
خال	khaal	uncle (on mother's side)
خالة	khaalah	aunt (on mother's side)
خامس	khaamis	fifth
خبر، أخبار	khabar, akhbaar	news (sing. = an item of news)
خبز	khubz	bread
خدع	khada:a [S-I a]	deceive
خدمة، ات	khidmah, -aat	service
خروف، خرفان	kharuuf, khirfaan	sheep
خريطة، خرائط	khariiTah, kharaa'iT*	map
خفيف	khafiif	light (adj.)
خلال	khilaal	during
(الـ)خليج العربي	al-khaliij al-:arabii	the Arabian Gulf
خليط	khaliiT	mixture
خليفة، خلفاء	khaliifah, khulafaa'*	Caliph, head of the Islamic state
خور	khawr	creek
خير	khayr	(state of) well-being

 د

دائرة، دوائر	daa'irah, dawaa'ir*	(government) department
داخل	daakhil	inside, the inside of something
دخل	dakhala [S-I u]	enter
دراسة، ات	diraasah, -aat	study
درجة الحرارة	darajat al-Haraarah	temperature
درس	darasa [S-I u]	study
درهم، دراهم	dirham, daraahim*	dirham (unit of currency)
دش	dushsh	shower
دقيقة، دقائق	daqiiqah, daqaa'iq*	minute
دكان، دكاكين	dukkaan, dakaakiin*	small shop, stall
دمشق	dimashq*	Damascus

دهش	dahisha [S-I a]	*be surprised, astonished*
دور، أدوار	dawr, adwaar	*role, turn*
دولة، دول	dawlah, duwal	*country, state*
دولي	duwalii or dawlii	*international*
دينار، دنانير	diinaar, danaaniir	*dinar (currency)*

ذ

ذاكرة	dhaakirah	*memory*
ذلك	dhaalik(a)	*that (m.)*
ذبح	dhabaHa [S-I a]	*slaughter*
ذبيحة، ذبائح	dhabiiHah, dhabaa'iH*	*sacrificial animal*
ذقن، ذقون	dhaqn, dhuquun (f.)	*beard, chin*
ذكور	dhukuur	*males*
ذهب	dhahab	*gold*
ذهب	dhahaba, [S-I a]	*go*
الذي (f. التي allatii)	alladhii	*who, which, that*

ر

رائحة، روائح	raa'iHah, rawaa'iH*	*smell, scent, perfume*
رائع	raa'i:	*splendid, brilliant, marvellous*
راديو، راديوهات	raadyo, raadyohaat	*radio*
راكب ، ركاب	raakib, rukkaab	*passenger*
راية، ات	raayah, -aat	*flag, banner*
رئيس، رؤساء	ra'iis, ru'asaa'*	*boss, chief*
ربح	rabaHa [S-I a]	*win, gain, profit*
ربع	rub:	*quarter*
رجع	raja:a [S-I i]	*return, come back*
رجل	rijl	*leg (f.)*
رجل، رجال	rajul, rijaal	*man*
رحب ب	raHHaba [S-II]	*welcome (requires bi-)*
رحلة، ات	riHlah, -aat	*journey, voyage*
رد	radda [D-I u]	*return something to someone*

رسالة، رسائل*	risaalah, risaa'il*	letter, message
رش	rashsha [D-I u]	sprinkle, spray
رشيد	rashiid	Rashid (man's name); also Rosetta (a town in Egypt)
رصد	raSada [S-I u]	observe, watch
رعى	ra:aa [Lh-I]	take care of, look after
رغبة، ات	raghbah, -aat	desire, wish
رف، رفوف	raff, rufuuf	shelf
رفع	rafa:a [S-I a]	lift, raise
رقم تلفون	raqm tilifuun	telephone number
ركلة، ات	raklah, -aat	kick
ركن، أركان	rukn, arkaan	corner
ركني	ruknii	corner (adj.)
رمز، رموز	ramz, rumuuz	code, symbol
رواية، ات	riwaayah, -aat	novel, story
رياضة، ات	riyaaDah, -aat	sport, exercise

ز

زائر، زوار	zaa'ir, zuwwaar	visitor
زاحم	zaaHama [S-III]	compete with
زار	zaara [Mw-I]	visit
زبون، زبائن	zabuun, zabaa'in*	customer, client
زمان، أزمنة	zamaan, azminah	time
زوج	zawj	husband
زوجة، ات	zawjah, -aat	wife
زورق، زوارق	zawraq, zawaariq*	boat
زي، أزياء	ziyy, azyaa'*	clothes, fashion, style
زيارة، ات	ziyaarah, -aat	visit
زيت	zayt	(edible) oil

س

سائح، سواح	saa'iH, suwwaaH	tourist
سائق،ون/ساقة	saa'iq, -uun/saaqah	driver
سؤال، أسئلة	su'aal, as'ilah	question

سادس	saadis	sixth
ساعة، ات	saa:ah, -aat	hour, time, watch, clock
سافر	saafara [S-III]	travel
ساكن	saakin	living, residing
ساكن، سكان	saakin, sukkaan	inhabitant, resident
سالم	saalim	safe, sound
سباحة	sibaaHah	swimming
سباق، ات	sibaaq, -aat	race
سبح	sabaHa [S-I a]	swim
ستة	sittah	six
سجل	sajjala [S-II]	register, score
سحر	siHr	magic
سد، سدود	sadd, suduud	dam
سدد	saddada [S-II]	aim; (football) shoot
سرعان ما	sur:aan maa	quickly, before long
سرعة	sur:ah	speed
سعر، أسعار	si:r, as:aar	price
سعيد، سعداء	sa:iid, su:adaa'*	happy
سفيرة، ات	safiirah, -aat	(female) ambassador
سفينة، سفن	safiinah, sufun	ship
سكب	sakaba [S-I u]	pour out
سكر	sukkar	sugar
سكن	sakana [S-I u]	live, reside
سلاح، أسلحة	silaaH, asliHah	weapon, arm
سلق	salq	(the action of) boiling something
سماح	samaaH	permission
سمع	sami:a [S-I a]	hear, listen
سمك	samak	fish (collective)
سمن	samn	ghee, clarified butter
سندويتش، ات	sandawíitsh, -aat	sandwich
سنة، سنوات	sanah, sanawaat	year

سور، أسوار	suur, aswaar	*wall*
سوق، أسواق	suuq, aswaaq (usually f.)	*market*
سونا	sawnaa	*sauna*
سيارة، ات	sayyaarah, -aat	*car*
سيدة، ات	sayyidah, -aat	*lady*
سيطر على	sayTara :alaa [Q-I]	*dominate*
سيطرة	sayTarah	*domination*
سينما، سينمات	siinamaa, siinamaat (f.)	*cinema*

ش

شارع، شوارع	shaari:, shawaari:*	*street, road*
(الـ)شارقة	ash-shaariqah	*Sharjah*
شاشة	shaashah	*screen*
شاطئ	shaaTi'	*shore, beach*
شاعر، شعراء	shaa:ir, shu:araa'*	*poet*
شأن، شؤون	sha'n, shu'uun	*affair, important matter*
شاهد	shaahada [III]	*see, look at*
شاي	shaay	*tea*
شبكة، شباك	shabaka, shibaak	*net, netting*
شتاء	shitaa'*	*winter*
شجرة، أشجار	shajarah, ashjaar	*tree*
شخص، أشخاص	shakhS, ashkhaaS	*person*
شديد	shadiid	*strong, mighty*
شرب	shariba [S-I a]	*drink*
شرح	sharaHa [S-I a]	*explain*
شركة، ات	sharikah, -aat	*company, firm*
شريحة، شرائح	shariiHah, sharaa'iH*	*slice*
شعب، شعوب	sha:b, shu:uub	*people, folk*
شعبي	sha:bii	*folk, popular*
شعر	sha:r	*hair*
شعر	shi:r	*poetry*
شقة، شقق	shaqqah, shiqaq	*flat, apartment*

شكراً	shukran	*thank you*
شكراً جزيلاً	shukran jaziilan	*thank you very much*
شكل، أشكال	shakl, ashkaal	*type, shape*
شوكولاتة	shokolaatah	*chocolate*
شمال	shamaal	*left*
شمس	shams	*sun*
شهير	shahiir	*famous*
شوط، أشواط	shawT, ashwaaT	*heat, race; football: half*
شيء، اشياء	shay', ashyaa'*	*thing, something*
شيد	shayyada [My-II]	*erect, construct*

ص

صاحب، أصحاب	SaaHib, aS-Haab	*owner, master; also sometimes friend*
صادق	Saadiq	*truthful, true*
(الـ)صافي	aS-Saafii	*pure, clear*
صالح	SaaliH	*doing right*
صالة	Saalah	*sitting-room, lounge*
صالون تجميل	Saaluun tajmiil	*beauty salon*
صباح الخير	SabaaH al-khayr	*good morning*
صبح	SubH	*morning*
صحن، صحون	SaHn, SuHuun	*dish*
صحيح	SaHiiH	*correct, right*
صديق، أصدقاء	Sadiiq, aSdiqaa'*	*friend*
صغير	Saghiir	*young (person), small (thing)*
صف، صفوف	Saff, Sufuuf	*class (school)*
صفى	Saffaa [Ly-II]	*drain, strain*
صلصة	SalSah	*sauce*
صلى الله عليه وسلم	Sallaa l-Laahu :alay-hi wa-sallam	*Prayers and peace be upon Him (said after mentioning the name of the Prophet)*
صندوق بريد	Sanduuq bariid	*post office box*
صوم	Sawm	*fast, fasting*

| صيدلية، ات | Saydaliyyah, -aat | pharmacy |
| صيف | Sayf | summer |

ض

ضربة، ات	Darbah, Darabaat	blow, beat
ضرورة، ات	Daruurah, -aat	necessity, requirement
ضم	Damma [D-I u]	include, comprise
ضيف، ضيوف	Dayf, Duyuuf	guest
ضيق	Dayyiq	narrow

ط

طائرة، ات	Taa'irah, -aat	aeroplane
طالب، طلاب/طلبة	Taalib, Tullaab/Talabah	student
طالبة، طالبات	Taalibah, -aat	female student
طبخ	Tabakha [S-I u]	cook
طبع	Taba:a [S-I a]	print, type
طبعا	Tab:an	naturally, of course
طبق، أطباق	Tabaq, aTbaaq	plate, dish
طبقة، ات	Tabaqah, -aat	layer
طبيب، أطباء	Tabiib, aTibbaa'*	doctor
طبيب أسنان	Tabiib asnaan	dentist
طبيخ	Tabiikh	cooking, cuisine
طبيعة	Tabii:ah	nature
طبيعي	Tabii:ii	natural
طرد	Tarada [S-I u]	banish, drive away (football: send off)
طريق، طرق	Tariiq, Turuq	road, way
طريقة، طرائق	Tariiqah, Taraa'iq*	method, way
طعام	Ta:aam	food
طفل، أطفال	Tifl, aTfaal	child
طفولة	Tufuulah	childhood
طماطم	TamaaTim*	tomatoes
طمح إلى	TamaHa ilaa [S-I a]	aspire to

طموح	**TumuuH**	*aspiration, ambition*
طنطا	**TanTaa**	*Tanta (town in Egypt)*
طوال اليوم	**Tiwaal al-yawm**	*all day*
طويل	**Tawiil**	*tall (person), long (thing)*

ظ

ظهر	**DHuhr**	*noon*

ع

عائلة،ـات	**:aa'ilah, -aat**	*family*
عادة، ات	**:aadah, -aat**	*custom, habit*
عادل	**:aadil**	*just, upright*
عاش	**:aasha [My-I]**	*live*
عاصمة، عواصم	**:aaSimah, :awaaSim***	*capital (city)*
عالمي	**:aalamii**	*worldwide*
(الـ)عالي	**al-: aalii**	*high*
عام	**:aamm**	*general*
عام، أعوام	**:aam, a:waam**	*year*
عامل، عمال	**:aamil, :ummaal**	*workman*
عبارة، ات	**:abaarah, -aat**	*phrase, expression*
عجلة، ات	**:ajalah, -aat**	*wheel, bicycle*
عجيب	**:ajiib**	*wonderful*
عجيبة، عجائب	**:ajiibah, :ajaa'ib***	*(object of) wonder*
عدد، أعداد	**:adad, a:daad**	*number*
عدس	**:ads**	*lentils*
عدن	**:adan**	*Aden*
عراقي	**:iraaqii**	*Iraqi*
عربي، عرب	**:arabii**	*Arabic, Arab*
عرض	**:arD**	*showing, displaying*
عرض، عروض	**:arD, :uruuD**	*offer, deal*
عرف	**:arafa [S-I i]**	*know*
عريض	**:ariiD**	*wide*

عسكري، عساكر	:askarii, :asaakir*	soldier
عشاء	:ishaa'	late evening (prayer time)
عشرة	:ashrah	ten
عصر	:aSr	mid-afternoon
عضوة، عضوات	:uDwah, :uDuwaat	member (f.)
عضوية	:uDwiyyah	membership
عطشان	:aTshaan	thirsty
عفوا	:afwan	you're welcome, don't mention it (reply to thanks)
عقب	:aqaba [S-I u]	come after, follow
عم	:amm	uncle (on father's side)
عمة	:ammah	aunt (on father's side)
عمان	:ammaan	Amman (capital of Jordan); :umaan Oman (Sultanate of)
عمر	:umr	life, age
عمل، أعمال	:amal, a:maal	work, job, business
عمل	:amila [S-I a]	do, work
عمومي	:umuumii	general
عن	:an	about, concerning
عند	:inda	at, with
عندما	:indamaa	when
عنوان، عناوين	:unwaan, :anaawiin*	address
عيادة، ات	:iyaadah, -aat	clinic
عيد، أعياد	:iid, a:yaad	festival
عيد الأضحى	:iid al-aD-Haa	Festival of the Sacrifice
عيد الميلاد	:iid al-miilaad	Christmas
عين، عيون	:ayn, :uyuun (f.)	eye; also spring (of water)

غ

غاية	ghaa yah	extreme, most
(الـ)غرب	al-gharb	the West
غربي، ون	gharbii, -uun	Western
غرفة، غرف	ghurfah, ghuraf	room

غسالة، ات	ghassaalah, -aat	*washing machine*
غسل	ghasala [S-I i]	*wash*
غلى	ghalaa [Ly-I]	*boil, come to the boil*
غنم	ghanam	*sheep (collective)*
غني، أغنياء	ghanii, aghniyaa'*	*rich, rich person*
غير	ghayr	*other than, apart from*

ف

فاضل	faaDil	*favourable, good*
فاكهة، فواكه	faakihah, fawaakih*	*fruit*
فاهم	faahim	*understanding*
فتاة، فتيات	fataah, fatayaat	*girl, young woman*
فتح	fataHa [S-I a]	*open*
فترة، ات	fatrah, -aat	*period, time, spell*
فجر	fajr	*dawn*
فحص	faHaSa [S-I a]	*to examine*
فخم	fakhm	*magnificent*
فراغ	faraagh	*leisure*
فردي	fardii	*single*
فرسا	faransaa	*France*
فرنساوي	faransaawi	*French*
فرصة، فرص	furSah, furaS	*chance, opportunity*
فرض	faraDa [S-I i]	*impose*
فرع، فروع	far:, furuu:	*branch (of a tree, company, etc.)*
فرعوني	far:uunii	*pharaonic*
فريق، فرق	fariiq, firaq	*team*
فستان، فساتين	fustaan, fasaatiin*	*frock, dress*
فصل، فصول	faSl, fuSuul	*section, season (of the year)*
فضل	faDDala [S-II]	*prefer*
فطر	fiTr	*breaking of a fast*

فظيع	faDHii:	shocking, awful
فعل	fa:ala [S-I a]	do, make
فعلا	fi:lan	really, actually, in fact
فقط	faqaT	only
فقير، فقراء	faqiir, fuqaraa'*	poor, poor person
فلفل	fulful/filfil	pepper
فن، فنون	fann, funuun	art, craft, technique
فني	fannii	artistic, technical
فندق، فنادق	funduq, fanaadiq*	hotel
فهد، فهود	fahd, fuhuud	leopard
فهم	fahima [S-I a]	understand
فورا	fawran	immediately
فوز	fawz	victory
فوق	fawqa	above, over
في	fii	in
فيروز	fayruuz	Fairuz (female name); turquoise (gem)
فيلل، فيلا	fiilla, fiilal	villa
فيلم، افلام	fiilm, aflaam	film

ق

قائمة، قوائم	qaa'imah, qawáa'im	list
قابل	qaabala [S III]	encounter, meet
قاد	qaada [Mw-I]	lead
قارب، قوارب	qaarib, qawaarib*	(small) boat
قال	qaala [Mw-I]	say
القاهرة	al-qaahirah	Cairo
قبل	qabila [S-I a]	accept
قبيح	qabiiH	ugly
قدم	qaddama [S-II]	present, serve
قديم	qadiim	old, ancient (of things)
قرأ، يقرأ	qara'a, yaqra' [S-I a]	read
قرار، ات	qaraar, -aat	decision, resolution

قرص ثابت	qurS thaabit	hard disk
قرفة	qirfah	cinnamon
قرن، قرون	qarn, quruun	century
قرنفل	qurunful	cloves
قريب	qariib	near
قسم، أقسام	qism, aqsaam	section, division
قصة، قصص	qiSSah, qiSaS	story, tale
قصر، قصور	qaSr, quSuur	palace
قطر، أقطار	quTr, aqTaar	region, area
قطعة، قطع	qiT:ah, qiTa:	piece
قفل	qafala [S-I i]	close, shut
قلب، قلوب	qalb, quluub	heart
قلعة، قلاع	qal:ah, qilaa:	fort, fortress, citadel
قلم، أقلام	qalam, aqlaam	pen, pencil
قليل	qaliil	little, few (quantity, number)
قليلاً	qaliilan	slightly, a little
قمر	qamar	moon
قميص، قمصان	qamiiS, qumSaan	shirt
قهر	qahara [S- a]	conquer
قهوة	qahwah	coffee
قوة، ات	quwwah, -aat	force, power, strength
قوسي	qawsii	curved, bowed
قيادي	qiyaadii	leading
قيم	qayyim	valuable

ك

ك	ka-	as, like
كائن	kaa'in	being, existing
كأس، كؤوس	ka's, ku'uus	cup, trophy
كافة	kaafat	all
كامل	kaamil	complete, whole
كبير	kabiir	big, old (of people)

كتاب، كتب	**kitaab, kutub**	*book*
كتب	**kataba [S-I-u]**	*write*
كتيب	**kutayyib**	*booklet, brochure*
كثافة	**kathaafah**	*density*
كثير	**kathiir**	*much, many*
كرة، ات	**kurah, -aat**	*ball; also used as a shortened form*
		of كرة القدم **kurat al-qadam** *football*
كرسي، كراسي	**kursii, karaasii**	*chair*
كره	**kariha [S-I a]**	*hate*
كريم	**kariim**	*noble, generous*
كسلان	**kaslaan**	*lazy*
كشري	**kushari**	*(name of an Egyptian lentil dish)*
الكعبة	**al-ka:bah**	*The Kaabah (Holy Shrine in Mecca)*
كعك	**ka:k**	*cake*
كفى	**kafaa [Ly-I]**	*suffice, be sufficient for*
كل	**kull**	*each, every, all*
كلام	**kalaam**	*speech*
كلية، ات	**kulliyyah, -aat**	*college, faculty*
كم	**kam**	*how many, how much*
كما	**ka-maa**	*just as, also*
كمية، ات	**kammiyyah, -aat**	*amount*
كوب، أكواب	**kuub, akwaab**	*glass, cup*
كيس، أكياس	**kiis, akyaas**	*bag, sack*
كيف	**kayf(a)**	*how*

ل

لـِ	**li-**	*to, for*
لَا	**laa**	*not, no*
لازم	**laazim**	*necessary*
لاعب، ون	**laa:ib, -uun**	*player*
لأن	**li' anna**	*because*
لحظة، ات	**laHDHah, laHaDHaat**	*moment*

لحم، لحوم	laHm, luHuum	meat
لذلك	li-dhaalik	because of that, for this reason
لذيذ	ladhiidh	delicious, tasty
لطيف	laTiif	pleasant, nice
لعب، ألعاب	la:b, al:aab	playing, game
لعب	la:iba [S-I a]	play
لماذا	li-maadha(a)	why
لمدة	li-muddat	for the period of…
لندن	landan	London
ليلة، ات، ليال	layla, -aat, layaalin	night
ليمون	laymoon	lemon

م

ما	maa	(before nouns and pronouns) what?;
		(before verbs) not
ماء، مياه	maa', miyaah	water
مائدة، موائد	maa'ida, mawaa'id*	table
مؤتمر، ات	mu'tamar, -aat	conference
مؤخرا	mu'akhkharan	recently
ماذا	maadhaa (before verbs)	what?
مارس	maarasa [S-III]	practise, carry out, perform
مالئ	maali'	filling, filler
مالي	maalii	financial
مؤلف، ون	mu'allif, -uun	author
مؤمن، ون	mu'min, -uun	believing, believer (in something)
مئوي	mi'awii	centennial, hundredth
مباراة، مباريات	mubaaraah, mubaarayaat	match (sport)
مباشرةً	mubaasharatan	directly
مبسوط	mabsuuT	contented, happy
مبلغ، مبالغ	mablagh, mabaaligh*	sum of money
متجاور	mutajaawir	adjacent, adjoining
متجر، متاجر	matjar, mataajir*	trading place, shop, stall

متحد	muttaHid	united
متحف، متاحف*	matHaf, mataaHif*	museum
متر، أمتار	mitr, amtaar	metre
متزوج	mutazawwaj	married
متفرج، ون	mutafarrij, -uun	spectator
متميز	mutamayyiz	distinctive, prominent
متى	mataa	when
مجتهد	mujtahid	diligent, hard-working
مثل	mithl	like
مجال، ات	majaal, -aat	field, sphere of activity
مجانا	majjaanan	free, gratis
مجنون، مجانين	majnuun, majaaniin*	mad
محطة، ات	maHaTTah, -aat	station
محل، محلات	maHall, maHallaat	shop, store
مخرج، مخارج	makhraj, makhaarij	exit
مخطط	mukhaTTaT	striped
مدافع، ون	mudaafi:, -uun	defender
مدخل، مداخل	madkhal, madaakhil	entrance
مدة	muddah (period of)	time
مدرس، ون	mudarris, -uun	teacher
مدير، مدراء	mudiir, mudaraa'	manager
مدينة، مدن	madiinah, mudun	town, city
مذاق	madhaaq	flavour
مربع	murabba:	square (adj.)
مرة، ات	marrah, -aat	time, occasion
مرحبا	marHaban	welcome
مركز الشرطة	markaz ash-shurTah	police station
مركز الفنون	markaz al-funuun	craft centre
مرمى	marmaa	goal, goalmouth
مريض، مرضى	mariiD, marDaa	(adj.) ill; (noun) patient
مساء	masaa'	evening
مساء الخير	masaa' al-khayr	good evening

مسابقة، ات	musaabaqah, -aat	competition
مسؤول، ون	mas'uul, -uun	official
مسبح، مسابح	masbaH, masaabiH*	swimming pool
مستشفى، مستشفيات	mustashfaa, mustashfayaat	hospital
مسرح، مسارح	masraH, masaariH*	theatre
مسرحية، ات	masraHiyyah, -aat	play (theatrical)
مسروق	masruuq	stolen
مسلسل، ات	musalsal, -aat	serial, series
مسلم، ون	muslim, -uun	Muslim
مسموح	masmuuH	permitted
مسيحي، ون	masiiHii, -uun	Christian
موسيقى	muusiiqaa (f.)	music
مشاهدة	mushaahadah	seeing, viewing
مشغول	mashghuul	busy
مشكلة، مشاكل	mushkilah, mashaakil*	problem
مشهور	mashhuur	famous
مصباح، مصابيح	miSbaaH, maSaabiiH	lamp
مصر	miSr*	Egypt
مطار، ات	maTaar, -aat	airport
مطبخ، مطابخ	maTbakh, maTaabikh*	kitchen
مطحون	maT-Huun	ground, milled
مطربة، ات	muTribah, -aat	(female) singer, musician
مطعم، مطاعم	maT:am, maTaa:im*	restaurant
مع	ma:a with,	together with
مع الأسف	má:a l-asaf	sorry
معجون	ma:juun	paste
معكرونة	ma:karuunah	macaroni
معنى، المعاني	ma:naa, al-ma:aanii	meaning
مغربي، مغاربة	maghribii, maghaaribah	Moroccan
مغنية، ات	mughanniyah, -aat	(female) singer

مفتاح، مفاتيح	miftaaH, mafaatiiH*	key
مفترض	muftaraD	assumed, supposed
مفروض	mafruuDH	necessary, obligatory
مفروم	mafruum	chopped, ground
مفضل	mufaDDil	preferring
مقدار، مقادير	miqdaar, maqaadiir*	quantity, measure
مقشر	muqashshar	peeled, skinned
مقطع	muqaTTa:	chopped
مقيم	muqiim	residing, resident
مكان، أمكنة	makaan, amkinah	place
مكة المكرمة	makkah l-mukarramah	Holy (City of) Mecca
مكتب، مكاتب	maktab, makaatib*	office
مكتبة، ات	maktabah, -aat	library, bookshop
مكتوب	maktuub	written
مكتوم	maktuum	concealed
المكسيك	al-maksiik	Mexico
ملابس	malaabis*	clothes
ملامح	malaamiH*	features
ملح	milH	salt
ملعب، ملاعب	mal:ab, malaa:ib*	sports ground, pitch
ملعقة، ملاعق	mil:aqah, malaa:iq*	spoon, spoonful
ملك، ملوك	malik, muluuk	king
مليونير	malyoonayr	millionaire
ممتاز	mumtaaz	excellent
ممثل، ون	mumaththil, -uun	actor, representative
ممنوع	mamnuu:	forbidden
من	man	who? (in questions)
من	min	from
من الممكن	min al mumkin	maybe
من فضلك	min faDlak	please
مناسبة، ات	munaasabah, -aat	occasion
منتج، ون	muntij, -uun	producer

منتجع صحة	muntaja: SiHHah	fitness centre
منذ	mundhu	since
منطقة، مناطق	minTaqah, manaaTiq*	region, area (football: penalty area)
منظم، ات	munaDHDHim, -aat	regulator
منظمة، ات	munaDHDHamah, -aat	organization
منقط	munaqqaT	spotted
منبعث	munba:ith	emanating
مهاجر، ون	muhaajir, -uun	emigrant
مهرب	muharrab	smuggled
مهرجان، ات	mahrajaan, -aat	festival
مهم	muhimm	important
مهنة، مهن	mihnah, mihan	job, trade, profession
مهندس، ون	muhandis, -uun	engineer
مواقيت	mawaaqíit	opening hours
موجود	mawjuud	found, situated, existing
موقع، مواقع	mawqi:, mawaaqi:*	site, situation, place
موقف، مواقف	mawqif, mawaaqif*	stopping, parking place
مولد النبي	mawlid an-nabii	(festival of) the Prophet's Birthday
مولود	mawluud	born
ميدان	maydaan	square (in a town)
ميناء، المواني	miinaa', al-mawaanii	(sometimes f.) harbour, port

ن

نائم	naa'im	sleeping, asleep
نادي، أندية	naadi, andiyah	club (social)
نار	naar (f.)	fire
ناس	naas	people
ناشف	naashif	dry
ناظر	naaDHara [S-III]	equal, compete with
نافع	naafi:	useful
نام	naama [Ma-I]	sleep
نتيجة، نتائج	natiijah, nataa'ij*	result, outcome

نجمة، ات	najmah, -aat	star, (female) film star
نساء (pl.)	nisaa'* (pl.)	women
نسمة	nasamah	individual (used in population counts only)
نشاط	nashaaT	activity
نصف، أنصاف	niSf, anSaaf	half
نظيف	naDHiif	clean
نفس، نفوس (f.)	nafs, nufuus (f.)	self, soul
نقد، نقود	naqd, nuquud	cash, money
نقع	naqa:a [S-I a]	soak, steep
نقل	naql	transport, transportation
نمر، نمور	namir, numuur	tiger
نهائي	nihaa'ii	final (adj.)
نهار	nahaar	daytime, hours of daylight
نهاية	nihaayah	end
نور	nuur	light (noun)
نوع، أنواع	naw:, anwaa:	kind, sort, type
نيل	nayl	getting, receiving

ـه

هادئ	haadi'	quiet, gentle
هال	haal	cardamom
هجين، هجن	hajiin, hujun	racing camel
هدف، أهداف	hadaf, ahdaaf	target, aim, goal
هدية، هدايا	hadiyah, hadaayaa*	gift, present
هذا/هذه	haadha/haadhihi	this (m./f.)
هرم، أهرام	haram, ahraam	pyramid
هنا	hunaa	here
هناك	hunaaka	there, there is/are
الهند	al-hind	India
هو	huwa	he
هو،هي	huwa/hiya	it (lit. 'he/she')
هواء	hawaa'	air

هواية، ات	**hawaayah, -aat**	*hobby*
هي	**hiya**	*she, it*

و

و	**wa-**	*and*
واحد	**waaHid**	*one*
واسع	**waasi:**	*roomy, spacious*
واقف	**waaqif**	*standing, stationary*
والد	**waalid**	*father*
والدة	**waalidah**	*mother*
وجبة، ات	**wajabah, -aat**	*meal*
وجه، وجوه	**wajh, wujuuh**	*face, (media) personality*
وحيد	**waHiid**	*sole, only, singular*
ود	**wadd**	*love, friendship*
وراء	**waraa'(a)**	*behind*
وسخ	**wasikh**	*dirty*
وسط	**wasT**	*middle, centre (of town, etc.)*
وصل	**waSala [Fw-I i]**	*arrive*
وصل	**waSSal [S-II]**	*connect, transport*
وضع	**waD:**	*putting*
وضع	**waDa:a [Fw-I a]**	*put, place*
وقت، أوقات	**waqt, awqaat**	*time*
وقع	**waqa:a [Fw-I a]**	*fall*
وقف	**waqafa [Fw-I i]**	*stop, stand*
ولا	**wa-laa**	*and not, nor*
ولاية، ات	**wilaayah, -aat**	*administrative division of a country; state*
ولد، أولاد	**walad, awlaad**	*boy (pl. also children)*
ولكن	**walaakin, walaakinna**	*but*

ى

يا	**yaa**	O! (used before the name when addressing someone directly)
يقام	**yuqaam**	is held, takes place (passive verb)
يد	**yad (f.)**	hand
اليمن	**al-yaman**	Yemen
يمين	**yamiin**	right (hand)
يوم، أيام	**yawm, ayyaam**	day
يومي	**yawmii**	daily (adj.)

English–Arabic vocabulary

This is again based on the words in the Vocabulary builders and in the texts.

about, approximately	حوالي	**Hawaalii**
about, concerning	عن	**:an**
above, over	فوق	**fawqa**
Abu Dhabi	أبو ظبي	**abuu DHabi**
accept	قبل	**qabila [S-I a]**
according to	حسب	**Hasb**
activity	نشاط	**nashaaT**
actor, representative	ممثل، ون	**mumaththil, -uun**
add	أضاف	**aDaafa [My-IV]**
address	عنوان، عناوين	**:unwaan, :anaawiin***
Aden	عدن	**:adan**
adjacent, adjoining	متجاور	**mutajaawir**
adult	بالغ، ون	**baaligh, baalighuun**
aeroplane	طائرة، ات	**Taa'irah, -aat**
affair, important matter	شأن، شؤون	**sha'n, shu'uun**
after	بعد	**ba:d (before nouns),** بعد ما **ba:d maa (before verbs)**
afternoon; (in the) afternoon	بعد الظهر	**ba:d aDH-DHuhr**
aim, shoot	سدد	**saddada [S-II]**
air	هواء	**hawaa'**
air conditioning	تكييف	**takyiif**
airport	مطار، ات	**maTaar, -aat**
Alexandria	الإسكندرية	**al-iskandariyyah**
all	جميع	**jamii:**
all day	طوال اليوم	**Tiwaal al-yawm**
all together	جميعا	**jamii:an**
also	أيضاً	**ayDan**
ambassador (female)	سفيرة، ات	**safiirah, -aat**

342

America	أمريكا	amriika
Amman	عمان	:ammaan
amount	كمية، ات	kammiyyah, -aat
and	و	wa-
announce, state	أعلن	a:lana [S-IV]
appear, seem, show	بدا	badaa [Lw-I]
apple	تفاحة، تفاح	tuffaaHah, tuffaaH
approximately	حوالي	Hawaalii
Arab, Arabic	عربي، عرب	:arabii
Arabian Gulf	الخليج العربي	al-khaliij al-:arabii
archaeological	أثري	atharii
arrive	وصل	waSala [Fw-I i]
art, craft, technique	فن، فنون	fann, funuun
artistic, technical	فني	fannii
as, like	ك	ka-
as for	أمّا	ammaa
aside, to one side	جانبا	jaaniban
ask	سأل	sa'ala [S-I a]
aspiration, ambition	طموح	TumuuH
aspire, have the ambition	طمح إلى	TamaHa ilaa [S-I a]
assembly, society	مفترض	jam:iyyah, -aat
assumed, supposed	مفترض	muftaraD
at, with	عند	:inda
attain, achieve	أدرك	adraka [S-IV]
attend	حضر	HaDara [S-I u]
attention, concern, interest	اهتمام	ihtimaam
attract	جلب	jalaba [S-I i]
aunt (on father's side)	عمة	:ammah
aunt (on mother's side)	خالة	khaalah
author	مؤلف، ون	mu'allif, -uun
award, grant	احتسب	iHtasaba [S-VIII]

baby	طفل، أطفال	Tifl, aTfaal
bachelor, single	أعزب	a:zab*
bag, sack	كيس، أكياس	kiis, akyaas
bag, suitcase	حقيبة، حقائب	Haqiibah, Haqaa'ib*
balance, equality	تعادل	ta:aadul
ball, football	كرة، ات	kurah, -aat
banish, drive away (football: send off)	طرد	Tarada [S-I u]
bank	بنك، بنوك	bank, bunuuk
bathroom	حمام، ات	Hammaam, -aat
be able	استطاع	istaTaa:a [Mw-X]
be carried, transported	تنقل	tanaqqala [S-V]
be surprised, astonished	دهش	dahisha [S-I a]
beard	ذقن، ذقون	dhaqn, dhuquun (f.)
beautiful	جميل	jamíil
beauty	جمال	jamaal
beauty salon	صالون تجميل	Saaluun tajmiil
because	لأن	li'anna
because of that, for this reason	لذلك	li-dhaalik
become	أصبح	aSbaHa [S-IV]
beer	بيرة	biirah
begin	بدأ	bada' [S-I a]
behind	وراء	waraa'(a)
being, existing, situated	كائن	kaa'in
belief, faith	إيمان	iimaan
believing, believer (in something)	مؤمن، ون	mu'min, -uun
beside, next to	بجانب	bi-jaanib
between, among	بين	bayna
bicycle	عجلة، ات	:ajalah, -aat
big, old	كبير	kabiir
black	أسود، سوداء	aswad*, f. sawdaa'*

344

boat	زورق، زوارق	zawraq, zawaariq*, قارب، قوارب qaarib, qawaarib*
boil, come to the boil	غلى	ghalaa [Ly-I]
boiling, (the action of) boiling something	سلق	salq
book	كتاب، كتب	kitaab, kutub
booklet, brochure	كتيب	kutayyib
born	مولود	mawluud
boss, chief	رئيس، رؤساء	ra'iis, ru'asaa'*
boy (pl. also children)	ولد، أولاد	walad, awlaad
branch	فرع، فروع	far:, furuu:
breach	اخترق	ikhtaraqa [S-VIII]
bread	خبز	khubz
breaking of a fast	فطر	fiTr
bridge	جسر، جسور	jisr, jusuur
British	بريطاني	briiTaanii
broadcast	أذاع	adhaa:a [My-IV]
brochure	كتيب	kutayyib
brother	أخ، إخوان/ إخوة	akh, ikhwaan or ikhwah
brown, fry	حمر	Hammara [S-II]
building, construction	بناء	binaa'
busy	مشغول	mashghuul
but	ولكن	walaakin, walaakinna
Cairo	القاهرة	al-qaahirah
cake	كفى	ka:k
Caliph	خليفة، خلفاء	khaliifah, khulafaa'*
camel	جمل، جمال	jamal, jimaal
camel (for racing)	هجين، هجن	hajiin, hujun
capital (city)	عاصمة، عواصم	:aaSimah, :awaaSim*
car	سيارة، ات	sayyaarah, -aat
card	بطاقة	biTáaqah

cardamom	هال	haal
carry	حمل	Hamala [S-I i]
cash, money	نقد، نقود	naqd, nuquud
cause, make do something; place, put	جعل	ja:ala [S-I a]
celebrate	احتفل ب	iHtafala bi- [S-VIII]
centennial, hundredth	مئوي	mi'awii
century	قرن، قرون	qarn, quruun
certain, definite	أكيد	akiid
chair	كرسي، كراسي	kursii, karaasii
chance, opportunity	فرصة، فرص	furSah, furaS
cheese	جبنة	jubnah
child	طفل، أطفال	Tifl, aTfaal
childhood	طفولة	Tufuulah
chocolate	شوكولاتة	shokolaatah
choose	اختار	ikhtaara [My-VIII]
chopped	مقطع	muqaTTa:
chopped, ground	مفروم	mafruum
Christian	مسيحي، ون	masiiHii, -uun
Christmas	عيد الميلاد	:iid al-miilaad
cinema	سينما، سينمات	siinamaa, siinamaat (f.)
cinnamon	قرفة	qirfah
city	مدينة، مدن	madiinah, mudun
class, row, line	صف، صفوف	Saff, Sufuuf
clean	نظيف	naDHiif
cleaning	تنظيف	tanDHiif
clinic	عيادة، ات	:iyaadah, -aat
close, shut	قفل	qafala [S-I i]
clothes	ملابس	malaabis*
cloves	قرنفل	qurunful
club (social)	نادي، أندية	naadi, andiyah
code, symbol	رمز، رموز	ramz, rumuuz

346

coffee	قهوة	qahwah
cold	بارد	baarid
college, faculty	كلية، ات	kulliyyah, -aat
come	جاء، يجيء	jaa'a, yajii' [My-I]
come after, follow	عقب	:aqaba [S-I u]
commence, open	افتتح	iftataHa [S-VIII]
commercial	تجاري	tijaarii
company, firm, business	شركة، ات	sharikah, -aat
compete with	زاحم	zaaHama [S-III]
competition	مسابقة، ات	musaabaqah, -aat
complete	تام	taamm
complete, whole	كامل	kaamil
computer	آلة حاسبة	aalah Haasibah
concealed	مكتوم	maktuum
conference	مؤتمر، ات	mu'tamar, -aat
connect, transport	وصل	waSSal [S-II]
conquer	قهر	qahara [S- a]
consider, regard	اعتبر	i:tabara [S-VIII]
contented, happy	مبسوط	mabsuuT
cook	طبخ	Tabakha [S-I u]
cooking, cuisine	طبيخ	Tabiikh
cooling	تبريد	tabriid
corner (adj.)	ركني	ruknii
corner	ركن، أركان	rukn, arkaan
correct, right	صحيح	SaHiiH
count, census	إحصاء، ات	iHSaa', -aat
country	بلد، بلاد/بلدان	balad, bilaad/buldaan
country, state	دولة، دول	dawlah, duwal
craft centre	مركز الفنون	markaz al-funuun
credit card	بطاقة تسليف	biTaaqat tasliif
creek	خور	khawr

cultural	ثقافي	thaqaafii
cup, trophy	كأس، كؤوس	ka's, ku'uus
curved, bowed	قوسي	qawsii
custom, habit	عادة، ات	:aadah, -aat
customer, client	زبون، زبائن	zabuun, zabaa'in*
customs, excise	جمرك، جمارك	jumruk, jamaarik*
daily (adj.)	يومي	yawmii
dam	سد، سدود	sadd, suduud
Damascus	دمشق	dimashq*
daughter	ابنة، بنات	ibnah, banaat
dawn	فجر	fajr
day	يوم، أيام	yawm, ayyaam
daytime, hours of daylight	نهار	nahaar
deceive	خدع	khada:a [S-I a]
decision, resolution	قرار، ات	qaraar, -aat
defender	مدافع، ون	mudaafi:, -uun
delicious, tasty	لذيذ	ladhiidh
demanding back, reclaiming	استرداد	istirdaad
density	كثافة	kathaafah
dentist	طبيب أسنان	Tabiib asnaan
department (government)	دائرة، دوائر	daa'irah, dawaa'ir*
design, designing	تصميم	taSmiim
desire, wish	رغبة، ات	raghbah, -aat
diligent, hard-working	مجتهد	mujtahid
dinar (currency)	دينار، دنانير	diinaar, danaaniir*
directly	مباشرةً	mubaasharatan
director, manager	مدير، مدراء	mudiir, mudaraa'*
dirham	درهم، دراهم	dirham, daraahim*
dirty	وسخ	wasikh
discount	حسم	Hasm

discover	اكتشف	iktashafa [S-VIII]
discuss	ناقش	naaqasha [S-III]
dish	صحن، صحون	SaHn, SuHuun
distinction, privilege	امتياز	imtiyaaz
distinctive, prominent	متميز	mutamayyiz
division of a country; state	ولاية، ات	wilaayah, -aat
do, make	فعل	fa:ala [S-I a]
do, work	عمل	:amila [S-I a]
doctor	طبيب، أطباء	Tabiib, aTibbaa'*
dominate	سيطر على	sayTara :alaa [Q-I]
domination	سيطرة	sayTarah
door, gate	باب، أبواب	baab, abwaab
drain, strain	صفى	Saffaa [Ly-II]
drink	شرب	shariba [S-I a]
driver	سائق،ون/ساقة	saa'iq, -uun/saaqah
dry	ناشف	naashif
each, every, all	كل	kull
ear	أذن	udh(u)n (f.)
eat	أكل، يأكل	akala, ya'kul [S-I u]
educational	تعليمي	ta:liimii
Egypt	مصر	miSr*
emanate, be sent out	انبعث	inba:atha [S-VII]
emanating	منبعث	munba:ith
emigrant	مهاجر، ون	muhaajir, -uun
encounter, meet	قابل	qaabala [S III]
end	نهاية	nihaayah
end, last part of something	آخر	aakhir
engineer	مهندس، ون	muhandis, -uun
England	إنجلترا	ingiltarra
English, Englishman	إنجليزي	ingliizi

enjoy	تمتع بـ	tamatta:a [S-V]
enter	دخل	dakhala [S-I u]
entrance	مدخل، مداخل	madkhal, madaakhil*
entrust, vest in	أسند لـ	asnada [S-IV]
equal, compete with	ناظر	naaDHara [S-III]
erect, construct	شيد	shayyada [My-II]
European	أوروبي، ون	uruubii
evening	مساء	masaa'*
every, each, all	كل	kull
excellent	ممتاز	mumtaaz
except	إلا	illaa
exit	مخرج، مخارج	makhraj, makhaarij*
explain	شرح	sharaHa [S-I] a
extent, compass	اتساع	ittisaa:
extreme, most	غاية	ghaa yah
eye; also spring (of water)	عين، عيون	:ayn, :uyuun (f.)
face, (media) personality	وجه، وجوه	wajh, wujuuh
facilities	تسهيلات	tas-hiilaat
fall, happen	وقع	waqa:a [Fw-I a]
family	عائلة، ات	:aa'ilah, -aat
famous	شهير	shahiir مشهور mashhuur
far away, distant	بعيد	ba:iid
fashion, style	زي، أزياء	ziyy, azyaa'*
fast, fasting	صوم	Sawm
father	أب	ab, والد waalid
favourable, good	فاضل	faaDil
features	ملامح	malaamiH*
festival, anniversary	عيد، أعياد	:iid, a:yaad
festival (event)	مهرجان، ات	mahrajaan, -aat
field, sphere of activity	مجال، ات	majaal, -aat

fifth	خامس	khaamis
filling, filler	مالئ	maali'
film	فيلم، افلام	fiilm, aflaam
final (adj.)	نهائي	nihaa'ii
financial	مالي	maalii
finish, come to an end	انتهى	intahaa [Ly-VIII]
fire	نار	naar (f.)
first	أول	awwal
first (adv.)	أولا	awwalan
fish (collective)	سمك	samak
fitness centre	منتجع صحة	muntaja: SiHHah
flag, banner	راية، ات	raayah, -aat
flat, apartment	شقة، شقق	shaqqah, shiqaq
flavour	مذاق	madhaaq
flood, overflow with	أفاض ب	afaaDa bi- [My-IV]
fluently	بطلاقة	bi-Talaaqah
folk, pertaining to the people	شعبي	sha:bii
follow	تبع	tabi:a
food	طعام	Ta:aam
food, things to eat	أكل	akl
foot	قدم، اقدام	qadam
football	كرة القدم	kurat al-qadam
for the period of...	لمدة	li-muddat
forbidden	ممنوع	mamnuu:
force, power, strength	قوة، ات	quwwah, -aat
fort, fortress	حصن، حصون قلعة، قلاع	HiSn, HuSuun qal:ah, qilaa:
found, situated, existing	موجود	mawjuud
foundation, setting up	إنشاء	inshaa'*
four	أربعة	arba:ah
France	فرنسا	faransaa
free, gratis	مجانا	majjaanan

French	فرنساوي	faransaawi
friend	صديق، أصدقاء	Sadiiq, aSdiqaa'*
frock, dress	فستان، فساتين	fustaan, fasaatiin*
from	من	min
fruit	فاكهة، فواكه	faakihah, fawaakih*
game, playing	لعب، ألعاب	la:b, al:aab
garden, park	حديقة، حدائق	Hadiiqah, Hadaa'iq*
Giza (district of Cairo)	الجيزة	al-jiizah
general	عام	:aamm عمومي: umuumii
geographical	جغرافي	jughraafii
German	ألماني	almaanii
getting, receiving	نيل	nayl
ghee, clarified butter	سمن	samn
gift, present	هدية، هدايا	hadiyah, hadaayaa*
girl, daughter	بنت، بنات	bint, banaat
girl, young woman	فتاة، فتيات	fataah, fatayaat
give	أعطى	a:Taa [Ly-IV]
glass, cup	كوب، أكواب	kuub, akwaab
go	ذهب	dhahaba, [S-I a]
goal, goalmouth	مرمى	marmaa
God, Allah	الله	Al-laah
gold	ذهب	dhahab
golf	جولف	guulf
good	جيد	jayyid
good evening	مساء الخير	masaa' al-khayr
good morning	صباح الخير	SabaaH al-khayr
grain, seed	حبة، ات	Habbah, -aat
Great Britain	بريطانيا العظمى	briiTaanyaa l-:uDHmaa
green	أخضر	akhDar*
ground (sports), pitch	ملعب، ملاعب	mal:ab, malaa:ib*

ground, earth	أرض	al-arD (f.)
ground, milled	مطحون	maT-Huun
group, gathering	جماعة، ات	jamaa:ah, -aat
guard (football: goalkeeper)	حارس، حراس	Haaris, Hurraas
guest	ضيف، ضيوف	Dayf, Duyuuf
hair	شعر	sha:r
half	نصف، أنصاف	niSf, anSaaf
hamburger	برغر، ات	barghar, -aat
hand	يد	yad (f.)
happy, joyful	سعيد، سعداء	sa:iid, su:adaa'*
harbour, port	ميناء، الموانى	miinaa', al-mawaanii (sometimes f.)
hard disk	قرص ثابت	qurS thaabit
hate	كره	kariha [S-I a]
he	هو	huwa
heart	قلب، قلوب	qalb, quluub
heat	حرارة	Haraarah
heat, race (football: half)	شوط، أشواط	shawT, ashwaaT
heavy	ثقيل	thaqiil
hello	السلام عليكم	as-salaamu-alaykum
here	هنا	hunaa
high	العالي	al-: aalii
historical	تاريخي	taariikhii
history	تاريخ	taariikh
hit, strike	أصاب	aSaaba
hobby	هواية، ات	hawaayah, -aat
hospital	مستشفى، مستشفيات	mustashfaa, mustashfayaat
hot	حار	Haarr
hotel	فندق، فنادق	funduq, fanaadiq*
hour, time, watch, clock	ساعة، ات	saa:ah, -aat
house	بيت، بيوت	bayt, buyuut

how	كيف	kayf(a)
how many, how much	كم	kam
how much?	بكم	bi-kam
human being; pl. = people	انسان، ناس	insaan, naas
hungry	جوعان، جوعى	jaw:aan*, jaw:aa*
husband	زوج	zawj
I	أنا	ána
ice	ثلج	thalj
ice-cream	أيس كريم	ays kriim
if	إن	in, إذا idhaa, لو law
ill	مريض، مرضى	mariiD, marDaa
immediately	فورا	fawran
implementation, execution	تنفيذ	tanfiidh
important	مهم	muhimm
impose	فرض	faraDa [S-I i]
in	في	fii
in front of	أمام	amaam
include, comprise	ضم	Damma [D-I u]
India	الهند	al-hind
individual (used in population counts only)	نسمة	nasamah
inhabitant, resident	ساكن، سكان	saakin, sukkaan
inside	داخل	daakhil
international	دولي	duwalii or dawlii
Iraqi	عراقي	:iraaqii
is held, takes place (passive verb)	يقام	yuqaam
it (lit., he/she)	هو،هي	huwa/hiya
Jordanian	أردني	urduni
journey, voyage	رحلة، ات	riHlah, -aat

just, upright	عادل	:aadil
just as, also	كما	ka-maa
Kaabah	الكعبة	al-ka:bah
keep, preserve	حافظ على	HaafaDHa :alaa [S-III]
key	مفتاح، مفاتيح	miftaaH, mafaatiiH*
kick	ركلة، ات	raklah, -aat
kind, sort, type	نوع، أنواع	naw:, anwaa:
king	ملك، ملوك	malik, muluuk
kitchen	مطبخ، مطابخ	maTbakh, maTaabikh*
know	عرف	:arafa [S-I i]
lady	سيدة، ات	sayyidah, -aat
lamp	مصباح، مصابيح	miSbaaH, maSaabiiH
last	أخير	akhiir
late evening (prayer time)	عشاء	:ishaa'
layer	طبقة، ات	Tabaqah, -aat
lazy	كسلان	kaslaan
lead	قاد	qaada [Mw-I]
leading	قيادي	qiyaadii
leading roles	بطولات	buTuulaat
learn	تعلم	ta:allama [S-V]
leave, let be	ترك	taraka [S-I u]
left	شمال	shamaal
legend	أسطورة، أساطير	usTuurah, asaaTiir*
leisure	فراغ	faraagh
lemon	ليمون	laymoon
lentils	عدس	:ads
leopard	فهد، فهود	fahd, fuhuud
letter, message	رسالة، رسائل	risaalah, risaa'il*
library, bookshop	مكتبة، ات	maktabah, -aat

life, age	عمر	:umr
lift, raise	رفع	rafa:a [S-I a]
light (adj.)	خفيف	khafiif
light (noun)	نور	nuur
like	مثل	mithl
like, love	أحب، يحب	aHabba [D-IV]
limit, border	حد، حدود	Hadd, Huduud
list	قائمة، قوائم	qaa'imah, qawaa'im*
little, few (quantity, number)	قليل	qaliil
live	عاش	:aasha [M-y I]
live, reside	سكن	sakana [S-I u]
load, burden	حمل، أحمال	Himl, aHmaal
lobby (hotel)	بهو	bahw
London	لندن	landan
look! (to a woman)	انظري	unDHurii
love, friendship	ود	wadd
macaroni	معكرونة	ma:karuunah
mad	مجنون، مجانين	majnuun, majaaniin*
magic	سحر	siHr
magnificent	فخم	fakhm
males	ذكور	dhukuur
man	رجل، رجال	rajul, rijaal
manager	مدير، مدراء	mudiir, mudaraa'
map	خريطة، خرائط	khariiTah, kharaa'iT*
market	سوق، أسواق	suuq, aswaaq (usually f.)
married	متزوج	mutazawwaj
marry	تزوج	tazawwaja [Mw-V]
match (sport)	مباراة، مباريات	mubaaraah, mubaarayaat
matter, affair	شأن، شؤون	sha'n, shu'uun
maybe	من الممكن	min al mumkin

356

meal	وجبة، ات	wajabah, -aat
meaning	معنى، المعاني	ma:naa, al-ma:aanii
meat	لحم، لحوم	laHm, luHuum
meet, come together	اجتمع	ijtama:a [S-VIII]
member (f.)	عضوة، عضوات	:uDwah, :uDuwaat
membership	عضوية	:uDwiyyah
memory	ذاكرة	dhaakirah
merchant	تاجر، تجار	taajir, tujjaar
method, way	طريقة، طرائق	Tariiqah, Taraa'iq*
metre	متر، أمتار	mitr, amtaar
Mexico	المكسيك	al-maksiik
mid-afternoon	عصر	:aSr
middle	وسط	wasT
millionaire	مليونير	malyoonayr
minute	دقيقة، دقائق	daqiiqah, daqaa'iq*
mixture	خليط	khaliiT
modern, up-to-date	حديث	Hadiith
moment	لحظة، ات	laHDHah, laHaDHaat
moon	قمر	qamar
more/most	أكثر	akthar*
morning	صبح	SubH
Moroccan	مغربي، مغاربة	maghribii, maghaaribah
mosque (large)	جامع، جوامع	jaami:, jawaami:*
mother	والدة	waalidah
much, many	كثير	kathiir
museum	متحف، متاحف	matHaf, mataaHif*
music	موسيقى	muusiiqaa (f.)
Muslim	مسلم، ون	muslim, -uun
name	اسم، أسماء	ism, asmaa'*
narrow	ضيق	Dayyiq

nation	أمة، أمم	ummah, umam
nationality	جنسية، ات	jinsiyyah, -aat
natural	طبيعي	Tabii:ii
naturally, of course	طبعا	Tab:an
nature	طبيعة	Tabii:ah
near (to)	قريب من	qariib min
necessary	لازم	laazim
necessary, obligatory	مفروض	mafruuDH
necessity, requirement	ضرورة، ات	Daruurah, -aat
neighbour	جار، جيران	jaar, jiiraan
net, netting	شبكة، شباك	shabaka, shibaak
new	جديد	jadiid
newest, latest	أحدث	aHdath*
news	خبر، أخبار	khabar, akhbaar
newspaper	جريدة، جرائد	jariidah, jaraa'id*
nice	لطيف	laTiif
night	ليلة، ات، ليال	layla, -aat, layaalin
ninth	تاسع	taasi:
no, not	لا	laa
noble, generous	كريم	kariim
noon	ظهر	DHuhr
nor	ولا	wa-laa
not (before verbs)	ما	maa
novel, story	رواية، ات	riwaayah, -aat
now	الآن، الحين	al-'aan, al-Hiin
number	عدد، أعداد	:adad, a:daad
O! (when addressing someone directly)	يا	yaa
observe, watch	رصد	raSada [S-I u]

occasion	مناسبة، ات	munaasabah, -aat
occupation, work	عمل، أعمال	:amal, a:maal
occupy	احتل	iHtalla [D-VIII]
offer, deal	عرض، عروض	:arD, :uruuD
office	مكتب، مكاتب	maktab, makaatib*
official	مسؤول، ون	mas'uul, -uun
oil (edible)	زيت	zayt
old, ancient (of things)	قديم	qadiim
Oman (Sultanate of)	عمان	:umaan
one	واحد	waaHid
onions	بصل	baSal
only	فقط	faqaT
open	فتح	fataHa [S-I a]
opening hours	مواقيت	mawaaqiit*
or	أو	aw
organization	منظمة، ات	munaDHDHamah, -aat
origin, basis	أصل، أصول	aSl, uSuul
other	آخر	aakhar* (f. أخرى ukhraa)
other than, apart from	غير	ghayr
outside	خارج	khaarij
owner, master; also	صاحب، أصحاب	SaaHib, aS-Haab
sometimes friend		
palace	قصر، قصور	qaSr, quSuur
participate, take part	اشترك	ishtaraka [S-VIII]
passenger	راكب ، ركاب	raakib, rukkaab
past (noun)	الماضي	al-maaDii
paste	معجون	ma:juun
patient (sick person)	مريض، مرضى	mariiD, marDaa*
peeled, skinned	مقشر	muqashshar
pen, pencil	قلم، أقلام	qalam, aqlaam

people	ناس	naas
people, folk	شعب؛ ،شعوب	sha:b, shu:uub
pepper	فلفل	fulful/filfil
period, time, spell	فترة، ات	fatrah, -aat
permission	سماح	samaaH
permitted	مسموح	masmuuH
person	شخص، أشخاص	shakhS, ashkhaaS
petrol	بنزين	banziin
pharaonic	فرعوني	far:uunii
pharmacy	صيدلية، ات	Saydaliyyah, -aat
phrase, expression	عبارة، ات	:abaarah, -aat
piece	قطعة، قطع	qiT:ah, qiTa:
pilgrimage	الحج	al-Hajj
pitch, course, playing field	ملعب، ملاعب	mal:ab, malaa:ib*
place	أمكنة، مكان	makaan, amkinah
place	أودع	awda:a [Fw-IV]
plate, dish	طبق، أطباق	Tabaq, aTbaaq
play, game	لعب	la:b
play (theatrical)	مسرحية، ات	masraHiyyah, -aat
play	لعب	la:iba [S-I a]
player	لاعب، ون	laa:ib, -uun
pleasant, nice	لطيف	laTiif
please (go ahead, sit down, enter etc.)	تفضل	tafaDDal
please (when asking for something)	من فضلك	min faDlak
pocket	جيب، جيوب	jayb, juyuub
poet	شاعر، شعراء	shaa:ir, shu:araa'*
poetry	شعر	shi:r
police station	مركز الشرطة	markaz ash-shurTah
poor, poor person	فقير، فقراء	faqiir, fuqaraa'*
porter	حمال، ون	Hammaal, -uun

possible, be	أمكن	amkana [S-IV]
post office box	صندوق بريد	Sanduuq bariid
pound (money)	جنيه، ات	junayh, -aat
pour out	سكب	sakaba [S-I u]
practise, carry out, perform	مارس	maarasa [S-III]
praise God	الحمد لله	al-Hamdu li-l-laah
prefer	فضل	faDDala [S-II]
preferring	مفضل	mufaDDil
present, gift	هدية، هدايا	hadiyah, hadaayaa*
present, here	حاضر، ون	HaaDir, -uun
present, serve	قدم	qaddama [S-II]
presentation	تقديم	taqdiim
price	سعر، أسعار	si:r, as:aar
print, type	طبع	Taba:a [S-I a]
prize, reward	جائزة، جوائز	jaa'izah, jawaa'iz*
problem	مشكلة، مشاكل	mushkilah, mashaakil*
producer	منتج، ون	muntij, -uun
production	إنتاج	intaaj
programme	برنامج، برامج	barnaamij, baraamij*
pupil	تلميذ، تلامذة/تلاميذ	tilmiidh, talaamidhah/talaamiidh*
pure, clear	الصافي	aS-Saafii
put, place	وضع	waDa:a [Fw-I a]
putting	وضع	waD:
pyramids	الأهرام	al-ahraam
qualify	تأهل	ta'ahhala [S-V] (لـ li- for)
quantity, measure	مقدار، مقادير	miqdaar, maqaadiir*
quarter	ربع	rub:
question	سؤال، أسئلة	su'aal, as'ilah
quickly, before long	سرعان ما	sur:aan maa
quiet, gentle	هادئ	haadi'

race	سباق، ات	sibaaq, -aat
radio	راديو، راديوهات	raadyo, raadyohaat
raise	رفع	rafa:a [S-I a]
read	قرأ، يقرأ	qara'a, yaqra' [S-I a]
really, actually, in fact	فعلا	fi:lan
receive, meet	استقبل	istaqbala [S-X]
recently	مؤخرا	mu'akhkharan
red	أحمر	aHmar*
referee, umpire	حكم، حكام	Hakam, Hukkaam
region, area (football: penalty area)	منطقة، مناطق	minTaqah, manaaTiq*
region, zone, area	قطر، أقطار	quTr, aqTaar
register, score	سجل	sajjala [S-II]
registration, scoring	تسجيل	tasjiil
regulator	منظم، ات	munaDHDHim, -aat
renew, restore	جدد	jaddada [D-II]
rent, be a tenant of	استأجر	ista'jara [S-X]
repeat, renew	أعاد	a:aada [Mw-IV]
report	تقرير، تقارير	taqriir, taqaariir*
reside; hold (an event, etc.)	أقام	aqaama [Mw-IV]
residing, living	مقيم	muqiim
restaurant	مطعم، مطاعم	maT:am, maTaa:im*
result, outcome	نتيجة، نتائج	natiijah, nataa'ij*
return something to someone	رد	radda [D-i u]
return, come back	رجع	raja:a [S-I i]
rice	أرز	aruzz
rich, rich person	غني، أغنياء	ghanii, aghniyaa'*
right (hand)	يمين	yamiin
right, correct	صالح	SaaliH
road, street	شارع، شوارع	shaari:, shawaari:*
road, way	طريق، طرق	Tariiq, Turuq
role, turn	دور، أدوار	dawr, adwaar

room	حجرة	Hujrah
room	غرفة، غرف	ghurfah, ghuraf
roomy, spacious	واسع	waasi:
row, class (in school)	صف، صفوف	Saff, Sufuuf
run	جرى	jaraa [Ly-I]
sacrificial animal	ذبيحة، ذبائح	dhabiiHah, dhabaa'iH*
sad	حزين	Haziin
safe, sound	سالم	saalim
salt	ملح	milH
sandwich	سندويتش، ات	sandawíitsh, -aat
sauce	صلصة	SalSah
Saudi Arabia	السعودية	as-sa:udiyyah
sauna	سونا	sawnaa
say	قال	qaala [Mw-I]
screen	شاشة	shaashah
sea, large river	بحر، بحار	baHr, biHaar
section, division	قسم، أقسام	qism, aqsaam
section, season (of the year)	فصل، فصول	faSl, fuSuul
see, look at	شاهد	shaahada [III]
seeing, viewing	مشاهدة	mushaahadah
selection	تشكيلة، ات	tashkiilah, -aat
self, soul	نفس، نفوس	nafs, nufuus (f.)
sell	باع	baa:a [My-I]
send	أرسل	arsala [S-IV]
serial, series	مسلسل، ات	musalsal, -aat
servant	خادم، خدام؛ (.f) ات، خادمة	khaadim, khuddaam; (f.) khaadimah, -aat
service	خدمة، ات	khidmah, -aat
shape, kind, type	شكل، أشكال	shakl, ashkaal
Sharjah	الشارقة	ash-shaariqah
she, it	هي	hiya

sheep	خروف، خرفان	kharuuf, khirfaan; (collective) غنم ghanam
shelf	رف، رفوف	raff, rufuuf
ship	سفينة، سفن	safiinah, sufun
shirt	قميص، قمصان	qamiiS, qumSaan
shocking, awful	فظيع	faDHii:
shop, stall	دكان، دكاكين	dukkaan, dakaakiin*
shop, store	محل، محلات	maHall, maHallaat
shopping	تسوق	tasawwuq
shore, beach	شاطئ	shaaTi'
shot (football)	تسديدة، ات	tasdiidah, -aat
shower	دش	dushsh
showing, displaying	عرض	:arD
side	جانب، جوانب	jaanib, jawaanib*
signal	إشارة، ات	ishaarah, -aat
since	منذ	mundhu
singer (female)	مغنية، ات	mughanniyah, -aat
singer, musician (female)	مطربة، ات	muTribah, -aat
single	فردي	fardii
sister	أخت، أخوات	ukht, akhawaat
sit, sit down	جلس	jalasa [S-I i]
site, situation, place	موقع، مواقع	mawqi:, mawaaqi:*
sitting, seated	جالس	jaalis
sitting-room, lounge	صالة	Saalah
six	ستة	sittah
sixth	سادس	saadis
slaughter	ذبح	dhabaHa [S-I a]
sleep	نام	naama [Ma-I]
sleeping, asleep	نائم	naa'im
slice	شريحة، شرائح	shariiHah, sharaa'iH*
slightly, a little	قليلاً	qaliilan
small, young	صغير	Saghiir

smell, scent, perfume	رائحة، روائح	raa'iHah, rawaa'iH*
smile	ابتسم	ibtasama [S-VIII]
smuggled	مهرب	muharrab
so, therefore	إذا	ídhan
soak, steep	نقع	naqa:a [S-I a]
soldier	عسكري، عساكر	:askarii, :asaakir*
sole, only, singular	وحيد	waHiid
solution	حل، حلول	Hall, Huluul
some, part of something	بعض	ba:D
son	ابن، أبناء	ibn, abnaa'*
sorry	مع الأسف	má:a l-asaf
Spanish	اسباني	isbaanii
speak	تكلم	takallama [S-V]
special; private	خاص	khaaSS
specialize	تخصص	takhaSSaS [S-V]
spectator	متفرج، ون	mutafarrij, -uun
speech	كلام	kalaam
speed	سرعة	sur:ah
Sphinx	أبو الهول	abuu l-hawl
spice	تابل، توابل	taabil, tawaabil*
splendid, brilliant, marvellous	رائع	raa'i:
spoon, spoonful	ملعقة، ملاعق	mil:aqah, malaa:iq*
sport, exercise	رياضة، ات	riyaaDah, -aat
spotted	منقط	munaqqaT
spread, currency	انتشار	intishaar
sprinkle, spray	رش	rashsha [D-I u]
square (adj.)	مربع	murabba:
square (in a town)	ميدان	maydaan
standing, stationary	واقف	waaqif
star, (female) film star	نجمة، ات	najmah, -aat
state, express	أعرب عن	a:raba :an [S-IV]

station	محطة، ات	maHaTTah, -aat
step, degree	درجة، ات	darajah, -aat
stolen	مسروق	masruuq
stone	حجر، أحجار	Hajar, aHjaar
stop, stand	وقف	waqafa [Fw-I i]
stopping, parking place	موقف، مواقف	mawqif, mawaaqif*
story, tale	قصة، قصص	qiSSah, qiSaS
street, road	شارع، شوارع	shaari:, shawaari:*
striped	مخطط	mukhaTTaT
strong, mighty	شديد	shadiid
student	طالب، طلاب/طلبة	Taalib, Tullaab/Talabah (f. طالبة، طالبات Taalibah, -aat)
study, studying (noun)	دراسة، ات	diraasah, -aat
study	درس	darasa [S-I u]
suffice, be sufficient for	كفى	kafaa [Ly-I]
sugar	سكر	sukkar
sum (of money)	مبلغ، مبالغ	mablagh, mabaaligh*
summer	صيف	Sayf
sun	شمس	shams
sunset; Morocco	المغرب	al-maghrib
surround	أحاط بـ	aHaaTa bi- [My-IV]
sweetness	حلاوة	Halaawah
swim	سبح	sabaHa [S-I a]
swimming	سباحة	sibaaHah
swimming pool	مسبح، مسابح	masbaH, masaabiH*
table	مائدة، موائد	maa'ida, mawaa'id*
take	أخذ	akhadha [S-I u]
take care of, look after	رعى	ra:aa [Lh-I]
take, use up, occupy (of time)	استغرق	istaghraqa [S-X]
tall, long	طويل	Tawiil
target, aim, goal	هدف، أهداف	hadaf, ahdaaf

taxi	تاكسي	taaksi
tea	شاي	shaay
teacher	مدرس، ون	mudarris, -uun
team	فريق، فرق	fariiq, firaq
telephone	تلفون	tilifuun
telephone number	رقم تلفون	raqm tilifuun
television (adj.), televisual	تلفزيوني	tilifizyuunii
temperature	درجة الحرارة	darajat al-Haraarah
ten	عشرة	:ashrah
tennis	تنس	tanis
thank you	شكراً	shukran
thank you (to a man/woman)	أشكرك	ashkur-ak/ik
thank you very much	شكراً جزيلاً	shukran jaziilan
that	ذلك	dhaalik
that is	أي	ay
the	الـ	al-
theatre	مسرح، مسارح	masraH, masaariH*
then	ثم	thumma
there, there is/are	هناك	hunaaka
thing, something	شيء، اشياء	shay', ashyaa'*
third	ثالث	thaalith
thirsty	عطشان	:aTshaan
thirteenth (f.)	ثالثة عشر	thaalithah :ashar
this	هذا/هذه	haadha/haadhihi (m./f.)
thousand	ألف، آلاف	alf, aalaaf
three	ثلاثة	thalaathah
ticket	تذكرة، تذاكر	tadhkirah, tadhaakir*
tiger	نمر، نمور	namir, numuur
time	زمان، أزمنة	zamaan, azminah
time	وقت، أوقات	waqt, awqaat
time (period of)	مدة	muddah

time, occasion	مرة، ات	marrah, -aat
tired	تعبان	ta:baan
to, for	لـ	li-
today	اليوم	al-yawm
tomatoes	طماطم	TamaaTim*
tomorrow	الغد	al-ghad
tourist	سائح، سواح	saa'iH, suwwaaH
tower	برج، أبراج	burj, abraaj
town, city	مدينة، مدن	madiinah, mudun
track, trace	أثر، آثار	athar, aathaar
trade, commerce	تجارة	tijaarah
trade, profession	مهنة، مهن	mihnah, mihan
trading place, shop, stall	متجر، متاجر	matjar, mataajir*
transmission, sending	إرسال	irsaal
transport, take, give a lift	وصل	waSSala [II]
transport, transportation	نقل	naql
travel	سافر	saafara [S-III]
tree	شجرة، أشجار	shajarah, ashjaar
truthful, true	صادق	Saadiq
try out, taste	جرب	jarraba [S-II]

ugly	قبيح	qabiiH
uncle (on father's side)	عم	:amm
uncle (on mother's side)	خال	khaal
understand	فهم	fahima [S-I a]
understanding	فاهم	faahim
united	متحد	muttaHid
United Arab Emirates	الإمارات العربية المتحدة	al-imaaraat al-:arabiyyah al-muttaHidah
university	جامعة، ات	jaami:ah
until, even	حتى	Hattaa
upright, honest	صالح	SaaliH

use, employ	استخدم	istakhdama [S-X]
use, employment	استخدام	istikhdaam
use, usage	استعمال	isti:maal
useful	نافع	naafi:
valuable	قيم	qayyim
very	جدا	jíddan
victory	فوز	fawz
villa	فيلل، فيلا	fiilla, fiilal
visit	زار	zaara [Mw-I]
visit	زيارة، ات	ziyaarah, -aat
visitor	زائر، زوار	zaa'ir, zuwwaar
wall	سور، أسوار	suur, aswaar
wash	غسل	ghasala [S-I i]
washing machine	غسالة، ات	ghassaalah, -aat
watch, look at	تفرج على	tafarraja :ala [S-V]
water	ماء، مياه	maa', miyaah
weapon, arm	سلاح، أسلحة	silaaH, asliHah
welcome	مرحبا	marHaban; أهلا وسهلا ahlan wa-sahlan
welcome	رحب ب	raHHaba bi- [S-II]
welcome, welcoming (noun)	ترحيب	tarHiib
welcoming (adj.)	ترحيبي	tarHiibii
well, right, OK	حسنا	Hasanan
well-being (state of)	خير	khayr
West	الغرب	al-gharb
Western	غربي، ون	gharbii, -uun
what? (before nouns and pronouns)	ما	maa; (before verbs) ماذا maadhaa
wheel, bicycle	عجلة، ات	:ajalah, -aat
when	متى	mataa (in questions); when عندما :indamaa

where	أين	ayna
which	أيّ	ayy
while	بينما	baynamaa
white	أبيض، بيضاء	abyaD*, f. bayDaa'*
who? (in questions)	من	man
who, which, that	الذي	alladhi (f. التي allatii)
why	لماذا	li-maadha(a)
wide	عريض	:ariiD
wife	زوجة، ات	zawjah, -aat
win, gain, profit	ربح	rabaHa [S-I a]
wind tower	برجيل، براجيل	barjiil, baraajiil*
winter	شتاء	shitaa'*
with, together with	مع	ma:a
without	بدون	bi-duun
woman	امرأة، نساء	imra'ah, nisaa' (irregular plural)
wonder, wonderful thing	عجيبة، عجائب	:ajiibah, :ajaa'ib*
wonderful	عجيب	:ajiib
work, job, business	عمل، أعمال	:amal, a:maal
workman	عامل، عمال	:aamil, :ummaal
world	الدنيا	ad-dunya(a) (f.), العالم al-:aalam
worldwide	عالمي	:aalamii
written	مكتوب	maktuub
year	سنة، سنوات	sanah, sanawaat,
	عام، أعوام	:aam, a:waam
yellow	أصفر، صفراء	aSfar*, f. Safraa'*
Yemen	اليمن	al-yaman
yesterday	أمس	ams
you	أنت	anta/anti (m./f.)
you're welcome (in reply to thank you)	عفوا	:afwan